THE
SEASON

ALSO BY WILLIAM GOLDMAN

Novels
THE TEMPLE OF GOLD
YOUR TURN TO CURTSY, MY TURN TO BOW
SOLDIER IN THE RAIN
BOYS AND GIRLS TOGETHER
NO WAY TO TREAT A LADY
THE THING OF IT IS . . .

Plays and Musicals
BLOOD, SWEAT AND STANLEY POOLE (WITH JAMES GOLDMAN)
A FAMILY AFFAIR (WITH JAMES GOLDMAN AND JOHN KANDER)

Movies
HARPER
BUTCH CASSIDY AND THE SUNDANCE KID

WILLIAM GOLDMAN

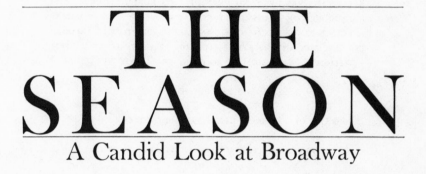

THE SEASON

A Candid Look at Broadway

HARCOURT, BRACE & WORLD, INC. | NEW YORK

FIRST EDITION

LIBRARY OF CONGRESS CATALOG CARD NUMBER: 69–14851

PRINTED IN THE UNITED STATES OF AMERICA

CHAPTER 1 WAS FIRST
PUBLISHED IN *Esquire Magazine*

AGAIN FOR ILENE

The Theatregoers Study referred to in this book was done by the Center for Research in Marketing, Inc. The Center, a market research organization, has done more than 150 studies for major American companies since its founding in 1957. Its president is William Capitman, who was visiting professor of Marketing in the Social Sciences at Yale University during the period that this study was made.

Contents

THE
SEASON

THE PALACE THEATRE
under the direction of
Messrs. Nederlander

SID LUFT

presents

A Group V Ltd. Production

JUDY GARLAND
at home at the Palace

> *Staged by*
> **RICHARD BARSTOW**

Costumes by
BILL SMITH
TRAVILLA

Lighting by
RALPH ALSWANG

Musical Director
BOBBY COLE

with

JOHN BUBBLES   **JACKIE VERNON**

FRANCIS BRUNN

THE PALACE THEATRE
under the direction of
Messrs. Nederlander

BUDDY   EDDIE
HACKETT   FISHER

Musical Director **COLIN ROMOFF**

Figures in the Carpet

At 11:43 she began to let them touch her. They had been after her flesh a long while, but it is only now, after she is done and it is ended, that she allowed them contact. Just the barest graze. Her fingertips to theirs as she moved, as always, jerkily, parallel to the footlights, first right to left, then back. And if she expected her flesh to quiet them, she was only wrong: the din, already painful, somehow went up a notch, now almost completely covering the noise from the pit where the band went wearily on with "Over the Rainbow," over and over, "Over the Rainbow," over again. For this was August 26, Judy Garland's closing night at the Palace. And the hysteria had been a long time building.

By 9:30 that night, before the first act of the show had ended, the large outer lobby was already almost full. (There was no point in going to the first act. She didn't appear in the first act. Everybody knew that.) Now, as the lobby filled up entirely, the audience itself began to become insistently noticeable. A stunning blonde walked by, in a lovely green jacket, sexy and confident, undulating with every step, and it comes as a genuine shock to realize the blonde is a boy. Two other boys flit by, chattering. First: "I got her pink roses and white carnations; you think she'll like it?" Second (angry): "Now why didn't I bring her flowers? Oooh, it's just too late for me now." Another flutter of fags, half a dozen this time, and watching it all from a corner, two heterosexual married couples. "These fags," the first man says. "It's like Auschwitz—some of them died along the way but a lot got here anyhow." He turns to the other husband and shrugs. "Tonight, no one goes to the bathroom."

But probably no more than a quarter of the house are obvious homosexuals. Two girls and a boy hurry through the lobby to their seats. "Wanna guess what I got her?" the first girl asks. "What? What?" from the second girl. "Would you believe a trunk of flowers?" "A *trunk?*" the boy says. "How you getting it on stage?" "I got a seat in the very front row," the first girl replies, homely but clearly triumphant.

By 9:50 most of the audience is seated.

At 9:52 there came the first burst of nervous applause, accompanied by the standard whispers preceding any Garland show: "Do you think . . . ?" "You don't suppose . . . ?" Rumor: Will she make it? Sure, she'll make it, she has to make it. I hear she's sick. No. She's fine. Well, if she's fine, then where is she? It's almost ten and . . . "Judy!" Someone shouts, and once the name is thrown, there is a burst of applause, then suddenly another, louder burst as Liza Minnelli, Garland's daughter, takes her seat. Everybody sighs because if the mother were sick, why would Liza come?

9:57, and everyone on the main floor starts to turn around, staring at the rear of the house. (She makes her entrance from the rear of the house. Everybody knows that.)

10:00, and the lights dim. A minute after that and the conductor starts talking to the men in the pit, and a minute after that: music. First the downbeat, then the drum roll, then "The Man That Got Away," a few notes of it, before the orchestra *segues* into another song, "The Trolley Song," and then another *segue,* and it's "Over the Rainbow." The audience is applauding the tunes. Of course they're applauding the tunes, why shouldn't they applaud the tunes, these are famous tunes, you'd expect the audience to applaud them, but what you wouldn't expect is that not only is the audience applauding the tunes, *tonight they're applauding the segues.*

10:05, and everyone stands up as if on signal, and the clapping and screaming, sporadic before, become concentrated, a force to be reckoned with. The screaming, unleashed, continues to build and build. She hasn't appeared yet, understand—no one's seen her—it's just that at 10:05 on the button everybody began to scream, and it didn't seem to matter that she wasn't there. The lady herself suddenly seemed almost superfluous, as if we could all have a terrific time standing there, shouting out loud, throwing kisses at the empty center aisle. I kept remembering that team—I think it's the Indianapolis Clowns—who play a few innings of baseball every so often without a ball, just miming the whole thing, and their crowds love it as this one loved the empty center aisle of the Palace.

Then at 10:07 it wasn't empty any more. Because at the rear, she had finally put in her appearance, and you knew she wasn't super-fluous, because the earlier screaming, the pre-Garland screaming, that was nothing. Down the aisle she came, slowly, slowly, throw-ing kisses to the people, mouthing, "Thank you, thank you," as the noise somehow grew, and along with the cries of "Judy!" came "We love you! We love you!"

10:09, she reaches the stage and just stands there. The screaming is coming in waves now, and in a trough of quiet someone begs, "Never leave us," and with that the noise again somehow grows, and she still just stands there, holding a mike, the center of the world. The noise cannot get any louder, there is just no way, and perhaps she senses this, because suddenly she is into "I Feel a Song Coming On," the hand mike close to her mouth, almost, but not quite, inside it. She stands there singing, legs spread wide and firm, her free arm jerking in the air, and somehow she seems mechanical, like Frank Gorshin's mimicking of Burt Lancaster.

And after the song and the screaming for it end, she moves into other songs—"Almost Like Being in Love" and "This Can't Be Love" and "Just in Time"—which is a mistake. It's bad for her, hard for her, because the voice is incapable of holding a note any more, and "Just in time" goes "Just in tiiiiimmme" and she can't make it last, so she makes a sudden campy gesture, and they love it and scream over it, and by the time they are quiet again she's out of the song. Next, a new song, and the audience doesn't like it much, probably because it is new, and for the first time there is almost quiet in the house.

But not for long. Because pretty soon it's "The Trolley Song," and at the very end of it there are the words "with his hand holding mine," and "mine" is a tough note, high and climactic. As she gets to it, she spreads her feet just a little wider, and suddenly she's eating the mike—it's down her throat, jammed—and from some-where she found it, because at precisely 10:30, on the word mine, she hit the high note with all she had and on the button perfect, and you could actually hear them gasp because she did it, she got a note right, a loud note yet, and she got it. It wasn't just that she was on pitch—she's almost always on pitch, or at least you know she knows where pitch is if she's off it—it was pitch plus volume plus timbre plus whatever else it is that distinguishes one voice from another, and this was Garland's voice, the old Garland's voice, back again, just like in the movies, and even though it was only for one note it was enough to tear the place apart.

There then followed half an hour of vamping: she did a dance; she introduced her daughter Lorna, who can't sing either; then her son, Joey, did a few minutes of drum solos; after that, Liza came up from the audience and talked with her mother awhile before singing, stunningly, "Cabaret." As Liza goes back to her seat, Judy says, "Liza, you've been marvelous all your life and so have Liza and Joey," instead of "Lorna and Joey," maybe a Freudian slip, meaning either Lorna wasn't good enough to be worth mentioning or Liza was so good it bugged her, and so she had to name her twice, or maybe it was just a plain old slip of the tongue.

Then she sings "Ol' Man River" followed by "That's Entertainment," where she intentionally fluffs the lyrics. The audience is clapping staccato now, and a young girl runs up to the stage and throws flowers to Judy, and that triggers it, because suddenly another girl is up there throwing flowers, and then a man charges to the footlights carrying a wrapped box of something, and she's singing "Rockabye Your Baby" as they begin closing in on the stage.

The aisles are filling, all of them, and now the trunk of flowers is pushed up from the front row; it's not a big trunk, not a steamer trunk or anything like that, but it is a large box, and it is full of flowers. And then a man, maybe forty, pushes close and hands Judy a drawing he's made of her, and cameras are everywhere, and more girls with more flowers wedge in toward her, and as the aisles pack tighter it's like Billy Graham at the end of his sell, standing on the dais, arms folded, going, "Y'all come now . . . come on . . . come on . . . we'll wait. . . . Christ went to the cross for you, you can come this far for him, come on, come on, y'all come. . . ."

11:32, and "Swanee," and someone in the mass of the center aisle shouts, "Over the Rainbow," and everybody whirls on him because part of the sacrament is that "Over the Rainbow" is the end, nothing after, ever, everybody knows that.

"Over the Rainbow" comes at 11:34. She is sitting on the stage floor now, and just before the final "Why, oh, why can't I?" she pauses long enough to shout: "AND I MADE IT!," a ringing reply to all the unbelievers who thought she was finished, the ones who make jokes about how the phrase JUDY TAKES OVERDOSE is set in permanent headline type at the New York *Daily News.*

And now, through the eleven minutes of curtain calls, more and more of the faithful press toward her. People sitting in the front rows who want to leave are simply trapped there. Curtain down and up. Curtain down and up. The clapping and the crying never die. And a young boy, maybe twenty-one, maybe less, is staring up at her and wringing his hands. He cannot and he will not stop with his hands, even though his constant wringing pressure has forced the skin to burst. He holds a handkerchief as he continues to stare up at her and wring his hands, and bleed.

And what is she to them that they should bleed for her? There are a lot of statements that will be made about homosexuals in this book, but I will save most of them for the chapter on Edward Albee. But two fairly obvious points can be made here. First, if homosexuals have an enemy, it is age. And Garland is youth, perennially, over the rainbow. And second, the lady has suffered. Homosexuals tend to identify with suffering. They are a persecuted minority group, and they understand suffering. And so does Garland. She's been through the fire and lived—all the drinking and divorcing, all the pills and all the men, all the poundage come and gone—brothers and sisters, she knows.

The following from a screenwriter: "I can't explain her appeal, but I saw it work once, in this crazy way. I was at a party in Malibu —my first big Hollywood let's-all-get-slowly-smashed-on-Sunday-type party—and there were all these famous faces, and I hid behind a Bloody Mary in the corner. There were a lot of actors there that the word on them was they were queer. But this was a boy-girl party; everyone was paired off, and all these beautiful men and gorgeous broads were talking and drinking together.

"Anyway, everything's going along, and it's sunny, and I'm getting a little buzzed in my corner position when this star-type female goes by me. I naturally look at her, and she's wearing this fantastically loosely knit sweater—I don't know what the hell it was, but there wasn't a lot of it, and also there's no bra, and these famous breasts are bouncing by. I'd never seen any before, I mean not famous ones anyway, and they weren't much, and I was thinking deep thoughts about that when I realized Garland was in the room. It's a patio, not a room, and there's a chaise in the center and the guy she's with, one of her husbands, he sort of supports her across the patio, and she plops down on this chaise and she says what she wants to drink, and he goes off to get it.

"I'm in the corner now, remember, and she's sitting all alone in the center of this patio and for a minute, there was nothing. And then this crazy thing started to happen: every homosexual in the place—every guy you'd heard whispered about, all these stars, they left the girls they were with and started a mass move toward Garland. She didn't ask for it. She was just sitting there blinking in the sun while this thing happened: all these beautiful men, some of them big stars, some of them not so big, they circled her, crowded around her, and pretty soon she's disappeared behind this expensive male fence.

"It may not sound like all that much, but I'm telling you, she magnetized them. I'll never forget all those famous secret guys moving across this gorgeous patio without a sound. And her just sitting there, kind of blinking, and then they were on her and she was gone. . . ."

She was gone from the stage of the Palace too, but ten minutes after the final curtain, the faithful still filled the aisles close to the stage. Watching them from the rear of the house, a Broadway professional shook his head. People were still trapped up front, unable to get by the followers in the aisles. The Broadway pro turned away. "What do you think?" someone asked him. "Is it theatre?"

"Theatre?" the pro said. "Is this theatre? You bet your ass it's theatre. It sure as hell ain't singing."

So ended the first production of the 1967–68 Broadway season. This book is about that season. All the plays and musicals that opened are touched on in one way or another, in more or less chronological order. By the time we reach the appendix on where to eat in Times Square, the reader, I hope, will have a reasonable knowledge about Broadway and why it works the way it does.

More than anything else, I wanted this book to be accurate. In the interests of accuracy I spent 18 solid months seeing as many shows and talking to as many people as I could fit into the day. For the statistically minded, I suppose I had fewer than 1,000 interviews, but not many. I saw every Broadway production, many of them more than once, some of them five times. I traveled to London as well as the usual tryout towns of Boston, New Haven and Washington. I commissioned a sociological study on theatregoers by the

Center for Research in Marketing, Inc., a leading motivational research firm, on such untouched subjects as what kind of person goes to what kind of play, and why do they want to see what they want to see. In addition, I have written and doctored Broadway plays and musicals, I have an advanced degree in drama, and many of my friends and acquaintances are active, some quite successfully, in the Broadway world.

With the above credentials, I am now in a position to ask the one crucial question about this book: *How accurate is it?*

Alas, not very.

Three reasons. First, and least important, there is a certain amount of lying, cheating and stealing in the Broadway theatre; nothing unusual, just the standard corruptions inherent in any American cash business. Some of the thieves I knew about before I interviewed them; others undoubtedly fooled me, and easily. In either case, the point is this: if a guy's working that side of the street, great faith cannot be put in his wisdom.

Second, a production can be made up of a hundred people, so that on any given day you can interview the director, who will say that all is going blissfully, while on that same day the author will tell you of his agony with tears behind his eyes. Both could be telling the truth or lying; both could be right or wrong. For when a show is shaping, no one can tell what the operative truth is at any given time. In a group endeavor, it's always *rashomon*.

Third, and most important, is this simple fact: people tend to glamorize, and for an example of what I mean, I give you Harold S. Prince.

As far as producers are concerned, Hal Prince may be the best there is. Since he became famous, in 1954, as the last of the boy-wonder producers, Prince has been connected with producing twelve musicals. Incredibly, only four have failed (and of the four, one won the Tony award as best musical of its season, while another was included in the *Ten Best Plays* of its year). A fifth musical, *New Girl in Town,* was only a mild success: it ran a year, won Tony awards for its costars, Gwen Verdon and Thelma Ritter.

That leaves seven musicals. *Pajama Game,* Prince's first, ran over 1,000 performances and won the Tony award. Then came *Damn Yankees;* it also ran over 1,000 performances and won the Tony. Next was *West Side Story;* no comment necessary. This was followed by *Fiorello!,* which shared the Tony and won the Pulitzer prize for drama. *A Funny Thing Happened on the Way to the Forum* won the Tony and ran within a month of 1,000 performances. *Cabaret,* which Prince also directed, won the Tony, and as of May, 1968, is well over 600 performances with a clear shot at 1,000. (Fewer than 20 musicals in history have run that long.)

But of all Prince's shows, his old-age pension is *Fiddler on the Roof.* In the season that this book covers—from the beginning of June, 1967, to the end of May, 1968—it was still, in its fourth year, the top-grossing show on Broadway, and there are experts who think it will eventually exceed the run of *My Fair Lady.* It is, even at its present stage, one of the great hits in the history of New York City.

But it isn't as big a hit, on the road, as *Hello, Dolly!*

Now, this is fact. All you have to do is check the weekly *Variety* grosses. *Fiddler,* successful enough on the road, has simply not pulled in the people that *Dolly!* has. You can't argue it. If someone asks you, "Which is taller, the Chrysler Building or the Empire State?" you can hedge: "I don't know, buddy; the Chrysler Building looks pretty tall to me." You can attack: "You should only own a building half as tall as the Chrysler, buddy!" But if pressed, you have to admit that, great as the Chrysler Building may be, glorious as are its splendors, the Empire State is taller.

And so it is with *Dolly!* and *Fiddler on the Roof.* On May 17, 1967, *Variety* wrote an article concerning trade disappointment that *Fiddler's* Chicago run was not up to expectations, *i.e.,* not up to *Dolly!'s.*

In June, when I asked Prince about the article, he erupted. (That is not hyperbole. He does erupt. Constantly. He has many virtues, but stillness isn't one of them. When we first met, years ago, there were four of us seated in his small office. He received a phone call, and I can still remember how he got up and crisscrossed the tiny room, stepping over people's feet, skirting desks and chairs, shifting the receiver from one ear to the other, never slowing down, winking at and nodding to the rest of us as he made his constant way, while at the same time continually brushing imaginary dandruff from his shoulders.)

"Where are those *Dolly!* figures?" he shouted now. *"Get me those Dolly! figures."* He paced around his office until a girl ran in with a sheet of paper. Prince glanced at it, handed it to me. It was a weekly tabulation of the money *Dolly!* grossed during its year run in Chicago. During the first weeks, with Carol Channing, business was $100,000 and change a week. Then, when Betty Grable and Eve Arden took over the title role, business fell off.

"You see?" Prince said. "Terrible with Grable and Arden. We're doing much better than that with *Fiddler,* so it's all going to average out. By the time we're done, we'll be just as big a hit in Chicago as *Dolly!* ever was."

In its July 26 issue, under the headline, CORRECTED FIDDLER GROSSES, *Variety* wrote: "Starting last May, the Harold Prince office in New York has been reporting inflated box-office figures to VARIETY on the touring company of 'Fiddler on the Roof' at the McVickers Theater, Chicago." *Variety* then went on to list both the reported grosses and the actual amounts taken in, the differences varying up to $12,000 a week.

On August 30, *Variety* reprinted a letter from Prince to his *Fiddler* backers, which went, in part, as follows: "The July 26th issue of VARIETY, which seems to come by our monthly statements with no difficulty (I assume turned over to it by one of our investors), corrected some Chicago grosses that we had given them earlier this summer.

"No question about it: *they caught us* [italics mine]."

The point to the above is just this: If one of the most successful theatrical figures of the century glamorizes the success of one of the most successful productions of the century, just how much glamorizing do you think an average Broadway figure does about a flop?

The mind, you should pardon the expression, boggles.

So those are the three reasons that this book isn't as accurate as I'd hoped: corruption, the group nature of the endeavor, and the natural human tendency to glamorize. One other thing you should be reminded of: Broadway isn't very big. Compared with television, for example, its audience is small. An NBC statistician reports that on a Monday in winter there are 120 million people who watch TV, at least for a moment, over the course of an entire evening. How many people do you think watch Broadway shows on an average Monday? (This isn't really fair, since Monday is a poor night for theatre, a strong one for television.) Still, think about it for a minute: guess the total number of all the people who pay to see all the shows on an average Monday. O.K.?

Maybe 12,000.

Broadway, then, is statistically trivial, and normally its product is trivial, too. But every so often, it isn't, and it's those "every so oftens" that we remember, because that's all Broadway really is: memories. Movies we can see again, TV is taped, but Broadway's strength is that the people are alive.

Memory may be the reason that a single showstopping musical number—"Hello, Dolly!," for example—can salvage an entire production. It marks that night in time. Years later, a flood of impressions will fill in the moment, like a pointillist painting. I can still remember what I was and who I thought I was the afternoon I stood through *Guys and Dolls* and saw the "Sit Down, You're Rocking the Boat" number. I can still summon the boy who watched Pulver pitch the palm trees after Mister Roberts died. But the "me" at mediocrities is gone. And I'll never get him back.

So, for the few of us who go, Broadway does mean something. Saul Lancourt, the marvelously astute manager of Leblang's Theatre Ticket Agency, has said, "People come in sometimes looking for tickets, and they've never seen a Broadway show before, and we look at them so strangely. But we've got to remember something: we're the phenomenon, not they." Just how small Broadway really is can be put in relief by a few comparisons:

1. No one can say for sure, since it's illegal, but probably more people smoke pot regularly than go to Broadway.

2. Between its opening, in December, 1967, and the end of the season covered by this book, May, 1968, one movie, "The Graduate," outgrossed Broadway.

3. During this season, 94 out of 95 TV specials each had a larger audience than all the people who attended all of Broadway all year long—the 95th special, incidentally, was about acting.

4. Less money was spent on Broadway tickets last year than on bathroom deodorizers. And speaking of deodorizers:

FISHER
Did you know Lincoln was a Jew?

HACKETT
You sure?

FISHER
Absolutely. He was shot in the temple.

It's the Palace Theatre again, another closing; Buddy Hackett and Eddie Fisher are holding forth, and the audience adores them. These are their people, and if the Garland closing was for the homosexuals, tonight is for the Jews, which is as it should be. For in the first two productions of the season, vague patterns are already starting to form, soon to become clearly textured figures in the carpet. These two minority groups don't just buttress the Broadway theatre; without either one of them, Broadway would be desperately enfeebled; without both, it would be a clear case of evisceration.

Hackett and Fisher received poor notices when the show opened,

Hackett for being foulmouthed, Fisher for being deafeningly miked. But now, by closing, the decibel level has been lowered and Fisher isn't half bad. He isn't half good either, but he sings as well as most Broadway musical-comedy leads, and is no stiffer than average. He seems very small, perhaps because he is small, or perhaps because there is no extension of personality. Garland, whatever her flaws, conjured size and a sense of history. Fisher is only Fisher and only of the moment: even when he sings "O Mein Papa" it's still *now*.

But Fisher isn't the disappointment; it's Hackett who makes a woman say out loud in anger, "I didn't know he was like this; he was never like this on the 'Johnny Carson.' "

Everything he says is smutty. Every story he tells seems to involve either his genitals or his hemorrhoids. The "craps" and the penis tugs are repeated endlessly. Sometimes he breaks into song (sung to the tune of "Flamingo"): "Flamingo . . . there's a bird in your ass. . . ."

After Hackett does his turn and Fisher sings his songs, they get together on stage, talking to each other and the audience, sometimes in English, sometimes in Yiddish. (*Everything* spoken in Yiddish gets a laugh.) After a while, Fisher sings a song, prefacing it with: "This one didn't sell like my old songs; it only sold 700,000 copies."

After the song, they start to pander to each other's public image. Hackett to Fisher: "If you had any more sex life, there wouldn't be enough left for the rest of the world. . . . Y'know, if you were any younger, they'd have to start a new Olympic event—hurdle this, baby. . . . I mean, for a Jew kid from Philadelphia, you been in a lot of good places," "in" being a euphemism for vagina. Fisher to Hackett: "When I say you're the funniest man in the world, that's not saying enough."

After the pandering, they ad-lib some more, and Hackett is so riotous, he keeps breaking Fisher up. Fisher simply cannot keep a straight face, Hackett is so fresh and original. Fisher gasps and giggles and staggers around, helpless, and it's all vegetarian-chopped-liver phony. Because there's a whole orchestra on stage behind them, and during all of Hackett's "ad libs," the boys in the band just sit there, deadpan, not one of them so much as even starting to smile.

They been there already.

LINCOLN CENTER FESTIVAL '67

Alexander H. Cohen

PRESENTS

The Unknown Soldier and His Wife

TWO ACTS OF WAR SEPARATED BY A TRUCE FOR REFRESHMENT

By Peter Ustinov

Brian Bedford
W. B. Brydon
Howard Da Silva
Bob Dishy
M'el Dowd
Alan Mixon
Melissa C. Murphy
Marco St. John
Christopher Walken

Directed by

John Dexter

Music by David Shire
Scenery and Costumes by Motley
Lighting by Jules Fisher
Associate Producer—Hildy Parks
Production Supervisor—Jerry Adler

GEORGE ABBOTT THEATRE

ALEXANDER H. COHEN

presents

BRIAN BEDFORD   **HOWARD DA SILVA**

in

THE UNKNOWN SOLDIER AND HIS WIFE

Two Acts of War Separated
By a Truce For Refreshment

by

PETER USTINOV

with

CHRISTOPHER WALKEN

JOHN DEVLIN   **MELISSA C. MURPHY**   **TOM ATKINS**
JAMES STORM   **MacINTYRE DIXON**   **NANCY REARDON**

Music by
DAVID SHIRE

Scenery and Costumes by
MOTLEY

Lighting by
JULES FISHER

Associate Producer
HILDY PARKS

Production Supervisor
JERRY ADLER

The play was originally presented at the Vivian Beaumont Theatre as part of the
Lincoln Center Festival 1967

2

Why Is Tonight Different from
Any Other Night?

Peter Ustinov's antiwar fantasy, *The Unknown Soldier and His Wife,* premièred at Lincoln Center's Vivian Beaumont Theater in July. It transferred to a Broadway house, the George Abbott, in September, where it ran a disappointing 64 additional performances before closing at an announced loss of $125,000.

The play is set around the televised burial of the Unknown Soldier. But almost from the start things go strangely—people seem to remember each other from other times with other names—and suddenly a long flashback begins that is to take up the great bulk of the play. First is a section in which the Roman legions were at war. Then follow segments set during the Crusades, the Age of Reason, World War I, etc. The same characters or character types reappear in most of the segments: the Unknown Soldier, the Wife, the Military Leader, the Religious Leader, the Scientist (mad), the Rebel. In most of the episodes the Unknown Soldier manages to get his wife pregnant and himself killed, until the very end, once more in the present for the televised funeral, when he refuses to die, and walks away from all the bloodshed with his wife and the child that he at last has lived to see.

Of the nine chief actors who opened with the play, four remained throughout the run. Of those four, three seemed much the same individually at the beginning and the end, while Melissa C. Murphy, as the Wife, had matured from a standard Broadway-type ingénue into a very pretty girl giving a very moving performance. For the rest, only Bob Dishy's marvelous mad scientist had not been adequately replaced. So adding it up, it would seem to come out about even: one performance damaged, one much improved, seven seemingly the same. Logically, what closed in November should have been just as valid a theatrical event as what started in the summertime, but that was just not so. What closed was defective; what opened had worked.

Why?

To begin with, the play had altered. At its first preview it ran 176 minutes, not counting intermission. The closing matinee took 38 minutes less. But this severe cutting didn't damage things: the play, repetitive in structure, was also repetitive in the writing. The play itself was better when it closed than when it opened. But when it opened it had a director. The Englishman John Dexter was enormously responsible for whatever appeal the evening originally possessed. But Dexter did not redirect the Ustinov play when it transferred. So whom did producer Alexander Cohen hire as director?

Nobody. And this was damaging because, among other reasons, the stage at Lincoln Center is a thrust stage, with the audience seated on three sides of the actors, while the Abbott has a standard proscenium stage, with the audience entirely in front. The actors were upset about the transfer. One of them said, "The only negative thing that happened was the way we were handled when we moved. There was no director." (And indeed, none was listed in the program.)

So the play was different, the actors were different, the stage was different, and there was no director. What else? Just this: by the time it closed, the production was well over 100 performances old and generally, by then, acting deterioration had set in. (Not always. Elia Kazan said this about *Tea and Sympathy:* "If there's an organic connection between the people backstage, a play will sustain in performance. Deborah Kerr—I haven't seen her really in 15 years, but she's an immaculate person, genuinely friendly—held the play together because of the cast's feeling for her.")

But this just doesn't happen often. It is miserably hard doing the same part over and over, making it seem fresh. Most actors cannot or will not do it. Ethel Merman is famous for "freezing" a performance after opening night and duplicating that identical performance throughout the run. This is her way of working, and no one works harder; still, after the opening, what you see is a Xerox of the original. Late in her *Funny Girl* run, I saw Barbra Streisand give a performance indistinguishable in all ways from what Jerry Lewis would have done with the part, and I mean that. She moved like Jerry Lewis, mugged like Jerry Lewis, and except when she sang, sounded like him. She was dying of boredom and very clearly didn't care about her performance, and it very clearly didn't matter to the audience, who loved her.

Audiences loved Zero Mostel in *Fiddler on the Roof* too, but most people connected with the show felt that the show improved after Mostel left it. For Mostel, brilliant as he is, can be destructive to a production. A *Fiddler* expert told me: "Mostel was good for about what people predicted—two months—and even at his worst he was still marvelous for 95% of the audience. But that other 5% would sit there and think, 'What in the hell is he doing?' It wasn't so much that he ad-libbed; what he did was really mysterious. He would extend pieces of business, and somehow—no one could ever tell quite how he managed it—he would reshape the relative weights of scenes so that they became about him, whether they were supposed to be about him or not."

Two actors known for their skill in sustaining parts over a long period of time are Robert Preston and Barry Nelson. Statistically, Preston is probably the most-sought-after performer on Broadway. This is because he can do it all: drama, comedy, both light and dark, and, of course, musicals.

Preston is fifty now, and he looks marvelous. The energy he generates on stage is more controlled in person, but it's there. He has a wonderful reputation around Broadway for working his tail off and never causing trouble, in good times or bad. One playwright told me: "We were dying out of town, it was miserable, and the leading lady was a bitch on wheels, but Bob just went about his business. You've got to work with him to know what it's like. He is this oasis, and you know you'd die without him. Once, I think in Philadelphia, he got this new speech and he said, 'No, I don't think I like this, I don't want to say it.' It was as if the earth had fallen open. Nobody knew what to do, and then he said, 'What if I cut this one line, would you mind that?' I said, 'No,' so he read it with the one line cut and then nodded. 'Fine,' he said. That was the extent of the turmoil he was responsible for."

As to staying fresh in a role, Preston says, "You have to do it consciously. It's a personal discipline, but it's how I was trained in the theatre; it was always expected of me. When I'm doing a musical, every night when I drive in, I repeat all my lyrics to myself. You can forget dialogue because you can fake it since you know approximately what the character is doing, but you can't fake a lyric. I say them over and over so that it becomes impossible to make a mistake. I remember saying to Art Tatum, whom I liked and admired, that he was playing sloppily on a recording of a song and he said—I'll always remember this—he said, 'I was seeing then.' Tatum was blind, you know, but he used to have periods when he could see shapes and colors, and what he meant was that when he made the recording he was able to see, and that's why the mistakes came; his fingers never made mistakes when he was blind.

"You want to be comfortable in a part. Out of town, during tryouts, at night, after a performance, you do what a bridge or golf player does if you're avid—*you play it again*. And you try to find those moments of discomfort and ask whether they're your fault or the play's fault, and you try to remove them. Because if one of them exists, let's say in the last act, it's going to color everything you do. It's the same as if there's something you have to do at night that you really don't want to do; it's going to color how you act all through the day."

When he talks about acting, Preston becomes suddenly serious. Lots of actors do, but somehow you get the feeling that Preston means it more. "Once I did a show with a girl, and she never really got her part. Then, after a long time, we did our Actors' Fund Benefit and she was marvelous. After it was over, she came into my dressing room and said, 'Well?' And I said, 'Well?' And she said, 'I got it, didn't I? I was marvelous, wasn't I?' And I said, 'Yes.' And she said, 'Is that all you've got to say?' And I said, 'No, where have you been the last six months?,' and she started to cry. I shouldn't have said it, probably, but I did. Where the hell had she been?"

Barry Nelson and I talked backstage at the Royale Theatre, where he was finishing a two-year run starring opposite Lauren Bacall in *Cactus Flower*. Nelson is the best actor I have ever seen at sustaining a light-comedy role. Comedy, an enormously intricate thing to sustain, can deteriorate faster than anything. Nelson says he has seen plays where it happened in five or six weeks.

"Two reasons, I think: actors settle down in a part after they open. 'I've already licked the part,' they say. It's an entirely different attitude from rehearsal or out of town. And along with the attitude goes setting the line readings. That kills it. The laughs start to go, actors begin to argue. 'I'm reading it the same way, so it can't be me,' they say. But the performance has become predictable. The spark's gone."

In the theatre then, tonight is always different from any other night. A show is a living thing, living and changing, usually for the worse. One of the reasons for this is that directors rarely return to check up on their productions. A leading casting expert explains why: "Two months after a show has opened a director can't bear to go back because the actors aren't doing exactly what the director told them any more. 'Oh, oh, look what she's doing,' he'll say. And he'll be in agony. Because a director really falls to pieces the day he realizes he isn't God. That's why failure is hardest for a director. I have never worked for a director who wouldn't rather be doing films; you can really play God out there. In two months it's still the same, right there on celluloid; you've captured a moment permanently."

After the opening, with the director gone, running the show is left in the hands of the production stage manager. It is his job to sustain the level of the show. But a problem arises. "Stage managers lose their authority to cranky actors," Barry Nelson explains. "If an actor says, 'Dammit, I'm sick of you giving me notes, cut it!,' what can a stage manager really do about it? Nothing."

So most shows go to hell, sometimes quickly. One of the reasons you may not like a show the critics loved is that you simply may not be seeing the same show. The acting may be flabby, the scene values changed or gone. It is always wisest to try and see a show as soon as possible after it opens. If the version of *The Unknown Soldier and His Wife* that closed had been as exciting as the one that had opened, I don't think it would have closed.

You can't blame the actors for the deterioration. Doing the same precise thing eight times a week, 416 times a year, becomes numbing to the soul. It has been said of Alfred Lunt, who is legendary for remaining fresh in a role, that the reason he can do it is that when he lifts a teacup, for example, he is obsessed with the notion of somehow lifting it right, lifting it perfectly, lifting it better than anyone else has ever lifted a teacup before. But in general, repeating a role endlessly is an assault to the sensitivity.

Barry Nelson says, "The longer you play the performance, the more your mind resents it. You're in the middle of a scene, and suddenly all you're thinking about is whether you should have Chinese food after the show." He quiets for a moment and fiddles with his glasses, staring around at the sets for *Cactus Flower,* a serious, intelligent man surrounded by two years of memories, two years of his life, maybe 800 performances, maybe 2,000 hours gone, 2,000 hours spent as a silly philandering dentist buffeted between a semifrigid receptionist and a nitwit mistress. Nelson puts his glasses on, turns to go. "I don't think any actor really likes long runs. I don't think humans were meant to do them."

And actors are humans. No matter what anyone says.

ANTA THEATRE

GENE DINGENARY   MIRANDA d'ANCONA   NANCY LEVERING

present

ALFRED DRAKE

in

SONG OF THE GRASSHOPPER

A New Comedy by
ALFONSO PASO

Adapted from the Spanish by
WILLIAM LAYTON and **AGUSTIN PENON**

Directed by
CHARLES BOWDEN

Also starring
JAN FARRAND

and

BEN PIAZZA

MICHAEL ENSERRO   *with*   ROBIN PONTERIO

and
DIANA DAVILA

Scenic production by **OLIVER SMITH**

Lighting by
MARTIN ARONSTEIN   *Costumes designed by*
NOEL TAYLOR

Production Stage Manager TOM SAWYER
Associate Producer EUGENIE SNELL

BELASCO THEATRE

SAINT SUBBER

presents

BURL IVES   KEIR DULLEA

in

DR. COOK'S GARDEN

A Melodrama

Written and Directed by
IRA LEVIN

with

BETTE   BOB   LEE
HENRITZE   BERGER   SANDERS

Set and Lighting by **DAVID HAYS**

Costumes by **NOEL TAYLOR**

Associate Producers: FRANK PRINCE and MANUEL SEFF

THE PLYMOUTH THEATRE

DAVID MERRICK

by arrangement with
Allan Davis, Ltd. and Michael Medwin

presents

PATRICK MAGEE   MAUREEN O'SULLIVAN

in

KEEP IT IN THE FAMILY

A New Play
by **BILL NAUGHTON**

Directed by **ALLAN DAVIS**

with
BURT BRINCKERHOFF

MARIAN HAILEY   TOM ATKINS
JEFF SIGGINS
and
KAREN BLACK

SUDIE BOND

Designed by
LLOYD BURLINGAME

Costumes by
MARY McKINLEY

Associate Producer
SAMUEL LIFF

CHAPTER

3

The First Week: Murphy's Law

The Broadway season officially
opened the last week in September with the arrival of three plays,
Dr. Cook's Garden, *Keep It in the Family* and *Song of the Grasshopper*. Before going into the plays in some detail, I'd like to
explain just what "the Broadway season" is, since that's what this
book is about, one Broadway season. I'd like to explain, but I can't
quite, because I'm really not sure.

Actors' contracts expire on the last day in June, so that is the
logical time to say that the season has ended. Only no one does.
The season ends the last day in May, according to most theatrical
records. No one quite knows why. Theoretically, then, anything that
opens at a Broadway house after the first of June should be the
start of the new season. But it doesn't work that way. Judy Garland
opened at a Broadway house in July, and Hackett and Fisher in
August, but they don't count officially, presumably because their
shows were vaudeville and not plays. *The Unknown Soldier and
His Wife* was a play, and it opened before the "official" opening,
but it doesn't count either, presumably because it premièred at
Lincoln Center.

At any rate, the bulk of openings takes place in a six-month
period. Counting plays that have opened in the sixties, over 75%

] 23 [

arrived between the first of October and the end of March. Producers don't much like coming in before October because their
feeling is that the audience "isn't thinking theatre." (*Fiddler on
the Roof* opened September 22.) And they don't like to open much
later than March because business tapers off for the summer.
(*Mame* opened May 24; *Wish You Were Here* opened June 25 and
ran a year and a half, but that was a long time ago and doesn't
count.) Whatever the season is, it began with *Dr. Cook's Garden*.

Broadway professionals instinctively gauge the potential success
of an incoming production as soon as it has been assembled. They
do this by weighing the skill and track record of the production's
chief creative people. And although many September production
staffs seem shaky, a pretty impressive bunch was involved in *Dr.
Cook's Garden*.

The play was a melodrama by Ira Levin. Levin is the author of
A Kiss Before Dying, an established classic in the mystery field,
and *Rosemary's Baby*, already a best seller by the time rehearsals
began. True, these were novels and not plays, but the point can
be made that Levin is thoroughly expert at thrilling an audience.
He was also not unfamiliar with Broadway success, having done the
adaptation of *No Time for Sergeants*. His producer, Arnold Saint-
Subber, universally known as "Saint," recently had produced *Barefoot in the Park* and *The Odd Couple,* and would certainly rate on
anybody's ten-best list. Burl Ives, an Academy Award winner, was
hired to play the title role, costarring with the up-and-coming Keir
Dullea. As director: the famous George C. Scott.

Impressive as the names were, there were also worries. Scott is,
of course, known as an actor, although he had directed before. However, his most recent Broadway shot at it had closed after two
performances. Not only that, the author of the failure was the same
Ira Levin, and, as Levin said of *General Seeger,* their earlier attempt
at collaboration, "it wound up sort of unpleasantly." Another
possible source of trouble was that Levin had never met Ives before
Ives was cast.

Scott had met Ives, but only briefly, for an hour, before the play
went into rehearsal. And Scott did not cast Ives. That had been
arranged by Saint-Subber before Scott came on the scene. Scott was
aware that Ives did not see the play the way he did, but he felt that
Ives's appeal might make up for any difficulty. "He's bled into
acting the last 15 years, and he has a wonderfully warm, folksy

quality." Scott was also worried about the play itself, but before getting into that, an explanation of why a warm, folksy actor was needed in the title role.

The melodrama concerns a doctor who kills people instead of curing them. It is set in a small New England town where Dr. Cook is the lone medical man. It's a terrific place to live, and everybody in town is nice-looking. Because Dr. Cook kills all the uglies. Any time a cripple or a bad guy crops up, Dr. Cook sees to it that he mysteriously dies. That is the situation as the play opens.

In the first act, Jim (Keir Dullea), a young doctor who adores Dr. Cook, returns to his home town for a brief visit. The afternoon of his return, through a series of incidents chiefly having to do with an abbreviation system that Dr. Cook uses for both his garden and his patients, Jim comes to realize that the older man is killing people.

In the second act, that night, Jim confronts Cook with the charge. Cook eventually admits the murders, but explains that he's really doing good deeds by getting rid of the mean and the crippled. Jim makes Dr. Cook promise he'll stop with the murders. Dr. Cook agrees. Jim goes upstairs to unpack, and Dr. Cook gets out a bottle of poison before preparing a little home-cooked dinner for the two of them.

In the last act, Cook poisons Jim, then gives him an antidote after Jim promises to leave Cook alone. Jim then tries to escape, he and Cook struggle, and Cook suffers a heart attack. Jim lets Cook die without trying to save him. The play ends with the possibility of Jim taking up where Cook left off as town doctor.

Scott was bothered that the play was superficial, that it didn't look deeply enough into the moral problems it inevitably raised. He talked about it while we had coffee in his office on East Fifty-fourth Street. Scott was about to turn forty at the time and was already, at least for me, one of the best actors in the world. There are a lot of unusual things about Scott but mainly it is his physical presence. Most male movie stars are stars from the neck up. Physically they are well enough put together, but what makes them magic is something in the face, usually the eyes. There are only two stars who are stars from the neck down, and they are Scott and Burt Lancaster. Both of them somehow give the feeling that if you say the wrong thing to them in an irritating enough way, they will kill you. Lancaster would kill you with grace and speed; Scott would brute-strength you to death. Understand, there is nothing in what

Scott does to suggest this: it's just part of him. What he says is in no way menacing. The man is bright and well-read and funny and self-effacing; for someone in his position, the lack of ego is astonishing. He really seems like a marvelous man. You just don't want to mess with him, that's all.

He picked up a copy of *Dr. Cook's Garden*. "There's no scene in here where Cook has doubts about his killing, his gardening of the community. Without it we have a play about a suspicious young man who points the finger and a villain who rationalizes 21 years of killing. It's another Warner Brothers 1940 movie, and I don't want Sydney Greenstreet; I want Pasteur gone wrong. Someone told me Ives saw it as a morality play; I think he's reading in a depth that doesn't exist. I think Ira won't deepen the play because he's worried that it'll confuse what he's written. But how deep should we go? That's my problem."

Levin indeed did not want Dr. Cook wandering around, wondering whether he'd been justified or not. "It would soften the character," Levin said. And as rehearsal time approached, he also said he wasn't worried. "I'm the eternal optimist; everything's going to be rosy, and not a line is going to be changed."

Saint-Subber was fatalistic before rehearsal. "I've never done a melodrama; that's why this appealed to me. By calling itself a melodrama it says it's not important. It's sleight of hand, a test for me. I've got to assemble just the right ingredients and then pray to God."

On September 11, *Dr. Cook's Garden* held its paid preview. At 8:05 that night, the Belasco lobby was completely empty except for a fat man with a poodle. The lack of activity was explained by a piece of paper taped to the inside of the door: "Preview Canceled." Now a canceled preview is not necessarily a sign of disaster. Trouble, yes; disaster, no. Four days later, more trouble: "George C. Scott quits job as Broadway director." This last from the New York *Times*. The article reported that Scott had bowed out as director because "a disagreement had arisen between Mr. Ives and Mr. Scott." Levin was to be the new director. (Levin had never directed before.) In the *Times* article, Levin praised Scott, saying, "Mr. Scott did 95% of the directorial job, and he did it beautifully too."

Clearly, things were going badly. But when previews finally did begin, things got worse: the audience was laughing in the wrong places. Warner Brothers, which had bought the film rights, was optimistic. A company man told me, "It's coming along, they're

making it better; most of the laughs have been gotten rid of." There
was a pause. "I never liked the play anyway. I always thought it had
problems. But they say that Jimmy Stewart wants to do the picture."
Another Warner's man confirmed that: "Stewart does want to do it,
and we don't care that it's in trouble. We expected it would be in
trouble. But it's going to make a marvelous movie from a not-so-
marvelous play."

The critics agreed that it wasn't so marvelous. DR. COOK'S GARDEN
IS PLANTED WITH STIFFS headlined Chapman in the *News*, while Clive
Barnes, the *Times* man, termed it "ridiculous" and congratulated
Scott for not being connected with it any more.

Scott, however, didn't feel much like being congratulated. What
had worried him before rehearsals—the play's lack of depth—had
never become a problem. What had become a problem was a good
deal deeper: Scott could not communicate with Burl Ives. "I
couldn't serve him. I refused to let him do those marvelous old
vaudeville turns of his. He's got wonderful qualities: he looks great,
speaks well, he's warm, easy to love, et cetera. What's working
against him is this incredible lack of acting ability. He's a personality, and nothing I did seemed to help. Ira and Saint said, 'Lean on
him,' but I'm not a taskmaster. I don't cope, I do what's worse; I
turn my back on the situation.

"I just couldn't get through to him—that's not his fault, it's mine
—and when I couldn't bear to sit out there and watch him any
more, I wanted to fire him. But I didn't have the power. I said to
Saint, 'Let me try for Eddie Robinson, Charles Boyer; let me get an
actor so I can talk to him.' Saint said, 'Take him to dinner.' Take
him to dinner? What the fuck am I gonna say to him? You can't
work around a table drinking Bloody Marys.

"When I found I couldn't get rid of Ives, I got rid of myself. I
didn't speak to Ira, simply to Saint. I said, 'I'm going,' and he said,
'I'll sue,' and I said, 'Lots of luck.' One of the things I feel worst
about is that I didn't even speak to Ira. And that nice thing he said
in the *Times* about me. I hadn't even told him good-bye, and he
said that. I feel bad about not speaking to Ira. I bought the package,
Ives included, and that was my mistake; I should have cast the part
myself. Still, I agreed to do it, and the fact that I couldn't bring it
off—I was there to serve and I couldn't find a way—I don't feel too
fucking good about that either."

Dr. Cook's Garden closed the week it opened at a loss of approximately $100,000. "It's not the money," Saint-Subber said later. He

was sitting on the sofa in his office on the fourth floor of his Sixty-fourth Street town house. "The money's not so painful, it's the time. What is it now, November, and I still haven't closed the books on the thing; I'm still burning the scenery and returning the props. The ingredients weren't right; the whole thing was utterly and completely my fault. Maybe I knew that." He shuffled some papers on the table before him. Then he put the papers down. "The most difficult thing to learn is to turn back, to forget the whole thing. Turning back; that's hard."

Months after the play closed, Levin was having a drink in the Algonquin Hotel. "I'm doing a book now," he said. "And after that, another book. And another book." He is a big man, bearded, and his movements are slow. "No, actually, it wasn't a bad experience with *Dr. Cook*. The problem with Scott and Ives only developed a week before Scott left. I thought we were going to be all right, I really did, though looking back now, I can see signs: all the people who didn't show up at the previews to give their reactions. Still, all in all, it wasn't so bad. Saint-Subber didn't come opening night. Anyway, I didn't see him. I don't think I saw him after the day Scott left, when he made a nice speech to the company. Then, of course, Ives got sick. That night we opened, Monday, he hadn't done the play since the Wednesday before. And, of course, I'd never directed. And then the previews being canceled, I'm not so sure that helped, but Ives had the right in his contract to an extra week of rehearsal by canceling the previews, and he exercised the right. And people began meddling—friends of his. Once—right here in the Algonquin—someone said that what the play really needed to work was for Ives to sing a hymn—*a hymn*—he and Keir should sing this hymn, and the other characters should join in. There was this big talk about that idea; they should all sing this hymn, and maybe if they did, it would save the play and . . ." Suddenly he was sitting up straight, staring out across the Algonquin. "Omigod—it was horrible—horrible—and it's all coming back to me now!"

On August 14, Bill Naughton's play *Spring and Port Wine* played its 750th performance in London's West End. That same day, Naughton's *Keep It in the Family* went into rehearsal in New York. Allan Davis directed both plays, and the similarities between the two do not end there: the London smash was about a North Country Englishman, living with his wife and four grown children, who becomes enmeshed in a family row when his youngest daughter refuses to eat a piece of herring. The American play was about a Massachusetts man, living with his wife and four grown children, who becomes enmeshed in a family row when his youngest daughter refuses to eat a piece of mackerel.

Obviously, you don't write two plays about fish fights, and Naughton didn't. The play entering rehearsal, *Keep It in the Family,* was an Americanization of *Spring and Port Wine.* The first question that comes to mind is: Since the play was a smash in London, and a smash is what everyone is after, why change it at all? The answer is that bringing a play over is an enormous gamble because there is little similarity in taste between London and New York. Of all the great hit plays, only one, *Arsenic and Old Lace,* managed to run 1,000 performances in both cities. *Boeing-Boeing,* which went into a fifth year in London, couldn't last three weeks here in 1965. And *The Mousetrap,* which has presently run more than 6,000 London performances, lived less than 200 here, and those at a smaller, off-Broadway house.

The problem of the transplant cannot be exaggerated in relation to Broadway: in the 1967–68 season, almost half of the straight plays were to have foreign origin, the great percentage English. Some plays are brought over unchanged; some are changed enormously but keep their original locale; some are Americanized, as was the case here. The decision of what to do with the transplant is usually left to the producer.

David Merrick, famed in song and story, was the producer of *Keep It in the Family,* and it was apparently his idea to Americanize Naughton's play. He explained why: "Naughton is deeply entrenched in North Country colloquialisms. Both his previous plays, good plays, failed in New York *and* in the West End too. If it's American, the audience can associate with it more."

To effect the transplant, Merrick went after N. Richard Nash, who was to suffer greatly this season. But Nash (best known for his wonderful romantic comedy, *The Rainmaker*) did not take much to the notion. "Merrick asked me to do it and I said 'No.' He said, 'At least go see it,' so I did, and I thought it was successful because of the monumental contribution of the director. I think that without the accumulation of telling detail he put into it, it would have failed in London." Merrick persisted. "Merrick called me in France, and I remember exactly what he said. He said, 'I'll make you two promises: we'll have the same director, and you don't have to have your name on it. And since you don't, you're now in the position of doing me a favor or not with no harm to yourself. Which do you want to do?' " Later, Nash was to say, "David shouldn't have insisted, and I shouldn't have done it." But he did do it. He agreed to attempt the transplant, even though he hated the play.

Allan Davis, the director, was all in favor of Americanizing the play. "I was here in New York when one of Bill's [Naughton] plays came in; it seemed doomed from Princeton on. With Bill, it's all character. Simple plot. Character. And with North Country working-class people. Now, if the audience can't identify, you're in trouble. Before Merrick, I wanted to make it Manchester Jewish. Sam Levene, Molly Picon—their speech patterns would be close to Manchester Jewish. But Bill didn't like the idea of making them Jewish. Then I thought, 'They ought to be from your Midwest.' "

Nash thought they ought to be from Pennsylvania, and that is where he set it originally. But then one night in London, he and Merrick saw the Irish actor Patrick Magee in *Staircase*. When Merrick suggested Magee for the lead role of the tyrannical father, the family became Catholic and the setting jumped to Massachusetts.

The Americanized version of the play that eventually opened in New York was probably, academically speaking, a better play than the long-running London hit. Not only that, but, according to the director, "the Nash jokes went better than the Naughton jokes." In other words, *Keep It in the Family* was a better and funnier play than the original. It opened in New York on Wednesday, September 27, and closed three days later to a loss of approximately $95,000.

Why?

Before making an educated guess, a small briefing on the story. The English version, *Spring and Port Wine,* centers around a family war between a peculiar man who is a tyrant and his wife and four children. The man is a no-nonsense workingman—his wife has to account for every penny in her weekly accounts—and the four kids, though they may mock him in private, snap to when he is around. "Kids" is really the wrong word here. They are, more accurately, young men and women, ranging from eighteen to their middle twenties. They all live at home, and they all pay board to their father for the privilege of doing so. Then the youngest daughter, nineteen, and secretly pregnant, stands up to her father: she refuses to eat a piece of herring. He insists. She will not budge. He decrees that the same piece of herring will be served to her at every meal until she does eat it, and until that time, nothing else will be given her for sustenance. The battle goes on until the eighteen-year-old son feeds the herring to the family cat. The father berates the boy, who collapses under the pressures. Eventually, everyone rebels, and the family seems about to split apart. But in the end, everyone is back together, sadder and wiser. In other words, the revolt of the younger generation has taken place in a small mill town outside Manchester, England.

But we've had that revolt in America. Looking around today, can anybody doubt that not only is the battle over, but the young people won in a walk? So when you put that situation in America, it all turns phony. What was real and compelling in England becomes ludicrous in America of the late sixties. How many families do you know where the four children, ranging from eighteen to, say, twenty-five, still live at home? *And pay rent?* What happened with the play here was that the reality, crucial to the success in London, simply evaporated with the anachronistic situation.

So, out of town, they set the play back 20 years. The idea of changing the time had occurred to Merrick, Nash and Davis while they were still in rehearsal. But the decision then was not to do anything and hope that the anachronism would work *for* the play; in other words, point up that the father was an old-fashioned man behind the times, and this, theoretically, would disarm the audience about the falseness of the general situation.

They opened in Boston to mixed notices. Elliot Norton, probably the most influential out-of-town reviewer, pointed out that the play was anachronistic. So then they set it back 20 years, hoping that the audience would think that this was how the revolt of the young people all started, because of situations like this.

But though the program said it was 20 years ago, the feel of the play was still 1967, and they couldn't shake it. The whole situation of the children at home paying board just didn't wash. No one believed it, neither the audience nor the creative people. Nash said, "The kids paying board is ridiculous. But it could be made to work. I wanted to investigate it, to see what happens if you bring the problem into the open and have the oldest son complain and the father say to him, 'You're right. Now go find a room of your own.' Then you could see what would happen to the son when he is offered his freedom and is frightened. Then you could really get at what a tyrant is and what a weakling is." But this kind of scene, valid as it may be, would likely have ripped the fragile fabric of a play that was, at heart, pleasant family bickering. Nash was right to want to do the scene, and Merrick and Davis were right in not allowing it.

I talked to Nash the day that *Keep It in the Family* opened. He was at the Sovereign Apartments in Westwood, California, working on the Merrick musical *The Happy Time* and feeling very much like Cassandra. "I don't think the play's going to make it," he said. "I feel even more strongly about its problems now than when I began on it. There isn't a genuine conflict in the whole play—just squabbles. And if you're going to write a comedy, it has to be about something serious."

A few days after the play opened and closed, I spoke again with the director, Allan Davis. He was packing for the trip back home. "The characters just weren't as real as Americans. No one identified with them. We got the facts of American life right—coffee for tea, mackerel for herring—but it all seemed silly here, the fish business. And the audience wouldn't rise to the play . . . they just wouldn't rise."

Then was Americanizing the play a bad idea? Merrick himself wasn't sure. "Could be terrible," he said before the opening. Davis was positive, even after the opening, that they had done the right thing. "We never would have left Boston if the setting had stayed English, I'm sure of it. We absolutely would have closed out of town." No one's ever going to know how, just as no one will ever be able to state an accurate rule about how to effect successfully a transplant without rejection. Certainly the play was a failure here. And certainly a real play had been turned phony. But how much does it matter that it was phony—does anybody actually think *Cactus Flower* is real? And *Cactus Flower* is an Americanized version of a foreign play.

Is it fair to generalize about a phony play failing? Naughton's other plays failed here, including *Alfie,* and they were as real here as in England. Maybe the answer is not to bring over playwrights like Naughton, who seem particularly indigenous to their terrain. There is, after all, no law that states that *all* English hits must be given to us. But as long as English plays keep running, American producers are going to knife each other for the chance to bring them over. And God knows, *Spring and Port Wine* kept on running; it gave its 800th consecutive performance on the day director Davis returned to England. He seemed anxious to get back.

As has already been pointed out, Broadway professionals gauge the potential success of a production as soon as the creative elements have been contractually assembled. Some shows start out big and open big: *The Odd Couple.* Some start out big and open small:

Kean. Some start out big and just don't open: *Breakfast at Tiffany's.*

On any rating system, the lowest rung is reserved for what is called the "Kiss of Death" production. This is the show that under no conceivable conditions can work. When a show feels like the Kiss of Death, it dies. "Feel" is really the operative word here. Louis Armstrong said of jazz that "if you can't feel it, I can't explain it to you," and the same holds true for the Kiss of Death. It's like Matthew Arnold's touchstone theory in reverse: no matter how talented the individual members of a production may be, the show is just going to lie there. Something in the combination presages disaster.

Song of the Grasshopper was the first Kiss of Death production of the season. Just why this was so cannot be definitively stated. But a brief study of the billing might prove at least a little instructive:

Gene Dingenary   Miranda d'Ancona   Nancy Levering
present
ALFRED DRAKE
in
SONG OF THE GRASSHOPPER
A New Comedy by
ALFONSO PASO
Adapted from the Spanish by
WILLIAM LAYTON and AUGUSTIN PENON
Directed by
CHARLES BOWDEN

Taking them in no particular order: the producers not only had never produced on Broadway before, they had never produced together as a trio before. Granted that everyone has to start somewhere; still, first producers tend to suffer more than experienced producers, who suffer greatly.

The adapters had never written a Broadway play before. They had, however, written a daily radio serial for the Quaker Oats Company, "Don Quakero," which for five years was broadcast to eight South American countries. So far, then, we have two new writers adapting a play for three new producers. The author of the original play, of course, was that incredibly successful figure, the author of 112 produced plays by the age of forty, the famous Alfonso Paso.

Who?

Now the feel is starting to come. If Paso is so famous, why hasn't anyone heard of him? Obviously because his plays haven't been done here. But if he's so successful, why haven't his plays been done here?

Whatever the reasons, valid or not, it must be admitted that there hasn't exactly been a bull market for Spanish plays on Broadway lately. The last Spanish smash was _____ (fill in your own blank). There may never have been a Spanish blockbuster, which doesn't mean there couldn't be one, and if *Song of the Grasshopper* was going to make it, the director was going to be crucial. For director: Charles Bowden.

Who?

Charles Bowden, the producer. He produced Williams' *Night of the Iguana* and Camus's *Caligula,* and he worked for 14 years with the Lunts. But in the sixties, he had not been credited with the staging of a single Broadway production. So *Song of the Grasshopper* was going into production with three untried producers, two untried adapters and one at least recently untried director. For star: Alfred Drake.

No "Who?" here. Alfred Drake is famous, gifted, dynamic, intelligent, and he is a terrific musical-comedy performer, the only man active in the theatre who has starred in three blockbuster musicals: *Oklahoma!, Kiss Me, Kate* and *Kismet.* But *Song of the Grasshopper* wasn't a musical; it was a play. And in the sixties Drake had appeared twice previously as the chief star in Broadway plays: *Lorenzo,* boom, four performances and out, and *Those That Play the Clowns,* boom, four performances and out.

Total it up: producers who haven't produced, writers who haven't written, a director who hasn't directed, and a star whose selection of straight plays, though admittedly adventurous, has not been much in keeping with the public taste. All of them turning their talents toward a seven-year-old Spanish play.

The Kiss of Death?

On August 9, *Song of the Grasshopper* went into rehearsal, and nothing concrete was heard of it for a while, one way or the other, which is standard: along the street, rehearsal period is generally a time of meaningless gossip, and a play can range from being a hit to a disaster and back on any given afternoon. For close to a month, *Song of the Grasshopper* was just one of any number of shows getting in shape.

Then, on September 6, it opened in Wilmington. There were two reviews—one pan and one qualified negative. (No one knew it then, but that was the high point, that qualified negative.) Business in Wilmington was bad, less than 25% of capacity, which was damaging, but not nearly so damaging as the troubles that were beginning to surface. By the time the show opened in Philadelphia a week later, everyone around Broadway knew that there was terrible trouble with *Song of the Grasshopper:* the authors weren't happy with the show, and the director wasn't happy with the authors.

All three Philadelphia reviews were negative. Business dropped to less than 15% of capacity. The producers waived their third week out of town and came back to New York early. By now a new writer had been brought in to doctor the script, and the old writers contemplated not allowing the action. A representative of the Dramatists' Guild was sent in to try and settle things as amicably as possible. A decision was reached that allowed the new writer to work. But this kind of thing can never be amicable. When *Song of the Grasshopper* opened in New York on September 28, the old writers did not attend. "We could not evidence with our presence what was on stage," one of them told me.

The critics, however, did come. One of them thought that *"Song of the Grasshopper* has all the subtlety and charm of a bull stabbing."* Another felt that "it is all dullness on the surface and, beneath that, more dullness." Still another: "At least now the season can only get better."

What was this play, and why did it die?

The main character, Aris (Alfred Drake), lives, separated from his wife, in a terrible pit of a house on the outskirts of Madrid. He has a lovely marriageable daughter, assorted younger children from assorted women, plus a crocodile in the bathroom. The latter, a recent addition, was found wandering on the property. He also has no money, the electricity is about to be turned off, the furniture taken away, and his last ten pesetas are invested in a raffle ticket.

He is also absolutely unperturbed about his situation. He knows that somehow everything is going to turn out all right. And the course of the play proves him right: he wins the raffle, returns the crocodile for a reward, etc. He is also reunited with his wife, who comes to see that his world view is the only one that really matters. So what if a grasshopper dies? You can never take away the singing it has done.

Clearly, this is a delicate play and must come across as such if it is to succeed. Said the authors: "The subject of the play was ignored in direction and interpretation; what we got was situation comedy, and the jokes aren't meant to carry it. Imagine *Harvey,* for example, being played as a situation comedy." Said the director: "What happened with us is what frequently happens when you have inexperienced writers: they become defensive; their ego becomes involved." Said Penon, one of the authors: "I had twelve conferences with the director. I thought he understood the play. I still don't know what happened; he talked so brilliantly about it." Said the director: "The authors thought they should see the finished product at once. In rehearsals they would say, 'Oh, no, no, that's not right,' and I would say, 'Of course it isn't right yet, but it will be by the end of the afternoon.' They made everybody nervous." Said Penon: "He didn't want us at rehearsals; run-throughs we could go to, but rehearsals were something else." Said Bowden, the director: "We didn't really keep them out of the theatre." Said Layton, the other author: "They didn't go so far as to forbid our attending rehearsals—I would have asked to have that put in writing—but there was that trouble in the second week of rehearsal and . . ." (What happened, as closely as it can be reconstructed, is that one of the actresses had a line she didn't like: "I feel beastly as ever." She asked the writers for a new line. One of them gave it to her: "I feel as low as ever." But he didn't go through the director to do it, and one of the producers said he had committed a cardinal sin of the theatre. After that, the authors were isolated from the actors. As a general rule, authors should not do anything without first getting the permission of the director. But this infraction, though infraction it clearly was, seems so slight compared with the repercussions that an educated guess would be that there was a desire to get the authors out of rehearsals, and this was as convenient an excuse as any.)

Communication, already strained, snapped. The writers were kept away from the director. Any notes the writers had were sent to one of the producers, who then explained everything to the director. Naturally enough, there is a difference of opinion today about how the producers behaved throughout all this. The director said, "They were fantastically co-operative and well organized," while the writers felt, "They acted out of panic."

What the producers did, as has been noted, was to bring in a doctor. "The writers took it so personally," Bowden said. "They felt it was a personal affront. But you've got to learn to take criticism in this business. I had several dear friends of mine down to see the show, and they all agreed that the trouble was with the script, not my direction." After Bowden's friends had made their judgment, a new writer was sent for. The old writers said, "The new man was a friend of Bowden's. He was brought in before we were consulted. He added jokes; we protested, vigorously, but . . ."

Now these are all men of good will, remember, and no one was setting about to sabotage anyone or anything. And remember, too, that this was a simple play, a play, as author Penon put it, "about a man who believes in Providence." He's got no money, he's deep in debt, there are mouths to feed, yet somehow it's all going to turn out. This is, naturally, a debatable notion, and during rehearsal period, Bowden and Alfred Drake wanted Aris to be given some kind of minor occupation for when Providence failed him— nothing big—maybe tutoring or doing small articles for the local papers. Bowden put it this way: "I feel he writes poems or takes in students. Occasionally. I don't think he does it for any set fee, but I think he does it."

At this point, I would like to talk briefly about the nature of Spanish and Portuguese comedy. (Ignore this paragraph; look at the one above.) Spanish comedy differs from Portuguese comedy in that . . . (Reread that paragraph above; do you see it?) . . . and, of course, one cannot estimate the effect of Franco and his consequent censorship . . . (You've got to have it by this time: the adapters were writing *a play about a man who believes in Providence,* while the director was directing *a play about a man who has an occupation for when Providence fails him.*)

That's the ball game. Right there. It's all over, and if you don't see why, the following is meant to put it in relief. We're writing a play about Columbus and Isabella. Scene: a great hall. Isabella on the throne at one end, Columbus kneeling before her. The room is lined with courtiers.

COLUMBUS
(*Rising*)
Your Majesty, I need three of your ships.

ISABELLA
(*Taken aback*)
Three . . . ? For what purpose, brave mariner?

COLUMBUS
(*He pauses, looks at the mocking courtiers. Then—a burst—*)
To sail around the world!

ISABELLA
Around the world? Fool, you'll sail clean off the edges.

COLUMBUS
(*Passionately*)
There aren't any edges, Your Majesty.

ISABELLA
How can there be no edges since the world is flat?

We have now arrived, as the hippies say, at the nitty-gritty. What can Columbus tell her? His existence is based on the lunatic notion that the world is round; and that is what makes him different from everybody else. (Just as Aris' thinking that Providence will take care of him *always* is what makes him different from everybody else.) Can Columbus say he's invented an edge rounder? No, he can't, because he's not a liar and because he hasn't invented one, and if he says he has, she'll sure ask to see the damn thing, and then where is he? Columbus could say that he isn't 100% sure: in other words, sometimes he thinks the world is round, but when he doesn't think it's round, he thinks it's flat. That is a perfectly valid line of reasoning, and you could write him that way, and if you did you would be writing about *a man who has doubts.* But that is exactly what the adapters of *Song of the Grasshopper* were *not* writing about. *Their man believed.* His entire existence is coupled with that mad belief: Providence will take care of me!

I know of no way of indicating the importance of this seemingly trivial disagreement between the writers and the director. It's like the Pentagon: no matter how big you're told it is, when you get there, it's bigger. The disagreement becomes reflected in every conceivable aspect of the production. Example: Aris, the believer, is a total innocent, and you get Alfred Drake to play him. Impossible. Drake is sophisticated, vital, a man who can't stand still. Aris is content to lie in his hovel with a crocodile in the head and wait for God to smile on him. Drake can't play that. Drake is Petruchio; he has to make things happen.

The breakdown of communication that began to surface in rehearsal was present from the beginning. But the crucial questions between the creative personnel simply were not asked. Why weren't they? A guess would be because everybody probably thought that everybody else understood. This kind of communications problem happens constantly on Broadway, and not just to newcomers. Bob Fosse, the experienced and wonderfully gifted musical-comedy director, said, "I was doing a show once; we had opened out of town, and the reviews were terrible—*terrible*—and we were sitting around, and I was talking and the book writer was talking and the composer was talking, and it turned out we all saw three different shows. In our heads. We were all working on three completely different musical comedies. Now why didn't we find that out sooner? We just didn't—don't ask me why." One of Jerome Robbins' great strengths is his ability to ask anyone any question, no matter what. Sheldon

Harnick, the lyricist for *Fiddler,* who worked with Robbins on that musical, says this: "Any show should be one man's vision. When Robbins takes over a show, it's his vision in every department. He drives the set designer crazy, he drives the orchestrater crazy, he has a total vision of what he wants. He presses you and presses you on every point, no matter how trivial, until it isn't trivial any more."

Song of the Grasshopper opened Thursday night, September 28, and closed two nights later, at a loss of its entire investment, about $100,000. Closings are generally sad; some become funereal. But the ending of *Song of the Grasshopper* was somehow angry; it was as if you were only there because you'd lost a bet. At 8:29 there was a total of 18 people in the lobby, counting the bartender. A woman with an eye patch walked by. At a hit she would have looked mysterious; here she just seemed wounded.

Inside, an usher was staring at the painfully empty orchestra. "Sit anywhere you want," she told me. "It's really a shame. No one walked out during the previews. It's just a shame 'cause it's not as bad as they say. It's no Pulitzer prize but . . ." She handed me my program, and then suddenly she was mad, her voice just the least out of control as she unloaded on Clive Barnes, who had cursed in his review of the play. "He said it was worse than *Dr. Cook's Garden.* He said 'goddam.' He used that word. In the *Times.*"

She stopped then, confused, staring front, for Murphy's Law ("Everything that can go wrong will go wrong"), which had been operating all week long in the theatre, was still going full blast. Because right then, with the house lights still on bright, with a few ushers slowly leading a few people down the carpeted aisles, at 8:42 P.M., five minutes before the curtain went up, the curtain went up. Not all the way up. Probably no more than 15 feet. But there was old Alfred Drake on stage, not doing much of anything, just waiting for the curtain to go up, and he turned slowly front, and there we were, the audience—*the audience!*

And I think I'll always remember *Song of the Grasshopper* like that, caught with its curtain up, its numbed star staring around, the audience staring around, everybody staring around, all of us confused, a piece of Pirandello in the night.

THE BOOTH THEATRE

HAILA STODDARD   MARK WRIGHT

LEONARD S. FIELD

present

HAROLD PINTER'S
THE BIRTHDAY PARTY

a comedy of menace

Directed by
ALAN SCHNEIDER

with

RUTH WHITE   **HENDERSON FORSYTHE**   **JAMES PATTERSON**

ALEXANDRA BERLIN   **ED FLANDERS**   **EDWARD WINTER**

Setting and Costumes by   *Lighting by*
WILLIAM RITMAN   **THARON MUSSER**

Associate Producer
DUANE WILDER

CHAPTER

4

"We're Losing You, Darling"

The Broadway season really got
exciting with the October 3 opening of Harold Pinter's *The Birthday Party*. Pinter, born in London in 1930, has been called "the best
and most important young playwright now alive." *The Birthday
Party*, his first full-length play, was done in London in 1958, where
it died within a week, leaving Pinter just another out-of-work actor
for a while.

As everyone knows, *Bench* changed all that. *Bench*, written for
BBC television, proved his first overwhelming success. Many people
feel that Kenneth Tynan's lengthy essay on *Bench* in *The Observer*
did as much for Pinter as Tynan's review of *Look Back in Anger*
had done four years previously for John Osborne.

Bench, of course, is a 50-minute play, all of it taking place, as the
title suggests, on a lonely seaside bench in an (unnamed) English
resort town. The play, a series of seemingly disconnected encoun-
ters between men occupying the bench, comes to a climax in the famous scene reprinted below. (The two characters in the scene have,
if anyone has forgotten, appeared in the play once before, but not
together; this is the only time in the play that anyone returns to
the bench for a second visit.) It might be advisable here to give the
scene a glance again, along with some of what Mr. Tynan wrote

about it, to see what light it sheds on Pinter in general, and *The Birthday Party* in particular.

DUSK, TEDDY ON THE BENCH ALONE. A TREMENDOUS MAN. STAN APPROACHES, HESITATES. TINY. ABRUPTLY HE SITS ON THE BENCH, KNEE TO KNEE WITH THE GIANT TEDDY.

TEDDY
Hello.

STAN
What'd you say—what'd you say?

TEDDY
(*Pause*)
Nothing.

STAN
Oh.
(*Pause*)
The roses . . .

TEDDY
What'd you say—what'd you say?

STAN
I said the roses.

TEDDY
The roses what? Get on with it—*the roses what?*

STAN
(*Pause. Then rises, stands over the bigger man*)
You know what.

TEDDY
I do, do I?

STAN
(*Pause*)
You know and Frankie knows.
(*Long pause*)
Frankie knows better than you know.
(*Pause*)
But you know.

TEDDY
All I did was say hello.

STAN
You denied the roses!

TEDDY
Keep your damn roses.

STAN

(Longest pause)

I intend to, mate. Tell that to Frankie. Tell him the roses are . . . are . . .

TEDDY

Are what?

STAN

(Pause)

Bloody well mine . . .

STAN GOES. DUSK. TEDDY ON THE BENCH ALONE. TREMENDOUS.

FINAL FADE OUT

The following is excerpted from Tynan's *Observer* article of November 27, 1960. ". . . as good as the play is, and certainly for a television play it has been extraordinary, it is not until the terminal confrontation between Teddy and Stan that one realizes that one is not only in the presence of an artist, but incredibly (the man has just turned thirty), an artist already at the peak of his powers.

"I know of no other modern dramaturgy as compressed as this: 16 speeches, 85 words, and (most significantly) 8 pauses. At first, when the two men are seated 'knee to knee,' it seems we are to witness the most wearisome of modern theatrical clichés, the 'deviate pickup scene.' But very soon it is clear that what we are watching is, *for Pinter,* the ultimate violence: the announcement of a future murder. (A lesser artist would never be content with the indication of violence; he would have to show the crime.) Pinter hints at it, conveys it, then leaves it, and at the same time leaves us sick with frustration. For surely Stan is going to die. And surely we cannot save him.

"What is Stan's crime? Clearly he is not the least ashamed of it; no man ashamed would hurl a charge the way Stan hurls 'You denied the roses!' at Teddy. And that of course is Stan's crime: he is not ashamed. For he is Man and not ashamed of it, and for that he must die; for that, Teddy, tremendous Teddy, must kill him. Stan is Man. (Is the rhyme a hint? Probably. Pinter need not have done that.) Man: virile, proud of his red blood. Teddy is, of course, homosexual, which is why Stan sits knee to knee with him—a taunt. Stan is man unafraid, no matter how great the odds or how tremendous the enemy.

"Frankie, referred to twice—some think mysteriously—is not mysterious at all. He is, of course, St. Francis of Assisi, the founder of the Franciscan order, all this clearly indicated by the fact that the Franciscans have split into three orders, just as the human race is split into thirds: men, women and homosexuals such as Teddy.

"What *Bench* is then, finally, is a heterosexual outcry against the modern world. Telling, moving, painful in its honesty, brilliant in its conception, it is pure Pinter. One final note: some critics have wondered why, since *Bench* is concerned with the world being in thirds—men, women and deviates—there are no women characters. The obvious Freudian reply would be that Woman is indeed present: the Great Woman herself; the Sea.

"But Pinter is far past Freud, and the final answer is his alone, for his art is not really menace or fear. It is the God-given ability to infuse universal meaning through the use of secrets. And if you tell what your secrets mean, well, they would hardly be secrets any more, now would they?"

With Tynan's analysis in mind, let us proceed to *The Birthday Party*. American critics had a terrible time with it. John Chapman of the New York *Daily News* called it a "whatzit." Clive Barnes of the *Times* thought it was incomparably one of the two most interesting plays to appear on Broadway in some seasons, the other being Pinter's Tony-award winner from the previous year, *The Homecoming*. Richard Watts of the *Post* was in between, finding it both cryptic and dramatically artful. The television critics were similarly in disarray; one of them felt that it started slowly but really picked up speed as it went along, while another felt it had a terrific beginning but bogged down toward the end. Pinter, of course, is famous for leaving certain things unsaid, and this annoyed *The New Yorker* critic, who felt it would have been all right had Pinter been forced "to be mysterious because of political pressure or the like," while *Time* felt that "unwillingness to communicate is his central theme" and therefore crucial to his work. The *Newsweek* man felt . . . there's really no telling what the *Newsweek* man felt, because he kept putting these strange words down one after the other. The following strange words occur after a plot synopsis: "Into this orchestration of rock-bottom behavior and starkly pungent language, Pinter builds a polyphony of hints, insinuations, metaphysical tips and touts that add up, not to 'meaning,' but to a visitation of portentous activity."

Never mind what *The Birthday Party*'s about; what's *Newsweek* about?

Alan Schneider, who directed the production, has a notion what

The Birthday Party is about: "Somebody is after somebody else and gets 'em." Schneider, a Tony-award winner for his work on *Who's Afraid of Virginia Woolf?*, is probably the busiest drama director on Broadway. Schneider is fifty, looks a lot less, and is enormously articulate, which is interesting only insofar as most of his best-known work has been with playwrights who tend to defy articulation —Albee, Samuel Beckett and Pinter. "I've done a lot of plays that seem to have no meaning—*The Trial* is my favorite novel—I have a drive toward the thing that isn't defined. I'm Russian, maybe that's why."

Schneider had been with *Birthday Party* a long time. "Since 1958. I arrived in England the week it closed and happened to see the Sunday reviews. I thought it sounded interesting, but I couldn't find the play. I was casting understudies, and somebody said, 'Please take a look at this actor friend of mine; he desperately needs the work.' And this guy and his wife came in, and it was Pinter, using his actor's name, I think. Later, when we got to know each other, he said, 'I've got this play I wish you'd look at,' and it was *Birthday Party*.

"It's gone through three stages since then. I wanted to do it and I brought it home with me, but it was impossible for anyone to read it at that time—Beckett and the rest of them hadn't happened yet. Yale said no to it; the Actors' Studio said no to it; I just put it aside. Then Harold became respectable with *The Caretaker,* and there were lots of offers to do it off-Broadway, using *The Caretaker* as an example of why it shouldn't be done on Broadway, since *The Caretaker* failed financially. But Harold said 'No.' Finally, with *The Homecoming,* Harold is now commercial. So, after—what is it? —almost ten years, it's being done."

To understand just what was so difficult about *The Birthday Party,* a summary of the plot might be in order. A piano player is living as the lone boarder with an elderly couple in a house at the English seaside. Two men, a Jew and an Irishman, come to take rooms, and the piano player is upset. The landlady tells the two men that it is the piano player's birthday, and a party is arranged, a neighboring girl being among those invited. Before the party, the two men savagely interrogate the piano player, accuse him of leaving the "organization." At this point violence would probably erupt if the landlady didn't appear dressed for the party. The party begins, and during a game of blindman's buff, the lights go out. In the darkness there is confusion, and as the Jew and the Irishman advance with flashlights toward the piano player, he retreats, giggling wildly. In the third act, the piano player, now nearly catatonic, is taken away by the strangers to face someone called Monty.

To repeat director Schneider's words: "Somebody is after somebody else and gets 'em." Nothing particularly difficult about the skeletal plot. It's really a 1930's gangster movie: John Garfield is hiding out, having left the Mafia, and Peter Lorre and Sydney Greenstreet come and drag him back to face Edward G. Robinson.

Except that there are a lot of things that Pinter doesn't ever say. For example, it isn't the Mafia—oh, it might be, or it might be the American Dental Association. He never specifies. The reference is only to the "organization." And the big boss, Monty: that's all we ever know about him, his name. We don't really know that he's the big boss; we only know that the piano player is being taken to see Monty. We don't even know for sure if the piano player is a piano player; he tells us about a concert he played, but the circumstances are so strange, and so is he, that it all might be a figment. And, of course, it isn't his birthday. His landlady says it is, but he tells us it isn't.

The New York *Times* has called Pinterism "maximum tension through minimum information," and it was just this frustrating lack of facts that infuriated the Wednesday-matinee ladies at *The Birthday Party*. Now these were good women, doing their damnedest to keep up. Before the first-act curtain, two of them were talking about problems with their teen-age sons.

FIRST WOMAN
I put on the Lovin' Spoonful; Simon and Garfunkel I tried.

SECOND WOMAN
Good for you.

FIRST WOMAN
"Explain it to me," I said to him. "I would like to know."

SECOND WOMAN
What did he say?

FIRST WOMAN
Nothing. *Nothing.* I practically begged. "Help me," I said. "I don't understand. *Does my needle need changing?*"

Clearly, they were trying, these two. At the first-act intermission, they walked silently up the aisles. Finally, one of them spoke.

FIRST WOMAN
It's about the terrors of everyday life.

SECOND WOMAN
I don't get that too much.

The second act of the play contains the birthday party itself, which ends in semidarkness. One of the final moments before the curtain has the piano player on top of the neighbor girl, who is spread-eagled and motionless. The whole theatre was buzzing as the ladies moved to smoke. "It's always like this," an usher said. "This jabbering. Always." In the lobby, half a dozen women were inhaling angrily.

FIRST WOMAN
Why? That's all I wanna know—just *why?*
SECOND WOMAN
Why what?
FIRST WOMAN
Why does he do this? If I were an artist, I would *want* to communicate. That's my job. I'm an artist, I'm supposed to communicate. Something. It shouldn't just have form—form's not enough—gotta be content—anything to communicate. What's with this Pinter? Why?

I talked to Pinter about it. He said, "It's a bloody big bore when they can't accept a thing for what happens on stage. On the whole, the what's-it-all-about business is more pronounced over here. It's about what the people do on the stage. Otherwise you could just put a poster up on stage, couldn't you? 'This scene is about . . . the next scene is about . . .' I'm not a sociologist; I'm just a writer. And I don't conceptualize very much. Never before and very little after.

"The original idea was the domestic situation: someone upstairs sleeping in a house, a boarder. The lodger eventually comes down. The domestic situation by the seaside, that was the start of it. The other characters didn't arrive till later. One day, about 20 pages in, Goldberg and McCann turned up. I didn't know anything about them until they appeared.

"This what's-it-about business—one regrets it. I'm doing a play now; it's my first in three years, and it means a great deal to me. I've done less and less writing for the stage. Writing becomes more difficult the older you get, at least it does for me. I found some 1950 poems of mine recently; I was astonished by the freedom I had, the energy, a complete uncaringness about form. I can't write that way any more. I'm thirty-seven now. I feel as if I'm eighty." He sounded very tired as he spoke. He was in America for a few days, and there were at least 50 requests for interviews. Every radio station wanted him, most of the TV, many of the newspapers, the magazines. Everybody wondering what it was all about.

FIRST WOMAN
It's got a lot to do with menace, that much I can tell you.

SECOND WOMAN
Oh, yes, very much. Menace and terror, yes.

They moved back down the aisles, and the third act started. Halfway through, a "buzz-buzz-buzz" of wonder burst across the theatre: Lulu, the neighbor girl who had been motionless and spread-eagled at the second-act curtain, made her entrance, and the ladies had to get it straight.

SECOND WOMAN
What is this? I thought she was dead.

FIRST WOMAN
She was dead.

SECOND WOMAN
Don't tell me dead; she's standing there.

FIRST WOMAN
She's a symbol.

.   .   .

The street was stuffed with children. December; 60 degrees; 11:15 in the morning, and it's raining. They stand there, waiting. Above them, teachers hold umbrellas as they hem the children in toward the building line, doing their best to keep the sidewalk at least partially clear.

11:20, and the children are quiet, but now they are beginning to hop up and down in place, hop, hop, staring toward the front of the line which begins at the entrance to Loew's Eighty-sixth Street movie theatre on Third Avenue.

Inside the theatre lobby the ushers are getting ready for the onslaught. There are 3,000 kids already seated in the theatre, jamming it, but the special Christmas play is ending, and they have to be cleared before the 3,000 kids outside can come in for the second show.

11:25, and it's as if some giant vacuum cleaner is sucking the first-show audience toward the exit doors. Fffffft, and they're going, going, and in the lobby the ushers are looking at each other, getting

ready, making last-minute checks with the teachers standing outside
in the rain.

11:30, and in they come! Not slowly—no trickle—just *whoosh!*
and then the flood—

—this way—

—no no no *this* way—

—follow Irving everybody—

Out of the rain they come, silent, and maybe four feet tall on the
average, all colors, shapes, you name it, and gloriously wet and—

—up the stairs—

—hit it kids—

—*now don't move*—(This from a tough Italian teacher to part of
his group, who froze on the word *move,* while he went off after
some others. An usher came up to them and said, "Go on in, children," but they weren't budging, so the usher said, "Please, children,
you're blocking things." But they had been given the word, and the
word was *don't move.* So finally, one of them raised an arm and
pointed to the Italian, and the usher ran over to him and explained,
and the Italian nodded, that's all, just a quick nod, but his boys
knew an order when it was given and now, alive again, they filed
down into the theatre and sat.)

—quiet now—

—patience, Sandra—

—hold hands and here we go and—

—the balcony?—(This last from a Negro teacher with Negro children in reply to an usher who was pointing up, and suddenly you
could see it on the Negro teacher's face as she looked around to see
if any white children were being sent upstairs too. "Really," the
usher told her, "you'll see better, and the main floor's full." And
now the Negro teacher saw it was the truth, that the main floor *was*
pretty full and that all colors were heading up the stairs, so still
just the least suspiciously she gestured for her flock to follow, and
up she trudged, dragging her tails behind her.)

—quickly now—

—shhhh—

And most of them were in before the first great thing happened
(this is all going to make sense in time). As these lines of children
charged across the lobby of Loew's Eighty-sixth to get in for the
free Christmas show, in this wild confusion, one little kid accidentally splintered off from her group and didn't know it because
everybody was running one way or another, and instead of running

with one group she was running with another. Her teacher caught sight of her as she was about to disappear, and although the teacher had enough to do shepherding the rest of her babes, she set off across the lobby like Gale Sayers, and at the far entrance managed to grab hold of the girl. As she spun the kid around, what do you think she said? "I told you to watch where you're going!" No. "Can't you ever listen, what's the matter with you?" Never. Not even close. What she said to the small startled eyes was this: "We're losing you, darling."

. . . we're losing you, darling. . . . (Remember, this will all make sense in time.)

Inside, the 3,000 were seated, and a Negro group sang "I Believe," and after the clapping, out went the lights. Then a spot hit him jogging down the aisle, red suit and beard and ho-ho-ho, and when he got to the mike, he said, "Merry Christmas, ho-ho-ho, and stay in your seats 'cause I've got my helpers checking on you, and no eating lunches during the show." Then Santa said, "Now let's all sing 'Jingle Bells' together," and he took a breath and started to sing.

But he was already way behind them!

That was the second great thing. Because the minute he suggested "Jingle Bells," they were off, all 3,000; they didn't wait for his word "together," and they didn't need any deep breath. The man said sing "Jingle Bells," so they sang. Then he said he'd be back after the show, and the curtain began to open, and as it did, there was that sound again, the "buzz-buzz-buzz" of wonder.

And I couldn't help thinking of the ladies at Pinter and how angry they were because they didn't understand what it was all about; so they resisted. And they wouldn't have sung "Jingle Bells" either. They probably would have first had to know who the bells belonged to, and what did the one-horse open sleigh *really* represent, symbolically speaking.

Now this is very dangerous. Let's take the worst possibility: let's say that you think the Pinter play is about apples, and it turns out it's about oranges. If you liked the apples, what possible difference does it make? You want to know about Harold Pinter? He is an English stylist, talented as hell, and right now he is cresting for one, and only one, reason: he is appropriately obscure; *he allows intellectuals to theorize.*

And *The Birthday Party,* if you really want to know what it's about, is about this: there is no hiding place. Does that make it a better play? Does that make the two hours any more pleasant while you're sitting there? Pinter is also saying, "There is no God." Or maybe he isn't. But in either case, it's pretty cornball, right? Examine any art work done down to bone and you find cliché. That's one of the things that's so painful about graduate school. You take some pretty poem, some poem that really moves you, and you examine it and pore over its imagery and decipher the philosophy, and what do you come up with? Keats is saying, "Love thy neighbor."

So what? That's for us intellectuals. We can argue about it. What you have to worry about is just this: You like the poem? Say so. You don't? Say it's spinach, and say to hell with it. Looking at it logically, what conceivable message could Harold Pinter possibly have that the rest of us don't know or couldn't figure out? We intellectuals will lead you down the garden path every goddamned time. Want to know whom we named in the eighteenth century as the three greatest writers of all time? Catch this: Homer, Sophocles and Richardson. Richardson. You know, that great, *great* writer none of us could live without, Richardson. Richardson we were selling then; today we're pushing Pinter. But no one really knows what's worthy. Oh, we pretend; we make believe there are certain definable academic standards that must be met in order for an artist to be considered valuable, but that's our bag. Telling the masses who is good and who isn't is just our way of keeping the fire high and the wolves away.

But because we pretend to know, everybody gets upset if they don't completely understand something. There is nothing, *nothing,* you *should* like because some intellectual tells you to. Did you like the scene from *Bench* any more because Kenneth Tynan said you should? Did that make it better for you? Would it bother you to learn that I wrote them both, the play and the essay? Well, I did, so think about that for a second. Did you actually believe the part where "Tynan" said the scene was about how Teddy was going to kill Stan and we were helpless to stop it? And what about that St. Francis of Assisi business? Did you believe that? Look at it again now: "Frankie, referred to twice—some think mysteriously— is not mysterious at all. He is, of course, St. Francis of Assisi, the founder of the Franciscan order, all this clearly indicated by the fact that the Franciscans have split into three orders, just as the human race is split into thirds: men, women and homosexuals such as Teddy."

This is the kind of bilge you have to look out for. This is how the intellectuals of this world, the bad ones, make their living. And Pinter is their boy now because, being so obscure, he gives them one and all the opportunity to write reams for their little learned journals, and there's enough for everybody. Pinter's like a minor-league James Joyce, and as long as there's a Ph.D. candidate alive, James Joyce will never die.

But even if Pinter had written *Bench* and Tynan had done the essay, and more than that, even if Tynan were right about St. Francis, that still wouldn't make it good. Pinter may be a major dramatist some day, but forget about some day, think about now, and what goes on up there on stage and whether it moves you.

The intellectual wants you to take the trip from the Christmas show to the Pinter play; he needs you to take it, because he has you then. The artist wants to keep you at Christmas, ready to sing "Jingle Bells." It's a bone-dry journey that the intellectual wants you to set out on, and don't you do it. But you are, and that's what's so crippling to Broadway. You're taking that trip, and it's sad. Because, in the words of that sweet teacher, "We're losing you, darling."

Or are you already lost?

EDGAR LANSBURY

presents

TAMMY GRIMES   BARRY NELSON   JENNIFER HILARY   ROBERT REED   KEITH BAXTER

LEO GENN

in

THE ONLY GAME IN TOWN

by

FRANK D. GILROY

Scenery Designed by
GEORGE JENKINS

Lighting Designed by
JULES FISHER

Costumes by
THEONI V. ALDRE

Directed by
BARRY NELSON

present
in association with
RICHARD RODGERS

avanti!

a comedy by
SAMUEL TAYLOR

in

also starring
BETSY von FURSTENBERG

RIK PIERCE

with
FRANK NASTASI

LORETO CARINGI

Scenery and Lighting by
DONALD OENSLAGER

Costumes by
WINN MORTON

Fashion Consultant
GEOFFREY BEENE

Directed by
NIGEL PATRICK

BILTMO

Philip Rose, David Wilde *and*
Nederlander-Steinbrenner Productions

present

A MINOR ADJUSTMENT

E. & R. MIRVISH

present

A New Comedy by
ERIC NICOL

with

WILLIAM REDFIELD   AUSTIN WILLIS   PAUL COLLINS   MARGARET DRAPER   JOAN DARLING

Scenery by
LEO B. MEYER

Lighting by
JULES FISHER

Costumes by
SAUL BOLASNI

Directed by
HENRY KAPLAN

DYAN CANNON   MARTIN MILNER
RUTH FORD   WALTER ABEL

in

THE NINETY-DAY MISTRESS

by
J. J. COYLE

with

DORIS BELACK   NICOLAS COSTER

TONY LO BIANCO

Setting by
LEON MUNIER

Lighting by
CLARKE DUNHAM

Costumes by
PEARL SOMNER

Associate Producer Selma Leichtling

Directed by
PHILIP ROSE

THE MUSIC BOX

DIRECTION: IRVING BERLIN AND J. J. SHUBERT

SAINT-SUBBER and MICHAEL CODRON

in association with Columbia Pictures Corp.

present

GIG YOUNG   BARBARA FERRIS

JON PERTWEE   RITA GAM

in

THERE'S A GIRL IN MY SOUP

A New Comedy by
TERENCE FRISBY

with

GEORGE HALL   ERICA FITZ

and

GAWN GRAINGER

Original Production Designed by
HUTCHINSON SCOTT

Costumes Designed by
STANLEY SIMMONS

Lighting by
LLOYD BURLINGAME

Directed by
ROBERT CHETWYN

Directed by
ALEXANDRA BERLIN

Also Starring
ALEXANDRA BERLIN

Lighting By
JOHN HARVEY

SHIMEN RUSKIN
PHOEBE DORIN

By ARTHUR ALSBERG and ROBERT FISHER

A New Comedy in Two Acts

Also Starring
LOUISE SOREL

and
LEE BERGERE

with
MARVIN LICHTERMAN
RAY FULMER

JUST A LITTLE THING CALLED A ROLLS ROYCE

HAPPINESS IS

PAT HARRINGTON

in

JOHN McGIVER

ANMARK PRODUCTIONS Presents

CHAPTER

5

Sex Comedy

Sex comedies generally revolve around vagina possession. Traditionally featherbrained, wildly plotted, gag-ridden, they are probably more closely associated in the public's mind with Broadway than any other kind of show except the musical.

Of the approximately 40 plays that opened officially during the season, six more or less fitted the standard sex-comedy form. Of the six, four were disastrous failures, lasting a total of 49 performances, losing at least $500,000. Now this may be after-the-fact thinking on my part, but it is my contention that by being given a short summary of the plots, it is possible to ascertain which four were the bombs. One refresher fact to serve as a guide: the three longest-running sex comedies of the sixties were *Mary, Mary, Cactus Flower* and *Any Wednesday*. Here are the plots. See how you do.

1. The Voyeurism Comedy. A Canadian tycoon is upset because his son, not yet twenty-one, is too goody-goody and is becoming too serious with a girl of similar nature. He arranges, through his public-relations man, for a woman to come and deflower the son. The woman, who is the PR man's girl friend and a wacky lady artist, honest in her own crazy way, agrees to the seduction if for reward she is given a one-woman show in the leading art gallery in town.

The tycoon installs a closed-circuit television set in his house and has it focused on his son's bed so that he and his public-relations man can follow the intercourse. At the crucial moment the set breaks, and whether the deflowering actually goes on as scheduled is kept vague. But the lady artist ends up marrying the public-relations man, while the son, a flower child just three days after his "experience," goes off to visit Red China.

2. The Mod Comedy. A Cary Grant-type American is in London, making a very good living writing about food and drink. He is devastating to women, and after a party he returns to his flat with a pickup, a wacky mod English girl, honest in her own crazy way. The girl, a Julie Christie type, is clearly a simple seduction, only it turns out that she isn't: she is not only cleverer than Cary, she is probably more experienced, and the act ends with her sleeping in his bed, but alone. In the second act, her boy friend appears, a Ringo Starr type who plays drums in a rock group. She dumps Ringo, goes off for a two-week vacation in France with Cary. The last act takes place after their return. They really like each other now and are happily sleeping together, but Ringo is still around. Even though she cares for Cary, she chooses Ringo, and the play ends with Cary, about to seduce a new creature, passing the time by admiring himself in the mirror.

3. The Fear-of-Marriage Comedy. A rich, wacky girl, honest in her own crazy way, picks up a guy in a Mayflower Coffee Shop. She brings him home to her apartment. They sleep together, and the next morning she says that she will be the guy's mistress for 90 days and no more, because after that it all becomes repetitive and dull, and it's time to change bed partners. She goes off shopping with her mother, who is very big in birth control. When the guy is alone, he phones his boss, and it turns out that he is really a private detective and that someone had hired his agency to trail the mother. By coincidence, he got picked up by the daughter in the coffee shop. Six weeks later the detective and the rich girl are in love, but her mother has discovered that he's really a detective, and they break up. Enter the rich girl's father, who has been living in Hawaii for 25 years where he has a mistress and seven sons. He wants to marry his mistress now, so he has hired detectives to find out if he is still married to the birth-control lady. He meets the detective and within five minutes offers him a job running his sugar plantation in Hawaii. The detective decides to accept the job. The girl reads the reports he has written about her and from that realizes he really

does love her. She also deduces that her birth-control mother had planned to have her aborted. She runs off to Hawaii with the detective and her father.

4. The Corpse Comedy. A two-fisted American businessman is in Rome trying to gather up the corpse of his dead father and bring it back to St. Louis. The father has been killed in a car accident while taking his annual monthly Italian vacation. But the red tape that Americans always find in Europe is defeating the American. To help expedite matters, the American hires an aide with limitless contacts, an Italian who loves love. Enter an English actress, classy but shy, who is also having trouble with Italian red tape in her questing after her mother's corpse. The American is surprised to learn that the shy English girl's mother was a passenger in his father's car and was killed with him. The Italian who loves love takes the two of them out to dinner. The American gets a phone call after dinner from his wife back in St. Louis, wondering why it is taking so long to get the corpse home. The Italian who loves love tries to seduce the American (he has tried to seduce the shy English girl off stage at dinner) and failing, leaves. Alone, the American makes a pass; the English girl rebuffs it and knocks him down. He is upset at his cloddishness; she is upset that he is upset; they sleep together. A few days later they are in love, and she tells him how her mother and his father had been having an affair for one month each year in Italy for twelve years, and she says she doesn't want that. Both corpses have by this time been lost, but they are eventually found, and all red tape is mysteriously cleared away. The mystery of who has cleared everything up is solved with the appearance of the two-fisted American's efficient wife. She does not guess that her husband has fallen in love with the shy English girl, who has in the meantime been given a film job in Spain. This has been arranged by the Italian who loves love, who is going along too. The two-fisted American and the shy English actress part but probably will get together later.

5. The Success Comedy. A young lawyer has a pushy wife. There is an opening for a partnership in his law firm, and he doesn't get it because he has difficulty exuding surface charm and also because other people's afflictions bother him. So when, for example, the head of the firm has his nose fixed, the young lawyer inadvertently makes a *faux pas* on the subject. When he finds out that he has not got the partnership, he gets terribly depressed and drunk, and in that condition takes every cent of cash from bank accounts and in-

surance that he can get his hands on and buys his wife a new Rolls-Royce. She walks out on him. The next morning, the young lawyer's landlord enters with a wacky lady artist, honest in her own crazy way, who has spent the night in the back seat of the Rolls. She explains when alone with the lawyer that she needs $100 for rent so that her landlord will let her back into her apartment to get her paintings for a one-woman show. Her honesty captivates the young lawyer, and he gets high on some of her marijuana, at one point taking a can opener and opening the cans of Campbell's soup in an Andy Warhol painting he owns. It turns out, however, that he has been smoking Pall Malls, and that brings down the first-act curtain. His boss, finding out that he has purchased a Rolls-Royce with cash, realizes that the young lawyer, who has always seemed like a poor simpleton, must actually be enormously rich and powerful, and decides to offer him a large raise plus a partnership. But the young lawyer, who has spent the day with the lady artist doing fun things in New York such as feeding the seals and spear-carrying in *Aïda,* turns down the offer because he realizes the rat race is not for him. His wife returns and leaves. The boss returns, ups the offer, and leaves. The girl artist leaves too, because she knows that even though she and the lawyer are fond of each other, now isn't their time. The lawyer is reunited with his wife who, it turns out, didn't want all those superficial success things so much after all.

6. The Losers Comedy. A second-rate Las Vegas dancer, wacky but honest in her own crazy way, picks up a second-rate Las Vegas piano player. They sleep together, and eventually she asks him to move in with her because it turns out that she has been having a ten-year affair with a successful San Francisco tycoon, and every time she breaks up with him because he won't get a divorce, she soon becomes lonely, relents, and takes him back. The piano player is a compulsive gambler who hates Las Vegas, but every time he comes close to having enough money for a stake to set up somewhere else, he blows it all gambling. They live together until the tycoon shows up, divorced and ready to marry. The dancer rejects him but lies to the piano player, explaining that the tycoon had only wanted to take up as before and is still married. The gambler saves up almost enough money to leave and, out of fear of blowing it gambling, has the dancer hide it. She does. A little later he wants it. She refuses. He pleads. She says no. He wrecks the apartment until she gives him the money, and he goes off to gamble. The next morning he returns, loser written all over him. Only this time he's won. And quit

while still ahead. Together they contemplate the possibility of marriage and the panicking responsibilities that go along with it.

Two of the six comedies can be marked off right away. (This is always excluding the possibility of an Alan King in the lead role and the resulting gigantic advance sale. I am speaking now of plays as plays, not as star vehicles.)

The voyeurism comedy, with the father and the public-relations man watching the father's son and the girl friend of the PR man have sex via closed-circuit television, is one of the two. I am not saying that voyeurism is not a fit subject for comedy: I think it's a terrific potential subject for comic investigation. But for this kind of play, it poses problems. The three central characters are the father, the PR man, and the wacky, honest girl. And I think there is something—how can I put it?—unbecoming in their situation. When the PR man gets his girl friend to screw with his boss's kid, I begin to doubt the sincerity of his affection. And when he is persuaded to watch the whole thing, something worse happens: I don't much like him any more. And I don't like the girl for agreeing, and I don't like the father for having the idea in the first place. I am not, in other words, enjoying their company. And I think that their actions, as dictated by the plot, are without excuse: the PR man's objection to watching the sex act of his beloved on the grounds that it's voyeurism only lets us know the author knew what he was doing, but it doesn't make it any less voyeuristic. If the PR man had refused, then I might conceivably have liked him. But if you don't like people, going to their house becomes a drag, then a bore, then unpleasant. And I think that was what precluded any chance of success for *A Minor Adjustment:* it was an unpleasant notion that eventually made its people unpleasant to be with.

The corpse comedy, *Avanti!,* had much the same problem: I mean your father dies, and the next thing you're having an affair with a girl you've known for maybe a day. Or, from her point of view: her mother has been having an affair with an American for twelve years and she, the daughter, disapproves, so as soon as she meets the son of the man who was doing something she disapproved of, she hops in the sack with him. And neither one of them is remotely upset about the dead parent. That's where it gets binding. In other words, if they don't care about their parents, why should we in the audience care about them? They are cold; they are selfish; to hell with them. Again, I think a comedy concerning young lovers meeting while collecting corpses is conceivable, but probably it is beyond Samuel Taylor's comic vision to write one at this point.

What I am suggesting is that these were Marley plays, dead to begin with. They were trying to creep into the standard sex-comedy genre, but something sticks when you try to be light and carefree with this kind of material. I'm not sure how unnatural a desire it might be for a father to watch his son's first fumbling climaxes, but the questions I might like answered are: Why would a man go to the extreme of actually inserting closed-circuit TV into his house? What drives such a man? Hatred maybe; maybe envy; maybe fear. Conceivably, there might be something there, but not for light comedy.

That leaves four. The success comedy, *Happiness Is Just a Little Thing Called a Rolls Royce* (the one about the lawyer and the pushy wife), had the opposite problem of the two plays discussed above. It had all the time-proven materials of the sex-comedy genre, and I think that if the time were 40 years ago, it might have had an enormous success. The dedicated young painter, a girl on her own: that was an exciting twenties notion. And the fact that this wacky but honest girl put out; well, you've got something there. That would have been good for a season's run 40 years ago. But the by-now paralyzing familiarity, I think, killed it. Plus the fact that the basic notion—a man buys a Rolls-Royce—is kind of limited. Either you know he hasn't got the money, so you think he's crazy—like the wife—or you don't know he hasn't got the money, and you think he's important—like the boss. And once they have reacted to this, the one by leaving, the other by offering a job, there's not much else they can do except just what they've already done all over again. And that's exactly what happens: the wife keeps coming back so that she can leave again, and the boss keeps coming back so that he can up the ante on the job offer. But neither action increases in comic richness by repetition. This was another Marley play then, except that, unlike the other cases, where we didn't like the people because they were so unpleasant, here we didn't like them because they eventually became so predictable it was beneath us to enjoy them.

Which leaves three: the fear-of-marriage comedy, the mod comedy and the one about the losers. The fear-of-marriage comedy, *The Ninety-Day Mistress,* had the most laughs. That's simply a statistical comment and means nothing: you can laugh and laugh and leave dissatisfied. If comedy were a matter of statistics, I suppose Jack E. Leonard would be Jack Benny. *Ninety-Day Mistress* had more than enough laughs to succeed. What killed it, I think, was that it was a masquerade and not well enough disguised: the notion of constantly compulsively changing partners because it gets so dull if you don't is basically a homosexual one, and I think the play was basically a homosexual play. The author, a former dancer with José Limon and Pearl Lang, would certainly have had plenty of opportunity to observe homosexual behavior. The girl in the play was the one who wanted to keep changing partners, and I would like to offer the heretical notion that if the girl had been cast as a boy, the play might have worked. It was somehow funny and false as it was, irritating and dissatisfying. The sex change would be valid psychologically, since the "girl" in the play sees her powerful mother a lot, and psychiatrists tend to agree that one of the causes of homosexuality is a dominant mother and/or a weak or an absent father. The "girl" here has as absent a father as it's possible to have, since he's been off populating Hawaii during her first, formative 25 years. Homosexuals also tend to fear marriage, as does the "girl" here; that is the whole point of "her" 90-day notion—to avoid permanent entanglement. People are always talking about how they'd like to see *Virginia Woolf* and *Streetcar* done all male. I'd like to add *Ninety-Day Mistress* to the list.

Which leaves the two successes, *There's a Girl in My Soup,* the mod play, and *The Only Game in Town,* the one about the losers. I think they were the only ones that ever really might have succeeded. They were the best plotted in that they were the least plotted, and this is one of the changes that has come over Broadway sex comedies. All those wild plot moments don't play well any more; television has educated us, and we're too smart now. Granted, *Girl in My Soup* has a certain air of improbability about it; there can't be too many Americans in London living high on the hog as gourmets. But this doesn't matter much, since the play was and is an English comedy, in which the nationality of the lead character was simply changed to fit the star, Gig Young. (The play, by the way, was not as successful here as it was in England, possibly for the perfectly logical reason that it wasn't as good here. Not only was the nationality change a hurt; there were others. Chiefly, the play had been cheapened for America. Example: in the opening scene, the gourmet and his publisher engage in a pointless push-up contest, which ends when the publisher accidentally is bumped in the posterior region. In London, his line was, "That's a foul; I was interfered with." In America, he says, "That's a foul, I was goosed." I think it is clear that while we are not dealing with wit on a Shavian level, there is still a certain delicacy and style to the wording "interfered with" that is lacking in "goosed." This kind of coarsening went on throughout the play and was, I think, damaging.)

The play ran the season, got a movie sale, and the indications are that it will have a successful road tour next year. One of the men who bought the piece for films said to me that it was "indistinguishable from any number of little British comedies that come over here periodically, only to be shot down in flames; it's pure luck that it was a hit in America."

I don't think so. Not that it's so funny, because it isn't funny, not really; there are laughs, but very few in the dialogue. There are some "business" laughs; that's about all. What the play has, I think, is an enormous contemporary quality. It is the first play, at least to my knowledge, where Cary Grant *loses* the girl to Ringo Starr. In most of these other sex comedies, the husband meets this great wacky but honest girl and falls in love, but in the end he stays with his wife, who is young and dull and already done with menopause. And he stays only because the playwright is trying to appeal to some kind of morality that never was true, and more and more we are coming to admit that. This is a wild world today. Ten years ago, *Confidential* might have thought twice before accusing Hayley Mills of living with her fifty-four-year-old lover; today it's in *Look* magazine.

Girl in My Soup also brings together a couple of characters who are kind of standard alone, but juxtaposed, prove kind of fresh: the mod girl and the suave man about town, with the kicker being that she turns him down. An amoral girl demoralizing an immoral man. We aren't used to that yet. I think that if *Girl in My Soup* had also been funny, it would have run for years.

And there's something else going on here that's pleasantly fresh: they sleep together, they really do, they hit the sack. And they aren't coy about it, and we aren't in doubt because the closed-circuit TV pops its cork at the wrong time. There is, verbally, the admission of intercourse without shame. Terrific. And one final difference, one that is so numbing I want to set it off by itself in a separate paragraph.

The game is worth the candle.

That's obscure, but I'll get to it. As previously stated, the three longest-running sex comedies of the sixties have been, in order of run, *Mary, Mary, Cactus Flower* and *Any Wednesday*. They starred, respectively, Barbara Bel Geddes, Lauren Bacall and Sandy Dennis. Look at those names again: Bel Geddes, Bacall and Dennis. *Those are sex objects?* Bel Geddes 20 years ago maybe, and Bacall killed me when she was a kid. Dennis was always charm—the kind of girl who people would describe as having a terrific personality when they tried to fix you up with her. Well, that fits all three of them now: personality is all that's left. Bacall is no broad any more, and Bel Geddes should lose a little weight. But Barbara Ferris in *Girl in My Soup* was young and cute as hell, with one of the splendid bottoms and good legs for mini-skirts, and you might conceivably have double-crossed your loved one for a shot at her. But my God, who's going to risk it to hit the sack with Sandy Dennis?

So *Girl in My Soup* had enough newness to carry the day. It got by Clive Barnes of the *Times,* which is all a sex comedy really has to do to survive—get by the *Times.* Frank D. Gilroy's *The Only Game in Town* did not get by the *Times,* and it didn't run either, which was too bad, because in the opinion of many Broadway people, it was the best sex comedy in years. It landed in the success column only because of an enormous preproduction film sale, which more than covered the losses of the brief Broadway run.

Broadway people had various reasons why the Gilroy play died. Here are some of them:

1. The size of the film sale (over $500,000) irritated some critics.

2. The play came in with an acknowledged history of disastrous road difficulty; all three original actors plus the original director were eventually replaced.

3. It was the last play of the season, so not only was there small chance for an advance sale but also a mood of departure in the air.

4. The theatre was too big for the small one-set play, and the actors were apparently miked, which irritated other critics.

5. Gilroy, who had won the Pulitzer prize for *The Subject Was Roses,* disappointed some opinion makers by dealing with an effort as slight as this.

Whether it was really all that slight or not is a matter of some debate. The play, a tough and touching story of two losers backing into a commitment, seemed wonderfully real, and the playing of the key roles by Barry Nelson and Tammy Grimes was first-rate. But the show, like so many others each season, was basically a charm show. It possessed no galvanizing power; you either went with the people or you didn't. A charm show—comedy, musical, or even drama—desperately needs the breaks. *The Only Game in Town* didn't get them, which was sad, because it was the best of the *Any Wednesdays*.

One final note about the play: like *Girl in My Soup*, it possessed a certain sensuality—no virgins giggled on these premises. Maybe it's all the start of a trend, which wouldn't be the worst thing that ever happened. Because the great sex-comedy hits of the sixties have all been sexless.

Sociologists, take note.

PREMIERE PERFORMANCE, MARCH 27, 1968

ETHEL BARRYMORE THEATRE

DAVID MERRICK

presents

HARRY
GUARDINO

ESTELLE
PARSONS

BRIAN BEDFORD

in

THE SEVEN DESCENTS OF MYRTLE

a new play by

TENNESSEE WILLIAMS

Setting and Lighting by
JO MIELZINER

Costumes by
JANE GREENWOOD

Associate Producer **SAMUEL LIFF**

Directed by

JOSE QUINTERO

THE MOROSCO THEATRE

ROBERT WHITEHEAD

in association with

ROBERT W. DOWLING

presents

ARTHUR MILLER'S
THE PRICE

starring

PAT
HINGLE

KATE
REID

DAVID
BURNS

and

ARTHUR KENNEDY

Directed by

ULU GROSBARD

Setting and Costumes Designed by
BORIS ARONSON

Lighting by
PAUL MORRISON

PREMIERE PERFORMANCE, JANUARY 25, 1968

LONGACRE THEATRE

GILBERT CATES
In Association with Doris Vidor

Presents

HAL
HOLBROOK

ALAN
WEBB

TERESA
WRIGHT

LILLIAN
GISH

in

ROBERT ANDERSON'S

New Play

I NEVER SANG FOR MY FATHER

with

Laurinda Barrett
Daniel Keyes

Matt Crowley
Sloane Shelton

Allan Frank
Earl Sydnor

Scenery and Lighting by
JO MIELZINER

Costumes by
THEONI V. ALDREDGE

Directed by

ALAN SCHNEIDER

PREMIERE PERFORMANCE, OCTOBER 8, 1967

CORT THEATRE

THEATER 1968

RICHARD BARR   CLINTON WILDER   CHARLES WOODWARD, JR.

presents

PAT
HINGLE

SADA
THOMPSON

JAMES
BRODERICK

in

JOHNNY NO-TRUMP

BY

MARY MERCIER

with

BERNADETTE PETERS   BARBARA LESTER

and

DON SCARDINO

Scenery, Lighting and Costumes by

WILLIAM RITMAN

Directed by

JOSEPH HARDY

CHAPTER

6

The Approvers

Johnny No-Trump was the best new American play of the season. It was written by Mary Mercier, a nervous, thin woman, forty now, and very bright. During rehearsal period, she was living in an efficiency apartment in a new building in the theatre district. There were a lot of books and, in the sleeping alcove, a mattress on the floor. While she talked, she smoked. "I never wanted to be a writer, but I remember being in Rome in 1962 and thinking how wonderful it would be—to be able to describe what I was seeing. About nine months before I started the play, a group of characters came into my head; eventually they changed sex, age, occupation, relationships, everything. The first time I sat down to write I continued until the first scene was written straight through—I was so shocked at what I'd done I put it away in a drawer and left it there a month—then I read it through, and it seemed to me as an actress to be playable. I was a bit player, understudy—that kind of thing—I haven't much of a career to discuss. After I reread that first scene and went back to work on it, it was as if I was the typist for the characters—sometimes, if I took a job and left them for two or three weeks, the snide remarks that would come out of them—I'm not a very good typist, and with all the cross cuts and erasings and them telling me what to do, I felt like the maid."

She doesn't write like the maid. Her play takes place on Long Island, and the following is taken from a scene between Florence, the mother of the title character—a boy of sixteen—and her brother Harry. He is sixty, a taxi driver, and he has just discovered that the kid wants to be, of all things, a poet. Florence's husband was also an artist—a painter—and a failure at it. She is a teacher, and shares a house with her brother. They are at lunch, and Harry has begun making some remarks indicating that Johnny, who is upstairs during this, is heading for trouble.

FLORENCE

. . . why'd you have such a sudden interest in his welfare?

HARRY

Cos I'm around the place now, and I *see,* and you're off out and ya come back tired and ya don't see!

FLORENCE
(*Pushes aside her plate*)

Out of a large family, that you and I should finish up together under the same roof! Well, I wish it amused me more. Harry, you're my very own North Star. Your ignorance is the one constant on this witless earth. Without fail, I can absolutely rely on you to come up with hopeless and aimless suggestions. . . .

HARRY

Ah-h, your sarcasm don't reach me. And too bad ya don't care for livin' under a roof that happens to be half mine. Also listen out one of my more aimless suggestions.

(*Points upstairs*)

Watch out where he's headed, cos give or take a coupla years, they're gonna call him a *Man.* Now what cards is he gonna play with? Answer me that! What cards? Number One . . . he's short.

(*He throws up his arms*)

It's already a bust! The end! Finish! Good-bye Charlie! Number Two . . . he's homely . . . so comes the insult on top of the injury! And Number Three . . . he's a KOOK! . . . Well, happy days! Ya look at that hand an ya say NO TRUMPS! The kid's got no trumps! Number Three at least ya can do something about—change him around in his ideas a little. The other two! Ya know the agony? . . . the *agony?* of every short, homely guy in this world. Who the hell ever gives 'em the real time of day, unless they got dough. And they all just happen to manage to want MISS RHEIN-GOLD or MISS RHINESTONE, or what the hell she calls herself! The American Rose they all want! And she goes to the pretty ones. Because, Miss Teacher, the pieces of cake always goes to the pretty guys. And I should know, cos nobody ever looked at me. And if I ever get born over again, and have to go through ALL THIS CRAP all over, PLEASE GOD, make me handsome and cute!

FLORENCE

Harold, you're my brother, and if you ever get sick, God forbid, I'll take care of you, but you are a fat ignoramus, and an old fart into the bargain! And I'm also past forty and too tired to be tolerant! You take up space! . . . you hear me? . . . an ignorant man in this world takes up *space!* and if you all dropped dead! . . . well, I'm sorry, my dear, but for me, Christ would have risen at last!

Is there any doubt the lady is a writer? There's a rhythm to her work, a build to her sentences. She possesses a marvelous flair for invective and, although you can't tell it from such a short excerpt, she puts people up there, weary, vulnerable people. Her play is in the tradition of "family" plays, and it is lovely. Not a master-piece—no *Long Day's Journey into Night*—it was too small in scale to be that. It reminded me most of Frank D. Gilroy's *The Subject Was Roses*. Gilroy's play was better plotted, but although he writes well, she writes better, and that extraordinary writing skill of hers makes up for any plot deficiencies. On the whole, the emotional impact of the two plays was about the same, and I would rate the two a tossup.

Gilroy's play, of course, established him, made him a small fortune, won him a Pulitzer prize, and ended up being the longest-running drama of the decade. Mary Mercier's play got her nothing —literally. It opened and closed the same night, Sunday, October 8, 1967.

To understand why, it is necessary to understand critics. There are two widely held notions concerning the New York drama critics, and they are both wrong: (1) they are not very nice; (2) they are not very good.

I don't think anybody along the street thinks that critics are half as harsh on plays as theatre people are. At least 60 nights a year, twice that if he covers off-Broadway, the critic trudges into ancient, forbidding structures and, if this year is representative at all, for an indecent percentage of the time, his intelligence is insulted. But he sits there, leaves promptly at curtain, and usually manages to find something civilized to say about what he has been forced to witness.

Most people simply do not know how bad much of what opens on Broadway is. There are plays, many plays, about which you can almost say that they are seen by no one who isn't related to somebody in the production. These shows close within a week, or out of town (20% of all productions do), and the public simply is not

there. What the public sees is the best of Broadway. The critic sees
it all.

There are critics, a minority, who are cruel. *Time* and *The New
Yorker* quickly come to mind. But they are outweighed by their
peers: *Cue* is rarely mean, Channels 2 and 4 the same, and Richard
Watts's *Post* notices are never nasty. Most people don't know this
and will undoubtedly continue to think of critics as assassins, but
believe me, until you've sat through a season with them, you just
don't know.

Now, for the second misconception, that they are not very good:
this is simply untrue. They are putrescent. And there is a reason
why most people don't know this either: most people have not seen
the production when they read the review. So if a notice makes
internal sense, there is every reason to believe that it is accurate.
And this is exactly why the critics are so execrable: they are the
opposite of accurate. They do not report what's there.

Before getting into specifics, I'd like to explain why this overwhelming critical inadequacy should not be surprising. There is
one thing that 99% of all critics share with one another: they are
failures. I don't mean failures as critics—my God, that's understood.
I don't even mean they are failures as people; I mean something
more painful by far. These people are failures in life.

It's a second-rate job, folks. Being a drama critic on Broadway
wouldn't keep a decent mind occupied 10% of the time. So you
don't even get second-raters. You get the dregs, the stage-struck but
untalented neurotic who eventually drifts into criticism as a means
of clinging peripherally to the arts. And most of your cruel critics
come this way: they are getting their own back. They failed, and
they're going to do their damnedest to see that everybody else falls
flat too.

I talked to a radio critic who had written a painfully sadistic
notice of *Here's Where I Belong,* a serious, flawed musical based on
John Steinbeck's *East of Eden.* "I wrote a terribly funny review of
that one," he told me. "It was all an imaginary scene set in the
producer's office in which the producer decided to cast a white man
in an Oriental part to cash in on the box-office controversy. It was
a helluva funny notice if I say so myself." (The authors of *Here's
Where I Belong* worked eight years for their one night on Broadway. That doesn't entitle them to raves, but I think they do deserve
some cogent criticism pointing out their failures.)

I then asked the radio critic if he ever prepared for a review by reading the play in advance. He said, "I was a director for ten years, so when I read a play, I direct it in my head as I go along. Anything I see on stage I automatically think is wrong, because I would have done it differently. So I never read before."

This is certainly reasonable, but the point of import here is he *was* a director for ten years. He *tried* to be a director. He *wanted* to direct in the theatre, but he couldn't cut it. He failed, man, and that's why, when somebody comes in with a serious musical based on *East of Eden,* he shreds it with a sketch about a producer trying to cash in on controversy.

Critics also tend to be petty. Example: it is standard practice for reviewers to get their notices to press agents after they are written. But this year a wire-service critic wouldn't let a press agent have his review of a play. Why? Because the wire-service critic was *seated behind* a television critic, and he was damned if he was going to give the press agent his review. (Where you seat these people, by the way, is a matter of international protocol. No one dares sit in front of the *Times* critic, except Winchell, but he sits on the side so it's all right. You have to be desperately careful where you place the newspaper people in relation to the television people, the magazine writers, etc.)

Something else to remember: not only are we dealing with failures —men who could not make it in their chosen line of endeavor— we are dealing with failures who have suddenly been given POWER. (But not enough. That's what kills them.) The influence of the critics has been debated for years. The Theatregoers Study indicates that 20% of New Yorkers and 10% of out-of-towners say they are chiefly influenced by the notices. These figures, of course, are only what people admit; still, it's probably fair to estimate roughly that one person in six attends a production because of critical enthusiasm.

"Enthusiasm" is really the key word as far as critical influence is concerned. Simply liking or not liking a show doesn't mean that much. If a critic calls a show "a genuinely thought-provoking evening of literate theatre," he is dooming it to a quick death. If, on the other hand, he says, "I had one helluva time at this musical, in spite of its flaws," he is writing what is called in the trade "a money review."

Perhaps the most painful point to be made about the critics is this: their influence is inversely proportional to their adequacy. They have the least influence over unambitious musicals, and they are best equipped to evaluate them. They have the most influence over what they are least qualified to judge: serious drama. A serious drama needs every conceivable break to survive. *Johnny No-Trump* had nothing whatsoever going for it: a new writer, a director new to Broadway, a cast without box-office appeal. It got, on the whole, mixed notices. It needed raves. It closed.

The critics' importance, then, is enormously variable from one kind of play to another. But, in any case, their influence is considerable, and this shouldn't be surprising, because do you know how many critics there are? (I am using the widest possible sense of the word critic here: anyone from any communications media who gets in free to a Broadway opening or second-night performance, and whose public comments might affect, theoretically, the success or failure of the play.) There are 199 Broadway critics. Or at least there were at one important drama this season. Now, logically, they can't all be bad, and they're not. When I said before they were putrescent, that was an exaggeration. Only 190 of them are.

Some of them are very intelligent. Kroll of *Newsweek,* for example, is the only one of the large-circulation reviewers who aspires toward being a "supercritic." This term, as I use it, means a critic who places the value of his own writings above that of the art object. Usually, the supercritic inhabits the literary world, as Dwight Mac-Donald or Norman Podhoretz does, although Pauline Kael has found her place in films. The point about supercritics is that you never have to read them to know what they think. They are predictable through the use of quiz psychology. Are the early notices of a novel splendid? The supercritic will pan it. He has to. Supercritics are dangerous for only one reason: what they say has nothing whatever to do with the art object. But, as I said, the theatre is relatively free from them. Brustein of *The New Republic* is a supercritic. He has made his place in this world panning Arthur Miller. When an Arthur Miller play comes along, Brustein is conditioned. If it turned out that Arthur Miller had written all of Brecht (which would almost kill Brustein), he would still somehow manage to turn out a learned essay explaining why Brecht, although at first glance a GREAT writer, becomes on deeper scrutiny morally obsessive and wearisome.

Kroll of *Newsweek* is sort of a secret supercritic. His pan of Neil Simon's *Plaza Suite* was so hysterical and had so little to do with what happened on stage, that even *Variety* paused in print to wonder what was wrong with Kroll. Kroll really came into his own at the annual voting for the best American play of the year. Kroll was the only critic to vote for Michael McClure's *The Beard.*

The Beard is a poetic, symbolic, one-act, two-character play set in heaven, which culminates in Billy the Kid blowing Jean Harlow. It opened to a set of genuinely murderous notices and offended a lot of people with its language. Perhaps that is because of a certain repetitiousness of vocabulary. The phrase "full of shit" occurs 14 times, "sack of shit" once, "I wouldn't listen to you shit in a rain barrel" once. The number of poetic uses of the word shit totals 37, making it second only to "fuck" in symbolic importance. Kroll's choice for best play contains the phrase "fuck you" 16 times, "give a fuck" thrice, "oh, fuck" once, "dumb fuck" twice, "crazier than fuck" once. There are also variations on the root word: "fucker," "little fucker," "dirty fucker," etc. "Cock" is of but tertiary significance, appearing a scant 14 times, not counting one time when it is used in a stage direction. "Cunt," as in "you're a cunt," is voiced 13 times, but (perhaps significantly) the phrase "prim little cunt" happens but once.

Whatever one may think of Kroll's taste, at least he had the courage to voice it, which is more than can be said of *Time*'s critic, Ted Kalem. When asked to name a best American play this year, Kalem abstained: nothing was worth it. That is certainly his opinion, and no one can mock it. However, there was a play that opened on Broadway called *Before You Go.* Among the things Kalem said of it were: "Wry, perceptive, honest, sad, funny and tender, it is compassionately discerning about two people who are not quite wise to themselves." And at the end of his notice: "The way of a modern man with a modern maid is surpassing strange, but Playwright Holofcener has got it on stage, got it laughing, got it right." Clearly he liked the play more than somewhat. The extent of his pleasure, however, is more apparent in a letter Kalem sent to a member of the production: "Would you be kind enough to pass this along to the appropriate parties," Kalem begins, going on to say, ". . . when a drama critic loves a play and it closes quickly, he feels dreadful, and that's the way I feel about the fate of *Before You Go.*"

Now come on—if you "love" a play and go out of your way to write a note about your "dreadful" feelings at its closing, and you've already written a glowing notice about the thing in print, doesn't that make the play worth *one* teeny vote for best play of the year? Ordinarily yes, but *Time* critics must, underline *must*, have snobbishly intellectual pretentions, and as Joseph Krutch once commented, the problem with being snobbish is that you can never say you like something, because then someone snobbier than you can look at you snobbishly and say, "Oh, so *that's* the kind of thing you like."

Now to the business mentioned before—the crucial error of not reporting what's there. Let me begin with the most trivial example that I can find: in a recent play, a critic liked the set for a library in a stately home, which "looked not only stately but also lived in." "Lived in" is the thing here. The greater part of the entire back wall of the set was taken up with book shelves. Floor-to-ceiling book shelves. The play was a little on the dull side, and I'm a library nut, so for want of something better to do, I started to count the book shelves. There were 78 of them, maybe three feet wide and eleven rows high, extending upwards perhaps twelve to sixteen feet. The majority of the shelves were certainly over eight feet high. *And there was no library ladder.* Wilt Chamberlain, given a running start, could not have reached the upper two rows, and a person of ordinary height couldn't have come close to the upper six. The books were simply out of reach. So what we had was a library set that was certainly stately, and completely *unlived in.*

Another example, a little less trivial now: John Colicos played Winston Churchill in *Soldiers* and got a set of absolutely glorious notices: "Brilliant," "Masterly," "Magnificent"—along those lines. You read those words, you figure this Colicos is some kind of an actor. And he is. Usually. But then, one of the weekly critics let a little something slip: "One part of Colicos' technique is to use a considerable amount of grunt and groan, so that the audience must sit up and listen to make out what was said."

Close.

Then, a daily critic, in his weekly summation, said: ". . . I can't say Mr. Colicos ever succeeded in being completely clear-spoken."

Closer.

What really was the truth? Hobe Morrison said it in his review in *Variety* when he put down that although Colicos was impressive visually as Churchill, "much of what he says is unintelligible."

That's it, boys and girls: unintelligible. You could see the mouth working and you heard the sounds come out, and they were brilliant, masterly, magnificent sounds all right, only they didn't end up as words. I couldn't understand him, my wife couldn't understand him either, and in the little private poll we conducted the night we were there, nobody we asked could understand him either. And we did not approach people and say, "I can't understand Coli-ços, and neither can anybody else we've asked; can you?" What we did ask was, "What do you think of the guy playing Churchill?" The unanimous answer was simply that he looked terrific but you couldn't understand what he was saying.

In other words, what the overwhelming proportion of the magic 199 reported was simply not to be seen on the stage of the Billy Rose Theatre.

Now there are infinite examples of this kind of thing that could be given, culled from a season of review reading, but it's pointless. Please believe that I have the examples, and if you don't believe me, go see any play at a preview and then, when the show opens, quick run and get all the reviews and see for yourself. It is, I guarantee, astounding.

Not reporting what's there can be considerably less than trivial. For example, Zoe Caldwell's performance in *The Prime of Miss Jean Brodie* was the most lavishly praised of the season. It won her the Tony award as best actress of the year. It would be very difficult, under any conditions, to give her less than passing marks. Here is what one critic said of her: ". . . Zoe Caldwell gives a performance of a sustained outrageousness and vulgarity that would have shamed one of the exhibitionist actor-managers of the Belasco period."

But even this is still a matter of possible taste. Where things get wild, and where I will leave this little notion of not reporting what is there, is best exemplified by what one of the leading learned critics said about *A Day in the Death of Joe Egg*. Briefly, *Joe Egg* is about an English couple with a spastic child, and this situation is ripping their marriage apart. Given this material, the play miraculously manages to be a warm and tender comedy. It is incredible, and how it is pulled off I'll never know, but one critic said this: " 'Joe Egg' comes across as a thin run-through of conventional English material." *Conventional English material!* In other words, "Ho-hum, another spastic-child comedy."

The things that these people claim they see defies belief, but there are other flaws in their collective make-up, and one of them is their astonishing ignorance concerning their material. One leading critic says this about Arthur Miller: "The man who was once considered the logical heir to O'Neill and Tennessee Williams as our most articulate playwright . . ." Now how in the name of God can Miller be considered the "heir" to Williams when Miller got to Broadway first? Another critic set out to try and explain why Robert Anderson's *I Never Sang for My Father* was proving almost as popular as the same author's better received *You Know I Can't Hear You When the Water's Running*. Well, it wasn't. The *Water* plays opened and jumped almost immediately to capacity and stayed there. The *Father* play (these are Anderson's own names for them) *never* sold two thirds of its tickets and was dying when the critic wrote his erudite explanation of why it was so popular. Another note on Zoe Caldwell: a critic raved about her for "filling out a part that, on paper, might possibly have been just a little too thin . . ." Well now, come on: Didn't he know that the "too-thin" part had already made an international star out of Vanessa Redgrave? It's a star-making role, and every actress who gets to play it is going to get screams at the curtain. Another critic, reviewing *Tiger at the Gates,* criticized one of the supporting actresses for playing Helen of Troy as a "dumb, dumb blonde." Well, in the first place, the character doesn't talk like John Stuart Mill but, more important, when a minor actress plays a part a certain way, that is because the director said: "Play it that certain way!" It's not the actress, it's the director, and anyone around the theatre knows that.

Easily the outstanding show of theatrical ignorance this season came, as one would expect, from *The New Yorker*'s Brendan Gill. In panning *The Happy Time,* a musical about a photographer, Gill wrote: " 'The Happy Time' is of interest for one thing only— proof of how influential Antonioni's meretricious 'Blow-up' has become. That photographers make a career of taking pictures because they are incapable of ordinary human feeling is now an accepted part of the cultural slag heap from which second-rate 'creative' people pluck their so-called ideas."

Gill is certainly clear: the people who did *The Happy Time* got their idea and, indeed, did their musical because of the impact that Antonioni's film about a photographer had on them.

Know when "Blow-up" opened in New York? Christmas, 1966.

Know when *The Happy Time* was looking for composers? *Before* November, 1966, because Kander and Ebb, who wrote both *Cabaret* and *Happy Time,* did half a dozen songs "on spec" (that means without a contract, to try and get the job) before their *Cabaret* opened in November. They were at first turned down for *Happy Time,* and the job was originally given to Cy Coleman and Dorothy Fields. All this was public knowledge, so Gill might have known that. But even if he didn't, he sure should have known that major musicals just aren't assembled that quickly. Everyone else around the theatre knows it; why not Gill? The book for *The Happy Time* had been in the librettist's mind for years. The average length of a musical, from conception to opening, might conservatively be set at two years. It's not just getting the material ready; it's finding a theatre out of town and in town and a costume man you want *and* who's available *and* a set man who's available at the same time as the costume man, not to mention the impossible job of trying to cast a show, especially a show with stars.

But Gill's notion conjures the following: picture David Merrick, the *Happy Time* producer, skulking from movie theatre to movie theatre for the noon show on opening days, desperate to find a sensationally commercial box-office idea like doing a musical about a photographer. I mean, there's a notion that's got ticket appeal all over it. Merrick watches "Blow-up"; his hands start to sweat. Without so much as waiting for the nude scenes, he makes it to a phone and gets Gower Champion in sunny Cal. "Get this," Merrick manages, "a musical about a photographer." "Send me the contract, we'll get rich," Champion says, and he flies in on the next plane, first nailing Richard Nash at home and having him rough out a story line in enough detail that the songs can be fitted around it. Then, all together, the creative personnel jet to wherever Goulet is doing his club act, because if you're going to do a musical about a photographer you've got to have Goulet on account of his terrific Kodak identification, and they all hop back to Big Town, first locking in David Wayne in case there turns out to be a part for an older guy. Everybody goes full out (Champion is fresh as hell, having finished staging and choreographing the two-character musical *I Do! I Do!* several weeks before), and the rest just falls automatically into place: bookings, casting, designers, all.

Gill is really beyond belief. That a man who earns his living pontificating on the value of theatrical productions should be so ignorant of the realities of those same theatrical productions is, I don't know what, shameful. "They all stink," a leading playwright once said of the critics.

Some of them sure do.

One final point about the 199. With the exception of perhaps half a dozen of them, they are individually meaningless in their importance to the theatre. Taken as a group, they can provide a certain backwash of approval for a production, or the reverse, but individually, and this is what eats away at them, they don't matter.

Walter Winchell doesn't matter either. Not any more. But he deserves separate mention because once he mattered very much. He is still credited, practically by himself, with plugging *Hellza-poppin* into being the longest-running revue of all time. But now Winchell lacks a first-rate outlet in New York, and he is reduced to being quoted for sad raves over sagging shows: "How Now Dow Wow" is a Winchell coining. Believe me, if they'd got a notice from the *Times,* they'd have used that instead.

John Chapman doesn't matter much any more either. He is the critic of the *Daily News,* the largest-circulation paper in America, over 2,000,000 daily. Once upon a time, they used to say around the street that "Atkinson fills your orchestra and Chapman fills your balcony." But as theatre tickets have gone up in price, Chapman's work has gone down in caliber, so that now he is in the position of being the critic you read last and care about least. Chapman is sometimes capable of spotting a pretentious play, and his work on theatre annuals was absolutely fine. But he has been drama editor of the *News* since 1929, and in all the interviews I had with all the theatre people all year long, not one had a decent thing to say for Chapman. Many of them felt he was even damaging to the theatre now. Because there is a part of everybody that wants to read the *News,* and with that 2,000,000 daily circulation, a really bright, incisive, enthusiastic critic might be a help to the theatre. It couldn't hurt.

Chapman is generally held suspect as far as his personal theatre taste is concerned. Example: if a poll were taken of theatre people to name the ten best plays of the last 100 years, one of the plays that would have to be listed would be Chekhov's *The Cherry Orchard.* A lot of theatre people feel that Chekhov is the greatest playwright of the last 100 years, period. And a lot more feel that of his four major full-length plays, *The Cherry Orchard* is the greatest. Chapman, reviewing the play this year, said the following: "Chekhov's 'Cherry Orchard' was the original soap opera, and it is time we put it away and forget about it." This is a terrifying statement, not so much because it shows Chapman's ignorance of Chekhov but because it shows his ignorance of soap opera.

All that this season really proved about Chapman, which was unknown before, is that he simply cannot tolerate homosexual plays. When the English homosexual play *Staircase* opened—it had been done in London to considerable acclaim by the famous Royal Shakespeare Company—Chapman could not sit through it. He left in the middle and reviewed no more plays all season that smacked openly of homosexuality: the *News* let someone else pan *Loot*.

If Chapman is now known as a critic who dislikes homosexuality on stage, Richard Watts of the *Post* has always been known as a critic who is not remotely disturbed by it. (Watts is even older than Chapman, having started New York work in 1924, and he is held in somewhat higher esteem, but not much. "Watts tries hard" is the best that theatre people have to say of him.)

Watts is still remembered as the only major critic who approved of Franco Zeffirelli's production of *The Lady of the Camellias,* the acknowledged champion homosexual production of the sixties. And the feeling was strong this year during the previews of the Albee play *Everything in the Garden* that Watts would love it, which of course he did.

Now there is nothing remotely wrong with liking plays that have homosexual themes, productions, or performances. Many of our leading critics have had what might be called "homosexual taste" and have been skillful critics at the same time. But when homosexual taste becomes distorting to the play itself, there is cause for concern.

Robert Anderson's *I Never Sang for My Father* is about a father-son relationship, and it had a very weak first act in which the mother is very much around. The act climaxes with the mother's death, and Anderson himself was aware of how superfluous and how weak the entire first act was: "I know it could all be summed up by saying, 'And Mother died.' " But Anderson felt that the first act was necessary as a foundation for the crucial second act to set up the father-son relationship, which is the strength of the play. Anderson only hoped he could get away with his weak first act.

Every critic, of course, recognized the problem with the play, no matter how they might have felt about it. The first act—the mother act—was weak; the second act—the father act—was stronger. Not Watts. He didn't like the second act much, but he loved the part that dealt with the old mother. A case can be made that homosexual taste often runs along these lines. Homosexual playwrights, for example, are frequently at their most perceptive when dealing with women, particularly elderly ones: they understand them better; they care more for them. Among the critics who saw Anderson's play, Watts is the *only* one who liked the first act best.

Watts is seventy now. Broadway legend has it that he reviewed the original production of *The Desert Song*. Both he and Chapman should be given Broadway's blessings and sent to pasture. That seems cruel, but the level of daily newspaper reviewing has sunk so low in New York, partially because of the deterioration of these men, partially because of the deterioration of Manhattan's newspaper business, that they are now damaging to the theatre. Broadway needs all the help it can get, and these two simply aren't capable of providing it any more. Their loss can only be the theatre's gain.

Walter Kerr's loss was the theatre's loss too. Kerr was the best. He wrote funny and he wrote smart, and he got better as he went along. When he started, many people felt he was more concerned with his own wit than with the play. The saying at the time comparing Kerr and Brooks Atkinson was: "Kerr knows what he's going to say before he goes into the theatre, Atkinson doesn't." Whatever the case, Kerr just kept on improving, writing really remarkable drama reviews under deadline pressure. (He has never been as sound at judging musical comedy.) He had a wild enthusiasm for the theatre. No one wrote a rave the way Walter Kerr wrote a rave. Writing for the *Herald Tribune,* Kerr was a perfect buffer for the much more conservative Atkinson on the much more powerful *Times.* When Kerr finally got the *Times* job in 1966, most Broadway people were delighted; the best critic was in the most influential post.

Then, after one season, Kerr decided to take the Sunday drama column and left the daily reviewing to a colleague. The theory was that this would split the power of the *Times,* so that one man would not rule quite so much as before. It didn't work out that way. Kerr simply castrated himself, and his Sunday pieces carry no perceptible weight at the box office. He is yesterday's news now, and that is a shame.

We talked about his present job in Bleeck's, a newspaperman's restaurant on West Fortieth Street. Kerr is so full of energy, so passionate about the theatre, that it comes as something of a shock to realize he is fifty-five. "Why did I change? I wanted the Sunday job not so much to get off the deadline as to get off the day. I was afraid of blowing the energy—I couldn't do any work of my own—if you're going to hit that deadline, you better save up all that energy. It doesn't matter if the play's a light comedy or whatever; you've got to give it all you have, and the days were going by. I wanted to take a longer look at things.

"It hasn't worked out the way I thought. The time pressure now works almost the same way. The paper wants it in sometimes Friday or Saturday of the week before. I'm always reviewing what I've just seen. I thought it would be looser. I thought I could have more time to think. I'd hoped that if I saw a play this week and another, say, six weeks from now, and they seemed to me to fit together, I could review them both at that later time. But it just hasn't worked out."

Regardless of how it has worked out, Kerr is stuck with what he wanted, and it's a shame. Because not only is his influence gone, but he isn't writing as well as he used to. He's scrambling in his Sunday pieces; they're neither reviews nor contemplative essays, but some sort of mishmash in between. Perhaps he'll find some way of handling it and getting what he wanted out of the change—that chance to take a longer view. But right now, like it or not, our best critic is in deep trouble: he has lost his style, he has lost his way, he has lost his power.

Any mention of power in connection with Broadway brings up the New York *Times.* How powerful is it really? And what form is that power taking now? I will keep this as brief as I can, because I love the New York *Times,* and I do not relish saying uncomplimentary things about it.

For openers, nowhere in all the theatre did I sense as much fear as I did while talking to employees of the *Times.* Example: I asked an employee of the daily *Times* when the Sunday *Times* closed. This was early in the season; no one knew that Kerr's power was going to be so totally eviscerated, and the possibility of a good review from Kerr saving a play was much talked about. How long, though, would it take before the Sunday review could come out? Certain sections of the Sunday *Times*—the book review, the magazine, entertainment— are set in print well before Sunday. Could a show that opened, say, on a Thursday night get reviewed by Kerr on Sunday? Or would it have to be Wednesday night? Or when?

"Don't ask me when it goes to bed," the daily *Times* man answered. "You want to know when the Sunday *Times* goes to bed, go ask someone on the Sunday *Times.*"

"It can't be a secret," I said.

"Nobody said it was a secret."

"Then just tell me. You know. So when does the Sunday *Times* close?"

"I already told you. You want to know when it closes, quit asking me—"

"You mean you won't tell me anything about the Sunday *Times?*"

"I'm not saying that—nobody's saying that—I'm just saying that if you want to know anything about the Sunday *Times,* ask the Sunday *Times!*"

Daily *Times,* Sunday *Times:* for more than 30 years it didn't matter; the wonderful Brooks Atkinson was critic, and the following he developed was enormous. When he retired in 1960, speculation was that Kerr would be his successor. The *Times,* alas, operates on the belief that any of its arts experts can operate equally expertly in any art. So the theatre job went to the *Times*'s music critic, Howard Taubman. The musical community was hardly unhappy, since Taubman had long been held as something of a joke. Broadway didn't know what to expect, but it turned out that by shifting Taubman, the *Times* had got rid of a bad music critic and gained an equally inept theatre man.

Taubman, serious beyond belief, was a passionate believer in Good Theatre. In the opening months of his tenure, stiff after stiff would come in to glowing notices from Taubman, provided it was a well-meaning stiff, a play of Import. At first, the public, conditioned for years to Atkinson, responded. But gradually, the influence that Atkinson had built began to lessen. Of Taubman it has been said: "He doesn't mind being bored." And that was what was so dangerous about him: he could not distinguish between good serious theatre and bad serious theatre. Simple seriousness was enough to please him.

Taubman obviously had to go, and he did, kicked upstairs, becoming a kind of cultural expert. In his place came Stanley Kauffmann. Kauffmann, a supercritic in good standing, was a major disaster. He had only one large flaw for a Broadway reviewer: he hated Broadway. Kauffmann was dispensed with after a season and is now back at *The New Republic.* Indicating, incidentally, that it really is the paper, not the man. No one on Broadway cares remotely what Kauffmann comes up with nowadays, but for one year people lived and died on his pronouncements.

The *Times* has the power. And they use it. One Broadway press agent said, "*Times* people call up and demand free theatre tickets. How many depends on the show. I think they accept it as their right. They're not as generous with their advertising rates." Harold Schonberg, a *Times* music critic, got free tickets for the Edward Albee play. So did Robert Alden, whoever he may be, twice. Hilton Kramer, a *Times* art critic, got free tickets for Pinter's *The Birthday Party.* Close to a dozen *Times* employees asked for and got free tickets for the Pinter play. The publicity agent for a leading musical estimates that in the last few months the *Times* got 30 free pairs of tickets to the musical. This is a sell-out musical. Figure tickets at $10.00 a seat; 60 seats is $600. Figure how many musicals and plays come in each year, and it is clear that the *Times* is getting thousands of dollars of free tickets from the theatre for no reason other than that people are afraid to turn down the *Times*. As another press agent told me, "You know that taking care of them isn't going to buy you futures, but still you do it—you just do it—you've got other clients, and you don't want the *Times* down on you. When I first got into this business, I couldn't believe it. You expect to get muscled, say, from the *News*. But the *Times*! Now that I've been around awhile I can tell you this: the *Times* chisels just as bad as anybody else." The press agent paused. Then he spoke again: "No. Worse."

One minor *Times* note: I am a kind of collector of slips of the tongue, Freudian, etc., and the best I got all year long came from one of the *Times*'s top theatre reporters, who actually referred to the greatest musical hit of all time as *My Fair Girl*.

No play this season demonstrates the power of the *Times* as well as Robert Anderson's drama *I Never Sang for My Father*. One of the three leading television critics said: ". . . a play I can recommend, and another demonstration that Broadway is willing to come to grips with the human heart and mind." This is pretty good, but it was the least enthusiastic of the three notices. The other two called it "the most considerable work this season" and "one of the finest plays I have ever seen." One of the daily critics said it was "written with skill, insight and feeling, and it has the great advantage of being beautifully acted." Another daily called it "absorbing, touching . . . exciting drama . . . fine theatre . . . a beautiful new play." It had done sensational business in Boston, where it was unanimously well received. It starred Hal Holbrook, Teresa Wright, Lillian Gish, nice names as a package, and Alan Webb in the play's best role. It had an advance of $105,000, pretty good for a serious drama.

Naturally, it bombed.

It was dead from the opening sentence on of the *Times* notice: "A soap opera is a soap opera, whichever way you slice the soap." The rest of the review was all downhill. The play closed to an announced loss of $180,000. The power of the *Times*, then, is this: it can kill serious drama. Almost without exception, a blast from the *Times* will destroy a serious play. But this is nothing new; what is new is that the *Times*, because of the ineptness of its recent critics (excluding Kerr), has lost the power to create.

I keep remembering a play that opened toward the end of Atkinson's reign, *The Rope Dancers*. It was a somber, brooding piece with no star power, and it got bad notices from the critics. But a rave from Atkinson. It ran close to 200 performances. His influence was such, his following so faithful, that if he said a piece was of value, enough people would go to see it to keep it alive awhile. A positive review from the *Times* means less now than at any time in memory.

And I think, with Clive Barnes as its present critic, nothing very good is going to happen to Broadway drama. Let me be quite blunt about this at the outset: I think Clive Barnes is the most dangerous, the most crippling critic in modern Broadway history, and I only hope he is dispensed with before these words reach print. The following is an attempt to explain why.

Barnes was already the ballet critic on the *Times* when he came to his present job. But unlike Taubman, who gave up one job to get another, Barnes kept his old post and thus became the man most responsible for the future of both American ballet *and* American theatre.

He is English. That, as we shall see, is one of the problems. And he is also primarily a ballet critic. That presents another problem. The theatre is of secondary importance to Barnes—sloppy seconds, some theatre men feel—and when there is a ballet opening, he often prefers to go to a preview of a play that might coincide with it. I am all for avoiding Broadway opening nights, but since they exist, they should take preference over ballet openings, since, as a rule, ballet is repertory, will be repeated, is usually in for a certain set run, and is not in any degree comparable with Broadway, which is at the financial mercy of the *Times*.

Barnes is a terribly busy man. Unlike Atkinson, who shunned publicity, Barnes likes it. He has appeared on the "Tonight" show. Fine. He has also appeared on local TV programs such as the astrology quiz show, "What's My Sign?" He also was one of several narrators for a fashion show held at Bergdorf Goodman on April 2. I have no idea what Barnes received, if anything. I don't think it matters much, using your position for a little extra now and then. What does matter is that on the night of the fashion show there was an event opening that Barnes was scheduled to review, and he called the press agents for the event and told them he might be late, since he had the fashion work at Bergdorf's. (He was not late, incidentally.)

He was late, though, for *The Happy Time*. It is not enough that he is ballet critic for the most influential paper in America as well as theatre critic for the most influential paper in America; he also gives lectures on the side. This lecture was in Pittsburgh. The plane back was late. The producer held the curtain 25 minutes, hoping that

Barnes would arrive. Finally, the producer had to start the show because many of the other critics were getting angry. Barnes arrived 15 minutes after the curtain went up and gave the show a nice enough notice, basing his knowledge of what he saw on Doctor Johnson's theory that a man does not have to taste an entire keg of wine to comment on its contents.

True enough. But the opening to *The Happy Time* not only is generally held to be the best part of the show, it is also the most important, in that it sets the style, tone, pace, everything. Barnes's giving a lecture in Pittsburgh when he should have been in New York had several possible consequences: he might have liked the show more had he seen it all, and given it a rave, or he might have liked it less and panned it. (The feeling was that he could not very well have panned it after being late; the ensuing anger along the street might have been enough to get him in genuine job trouble.) More important, many of the other critics might not have been as hostile to *Happy Time* had Barnes been in his proper place. Some of the notices were unexpectedly blistering, and there was general agreement that the critics were sore. One of them turned on a member of *The Happy Time* management and said angrily, "We're sitting around here waiting for that guy like a bunch of pigs." Obviously, the other critics knew that no curtain would be held 25 minutes for them.

Coming from ballet, Barnes had a good excuse for being ignorant about the business of Broadway. So before the season started, when he was quoted as saying that the *Times* was not crucial for success, as witness the musical *Sherry,* which he said was not pleasing to the *Times* but running happily nonetheless, and then *Sherry* closed shortly thereafter to a loss of over $500,000, Barnes was to be excused. (Actually not. I mean, if you're going to comment in print on your influence, and the example you use is clearly an inept example, which you could have found out simply by flipping open *Variety* to the grosses page, it indicates you're not doing your homework.) A year later, Barnes, experienced now, said the same thing all over again on one of his television appearances: the *Times* really had no great influence, as witness a play he disliked that was doing splendidly. The play closed shortly thereafter to a loss of almost $200,000, the coming death again clearly visible in *Variety* as Barnes spoke. In other words, Barnes knew nothing of the business of Broadway or his influence on that business, and during the course of the season never happened to learn.

Ballet reviewing requires a very special talent: it needs patience, because the essence of ballet reviewing (although new pieces are being done continually) is *re-reviewing*. And commenting on the stars: Has Margot got her left arm under control? Is Eddie doing too much? Is Rudy swishing less this season? A ballet reviewer is constantly reassessing. But a Broadway man, especially the overnight Broadway man for the *Times,* has got to *say it right then.* When Barnes says it, if he says it at all, it is usually later. Example: *Loot,* the black comedy from England, couldn't have asked for a better word from Barnes than this: "Hilarious." That is what he called it. "Hilarious." But that was later, in a passing reference in an entirely different article. What he said on opening night, when it counted, was this: "There is something for everyone to detest in Joe Orton's outrageous play, 'Loot,' which opened last night at the Biltmore Theatre. To like it I think you might have to have a twisted sense of humor. I liked it. But I do trust it's not for you, for you would be a far nicer person if it were not." Now, telling an audience that a play is probably not to its taste is quite a way from calling it hilarious. If he had said what he meant the first time, *Loot* might have had a run.

Jean Brodie. "This is one of the best plays in many a season. . . ." A producer couldn't ask for more. And if the producer had got that notice on opening night, some people think *Brodie* might have been the smash it was in London instead of the disappointingly small success it was here. But that quote came weeks later. The Barnes opening-night review began like this: "The two themes of 'The Prime of Miss Jean Brodie,' seen last night at the Helen Hayes Theatre, seem to be the folly of the romantic imagination and the imprint made upon a child's character by an inspired teacher. Jay Allen's play, based upon Muriel Spark's original novel, is at its far from inconsiderable best when concentrating upon the character of Miss Brodie herself—indeed, here it is fascinating in its insights into a marvelously portrayed eccentric human being. Where it is less successful—and it seems rather less successful here, after extensive rewriting, than it was originally in London—is in placing Miss Brodie's prime into its philosophical, emotional and even topical contexts."

There are many other examples that could be given, but these two are sufficient to outline the first conclusion: if the job of the overnight critic of the *Times* is to say what he thinks fast and clear, Barnes has trouble measuring up.

Barnes is also known in the trade as a smart ass. He is constantly throwing in little bitch asides. One example out of, believe me, hundreds: Frank D. Gilroy's *The Subject Was Roses* won him a Pulitzer prize. When Gilroy's play *The Only Game in Town* opened, Barnes commented in the opening paragraph of his notice: " 'The Only Game in Town' was written by Frank D. Gilroy (and how many playwrights do you know who have achieved real distinction with a middle initial?) . . ."

Now what in the name of God does what a man chooses to call himself have to do with what goes on up there? Is Tennessee Williams a lesser writer because he didn't call himself Tom? Does it matter that Sam Clemens took a funny name or that George Shaw liked his middle moniker, Bernard? If an author wants to be published as J. M. Barrie, let him; if he wants to be known as George S. Kaufman, that's his business. And of all things, how does a man named Clive come off knocking a serious writer because he uses his middle initial?

But still, all of this—the smart assness, the ballet preference, the lack of interest in Broadway, the self-glorification via television—all of this together is less important than one simple fact: the man has a wild English bias.

This is so well known, so clear, that one of England's best directors was forced to comment on it. "It really is embarrassing," he said to me. "It's outrageous. Of course, I'm getting rich from it, but I shouldn't think it would be pleasurable to you people."

Barnes's English bias established itself early. He didn't like *Keep It in the Family* because it had been changed from its English locale, and that is a reasonable position. Then came Pinter's *Birthday Party*, done with an American cast, which Barnes said was the most interesting play to be seen on Broadway in some seasons, not counting Pinter's *Homecoming*. He also said that the acting, *"by normal standards was exceptional* [italics mine]." He also said (italics again mine): *"The play would have been far better acted by a British cast."* He didn't even say a "good" British cast. Exceptional American acting simply isn't as good as any British acting, period. (Much later, Barnes was to write, "British actors do seem to have a way of making characters seem people and not just characters." The other side of that coin has got to be that American actors don't.)

Following wonderful notices for *After the Rain, Rosencrantz and Guildenstern Are Dead* and *Girl in My Soup*, Barnes did a piece on the first month of the theatre season, in which he commented on the fact that the best things were all English. He concluded his piece by saying: "The lesson of the last few seasons, so strongly reinforced by the last few weeks, seems to suggest that Broadway may become the national shop window for our theatre, but not the workshop. This is perhaps a new function for Broadway, but not an ignoble one. It now remains for the producers and, even more, the theatre public (who, after all, control the whole situation) to ensure that the quality of the goods shown in the window are the world's finest."

This was a bit bothersome to some people. Barnes seemed to be saying that it would not be the least bit ignoble for Broadway, traditionally the heart of the professional American theatre, to change course somewhat radically and become, instead of something American, an international theatrical showcase. And in the context of Barnes's piece, "international" meant "British."

Let's turn that around. How would it sound to English theatre-goers if an American, suddenly thrust into their most influential theatrical post, suggested that the West End forget about showcasing British playwrights and concentrate instead on importing American writers? Being careful, of course, not to damage or change the merchandise en route.

(One minor point about Barnes's British background: he is obsessed, like all class-conscious English, with accents. And British customs are a similar obsession: in *The Birthday Party* he ended his review by saying that although the sets and costumes were evocative enough, "I could not believe a window seat in a seedy south coast boardinghouse, and the bottle of Grant's whiskey has an American rather than an English label on it.") When Barnes raved over Margaret Leighton's embarrassing performance in *The Little Foxes*, everybody knew you were in trouble if you weren't English. (Though, to be fair, he did have unkind words for Miss Leighton when she later took over the lead role; her southern accent was bothersome to him.)

The British preference, if that were all, would be devastating enough. But the fact is, it also distorts his views of American work. For example, he killed Robert Anderson's play *I Never Sang for My Father*, by slamming it as soap opera. Harold Clurman, presently among the best of the critics writing reviews of Broadway, called it "a play of decent sentiment." Clurman, I submit, is considerably closer to the truth. The Anderson play, dealing with two people, a father and a son who do not like each other much, who end up with the son guilt-wracked over his lack of emotion while the father dies alone and paralyzed and filled with hate, may be any number of things, but soap opera isn't one of them. If it were, the first-act curtain, which has the mother dying, would be a soap-opera scene. Think of the tears you could force: Lillian Gish gasping in a hospital, a son trying to be brave, a crying father, nurses scurrying around sympathetically. Anderson handles the whole thing in practically a sentence. The son tells the audience his mother is dead, wham, like that, no mother on stage, and curtain. The damaging thing about Barne's treatment of Anderson's play is that he was simply not qualified to judge it, any more than I am qualified to say whether Brian Rix should make a living in English theatre. There are some things that are native to countries, and the English love Rix's farcical buffoonery. And the English are stiff-upper-lip people —they prefer never to show any emotion. The Anderson play was an openly emotional evening, but not soap opera, and Barnes was simply unable, by heritage, intelligence or birth, to tell the difference.

But in the end, it all comes down to Arthur Miller.

I mean this: the critic of the *Times* has to be able to deal with the best of American playwriting. If he enjoys trivia like *Girl in My Soup* because it's English, and he feels at home with it, no one is going to be damaged in the long run. But it is the important playwrights that need decent criticism. It's the Millers that make the American theatre go. Or stop.

Miller's *The Price,* his first Broadway work in 13 years, was dogged by bad luck almost from the beginning. The play dealt with two brothers, one a failure cop, one a successful physician, who meet after long absence to sell the furniture that belonged to their father. It is a four-character play, the other two people being the cop's wife and an ancient Jewish furniture dealer who has been called in by the cop to give a price on the value of the father's belongings.

The play had so many things going for it, it seemed almost as if the misfortune that struck it resulted from *hubris.* Robert Whitehead, returning to the Broadway theatre after the anguish of Lincoln Center, was the producer. Ulu Grosbard, perhaps the most highly thought of young straight-play director in town, had been hired to direct, and the cast had Arthur Kennedy as the surgeon, Kate Reid as the wife. As the cop, Jack Warden, once the hottest young actor in the theatre before he disappeared into bad films and worse television, was returning to Broadway. The part of the ancient furniture dealer was probably the hardest to cast, and the biggest gamble was taken: David Burns, a musical-comedy funnyman was selected.

The play's opening, originally set for fall, was canceled and put back to late January. Casting problems. Finally, rehearsals began. The play, really an argument between the brothers refereed almost by the old Jew, had enormous potential: which one of the brothers was the success, which was the fool, and it wasn't always what met the eye. If the play had a problem, it was that although the brothers had at each other mightily, the climax was missing. Robert Anderson has said: "Comedy is like petting: it's fun and no one gets hurt. A serious play is more like intercourse: if you don't have the orgasm, you end up frustrated." The Miller play didn't have the orgasm; it ended just short of it. But there was every reason to assume that once the actors got in front of an audience and Miller could see his piece alive, a way out of the frustration might be found.

There was never any time.

Before the Philadelphia opening, Warden got sick and left the cast. It had taken months to cast the two brothers; now the sturdy Pat Hingle was put into the part within hours. But all the other actors had gone through their learning processes, the in-depth investigation of their roles. To go through it again with Hingle would have been difficult, if not impossible. The Philadelphia opening was postponed while Hingle simply went through the enormous task of learning his lines. Clearly, there was trouble in Philadelphia.

But as if to compensate, there was also David Burns. David Burns's performance as the wheezing octogenarian Jew was one of the best I have ever seen. For me, it rated with Bert Lahr in *Godot* and Mostel in *Rhinoceros*. It was simply so real, so fine, so goddam perfect that you could only marvel at the skill and warmth of the man. Nothing on Broadway this year touched it.

Two days before the New York opening, Burns had an emergency operation and was out of the play. His understudy took over and was, like Hingle, sound. More you couldn't ask. By this time, Miller was staging the play himself, Grosbard having been replaced. As the troubles of *The Price* kept on coming, a sad lady shook her head and said, "Poor everybody."

When the play finally opened, it proved enormously controversial, by which I mean it caused considerable critical disagreement. Before discussing Barnes's review in detail, the following quotes should give some idea of the direct conflict of opinions the play aroused. Speaking of Miller's career as a whole, a critic said, " 'The Price' is one of the most engrossing and entertaining plays that Arthur Miller has ever written." Against this, a critic said: ". . . the author of 'Death of a Salesman' is still waiting in the wings, unfulfilled."

As to *The Price* specifically, one critic felt is was merely "far better than average" when taken on its own level of psychological drama. Against this: "A great evening in the theatre . . ."

As to the story: ". . . Miller holds the interest with the skill of a born storyteller." Against this: "The action itself has ended before the play starts . . . the story itself is over. . . ." Another opinion: "The motivation of the story is paper thin and will not bear surveillance." Another: "The details of the story are extraordinarily clumsy."

Now to the characters: "The characters are paper thin. . . ." Against this: "Miller has provided wonderfully meaty parts for his cast. . . ."

Given these conflicting opinions, where did Barnes fit? Here's the kicker, folks: *all the quotes given above are directly from Barnes's opening-night review.* That's right: the most important man in the New York theatre loves all those meaty parts provided for all those paper-thin characters. And for Clive Barnes, a born storyteller is one who tells a story that is already over, with paper-thin motivations and details that are extraordinarily clumsy. Look over those quotes again if you want to; it's all there. And all it proves is this: the man cannot deal coherently with American drama.

Perhaps the most frightening new thing that *The Price* review revealed was Barnes's inability to deal with the American language. Again, from his first-night review: "I doubt also the language of these people, for Miller has them breathing the dust of the theatre rather than the air of the streets. Phrases such as 'What's it all about!' or 'It won't be solved in a day, Esther,' or 'Are we both running away from the same thing?' are pure fustian." (I had to look up *fustian* too: it means, among other things, pompous, pretentious talk, rant, bombast.)

Now I have checked this paragraph with any number of people who make their living writing American dialogue, and they all, without the remotest exception, found the quoted Miller lines to be perfectly standard, spoken, 100% American dialogue. They didn't say it was brilliant, understand. They just all agreed it was believable, idiomatic American talk, and not in any way ranting or pretentious or bombastic.

The picture of Barnes now is almost complete: (1) he has no ear for American speech; (2) he cannot deal with American drama; (3) he prefers, in all ways, English theatre to American theatre; (4) he would find it not at all ignoble if Broadway were to become primarily an importing agent; (5) he prefers ballet to theatre; (6) he is a smart ass; (7) he enjoys glorifying himself publicly through his position; (8) he changes his opinions constantly, which is certainly the right of free men, but not so helpful when the life or death of a play is based on a critic's having the courage to say what he thinks *now*, not a month later in a ballet column; (9) he has little interest in learning the financial aspects of Broadway, to which he is central.

Add one final trivial little thing: Barnes did not give an unqualified rave to a single American Broadway production all season long. *The Show-off?* Sure, but that was the APA repertory. *Hair?* Sure, but that was a transferred off-Broadway show. *Scuba Duba?* That was off-Broadway. So was *Your Own Thing.* So was *Jacques Brel.* So was *The Boys in the Band.* So was every other American show that got a rave. Most English shows, it goes without saying, got raves or the next best thing.

Late in May, Barnes wrote a column about U.S. theatre, in which he said that ". . . Broadway is only for Establishment playwrights, such as Neil Simon, Tennessee Williams, Arthur Miller or Robert Anderson, fine fellows all, but hardly the most interesting playwrights in the United States."

Taking them in no order: I like Robert Anderson's stuff; its open emotional quality is something I find admirable, but I'm not going to the mat over him; Neil Simon I think is interesting, perhaps not so much for what he has written but what he is going to write next.

But I'm sorry, Williams and Miller are two of the three best playwrights this country has produced, *ever,* and they are both alive and producing plays, and if they are to be dismissed as "hardly the most interesting playwrights in the United States," it's more than a bit disturbing. Maybe Broadway isn't San Simeon—God knows it isn't San Simeon—but if it is also slightly better than a pigsty, it's because of Williams and Miller. They are the best we have, order them any way you will, *and* the most interesting *because* they are the best. And when the one lethal voice in the American theatre—the one voice that can actually kill—dismisses them, something's wrong somewhere.

And what is wrong is that the New York *Times* has somehow summoned a chauvinistic British ballet lover and given him the right to influence the future of Broadway drama according to his whims. Barnes is forty. Drama critics live a long time.

There is some favorable news on the critical scene: the television critics are becoming increasingly important, and they are good. Two of them are, anyway, the two most important—Leonard Harris of CBS and Edwin Newman of NBC. Part of their increased importance is because of the decline of daily newspaper reviewing. But I think the main reason they are gaining in influence is because they are the two best people commenting overnight on the Broadway scene. They are first-class men and both are enormously intelligent, and their jobs, unlike those of their newspaper counterparts, are prestigious. Newman is estimated to make close to $75,000 a year, and his is already the most famous face of any reviewer.

Leonard Harris, the CBS critic, is thirty-six, married, with two children. He attended City College and graduated Phi Bete. He went to Yale Law for two years, got drafted, and after he came out, took stock. "I was twenty-eight, and I thought, 'What can I do without training, without schooling, without ability?' The obvious answer was newspaper work." He worked for a while in Hartford, then shifted to the *World Telegram and Sun* in New York. Since 1966, he has done the critic's job for CBS and done it excellently.

He's a handsome man—on television he seems somewhat stiffer than in person—and he dresses and talks well. A lot of people are critical of the television critics because they review their shows in about a minute, maybe a little more. (This is typical Broadway reasoning: no one has ever complained that the *Cue* notices are too short, and the Newman/Harris notices are as long as *Cue*'s or longer.) Harris says: "I usually get back from the theatre by ten. I have till 10:40 to get what I want to say on the teleprompter. Obviously, there's no trouble getting 75 seconds of stuff written in 40 minutes: the problem is narrowing it down. Locating yourself is the really hard thing, making it come out exactly as you think, and not better or worse than it is.

"I'm not by nature a gregarious person. I'm not close to the theatre crowd; I don't see Broadway people socially. I try not to be funny for the sake of being funny; it's so easy, and the play's helpless to defend itself. I try never to turn out a good piece at the expense of the play; you always have to guard against that."

Edwin Newman of NBC is probably somewhat less concerned with plays than with politics. He is nationally known for his political coverage, but he has been doing theatre criticism for four seasons. "I was assigned the job, I didn't ask for it. I had dealt with plays and books and movies in broadcasts. I imagine the assignment is permanent, but this is a somewhat unpredictable business; we work on contracts here."

Newman stands over 6 feet, weighs 190. He has a sardonic sense of humor and writes well; he's published articles and reviews in *Harper's, The Atlantic Monthly, Punch,* etc. Like Harris, he almost became a lawyer. He majored in political science at Wisconsin, served in the Navy during World War II, and afterward went to work for Eric Sevareid in Washington. He was married during the war, has one daughter. He spent most of the fifties in Europe, first free-lancing, then heading the NBC news bureaus in London, Paris and Rome. I had no idea how a television critic went about his job, so I asked Newman if I might accompany him after the late March opening of the new Tennessee Williams drama. Newman said fine. We arranged to meet outside the theatre following the play.

I arranged, long before that time, to visit Mr. Williams. . . .

Glaven meets me at the door. He lives with Williams; their names share the nameplate on the door: "Glaven/Williams." They live on the West Side, which is sort of surprising. But what is really surprising is that they live in one of those new buildings that are gradually taking over Manhattan. Glaven leads me through the foyer to where Williams sits on a living-room couch. I sit in a chair across from him. Glaven moves beside Williams on the couch and settles down. There is a small bulldog, and it comes and sits by me.

"Look at her," from Williams. "Going right to a stranger—look—she's taking to him. Isn't that typical of her."

"Just like a woman," Glaven confirms. He does a lot of that: confirming. He sits by Williams on the sofa, listening attentively, making suggestions, refreshing drinks and memories.

I ask about *Camino Real,* one of my favorite of all my favorite Williams plays.

"*Ca-mi-no Real,*" Williams corrects. "Oh God, that was a hard one. I was crazy that opening night. Kazan came in with the Steinbecks, and I said, 'How dare you bring those people in here?' "

"And you like the Steinbecks," Glaven reminds.

"They're marvelous people—Elaine is just wonderful. But that's how I am opening nights. I'm out of my skull opening nights."

I ask how *Kingdom of Earth* is coming. (It was to change titles later.)

Williams nods. "I think we'll curtain at 11:05 or 11:10. Jose doesn't hurry things up, does he?"

Jose is Quintero, the director, and on the question, Williams turns to Glaven for confirmation; Quintero was doing the show too slowly.

Glaven nods.

Then on to the reviewers. "The reviewers don't like me . . . they don't like me . . . I've got an outside chance . . . Charles Bowden and I . . . it was on *The Night of the Iguana* [Williams always calls his plays by their full names—never *Iguana*, never *Streetcar*, always *A Streetcar Named Desire*] . . . we were coming back to New York, and we said a special mass for the play . . . Bette Davis was upset that Margaret Leighton's part was bigger than her part; on opening night she finally decided that Miss Leighton's part would not be shortened, and she gave a wonderful performance . . . we got by the critics that time . . . but they don't like me. . . ."

Now to opening nights. "Opening nights?" He looks at Glaven. Glaven suggests nothing. Silence for a moment. Then: "Laurette Taylor in *The Glass Menagerie* was not to be believed. She was incandescent. I remember going up on stage afterward, and she said, 'Either they liked this play or there are an awful lot of liars down there.'"

I mumble some question about how many plays he has written.

Williams says, "My mother bought me a typewriter when I was thirteen, and I've been writing ever since."

I start to jot it down, but then I remember the little sigh that had preceded his answer, and suddenly I realize he's said it before, that remark, said it all before, everything I can possibly ask him, in thousands of interviews since 1945, and suddenly I feel terrible taking up his time. I go through my list of remaining questions, cutting the most obviously silly.

Then from Williams: "I was not a well-liked kid."

"Why do you say that?" from Glaven. "You think you're not well liked now, and you're loved."

"I would have died if I'd stopped writing."

Glaven confirms: "It's seven days a week, no matter how he feels. He's amazing."

Williams nods. "Sometimes I wake at two in the morning."

Glaven quotes, " 'Genius is a great ego and fantastic discipline.' "

"I don't think well of myself," Williams says, from somewhere in his mind. "I have nothing else to do but write. I have about five good days—when the play comes open to me and it's easy to write it. I was a professional typist, and I can write very, very fast—when I feel a play coming open to me."

Out of town is coming up. Does it bother him? "Out of town is for the actors and director. The writer has done all he can." Has he ever improved a play out of town? "Not at all." Then his mind is back on *Ca-mi-no Real*. "Cheryl Crawford, poor thing, produced it, and she cut out the confetti in the carnival scene after the reviews were bad." Now he is out of town again. "Tallulah, poor thing; she gave one of the great entrances [this is the revival of *The Milk Train Doesn't Stop Here Any More* he is talking of now]. The idea for the entrance was all hers."

Glaven says: "You so often talk about her entrance."

Williams: "It was wonderful. Such a wonderful entrance. I remember Merrick asked me if I wanted to close before we opened, and I said, 'No; it would break Tallulah's heart, poor thing.' Of course I didn't want it closed either. When you work that long on a thing, you love it."

The doorbell rings, and some young men come in. Glaven sees me to the door and is polite as always, but I can't hear what he's saying, because the young men are walking up to Tennessee Williams and holding out their hands, and one of them says to him, "Tom . . . Tom, you're looking wonderful. . . ." "Hello, Tom," the other young one says.

. . . Tom . . . ?

At 9:20, Wednesday, March 27, the limousines start to arrive. The fifth and sixth are white and black Rolls-Royces. They try to park in front of the Barrymore, but the police on duty direct them across the street.

Inside, Williams' retitled *The Seven Descents of Myrtle* is opening. It is a three-character play, not a comedy, no matter what you may think the plot indicates: a twenty-year-old southern transvestite homosexual (played by an unbelievably miscast thirtyish Englishman) marries a moronic stripper in order to deprive his animalistic half brother of their mother's estate, which the transvestite homosexual has promised in writing to the animal when he dies. The plot revolves around the possession of the piece of paper that the transvestite homosexual signed, and when the dam that is holding back the flood waters of the local river will give way and drown everybody. Eventually, the transvestite homosexual gets into one of his mother's nighties and dies. The dam bursts, and the animal hurries the dumb stripper up to the roof where they can presumably wait out the flood together.

At 9:25 the first autograph hunters arrive.

9:26, and Merrick appears. "There's a horse's ass for every light on

Broadway," he says to me. Then: "Are you still writing that silly book?"

I said I was.

"Have you put in that the theatre is obsolete? They don't want us."

I asked how the opening was going.

"I've just been in and out. They seemed coolish."

Glaven scurries across the street. "David," he says. "Come have a drink with Tennessee."

Merrick opens his pocket watch. "It's almost over."

Glaven urges: "Please come; he would appreciate it so."

"Of course," Merrick says, and he goes with Glaven toward the Edison Hotel.

9:30. Eleven limousines now. The limousine drivers are talking with the autograph hunters, exchanging celebrity anecdotes. "I took that movie girl—what the hell's her name? Stella . . ."

"Stevens?" one of the autograph hunters says.

The limousine driver can't remember. "I took her down to the place on Thirty-fourth Street that sells Nathan's hot dogs."

"Was she nice?" another autograph hunter asks.

"Yeah. She was very nice. She just wanted these hot dogs, I remember. She was with some actor."

"Who? Who?" from the autographers.

"Nobody; that's the point of my story," the limousine driver says. "He'd done maybe a couple TV shows is all. Nothing parts. But when they were getting in, this old broad—she musta known everything about everyone—she came up and looked at him like he was Gable and started listing his credits: 'Run for Your Life,' like that. And this Stella, she was the famous one, and she was in the car, so this old broad didn't see her, but she was excited by this nobody, that's the point of my story."

"I don't get it," one of the autograph people said.

"Well, Jesus, if she goes crazy over a nothing like a two-bit TV nobody, what do you think would have happened to her if somebody had told her that all the time she was talking to him, this Stella whatever-the-hell was in the car, and she didn't even know it?"

The autograph hunters listened till it was over, then left the limousine driver alone.

"You get it, don't you?" the limousine driver said to another limousine driver.

"I got nothin'," the other limousine driver said.

9:37, and a small, weary photographer puts down his heavy bag of equipment beneath the marquee. Another photographer with his own heavy bag is there. They look at each other, eye each other's burdens, and wearily shake hands.

9:41, and Merrick crosses toward the theatre with Williams and Glaven and the director, Quintero. And someone who looks like someone's mother but is probably an agent. They all enter the theatre. Merrick immediately exits again.

At 9:44 a laundry truck pulls up and makes a delivery; a different world heard from.

At 9:52 the first people leave, and inside there is the sound of applause.

At 9:54 Edwin Newman exits. "Gee, that was long," he says, pausing a moment before completing the thought, "which is the kindest thing I can say about it. I thought that flood would never come." He walks east on Forty-ninth Street until he comes to the RCA building. Then he elevators to the fourth floor, moves through the ticker-tape room into the main newsroom, which is the size of a basketball court. His office, which he shares with another newsman, is off the main newsroom. As he enters his office, someone says to him, "Well?"

"Not tonight," Newman tells him, shaking his head.

10:10, and he puts paper into his typewriter. He starts to type, stops, makes a phone call. "I wanted some extra time," he explains. "A minute and ten seconds, fifteen seconds; they gave it to me." He goes back to his typing. (He has been quoted as saying of his job: "One of the advantages of TV reviewing is what most people think is its disadvantage: brevity. When you have no time, you must pick out what you think is salient. Of course there are difficulties: the nuances don't appear as they should. Both the praise and the panning appear excessive.")

10:28, and the review is done. He reads it aloud, timing it. Then he begins the refining and cutting of phrases, words, all with considerable care.

10:30, and the make-up man comes in. He is Richard Nixon's present make-up man (not the one from 1960), and for the five minutes he lines and powders Newman, Newman talks. "You know what Williams has done, and you're terribly cast down by the knowledge of how long it has been since he has done it and how much greater the odds are against his doing it again." (. . . they don't like me . . . the reviewers don't like me . . .)

"You go to a Williams play hoping it's going to succeed, knowing what it can mean to the theatre. And then a night like tonight." Newman's words end abruptly. He has been terribly upset by the badness of the evening. The make-up man leaves; Newman returns to his review, fidgeting with it, smoothing it, reading it aloud again, for time. This was what he read:

There is no rational explanation of *The Seven Descents of Myrtle* except that Tennessee Williams is burlesquing himself, if that is rational.

Williams' exercises in southern degradation have sometimes illuminated the human condition, but this one is narrow, obsessively petty, and essentially ludicrous. He gives us an impotent and effete young man, mother-fixated, dying of tuberculosis, who marries an addlebrained, overage stripper. That is so that she will inherit his farm, and keep it from his brawny field hand half brother.

Williams brings them together on the farm, with a flood threatening, and as they go through their contrived paces, you pray for the levee to break. Williams tries to create an atmosphere of terror, heavy with sexuality. He manages only a nerve-wracking monotony, especially with the stripper, bravely played by Estelle Parsons, who is made to laugh uncomfortably in a cracked voice from the beginning to end.

None of this is Miss Parson's fault, nor is it that of Brian Bedford as the husband, or of Harry Guardino as the virile one. There are also a few moments when Williams' comic touch flashes as it used to. But what a sad evening.

Edwin Newman, NBC News.

What would you say if you had more time?

"I'd say that the funny moments have nothing to do with the play. And the guy dying in his mother's dress, I'd mention that. I'd like to say more, but enough's enough."

10:46, and he types up his review. Nine copies with a wide left-hand margin so that the director can mark picture cues. (Pictures of the performers will flash on during the reading.) In the middle of the typing he breaks off. "You know, the play doesn't even make sense: the sick one must have known he was going to die or he wouldn't have married the stripper, and yet the curtain of the first act is the sick one finding out he's going to die." He shakes his head, goes back to typing. Of the nine sheets, he keeps a copy for himself; one is for the director; one he mails to Hobe Morrison at *Variety;* the rest are distributed so they can be quoted on other shows.

10:55, and he walks down the back stairs to the floor below and enters the newsroom. Jim Hartz, the newscaster, is at his desk, and Kyle Rote, who handles sports, is moving around. Newman approaches a man with his review, and they go over some pictures of the performers and decide which should go where in his notice.

11:00, and he walks into the control room. To an outsider, the control room is bedlam. Eight people sit in it (with a ninth in the adjoining room separated by a large glass partition). Among them are the director and the producer and the assistant director and production assistants and a light man, and they are all talking across each other: "Five, four, three, two, one"; "start going in slow after the spot"; "film roll." In the front of the room are television sets. Twenty-three of them. Four are large and in color. Nineteen are small and black and white. Not all of them are on, and one of them is tuned silently to the opposition news broadcast on Channel 2. Some footage of Nixon comes on Channel 2. "That's '52 footage," someone says, and when you look closely, you realize that Nixon seems terribly young.

"I go on about 11:22," Newman says. "Sports gets about two minutes, fifteen seconds, weather gets five minutes." Someone makes a remark, and suddenly it is clear that these people are not overjoyed that one sixth of a news show is devoted to weather forecasting.

At 11:17 Newman starts out of the control room to where the show is being shot. He takes his place behind a desk, sips water. Jim Hartz, practicing the title of the play, stumbles over the word *Descents,* and everybody breaks up. But this is during a commercial, and when the news itself comes back, all are straight-faced again.

At 11:21 Hartz says, "A new play by Tennessee Williams, *The Seven Descents of Myrtle,* opened tonight at the Barrymore Theatre. Here to review it is Edwin Newman." Newman reads his review. It takes 70 seconds. It seemed to me an accurate summary, cogent, sound and kind, considering the painful pace of the play in performance.

At 11:25 Newman goes into a washroom and takes off his make-up. Kyle Rote comes in. "I guess you put some more people out of work tonight," Rote says.

Usually Newman does not go out afterward, but tonight he decides to hit the Brasserie. Sinking back in a cab, he closes his eyes. "It's a gladiatorial thing, theatre reviewing. Relatively speaking, we're at the beginning of reviewing on the air. But after a night like tonight . . . In the first act I was hoping for a miracle somehow. After that it was painful sitting there." (. . . they don't like me . . . I was not a well-liked kid. . . . Why do you say that? You think you're not well liked now, and you're loved. . . .)

At 11:37 he is almost to the Brasserie. It really got to him tonight —the reviewing—for perhaps the first time. "I really wonder," Ed Newman says, "how long anyone should have this job."

I hope he has it for a long time. Leonard Harris too. They are intelligent men, perceptive men, and they report what's there. They miss. They're not perfect; neither is Clurman or Kerr or Hobe Morrison, who writes for *Variety*. But they are the best we have, and better than that, they're good.

I left Newman at the Brasserie and went on up Park Avenue. The ladies were well dressed, as they often are, and I thought of the night I had seen the Williams play, and of the well-dressed woman who had walked out of the theatre just behind me. She was in her middle years, and she was clothed with expensive taste. She carried herself well, and so did her escort, to whom she turned as she left the theatre. "I thought that play was shit," she said to him.

Tennessee Williams needs the kindness of strangers now.

7

Producers

The following tale told by a movie nut is true. "At the Museum of Modern Art, in the middle fifties, there was a special movie. Someone from the museum had made a compilation of scenes from about a dozen Dietrich pictures, all the way from 'Blue Angel' through, I think, 'Witness for the Prosecution.' And the compiler narrated the film from the stage in the museum theatre. I think it was originally done by the museum for charity purposes, but they gave a special showing one Saturday morning for the very dedicated.

"*Early* Saturday morning. This girl I was dating had pull, and we got in and sat down, and everyone was bleary. Then this guy got up on stage and started the narration about Dietrich while the picture he'd spliced together was shown. All the scenes you'd expect were there: singing 'Falling in Love Again' from 'The Blue Angel,' chasing across the desert in high heels after Gary Cooper in 'Morocco'; you name it. I don't know how long it went on—an hour, hour and a half maybe—but gradually this thing came over the house: we realized for the first time that this woman was an *actress*. I'd never dreamed that she had such range or skill; I just thought of her always as this broad Hemingway called 'the Kraut,' and that made her A-O.K., this all being, of course, before we found out that Hemingway wasn't so A-O.K. himself, being something, as his memoirs have indicated, less of a man and more of a bitch than we thought then. Anyway, as I said, these Dietrich scenes just snowed that house full of film nuts, and after it was over, everyone went ape applauding.

"It's still early Saturday morning, remember, and the film is finished, and the guy on stage says, 'Ladies and gentlemen, Miss Marlene Dietrich,' and he gestures toward a side door, and there she was, in the flesh, coming on stage. I was in my twenties then, and that was the first time I realized that those people who are possessed of beauty are simply different from the rest of us. Her hair dazzled, and she was wearing what I remember as a kind of light-beige suit, maybe Chanel, and *it* dazzled and *she* dazzled, and the whole house just stood up and gasped. It was incredible.

"She spoke to us, thanked us for coming down, thanked us for liking it, which we so obviously had, thanked the guy who'd spliced the thing, and in general was sexy and gracious as hell. Then, instead of disappearing back through the side door, she made her exit up the aisle through the audience. When she passed my row I started to follow her—I just had to. I left my date flat (we chatted about that quite a bit the rest of the day) and took off after Dietrich. I tried to look as if I weren't following her: when she'd stop to greet someone, I'd stop and glance around as if I were looking for someone, or I'd pretend that I'd left something in my seat and was just trying to locate the row. She had better things to do than check on whether there were any creeps on her trail, so I stayed right behind her, out of the theatre, through that basement lobby, up the stairs of the museum toward the main entrance. I couldn't help myself, because I couldn't believe that any human being could look the way she did. I didn't know people like that existed, and I didn't know if I was ever going to have a shot at seeing one again, and what if I didn't?

"She reached the front door of the museum and out she went, and out I went, and as she hit the sidewalk she flicked her right hand high, and down the block a big black limousine started cruising toward her. Or toward us, I should say, because I was still in my allotted place, half a step behind her. The car stopped in the middle of the street, which had been all torn up for repairs, so I figured maybe she'd stop and let the chauffeur help her, but she didn't; she just glided through the rubble as if it were a golf green. I didn't glide so good. I stumbled and that made a sound, and by the car she turned: there I was, a grown man, humiliated, clumsy, you name it.

But when she looked at me, what I saw (what I obviously wanted to see) was not pique or irritation, because what she did, I swear, was give me a glance that said, 'Listen, relax; I only got this way for you.'

"Needless to say, I have been something of a fan of Miss Dietrich's since that time, which is why I went to see her show this year. I went feeling a little frightened that she might not be what she was.

"I was right to be frightened.

"She was introduced and came out and stood in front of the orchestra, and the first thing she did was 'I Can't Give You Anything but Love, Baby,' and I knew there was something wrong. But I couldn't zero in on what it was until the next song, 'You're the Cream in My Coffee.' (She's singing as well as ever, by the way, which is like saying that Esther Williams is acting as well as ever.) Anyway, it was during that second number I saw it: her mouth doesn't work right any more. The bottom lip—the right half of it—sags, as if the muscle were gone. And once I realized that, a lot of impressions clicked: her movement was stiff; it was as if she were so trussed up she couldn't move. And worse than that was her hair: it wasn't behaving like real hair. When a woman bows her head, real hair naturally falls over her face at least a little. Dietrich's hair didn't budge. Stiff as barbed wire. And suddenly, with the sagging lip and the trussed-up body and the barbed-wire hair, what she looked like was some female impersonator up there doing his Dietrich turn.

"I ought to add that this is a minority report. I saw her show at a matinee, and all I heard from all the old ladies around me was how impossibly beautiful she looked. So maybe I had this reaction because I had seen her once when she really was impossibly beautiful. One more thing: some of her numbers were sensational. Like many movie stars, she is basically a facial actress. And Dietrich's still got her eyes. And as long as they can flash, the lady will earn a living."

But what about the man who produced the show: Did he earn a living? And what about producers in general? Do they do well? How do they? And how well?

Dietrich's show was produced by Alexander H. Cohen, one of Broadway's most famous producers. The Dietrich show, according to *Variety*, was personally financed. It was a one-woman show (with orchestra), and it ran for six close-to-sell-out weeks, grossing a total of well over $400,000. Guess what the profits were, according to *Variety*.

There weren't any.

Variety reported that the show was "an approximate breakeven." Assuming *Variety* is close to accurate, Cohen made nothing as far as his producer's share of the profits was concerned. And it is this profit share that on a big hit makes a man rich.

Relatively speaking, producing on Broadway is an easy-entrance business—not as easy, maybe, as dress designing, where all you need to do is rent a sewing machine. But still, a recent edition of the New York Telephone Yellow Pages listed 326 entries under the heading "Theatrical Managers and Producers." To be a producer, all anyone need do is option something. You pay a few hundred dollars for the rights to a literary property for a negotiable number of months, and you're a producer.

In theory, a producer gets nothing until a show is out of the red and paying off. Then he splits the profits with the backers. If, for example, a musical makes $1,000,000 profit, the producer keeps half. If it loses money, the producer gets nothing.

Considering the rarity of a smash (maybe two shows a season), the logical expectation would be that producers are relatively impecunious, scrabbling from show to show, desperate for the one gusher that at last will make them solvent. This is, of course, all theory. In fact, a show need not make a profit in order for producers to do well: all it has to do is run awhile. Because producers get a flat percentage of a show's weekly gross; some get 1%, some get more. And to cover office expenses, a producer also gets a "cash office charge," which might vary from more than $350 a week for a straight play to upwards of $500 a week for a musical. Let's take the hypothetical case of a musical similar to *The Apple Tree* or *What Makes Sammy Run?* or *Milk and Honey,* or any other musical that ended its long Broadway run at a considerable loss.

Let's say our musical runs a year and loses half of its $500,000 investment. So the producer gets no profit piece. But for the 52 weeks of the run, he has got $500 a week for office expenses, and that's $26,000. Let's assume that over the entire year our musical does three-quarters of capacity, which is reasonable, and let's put capacity at $100,000 a week, which is reasonable too. That brings in another $39,000, making a total of $65,000 for the producer while the show is losing $250,000. (The figure $65,000 is actually high because, for the late weeks of a run, the producer will expect everyone to take percentage cuts, and that includes himself. So let's drop the total to a $60,000 total for the year.)

If a guy can luck into enough flops like that, he can retire.

But all musicals don't run a year, and straight plays don't do the business that musicals do, so a producer has to find other ways to augment his income.

Many of them "take."

An old theatre owner told me the following story: "I once booked a show into a theatre of mine because I knew the producer was such a thief. It was a one-set show, and as I recall, it had only about half a dozen actors—none of them names—so I figured it would break even at a low figure. I booked it, not so much because of the low break-even figure, but because the producer took. I'm telling you, this guy did everything: he had his wife down as one of the musicians . . . [Explanation: in many Broadway houses, there is a penalty that the musicians' union extracts from the theatre management —four musicians must be paid every week, regardless. Regardless of what? Regardless of whether the show is a musical or not. If it is a straight play and no music is required, the four musicians still must be paid their weekly salary. They don't play any music, obviously—they're not even inside the theatre—but they must be paid. For not playing. One of the ways that producers make a little extra is to become members of the musicians' union, or have their wives or children join, and then have them listed as one of the four nonplaying musicians. The musicians' union tends to be reasonable about this—no one knows why—and the weekly salary comes to over $200 per musician. If any newspaper printed the names of all the people "playing" nightly at Broadway houses, there would not be many smiles from the theatrical community.] . . . but not only was his wife a musician, he had himself down as some kind of special cockamamie publicity adviser and some other family member in as assistant stage manager or understudy, I forget which. I can't even remember all the angles he had going, but counting the legit stuff, the per cent and the cash office charge, I figured that even if business were terrible, he'd still make a fast $1,500 a week for every week it ran. Well, with money like that coming in, he couldn't let it close fast, could he? And he didn't. I never saw a guy sweat so over a turkey. But he kept the damn thing running close to a season."

More briefly now, other ways they "take." (Not all producers do this, understand, and even those who do don't do it all the time. But it is done, and unpleasant as it may be to talk about, it's one of the things that make the theatre work the way it does, and so it must be mentioned.)

Producers have been known to rent walls. Example: I am a producer and I have a show coming in. I find a nice empty wall somewhere that might be fine for billboard ads, and I rent it as the W. G. Company for, let's say, $2,000 a year. (All these figures are totally inaccurate, simply put down as examples.) My show comes in, and I go to the W. G. Company and I say, "I'd like to rent your wall for billboards," and then I put on my W.G. hat and say, "It'll cost you $1,000 a month," and under my producer hat now I say, "Deal," and I've made myself a profit of $10,000 if my show runs a year.

And then there's the kickback business. Various companies bid to make the set for my show, and the one that wins slips me—as producer—an agreed-upon sum, which is why he got the job. Or, if I've got two shows running, the advertising rates are less than twice as much as for one show. But I charge both my shows as if I were advertising them separately and pocket the difference. (One long-closed show's backers were surprised to find a total of $40,000 sent to them. The attorney general was about to grab the producer, which accounted for the windfall.)

Of course, the major taking done by producers is done in the area of tickets, but that will be gone into in some detail in a different place. In general, for now, I think it's enough to say that some producers take, that they probably would do it in any profession, but that some of them do it because they almost have to if they're going to survive as theatrical producers; it is that hard to do profitably.

Alex Cohen, the Dietrich producer, has become increasingly important and active in recent years. He had his own television talk show for a while this season; he produced the Tony-award TV program; he is also active in London. He is charming, intelligent and harried, leading the high-pressure telephone existence of so many top executives. A quick count revealed at least six telephones in his office, with an infinite number of buttons and extensions. Cohen is on the go constantly, living a lot on planes. His program listing for the Dietrich show was underplayed and factual: "ALEXANDER H. COHEN (Producer) has presented plays by Shakespeare and Pinter, Whiting and Shaffer, Sheridan, Chekhov, Rattigan and Shaw, along with shows by Flanders and Swann, Chevalier, Montand, Borge, Nichols and May; with players such as Burton and Boyer, Gielgud and Drake, Thorndike, Calhern, Bancroft and Page, Redgrave, Robards, Rutherford and Leigh, Richardson, Slezak and MacLiammoir." This is the kind of impressive credit list only a leading Broadway producer could have.

And I think that if you had been the sole backer of all the plays produced by Alex Cohen since January 1, 1960, in which public investing was solicited, you would have lost maybe $1,000,000.

Not that Cohen hasn't had hits. He's had an excellent percentage of successes, about half of his productions. Burton's *Hamlet* made money, and so did a limited run of *School for Scandal,* starring Gielgud. Nichols and May returned a profit, as of course did *Beyond the Fringe.* But none of these were blockbusters (even *Beyond the Fringe,* the longest-running revue of the decade and one of the longest ever, with a cast of four unknown Englishmen, only returned approximately $1.15 profit for every $1.00 invested up through July, 1967). A blockbuster might pay off four, five, six to one. Most of Cohen's hits have been tidy, while his failures have been monstrous: among straight plays, according to *Variety*'s figures, *The Devils* lost $175,000, while *Lorenzo* topped that, losing $180,000. And Cohen's three musicals, *Rugantino, Baker Street* and *Time for Singing,* closed to a total loss of over $1,250,000.

None of this is to belittle Cohen. He is, to repeat, one of Broadway's leading producers. Not to mention talented. He directed *Beyond the Fringe,* an unbelievable success for first-time-out directing. Cohen's wife is talented too: not only does she associate-produce a lot of his shows, but she also writes. The Academy Awards program this year was written by many authors, several of them famous, highly paid, honored, experienced screenwriters. Cohen's wife got sole billing for writing the entire Tony-award show. Again, unbelievable.

The two leading Broadway producers *now* (it may all be different in even two years' time) are David Merrick and Harold Prince. Prince did not have a new show this season, but his *Fiddler on the Roof,* four years old, was still the top-grossing show of the year, and his *Cabaret* ranked third, just behind *Mame.* So even though he wasn't active with a new show, Prince was very much in evidence. He has turned to direction lately, at which he does not excel to the extent he does as a producer. Whether his directing will damage his producing record is at this point unknown. He directed *Cabaret,* and it is a great success. But his four previous Broadway directing jobs all failed, losing over $1,500,000.

It is doubtful that David Merrick will ever turn to directing. It is well known that Merrick is too much of an actor-hater to purposely seek contact with them all day long. He is a much-maligned man. It's easier for magazine writers to sell pieces about him if they fit a pattern: nobody wants to read about what a neat guy David Merrick is; monster stories, great, but that's all. (There was a rumor along the street that the Sunday *Times* magazine section had been displeased with a Merrick profile because it wasn't negative enough.)

Merrick is a difficult and complex man, and there is no intention here of attempting to explain him. N. Richard Nash, who likes Merrick, has said of him, "He's the only man I know who's made a vice of honesty. He'll sacrifice tact for honesty any time." There seems to be little doubt that Merrick takes delight in being difficult.

This was not an outstanding year for Merrick. He put six new shows into rehearsal, but only five got to New York. Of the five, all except *Rosencrantz and Guildenstern Are Dead* ranged from disappointments to disasters. Merrick's real triumph this season was the black *Hello, Dolly!*, in which Pearl Bailey scored her great personal success. The color switch was a brilliant piece of producing on Merrick's part, transforming a long-running show that was starting to atrophy into one of the hot tickets in town all over again.

There is also something symbolic, at least for me, in the black *Dolly!* (I don't like the show itself, not at all, and interestingly enough, no one interviewed throughout the entire year liked it much either.) Just as our parents cannot explain the success of *Abie's Irish Rose* to us, I think we are going to struggle slightly to explain *Dolly!*'s success to our children. Irish *v.* Jews 40 years ago; black *v.* white today; happy ending; happy ending. Broadway makes money where it can.

Merrick and Prince produce in entirely different ways. Prince does one show at a time; Merrick might have three or more simultaneously in rehearsal or out of town throughout the fall season. Prince is known as an absolutely first-rate financial man, and his shows come in more cheaply, on the whole, than those of any other producer. He has said, "Unless you can do it sensibly, no project is worth it. There is absolutely no reason why a show has to get on. It's not even very important." Prince is an ubiquitous figure in any of his productions, constantly around, checking on this, keeping tabs on that. He is *there*.

Merrick tends to be *somewhere else*. This is a matter of logistics: if you do half a dozen shows a season, you simply cannot keep up with everything. But if Merrick spreads himself thin, he compensates with one remarkable skill: more than any of his peers, he is known for doing battle with adversity. Merrick's is the best publicity mind in the theatre, and if a show has any shred of public interest, Merrick will find it and exploit it. One might make the following comparison of Merrick and Prince: given the same show with the same notices, Prince would tend to make more or lose less, while Merrick would tend to run longer.

Together, their shows accounted for over 40% of the total Broadway gross this season. But good as they are, neither of them is as good now as he was in the fifties. Prince's first five musicals all made money. But between *Fiddler* and *Cabaret* he brought in two musicals that everyone forgets about: *Flora, the Red Menace* and *Superman,* which together lost over $900,000. And Merrick's fifties musicals averaged over 600 performances, including an opera that ran five performances. But in each of the last three seasons, Merrick has had a major musical close before it opened, and in the period between October, 1966, and January, 1968, Merrick had eight failures. Eight failures in 16 months just may be a modern theatrical-disaster record for one man.

Why the falling off? My guess is that neither of them is that hungry any more. In their own field, they are both a little legendary; what's left to prove? Their interests are fraying now: Prince has definitely been announced as the director of a new film next summer, and rumors have spread along the street all season that Merrick is going into movies. Merrick said this: "Sometimes I think I'm producing just for mischief; I like to sound off on TV. I enjoy the forum it gives me. I say I do it because it sells tickets, and it does, but really I enjoy baiting the critics, saying what I think about the theatre and politics. The mischief."

But even though they both may have crested, they are marvelous managers. And would you like to know the best original American play Hal Prince has done in 14 years of outstanding Broadway work? *Take Her, She's Mine.* And Merrick's leading original? You can have your pick between *Don't Drink the Water* and *Sunday in New York.* The point is this: neither of them has the least interest, time, taste, skill or knowledge to produce an original American play. Prince does mostly musicals, and Merrick, for all his enormous number of productions, is primarily an importer: he goes to London, buys what he wants, ships it back over. He is as much a force on the American drama as Sol Hurok. Look at Merrick's hit plays this decade: *Taste of Honey, Becket, Luther, Philadelphia, Here I Come, Marat/Sade, Cactus Flower.* French, Irish, English. The same thing holds true for his musicals: Merrick has had nine successful musicals in the sixties. Five of them were imports.

This means, naturally, that the author of original American plays cannot have the best management for his productions, which, of course, he so desperately needs. And this is terrifying, because do you know who the best producer on Broadway is for original American plays?

There isn't one.

The easy explanation for this is that there are no decent American playwrights. This may be true, but there is also another reason —a cripplingly important reason in relation to the original American play—and to understand it, one must understand the concept of "the Snob Hit."

The Snob Hit has its literary counterpart in the Unread Best Seller. Recent examples of this genre might include *Doctor Zhivago, By Love Possessed, Ship of Fools, Herzog* and, most recently, *The Confessions of Nat Turner*. But there is a certain logic to the Unread Best Seller: it looks good on your book shelf. No one's going to quiz you about it, because no one else finished it either. The five books mentioned above, clumped together in someone's living room, bespeak breeding. They indicate intellectual interests. And there's no effort, other than financial, to owning them. But you have to go to a play. It's work. Still, every season, annual as roses, the Broadway entertainment seeker marches through the muck to the Snob Hit.

Nothing comes from nothing, and I think you can date with reasonable accuracy the beginning of the Snob Hit phenomenon: January 21, 1950. Henry Miller's Theatre. T. S. Eliot's *The Cocktail Party* opened that night and began a run of over 400 performances.

The Snob Hit did not become completely formalized in the fifties, however. It was the sixties that made the event obligatory. This decade has seen the following Snob Hits open: *Becket, A Man for All Seasons, Beyond the Fringe, Luther, Dylan, Marat/Sade, The Homecoming.*

Now it is possible, from looking at those plays, to make several very precise statements about just exactly what a Snob Hit must be. First and absolutely crucial is this: *the power of the production must be British. Becket* was a French play, but the power was Olivier; *Man for All Seasons, Luther* and *Beyond the Fringe* were almost totally British in all departments. *Dylan* was written by an American, but it was about a Welsh poet and it starred Alec Guinness. *Marat/Sade* was a German play, but the Royal Shakespeare Company provided the seal of approval, as they did again with *The Homecoming,* although the fact that Pinter was the playwright was very helpful in getting the snobbishness across.

A second requirement of the Snob Hit is that it must manage somehow to be at least a little unintelligible. This is because the audience that goes to the Snob Hit must be convinced that the "average" theatregoer wouldn't understand it. Or, third, like it.

This last and third requirement, of course, is the greatest of all hypocrisies concerning the Snob Hit, because the people who go to see them don't like them either. Two examples:

1. Pinter's *The Homecoming* ran over 300 performances without the blessing of the *Times*. Pinter's *The Birthday Party* had infinitely more publicity, far better notices, including a rave from the *Times,* and it lost its entire investment while barely running one third as long a time as *The Homecoming.* Why? Because people hated *The Homecoming,* and they weren't about to get stung by Pinter again. I don't think Pinter is ever going to have another Broadway success unless he comes over packaged with Olivier or Scofield. The moment of Pinter has passed. I suppose a rule would be only one Snob Hit per author.

2. Robert Dhery's revue *La Plume de Ma Tante* ran over 800 performances. (This was back in the fifties, before the Snob Hit was as structured an event as it is now. *La Plume de Ma Tante* was French, and there was once even an American Snob Hit, MacLeish's *J.B.*) A few years after *La Plume* closed, Dhery returned with *La Grosse Valise.* It shut in less than a week. The point is this: it is inconceivable that a man responsible for something as successful as that first revue could have his next show die as quickly if the audience had really liked the first success. Enough people would have bought advance-sale seats to ensure a moderate run at least. But they didn't, and the reason they didn't is because they went to *La Plume de Ma Tante* only because they had to, and they were not about to be bored to death again.

Why did they have to go to *Rosencrantz?* For the same reason they have to go to any Snob Hit: it is socially necessary, and it is medicinally sound. The Snob Hit is rooted in two false beliefs: 1) theatre is "good" for you, and 2) British is better. The first accounts for so many Snob Hits being "lofty" in either subject matter or treatment, or both. Poets, clerics, historical figures from various ages; these are the grist of the Snob Hit. The second is the reason why the power of the show has to come from England.

What is dangerous about the Snob Hit is this: of all the money paid to see serious drama during the twelve months this book covers, almost 30% was spent to see the Snob Hits. In fact, this year's Snob Hit grossed almost as much alone as all original American dramas put together.

If we can rid our minds of the Snob Hit mystique and look at it from a primarily commercial point of view, *Rosencrantz and Guildenstern Are Dead* had less than nothing going for it. The title alone is enough to kill it. The word dead never draws them in droves, and when you add those jawbreaking names, it's perfect. (People did tend, eventually, to refer to it as "the cheese play.") Now if the title were a put-on and the whole thing masked a light sex comedy, you might have got away with it, but *Rosencrantz* is not sexy. It is, rather, an enormously complex conceit by a young British writer, Tom Stoppard, and it concerns itself with the last days of Hamlet's two inconsequential buddies, who are eventually caught up in the court intrigues at Elsinore and murdered. Add to this the fact that a certain knowledge of Shakespeare's effort is helpful to the understanding of Stoppard's play, since Stoppard weaves his action around scenes from *Hamlet*. In other words, we're dealing so far with a historical/literary/pageant/drama. One more thing: it is very definitely influenced by the Theatre of the Absurd—Beckett and Genet and Ionesco, none of them Broadway favorites. And in the title roles, two English unknowns, Brian Murray and John Wood. Couple all the above with the fact that audiences in general were enormously unhappy with the play, and you've got as perfect a Snob Hit as you could ever ask for.

Rosencrantz opened to stunning notices, won the Tony as the best play of the season, grossed lots of money, established lots of reputations. It was the undisputed dramatic triumph of the year. I thought it was terrific, but the audience I saw it with sure didn't. Derek Goldby, who staged the play so wonderfully, likes to tell the story of the man and wife coming up the aisle after the play was over. "I didn't understand any of it," the husband said, whereupon his wife whirled on him, whispering, *"Don't say that."*

David Merrick produced *Rosencrantz,* thereby extending his record as Broadway's most astute sniffer-out of Snob Hits. (He has now had four in the sixties alone; Alex Cohen, his closest competitor, has had but two.) Now there would be nothing dangerous about the Snob Hit if there were simply a wild back-stabbing session each year in London and the most astute slayer got to bring the next Snob Hit to these shores. But it doesn't work out that way.

It is very difficult to ascertain just what is American and what isn't, but this much can probably be agreed upon: Broadway isn't. At least, not Broadway drama. At least, not enough of it. It's English, and you can't realize it until you sit through a season of the stuff. London is my favorite city, but right now, having sat through an American theatre year, I'm sick of the English. I'm sick of rotten English actors and I'm sick of rotten English plays. The whole "British is better" syndrome eats cancerously across every Broadway level, and it is simply not true. Any American who has seen even half a dozen West End productions knows that the level of acting in the average West End play is perilously close to mediocre. English actors in general are very skilled and very surface, technically sound and emotionally empty.

And English taste, which we are in such awe of, is just as simple-minded on the whole as ours. The following is a list of English productions that are still, in late May, on the West End boards, having opened before the present year, 1968. First, there's Agatha Christie's *The Mousetrap*. It opened in 1952 (that is not a typo), and it is third-rate Christie. Then there's *The Black and White Minstrel Show,* which is the longest-running musical; it is a television program, done twice nightly for legitimate-theatre audiences. *Spring and Port Wine*—done here as *Keep It in the Family*—is still going strong and still negligible. *Girl in My Soup* is in its third trivial West End year. All the other plays are comedies. Mostly sexual: *The Flip Side, Let Sleeping Wives Lie,* etc. For musicals, there's Anna Neagle in *Charley Girl,* which even the locals think stinks, and a revival of *The Boy Friend.*

There's no decent drama here, folks; there's no pertinent comedy. That's not intellectual stimulation playing on the West End, that's junk. English junk, no better and no worse than ours, simply indigenous to the locale.

Yes, there is great English theatre. And it's in the repertory houses, which have as much to do with the West End as *The Fantasticks* has to do with Broadway.

This 1967–68 season was a terrible one in London, which is marvelous for Broadway. The season before was bad too, and hooray! The English had a burst of talent after Osborne—Pinter, Wesker, Bolt, etc.—but it is tapering off now. That's music to a Broadway lover's ears.

Because, though I may be sick of rotten English actors and rotten English plays, I'm sickest of all of rotten American producers who keep bringing over damn near anything that receives the gentlest London critical approval. They do it for several reasons, none of them happy:

1. It offers them intellectual protection; when the Broadway producer brings over some piece of English esoterica and it bombs, he

can fall back on the bromide: "It was too good for Broadway; let me show you my London notices."

2. Most producers simply cannot read. Oh, they know the words, or many of them anyway, but when it comes to putting them together, to visualizing, they are helpless. And seeing a London production rids them of the necessity of judging a script by literary standards. Merrick, for example, let it be known that he took *Rosencrantz* from a single reading of the text, which prompted an acquaintance of his to remark, "That is the single most inconceivable event in the history of the world, since David doesn't read anything; he simply sneaked in the back one night at the National Theatre, liked it, and decided to tell people it was the script that got him." Another acquaintance of Merrick's says he does read scripts: "I saw him reading a script once. It was open and so were his eyes. My conclusion can only be that he was reading." (To be totally fair to producers, it is easier to judge a production when you see it done. This does, however, make it a little hard on American playwrights, since you can't see their plays done until someone does them, which, if you're a producer, is what they want you around for.)

3. Producers think that doing English plays offers them a better chance of financial success. This is simply statistically untrue. Of the 17 plays this year that legitimately might be termed English, four were profitable. Of the 25 non-English plays, six ended in the black. The percentage of successes is approximately the same.

But the English percentage should be much greater; generally, they have had the incalculable advantage of a tryout, most often a successful one. There's an excellent reason for English plays not doing better here, and it's this: American audiences tend not to like English plays. No more than English audiences tend to like what we do.

The Broadway audience will suffer only one Snob Hit per season, and since the characteristics of the Snob Hit are so easily seen, it is madness for American producers, trying to capitalize, to inundate us with the annual amount of English bilge that reaches these shores. As brief examples, the following plays, which should be remembered on three counts: (1) they all lost money; (2) they all aroused an absolute minimum of public interest; (3) they all, at the very least, were received decently by the Broadway critics.

After the Rain really got notices: of the twelve overnight reviews, ten were good, the two that were unfavorable coming from the least important news service and the least influential television critic. The *Times* found it "extraordinarily welcome." The *Post* called it "a fascinating play." The *News* said that for the first time in the season there were cheers from a first-night audience. Harris of Channel 2 said that he "left the theatre with a pleasant tingling sensation," while Newman of NBC said it was a "really good play." The day after it opened, a newspaper article titled " 'Rain' Shines" reported that it was the first hit of the season.

The plot of John Bowen's *After the Rain* concerns a nut rain maker who starts it raining. The rain doesn't, and won't, stop. The flood starts. The water level becomes dangerous. A friend of the hero asks if the hero will take the friend's wife to high ground. The hero takes the wife in a dinghy, and they get lost briefly, paddling through the streets of London. They get out of town and tie up to a house for a while. Then there follows a terrifying scene in which the hero, leaving the safe second floor of the house, swims down into the kitchen looking for dry food and almost gets pinioned by a cupboard and drowns. Finally, he makes it back to the second floor. The hero and the friend's wife live in the house for three days, burning the banister of the stairway for warmth and dryness (the wife is sick and coughing terribly), and eventually they burn much of the house's floor boards. Then they leave the house and paddle on through the flooded countryside, soon finding Sonia, a dancer and the heroine of the novel, floating helplessly on top of a piano.

The astute reader will note that I called Sonia the heroine of the novel, and so she is—the novel *After the Rain,* by John Bowen, on which his play was loosely based. Unfortunately, none of the exciting adventure material outlined above lends itself to the stage.

The play *After the Rain* all takes place after the hero and Sonia are rescued and living on a houseboat with a lot of other people who represent, I suppose, humanity. The production got the notices, almost unanimously good notices, and it lost $125,000 in the 64 performances it managed to last. In only one week did it ever sell as many as half its seats. Now, this is not bonanza business, but *After the Rain* did one hell of a lot better financially than some of the other English successes that were brought over this year. (Actually, *After the Rain* was not an English success. It got, if anything, better notices over there; the *Times* of London called it "one of the richest and most stageworthy British plays of the past 12 months." But it bombed there too with the people.) None of this means that it wasn't a good play. But if it got the notices over there and still died, why bring it over here, unless you have $125,000 you want to pitch? Clearly, this is not a mass-market venture: if you want to bring it over, by all means do it, but give the poor thing a chance to live, a chance to find its audience. *After the Rain* belonged off-Broadway, if it belonged in this country at all.

"*By George*" was perhaps the most literate play of the year, not surprising when you consider that the spoken words all came from the nontheatrical writings of George Bernard Shaw, beginning with a description of his arrival in London and ending with his setting his house in order before his death. Michael Voysey, who "devised" the evening, did an enormous amount of research into Shaw's letters, dramatic and musical criticism, etc., to form the narrative of his little play. I say "little" because it was a one-man play, with the British actor Max Adrian impersonating Shaw. The ad quotes from London were something: "Superb. A dazzling piece of work." This from the London *Times*. The Sunday *Times* called it "Stunning. Masterful, witty and touching." The *Daily Mail* said, "Dazzling," the *Telegraph,* "Triumphant."

New York was somewhat less cordial. The production split the newspaper critics, but of the communications men, only one of six panned it. *Newsweek* loved it, and *Cue* said, "You simply cannot go wrong with this evening." Right or wrong, people simply did not go to the evening at all. It was announced as a limited run, but it couldn't even fulfill that obligation. It closed at a loss of 50 big ones, and in the one full week it played, it failed to sell half the seats in the house.

Would the English like an evening of O'Neill's music criticism? Let's pretend he wrote some, some really flashy blasts of the New York concert scene around 1910. Why in the name of sweet Jesus should the British give a damn? What's this play doing here, on Broadway, a one-man show of Bernard Shaw's letters and criticism? If you're going to do it, maybe book a college tour, maybe try for some offbeat TV special. But if you can't get them, leave it home. (I know I sound vituperative in this chapter, but dreck is dreck, even if it's upper-class British.)

One good thing that happened because of "*By George*" was that I got to talk with Hal Holbrook about one-man shows. Holbrook, a native of Cleveland, started acting there back in 1942, but it was not until 17 years later that, like Byron, he awoke to find himself famous. The occasion, of course, was the off-Broadway opening, on April 6, of his *Mark Twain Tonight!* Since then, he has done the one-man show on Broadway, earning a Tony for best actor of the year, and in 1967 he triumphed again with a TV special of the Twain material.

Holbrook talked about the Twain evening. "I built up the material working in night clubs—fifteen-minute pieces mostly—the idea of hooking it together just came about. I enjoyed the two-in-the-morning show most: I'd have had a few drinks by then, and the audience was small and not in any hurry to go anyplace. You could establish a wonderful contact with them if you just took your time.

"Eventually it became a full evening. I made it three acts rather than two because I was haunted by the fear that I wouldn't be able to hold the audience long enough, and with three acts the acts could obviously be shorter. I'm terribly sensitive about audience attention. One cough used to throw me like a knife in the gut: I hadn't held them.

"People are bound to come with the creeping feeling that they'll be bored to death. Who wants to see an evening about a literary figure? I knew in that first act I had to overcome that natural reluctance, so my biggest desire was to make them laugh their asses off at the start, so they'd go out at intermission and say, 'Hey, this guy's funny.' The second act became the social-comment act. I'd start with some funny material to get them again (but not too much of it, or they'd never stop laughing and take the show right away from you). In the last act I gave them the Twain they'd been expecting all along: warm, whimsical, memories of childhood. I think if I'd done the acts the other way around, the third act first, it would have killed it. Oh, the reviews would have had to say 'Good make-up' and 'Nice enough acting,' but it never would have really come home to an audience. Because the most important thing was never to give the audience a chance to figure what you're going to do next: surprise is the one thing you have going for you. In a one-man show, the little you've got takes on more importance. There's drama in a water pitcher if you use it right."

There was no drama in "By George." It was fatally predictable: Shaw was young and he talked a lot, and he was middle-aged and talked a lot, and nothing happened that you didn't know was going to happen. It was a genuinely dreary evening.

There are no rules on Broadway, and one of them is this: art must be both fresh and inevitable; you must surprise an audience in an expected way.

Brief Lives was another one-man show, perhaps the most costly in history: $106,000 down the drain. It split the Broadway critics, but got three out of four from the papers, including a particularly strong notice from the *Times*. In the two weeks it lasted, capacity would have been about $71,000; *Brief Lives* took in about $13,000. The *Times* thought the acting brilliant and felt that the evening, though not for the overdull or the overcultivated, was entertaining and sharply moving. *Cue* felt that the import was too good for Broadway.

Want to know what they were talking about? An adaptation of writings by the English antiquary John Aubrey, who only died in 1697. I think there were half a dozen "forsooths" in the first two pages of the text. The play takes place in a day of Aubrey's life, the day, one supposes, he dies. He goes through various tasks: cooking, urinating, etc., all the while chattering on about people he has seen and places he has known. The set, by Julia Oman, was a glorious mess; the Collyer brothers would have wept in recognition. And Roy Dotrice was really quite remarkable at his chore.

But I wonder again what the point is of bringing this to Broadway? It seemed so special, these gentle musings of an antiquary in his dotage; it seemed so unfair to both the historical figure and the actor to shove them out on the stage of the Golden Theatre and say, "Entertain the masses."

Nathan's Famous serves a great hot dog. If they decided to price it at five bucks the weenie, and the crowd started thinning, I don't think it would be fair to complain that the product was too good for the public. There was nothing to fault in *Brief Lives,* if you don't mind plotless seventeenth-century musings. Now come on—it's all very well for *Cue* to say it's a pearl and we're swine, but *Cue*'s critic has creamed over too many stiffs for anyone to take him seriously. A very good case can be made that *Brief Lives* had no business on Broadway.

The season's English-history course was far from finished. February brought us *Portrait of a Queen,* a recounting of much of the life of Queen Victoria. Now this is a decent enough subject for a play: the lady hung in there, and things happened while she was around. In a play like this, a lot depends on who you get to write it, and the producers got Victoria herself to do the job. Another writer put it together, and songs of the times were interspersed throughout, but mostly what we got was Victoria's reign as told through Victoria's letters, speeches and journal entries.

Of the nine overnight critics, only two were unfavorable. Dorothy

Tutin, who played Victoria, got hats-in-the-air notices and, eventually, a Tony nomination for her work. In spite of this, the show lost $180,000 and never did as much as half-capacity business. The show had been a triumph for Miss Tutin in London, as I assume an evening of Julie Harris portraying Eleanor Roosevelt in selections from that wise lady's writings might triumph in America. But just as I find it doubtful that the West End would welcome Eleanor, I see no reason for us to fall on our knees before Victoria. I mean, in the second act there is this endless section recounting Victoria's squabbles with Lord Palmerston. Look: I am a reasonably intelligent man, with a reasonable amount of interest in the world around me and a reasonable curiosity about the past, but why should anyone expect me to give a shit about Victoria and Palmerston? Or Prince Albert's troubles with his exposition hall? In the third act, they trotted out Gladstone and Disraeli. Fine. They were great and influential men, but showing them to me for a few minutes in the last act of a documentary play doesn't help them or me; it's like a musical in which you try to have an eleven o'clock number for the star so that the audience will leave the theatre happy and forget your earlier transgressions.

I think *Portrait of a Queen* would have made a splendid TV special. Free, it's a treat, and Miss Tutin is one of the best. But it cost $7.50 to sit in the orchestra, and you can buy a lot of paperback books on English history for that amount. And be better off.

I am aware that *Soldiers* was not written by an Englishman (Rolf Hochhuth was born in what is now West Germany), but the man who was the power of the production—Kenneth Tynan—is English. The play arrived in North America on a tidal wave of London publicity (it had been refused production in England), and the main character, W. Churchill, qualifies as British.

It was probably, along with *More Stately Mansions,* the most prepublicized straight play of the season. The New York notices were generally favorable, and John Colicos as Sir Winston received career reviews; the *Times* had a feature story on him right after the opening, all of which only reaffirmed what everybody already was aware of: *Soldiers* was news.

The controversy centered around the central character of Churchill: How much did he comply with the ghastly leveling of German cities by bombing? What, if anything, did he have to do with the death of the Polish leader Sikorski? This is all clearly combustible material and, theoretically, pertinent to Vietnam.

The play, for all its publicity and praise, died at the box office. I
think this is only partially because of the fact that it was English;
more to the point was that it was a stiff. I mean, the writing was on
this level: when Churchill is told that Sikorski has died, he says—get
this now—he says, "What? Where? How?" in that order. That is,
categorically, bad writing. And representative of the play. I think
the play was done only because the main character was named Winston Churchill. Take that element away, make him a fictitious
leader and don't have your actor wigged and outfitted to resemble
Sir Winston, and the play is simply dull polemic. It was a dreadful
experience sitting through it. You not only started to dislike the
theatre, you began getting angry at Churchill, not for allowing the
bombing but for being such a witless bore. There are a lot of criti-
cisms one can level at Churchill, but he was almost always witty,
almost never dull. The caricature on stage in *Soldiers* was in no way
a great man.

But people didn't know this without seeing it, and they didn't go
to see it, despite the critics and the newspapers, because the word-of-
mouth was bad. Unless you were the kind of theatregoer who enjoyed pure dialectic, there was nothing rewarding in *Soldiers*. Yet
producers were scrabbling over each other for the rights. Finally,
Herman Shumlin, the man who did *The Deputy,* Hochhuth's earlier soporific, was allowed to produce it.

Now these producers who wanted to put on *Soldiers* are not noted
for their philanthropy. They are money men, and they didn't want
Soldiers in order to introduce to Broadway the notion that bombing
was an evil. They thought they were going to make a pile. That's
why producers keep bringing over esoteric English curios and expecting our dollars in return. But there isn't that much money in
English productions, and I only wish to God someone would convince them of that fact. (I am stopping my list here, but I could go
on *ad nauseam: Loot* bombed here after London praise; *Staircase*
bombed, ditto; *The Promise* bombed; *Keep It in the Family*
bombed.)

This is not only madness on the part of our producers; it is harm-
ful. A producer who did one of the shows discussed here let loose a
blast after his offering died: "We had an overwhelming majority of
rave notices. The lack of attendance is a devastating commentary on
the New York theatregoing public." This is simply an excuse for rotten producing. I do not want to be put in the position of defending
the Broadway audience, but I think the plays discussed here repre-

sent not a failure of Broadway audiences but Broadway producers.

Granted there is money, big money, in a Snob Hit. But there is room for only one each season, and none of the five plays discussed had all the qualities necessary for becoming one. And it's cowardly, foolhardy and dumb to keep bringing this stuff over.

This is a free-enterprise country, thank God, but if producers want to produce for a limited audience, produce Israel Horovitz. Give a shot to Bruce Jay Friedman. *Before* off-Broadway does it. The insistence on trying for the Snob Hit and importing wave after wave of English special material is just one more reason why American writing talent is shying clear of Broadway.

I am not trying to sound jingoistic. Bless *Joe Egg*. Hooray for *Rosencrantz*. It's the secondary stuff that is so stultifying. Brought over by, for the most part, second-rate producers who lack the brains and guts to take a shot at something home grown. If American producers insist on losing money, let it be on an American play. Let the American playwright know that *somebody* wants him. He's just like any other animal; feed him, keep him warm, pet him every now and then.

Who knows? Someday he might even lick your hand.

Alternatives to Broadway

Off-Broadway" has always been
an imprecise name, but never more so than today, with a total of
two Broadway theatres out of 34 actually housed "on" Broadway,
the rest nestling in slummy side streets east and west of Seventh
Avenue.

Scuba Duba, by the novelist Bruce Jay Friedman, which opened
October 10 at the New Theatre, was a remarkably unusual off-
Broadway venture; in order to understand why, one first has to get a
grasp of what might be termed "usual" off-Broadway theatre.

Theatre is a constant war against the Establishment. Off-Broadway has been around for more than 50 years, but what is generally
meant today when one speaks of off-Broadway may be said to have
begun in 1951 with a revival of *Dark of the Moon.* The public con-
sciousness, however, was not really caught until the following year,
April, 1952, when the revival of Tennessee Williams' *Summer and
Smoke* opened at the Circle in the Square Theatre in Greenwich
Village, ran for 350 performances, and made a very definite somebody
out of Geraldine Page.

These productions set the tone, if one can generalize, for off-
Broadway: it was primarily a theatre for old plays and new actors.
(Besides Miss Page, Jason Robards and George C. Scott made their

reputations off-Broadway, before moving uptown.) Another thing tended to be true of off-Broadway: it was deadly serious, and not serious in any comic way. And economically, it was a precarious business: although there have been many off-Broadway runs of 500 performances and more, shows—with rare exceptions—survived only on weekend business and suffered at other performances. (Generally today, off-Broadway does five of its eight weekly performances between Friday night and Sunday night.)

Bruce Friedman's play was different from most off-Broadway productions in three central ways: (1) it was an original play, not a revival; (2) it was a lunatic sex comedy; (3) it was an immediate sellout, a blockbuster.

The play is basically about a guy with a problem, trying to get through a night. He is a nervous fellow, a liberal, and his name is Harold Wonder. He has taken a château in France for a month's vacation with his family, and on the night of the play, though his children are upstairs asleep, his wife has run off with a Negro skin diver, whom Wonder refers to as "Scuba Duba." The play has some of the finest comic writing in years, on or off. Example: Wonder has found a bikinied, nut-type girl, Miss Janus, in the neighboring château, and they talk through most of the play. At one point in the first act, the subject of being massaged comes up.

MISS JANUS

You know, a lot of people believe it's a homosexual thing. I don't. But I don't even believe homosexual relations really exist. Certainly not between two men. Why would they bother? There are so many other things they could be out doing. I don't think it's ever really happened. Maybe in Germany once or twice, in the thirties, but that was the only time. I think it's something someone made up to play a big joke on society. A couple of fags made it up.

Now that's first-rate work, and the play is shot through with it, and Friedman did not suffer after the opening. *Life* did a story on the show; the Sunday magazine section of the *Times* did an enormous article on Friedman and his play, referring to him as "The Hottest Writer of the Year."

Scuba Duba was almost done on Broadway. Alexander Cohen had it under option for a while, but nothing came of that. The present producer tried originally to do it on Broadway, but at the last minute, the whole thing came apart. Friedman said: "I was finished with it, sick over it, and went back to a book. The whole thing had just collapsed over one weekend. I said I couldn't get involved with it again." But eventually, enthusiasms rekindled, and the show was done off-Broadway.

Friedman wrote the play in Europe several years ago. The first notion he had was of "an evening and a guy in a pickle like this. I also had race on my mind, and this brought them both together. It always seemed like a play to me, rather than a novel, because it all takes place during one evening. I suppose what I wanted to do was expose the New York *Post*-reading guy to this most terminal of all situations."

Friedman, of course, is primarily known as a fiction writer, and he is presently doing a musical version of his novel *A Mother's Kisses* for Broadway. But he says, "If I get another play written, I'm not at all convinced I'd do it on Broadway." He paused then. "I may have to eat that," he added finally.

Maybe, maybe not. Because the differences between Broadway and off-Broadway, particularly financial, are nowhere near as great as they once were. *Scuba Duba,* a one-set show, cost $35,000, and the revival of the musical *House of Flowers* cost $60,000. Ticket prices are similar too: the top price at *Scuba Duba* is $6.50; at *Plaza Suite* it's $8.00.

And there's Hollywood money off-Broadway now. Published figures indicate that *Scuba Duba* was sold for $150,000, and *Your Own Thing,* the first off-Broadway musical to win the New York Drama Critics Circle Award as best of the year, went for $500,000.

Friedman's play triggered a sensational off-Broadway season: *Variety* was to call it the most successful ever, commercially, and it may have been the best artistically too. Israel Horovitz scored with his brilliant *The Indian Wants the Bronx,* and Mart Crowley with his enormously flicky *The Boys in the Band.* Joseph Papp's Public Theatre, where *Hair* started, had a good season, and the Negro Ensemble Company was well received.

At the end of the season, the *Times* reported that a Broadway house—Henry Miller's Theatre—had been leased for an entire year by none other than the Circle in the Square group, who had started the whole modern movement rolling with Geraldine Page, back before the flood, in '52. It would be nice to buy that symbol—the two theatres coming together, melding, all one now. But some shades of difference remain.

Example: the night I saw *Scuba Duba,* Harold Wonder, the cuckold liberal, was talking to Miss Janus of the "spade" that his wife had left him for.

"NEGRO!" from behind me. Loud and mad. I turned to see

which Negro was shouting. Whoever he was, he was sitting close behind me, but as I looked, I saw nothing but Caucasian faces. The theatre quieted. The play went on. Toward the end of the first act, Harold is still talking to the bikinied Miss Janus about his wife Jeannie and the Negro, Scuba Duba.

HAROLD

That black bastard told us he's got beautiful paintings on the wall. I can just imagine. I can just picture the colored shit he's got hanging up there. Haven't you heard? That's where Picasso is having all his shows these days. At that spade's apartment. The second Picasso knocks off a canvas, he rushes it over there, special delivery. It's the only place he'll show his paintings. Maybe he likes the colored smell up there; it really brings out the values.

It was somewhere during this speech that the guy behind me went bonkers.

"NEGRO!" he shouts. "NEGRO! SAY 'NEGRO'!"

Everyone turns, trying to locate the sound. The actors, visibly and understandably unnerved, get a little more unnerved, because now, right there, smack in the middle of the play, this white guy gets up from right behind me, edges to the aisle and starts slowly down toward the stage. He is neatly dressed, grey slacks, double-breasted blazer, red turtleneck sweater, and he is holding his program out in front of him as he makes his steady way. All the time he is yelling at the actors: "WHAT KIND OF FILTH IS THIS?"

I think, subconsciously, this is every performer's nightmare: that you're going to pee them off so much they're going to come up on stage and kill you. The two actors wait, frozen. The guy reaches the stage. The actors stay motionless. They are very close to the front of the stage. The guy stops. There is dead silence in the theatre now. Then the guy rips his program in half, throws it in the actors' faces, and methodically moves away, up the aisle, out of the theatre and gone. Now this is not conducive to comedy, and the rest of the act is done in silence.

At intermission, I run into Friedman, who happens to be there. "Jesus," I said, "you get this every night?" Friedman shakes his head, but he is obviously excited and pleased. He is a big, ruggedly handsome guy, and his size is always surprising when you see him, since all his writing is based on a kind of lunatic-timid fear.

"You sure don't get this kind of reaction from a novel," someone says.

"That's something I like about the theatre," Friedman says. "I like the dangerous atmosphere you can create."

From somewhere: ". . . No . . . no . . . please . . ."

"I've never seen anyone get up like that before, not at a play," somebody else says.

"I'll tell you the crazy thing," Friedman says. "The crazy thing . . ."

". . . Please, *please* . . . no . . ."

"The crazy thing," Friedman repeats, "is that at one time we actually toyed with the idea of having someone get up like that out of the audience. Have it be part of the play. We . . ."

". . . Oh, God, no . . . please, no . . . stop . . ."

"We were really thinking of doing it," Friedman goes on, "having someone yell at the actors, only we finally decided it wouldn't work because the audience wouldn't believe it, but tonight they believed it, so maybe we should have gone ahead and done it anyway. . . ."

And now his voice trails off.

Because now, on the far side of the crowded lobby, in the midst of all these well-dressed, middle-aged people, this youngish-type guy unloaded on this oldish-type guy, right there, *splat,* and the old guy staggered back, and his glasses went off down some stairs, and blood trickled near the old guy's eyes and streamed along his nose. And this old woman, who had been the one going ". . . No . . . please, no . . ." for the minute or so before the fight, started with, "God . . . God . . ."

"Who saw?" the old guy shouted, retrieving his glasses, the blood still coming down his face. (The young guy had fled back into the crowd.) *"Who saw, who?"*

"Ah did," said a young southern lady. "Ah don't know who did right or wrong or anythang, but ah'll tell everythang ah saw." Off they trooped to the manager's office.

They never fight with their fists on Broadway. . . .

Repertory theatre, theoretically, is the best of all possible worlds. When it works. It is working now in London with the English National Theatre under Olivier, and it is so good it makes you want to cry. Repertory rids actors of the curse of repetition; it provides them with the possibility of working at various roles in various styles simultaneously, letting them experiment and grow.

Broadway has one repertory company. It is called the APA. It is good and it is getting better. Any decent rep company needs a central figure, and the APA has Ellis Rabb. He produces, acts, directs, and, I suppose, does his best to raise money, for repertory is expensive. Basically this is because it is, in a sense, wasteful. You are hiring enough actors for, say, four plays, and you construct the sets for four plays, and your costs are not far from your costs for four plays, but your income does not come from 32 performances a week, but the standard eight.

The APA did four plays this season, and all of them were worth doing and most of them were done well. If they can survive their constant money struggle, they may be extraordinary in a few years' time. The best thing to do now is leave them to grow and wish them Godspeed.

Repertory companies can help writers grow too, or if not grow, at least stay alive. If a play remains in a company's repertory over a period of years, it is a living thing, and it was this possibility that made Paddy Chayefsky decide to give his new play, *The Latent Heterosexual,* to the APA for the 1968–69 season.

Chayefsky talked about why he had decided not to have the play done under standard Broadway auspices. (There had been considerable Broadway-producer interest in the play, all of which Chayefsky had rejected.) "I think every writer who's had a hit is disenchanted with Broadway; I think it's important to have that hit, just so you can see how little it really means. A lot of money has never been a good excuse for writing.

"I came in on the end of the great Broadway. And I belong to that generation that still thinks it does its best work for the theatre. So I write plays and I do movies to make a living. A Broadway production, even if it's a hit, is dead in a year and a half. That's the extent of the life Broadway can offer a drama. If a play stays in a company's repertory five years, that's got to be worth something. What's important to me is that the play should live. I want the life, not the money.

"When people ask me why I'm not writing for Broadway, I ask them, 'Why should I?' I don't want to patch things up; I want to start over. I don't think people should go on if they're not happy with each other. Here in the commercial theatre, it's a shabby shop. I don't mean the compromises—that's workaday stuff—I'm talking about a matter of dignity. Depending on the tiny inconsistencies: if you're a serious drama and you don't get the *Times* . . . There was a revival of a play of mine, and out of 27 reviews, 24 were good to rave. The *Times* was bad. Someone called up and said, 'I must be crazy, *I* liked it.' He didn't say, 'The *Times* is crazy.' And then he said, 'How can you account for these reviews?' Twenty-four out of 27, and he only reads the *Times.*

"I just want my plays to be around. From all over the world, offers pour in: 'We hear you hate Broadway; write us a piece about it.' I don't want to write an anti-Broadway piece, and I'm not going to. I just don't want to contribute to Broadway any more."

Chayefsky had written *The Latent Heterosexual* for Zero Mostel, and Mostel was available, so he allowed the play to be done by a regional theatre in Dallas with Mostel starring. The Dallas Theatre does not have the reputation in any way of being on the same level as a company like the APA, and Chayefsky wanted very much to stop Broadway critics from coming. The whole point of doing the play in Dallas, of giving it to the APA, was to get away from Broadway.

But Broadway was not to be spurned. *Time* reviewed it, *Newsweek* too; the *Saturday Review, Life.* And most important, of course, Clive Barnes of the *Times.* Barnes was pleaded with not to come; he was phoned from Dallas both at the *Times* and at the airport. There had been troubles with the production, a crucial role had been recently recast, and more than that, except for Mostel, the production was reputedly not up to professional standards.

Naturally, Barnes came. He thought it was splendid that Chayefsky had given his play to a regional theatre, "thus putting these theatres in the critical spotlight. . . ." (Which is exactly where regional theatre ought not to be. When regional repertory starts becoming a hit-or-miss business like Broadway, we might as well all throw in the sponge.) Barnes loved Mostel, and he gave Chayefsky credit for having written at least his most serious play ". . . if only because he seems at last to have lost the soft core of sentimentality that in the past has reduced his finest thoughts to the level of fortune-cookie mottoes."

That is rather a curt dismissal of a serious writer with a considerable sum of quality work behind him, and I wonder what was so fortune cookieish in *Gideon* and just which production of it Barnes saw, and what was so soft-core sentimental in the film "The Americanization of Emily," both of which are late Chayefsky works.

This is, of course, unimportant. What matters is that the critical attention changed the course of the play. It is no longer on the APA schedule for 1968–69. Chayefsky, when I spoke with him after Dallas, sounded tired and sore. It was, he said, "a very unhappy and bitter experience." There was much newspaper gossip of an enormous film sale. Chayefsky said it was all false. "Now on top of every-thing else that's happened, I've got to go around and explain to everybody I'm not rich."

No account of repertory in New York would be complete without a mention of the two centers, City and Lincoln. They are not really repertory, in that they generally do not rotate productions. They simply do revivals for limited runs. City Center tends to concen-trate more on musicals, while Lincoln Center does plays. City Center is an old building; Lincoln Center's theatre is very new. The acous-tics are better in Lincoln Center; City Center's seats are far more comfortable. You pays your money and you takes your choice.

Off-off-Broadway is the third chief alternative, and by far the most contemporary. It is hard to say just what it is, because as one off-off-Broadway theatre owner said, "Our real problem is that we have no definition as to who we are and what we do." Off-off-Broadway tends to exist in chartered clubs, churches, work groups, cafés. It can per-haps be understood vaguely if it is compared with off-Broadway. Off-Broadway was a product of the fifties; off-off is very much a move-ment of the sixties. Off-Broadway tended to be traditional: Broad-way for a highly select audience. Off-off is revolutionary; it wants to change theatre from a spectator sport to almost a participant sport. Off-Broadway was basically European: Genet, Chekhov, Brecht were the real strength of the operation; off-off is totally and completely American, in style, content, you name it. Off-Broadway was serious and solemn; off-off is serious and basically comic in outlook. Off-Broadway was primarily revivals; off-off, and this is crucial, is new plays, mostly short, by American writers. And finally, if one can really generalize and say that the acting style of off-Broadway was basically Method, then the acting style of off-off is basically impro-visational.

Early in April there was a meeting to try and attempt to organize the off-off-Broadway theatres. They were being closed down for vari-ous infractions by firemen, building inspectors, the police. In a small room in the West Twenties, a bunch of them sat, trying to figure out some action. They were all very passionate about what they were do-ing in the theatre, but none of them was sure that they were all go-ing to be able to do it much longer.

"I think we have to do something public," one of them said, "so we'll get the proper notice. The harassment is happening so fast it's all going to be over if we don't move."

"We'll demonstrate!" another of them said.

"Right!" several said.

"Won't we need a demonstration permit?" somebody wondered.

"We'll get one!"

"*Right!*"

"Anybody know how?" the wonderer went on.

There was this terrible pause.

"Uh . . . don't you just apply?" one of them said.

"Who to?" the wonderer said.

"I don't know," one of them replied. "But Jesus, everybody's demonstrating these days; how hard can it be?"

"I'm not saying it's hard," the wonderer explained. "I just don't know what the specifics are."

"Well, the first order of business is to figure how you apply, then who to."

"I wonder how long it takes," the wonderer came again. "If it takes too long, as somebody said, it's all over."

"They gotta let us demonstrate," somebody said. There was a pause. "Don't they? . . ."

The meeting went on, and the impression given was of a bunch of people who just want to be left the hell alone to do their plays, but who are so trivial in the Manhattan power structure (their great hope was that Mayor Lindsay liked the theatre) that their biggest enemies are the off-Broadway producers, who are angry that part of their audience is being taken away. One of the people in the meeting said, "We have powerful antagonists and, of course, what we're doing is illegal." (Many of their "theatres," for example, have only one exit, a fire-code violation.) "We have to try and get the police to adjust to our violations," one of them said. Then, hopefully, "Anybody got any suggestions on that?" It was all very serious, and sad, because none of them knew whether they were going to be around tomorrow.

Joe Chaikin's going to be around tomorrow. He is head of the Open Theatre, a group of actors, playwrights and directors who have been meeting for the past five years. They are responsible for *Viet Rock* and *America Hurrah*, responsible in that the plays were worked on in great part improvisationally by the authors with the Open Theatre actors.

The Serpent, the new play by the author of *America Hurrah*, Jean-Claude van Itallie, was given a rehearsal in late March. It was going to tour Europe in the summer, playing opera houses and union halls. *The Serpent* is a series of scenes, some of them closely based on Biblical episodes, some of them not. Even in rehearsal, the Cain and Abel section was incredibly powerful.

The whole cast is on stage, sitting around the perimeter, some of them making sheep sounds, some of them kneeling, pretending they are sheep. You know it's Cain and Abel coming up, and it's a bore: the one is going to nail the other, and let's get on with it. But what happens is that, for a while, Cain and Abel mime working in the field (they never speak throughout), taking care of the sheep, chopping wood. Then Cain stops and stares at Abel, and as he stares, four girls say in unison something like, "It occurred to him to kill his brother but not that killing his brother would mean death." Cain is big, a brutal young actor, and Abel is slender, and he sees Cain looking at him; there is this impulse in Cain that he doesn't know what to do with. He takes his brother's hand and he squeezes it terribly, wrapping his giant hands around Abel's slender fingers, until Abel's fingers break and Abel is in silent agony, and there is no sound except for the baaing of the sheep; then Cain goes back to his work. Because he thinks it's over—whatever it was that had him—he thinks it's gone. And now Abel comes to Cain in anguish and wonders, What is it? Why? And the impulse is back in Cain again, and Cain is helpless before it, and he cracks his brother's arm.

And then he goes back to work again. Because again he thinks it's over, whatever it was. Only now Abel knows that whatever is happening is a terrible thing and, fingers broken, arm cracked, he starts to get away. But Cain stops that; he doesn't know what he wants really, but he knows he doesn't want Abel gone. He lifts Abel high over his head, and then, curiously, almost tenderly, he puts him down and breaks his leg so that his brother won't be able to get away. Then he goes back to his work. Abel is in desperate agony now, and there is no sound except the baaing of the sheep and a soft breathing sound—quiet inhale, quiet exhale. Then Cain goes to his brother and straightens him out on the ground, trying to see where Abel's life is. The breathing sound is louder now: the breath is all that Cain finds left alive. He breaks his brother's stomach. Abel dies. The breathing sound stops. There is just the baaing of the sheep. Cain picks up his dead brother and gently gives him back to his sheep, lays him down across their backs, lays his brother down. . . .

Joe Chaikin lives in the Village. The people who worked on *The Serpent* had to give four days a week of their time for workshop rehearsals, obviously for no salary. Chaikin makes his living teaching at The New School and Sarah Lawrence. He teaches acting styles, character work and conventional Method work. Of Method acting he says: "There's a great value for Method actors in being dumb: you assume your feelings are what are crucial and all that matters."

Chaikin is, I would guess, in his thirties, short and curly-haired and quiet, totally nondynamic and absolutely not the kind of person you would expect to be able to draw about him the talent he has obviously drawn. He was an actor—a good one from all accounts—and he worked with the Living Theatre before they fled to Europe. "I felt a terrific longing for a kind of ensemble. I wanted to play with actors, actors who felt a sensitivity for one another. I felt it important to be in the same room, sort of. In order to come to a vocabulary, we had to teach each other: we had no ambitions other than to meet and play around.

"Off-off-Broadway's impulse was a terrific dissatisfaction with what is possible on Broadway. It's hard to unify it because the experiments are so different, but they all relate to dissatisfaction. Broadway's like a sign that says, 'Waitress wanted.' But the policy of the restaurant is already determined before the waitress is hired. You've got to fit within a certain shape. There's no more room for discovery."

Broadway theatre is primarily "fourth-wall" theatre: the curtain is the fourth wall, and when it goes up, the audience can eavesdrop. Off-off-Broadway tends to remind the audience constantly that what it is seeing is an event happening in a theatre, not "real life." In one play that originated off-off-Broadway, for example, the actors stop midway through the first act, take out cigarettes and sit around on stage smoking while they engage the audience in conversation on any subject the audience wants to talk about: how they like the play, what they think of Vietnam, whatever happens to be on anybody's mind at the moment. When this kind of thing happens, it is very hard to pretend you are eavesdropping at a fourth-wall play.

Chaikin says: "Off-off-Broadway is really an attack on the fourth wall. It wants to destroy the fourth-wall business. I have difficulty believing most of what happens on Broadway. Mary Martin's like a character in a television commercial; nobody's like that."

Chaikin has so far resisted any attempts to do anything with the Open Theatre that would move it into what the off-off-Broadway people call "the profit theatre," meaning both Broadway and off-Broadway. Many people off-off could not make a living uptown; Chaikin could.

What will happen to Chaikin? The hope is that he will stay where he is, doing what he's doing. "On Broadway," he says, "you have to try and get your money back. Some of us felt we had to find something to engage us other than that. People who are really interested in the theatre can't help it very much; they're sort of stuck. We can't become dentists. . . ."

Chaikin has said that Broadway doesn't care for off-off-Broadway, because one of the reasons for its being there is to repudiate Broadway. He may well be right, but nevertheless, in the Belasco Room at Sardi's (home of an infinite number of backers' auditions for theatre-party ladies) an attempt was made to bring the two groups together. It was the monthly Drama Desk meeting, in which critics are invited to eat a buffet lunch and then listen to a discussion of some aspect of the theatre.

On this particular April day the subject was, "Which contemporary forces will have the chief effect on the popular theatre of 1975?" Speaking for the off-off group were Gerald Freedman, who has directed all over and well, Tom O'Horgan, and several other creative people. The talk, however, was monopolized by a noncreative person, Richard Schechner, the editor of the *Drama Review*, which is to revolutionary theatre what *Variety* is to Broadway. There was a genuine sense of excitement during the meal, because although most of the critics were ignorant of off-off-Broadway, they knew that whatever it was, it was something, and it was alive. And besides, strange things had happened on Broadway lately: Kazan had left, and Jerome Robbins had as good as left, and even Neil Simon was growing disenchanted. The usual critical reaction, when Broadway is condemned, is to decide that the attacker is someone who couldn't make it, and it's all sour grapes. But no one has made it much bigger than Robbins or Kazan or Simon. So there was a genuine feeling of interest. Because there was a lot to talk about.

After the meal the panel was introduced, and some of the members made little speeches condemning the popular theatre. Then a member of the audience, an elderly man, started to talk. He said, "My name is George Oppenheimer, critic of *Newsday*. I've got just one question, and I wish you'd tell me the answer: Why do you hate us? We don't hate you."

Schechner got the floor. "I have no contempt for you," he said. "Broadway isn't worth being contemptuous of. It's disappearing into high-rise buildings anyway. Something can be important in one of three ways: economically, socially, artistically. Artistically, Broadway is of no importance. Socially, yes: we get together and talk, like now. Economically, it is of no interest: if it died, the New York tourist business would suffer slightly, but it has no effect on the gross national product, and no one would mourn. There's no point to whipping Broadway; one wants to preserve it because of its quaintness. It's like the Alamo—a tourist attraction we should all remember." He went right on, denying contempt again and again, and with every phrase came the bleeding-heart wail of a man who has *only* contempt, a man who wanted desperately to be invited to the party, but wasn't, because of a lack of taste, or talent, or probably both. And as he went into his peroration, you could feel the meeting going, as indeed it was. Because soon Schechner was saying, of nothing in particular, "It's a crock of shit." And then an old critic yelled, "That sums up this whole discussion," and from there they began firing shots across the water, neither side listening. And that was too bad. I mean, *why* did Kazan leave? And what *is* this off-off-Broadway thing? There were things to talk about.

All gone.

PREMIERE PERFORMANCE, OCTOBER 15, 1967

LONGACRE THEATRE

ROBERT LEDER and MICHAEL PRODUCTIONS

present

SANDY DENNIS

as

DAPHNE
IN COTTAGE D

a new play by STEPHEN LEVI

also starring

WILLIAM DANIELS

Scenery and Lighting Designed by
JO MIELZINER

Costumes Designed by
THEONI V. ALDREDGE

Associate Producer — PORTER VAN ZANDT

Directed by
MARTIN FRIED

Critics' Darling

Four years ago, Sandy Dennis played a businessman's mistress in *Any Wednesday,* and these are some of the things the daily critics said about her. The *Times* said, "Her hands flutter helplessly to punctuate her moods, and her lips and eyes express change like a lovely landscape in a summer shower. She can walk around in a glamorous peignoir and somehow manage to be seductive and bored with love as the whim strikes her. She can wear a party dress and long white gloves to make a dip for an *aperitif* and make it seem like the natural way to keep house." She was, in general, an "adorable thirty-year-old nymph." The *Journal-American* said that she "manages, with the wonderful use of her hands and a beautiful sense of timing, to creep into every heart. . . ." The *Post* said she was "enchantingly appealing," the *News* found her "irresistible."

But no one writes love letters like Walter Kerr: "Let me tell you about Sandy Dennis. There should be one in every home.

"She's dangerous, of course. She's got the tongue of a delectable cobra (don't say there's no such thing, I saw one last night), and while she never used it to strike dead anyone on stage, she can turn in a doorway, prepared to exit, and wipe out whole scenes with its adder-like leap.

"No explanation is ever offered for this peculiar conduct. Miss Dennis is not playing a femme fatale, or anything near it, in 'Any Wednesday.' She is playing an idiot child who claims to be thirty (it's her birthday) and who is described by one of the men in the company, in a wild overstatement, as looking about twelve years old. (Significantly, there is just one candle on her birthday cake, and my guess is that that's about right.)

"Behind all the cat-on-the-fence energy there's a faintly humiliated mouth, and behind all the haymakers there's a doll in bare feet who can't say anything angry without making it sound funny, and winsome to boot. Try listening to her do a simple line, something like, 'I'm just so touched,' or, with mournful pleasure, 'I never had a pill-box,' and you'll get the combination. Dumb, knowing, injured, and outraged in seven syllables or less. The girl is enchanting."

These reviews, regurgitating as they seem on rereading, heralded something very special in the theatre: Broadway had a new critics' darling. Miss Dennis was by no means the only one around. Carol Channing is a critics' darling. And so is Mary Martin. And Beatrice Lillie. There are others, but for purposes of definition, these will do.

The thing that makes them critics' darlings is, of course, simple and obvious: critics love them. All the time. Critics' darlings are always praised, overpoweringly, regardless of the caliber of their work. Another thing they have in common is that they are the products of the *daily* drama reviewers. On television or in films they may be panned. But on Broadway they are the trinkets of the overnight boys.

They are also freaks. All of them. All the time. Mr. Webster says a freak is "oddly different from what is usual or normal." That is certainly true of the people under discussion, but I would like to push the definition a good deal further: these are people that never breathed on this or any other planet. It is not possible that anybody ever met anyone like Carol Channing on the street. With those crazy popping eyes and that bizarre speech pattern, the lady would be hatched up on sight. And rightly so. Critics' darlings all share this in common: extravagance of gesture. They gesticulate; they overdo. They are, in all ways, enormous. And they are all women.

After her run in *Any Wednesday*, Sandy Dennis went to Hollywood. (She also appeared on stage in London with the legendary, disaster-ridden, Actors' Studio production of *The Three Sisters*. Her performance on opening night there, even more jittery than her usual work, has been described as resembling an ape looking for a banana. She received notices that would have upset Lou Nova. But this, as I said, was London.) Hollywood treated her better. She won the Academy Award for her supporting work in "Who's Afraid of Virginia Woolf?" Then came "Up the Down Staircase," and she was a star: *Boxoffice* magazine listed her as one of the ten leading female film attractions in the world.

She decided to return to Broadway in the title role of *Daphne in Cottage D*. It was a two-character play, and as far as can be gathered, the plot of the play, at the time she decided to do it, ran something like this: two people—Daphne and Joseph—meet by accident one day in a resort hotel along the New England coast. It turns out that she is the widow of a movie star and has a seven-year-old son named Billy living in California with a state-appointed guardian, because she's an alcoholic and can't be trusted with control. He is a doctor and has a case of the blues because two years before he accidentally ran over and killed his child, a son named Billy. And if his Billy were alive, he would be seven years old now. The play chronicles how they get to know each other, Daphne and the doctor, and how, at the end, she leaves him her Billy and kills herself.

A cursory reading of the plot indicates certain improbabilities, but the author, a young man named Stephen Levi, could write, and the play clearly contained two decent acting parts, and probably laughter. Miss Dennis set about having the production done, but there was trouble: no one liked the play enough to produce it. Not even with her in the title role.

Eventually, after more than a year, the play got on. William Daniels, a very good actor who had appeared with Miss Dennis in *A Thousand Clowns*, was given the other part. Daniels' reputation is not only that of a serious, skilled actor but also a quiet professional who doesn't make trouble. That was very important, for no new play this year was as tightly controlled as *Daphne* was by Miss Dennis. The director had never directed a success on Broadway, but rumor had it that his wife was a very close friend of Miss Dennis'. No trouble there. No trouble from the producer either: when no experienced management would touch the play, she got her business manager to do it.

The playwright, Levi, had put his faith in his director. There was considerable discussion about whether Daphne should give her child away to the doctor and commit suicide. Levi said: "I'm sure the plot will stay as it is. The director and I both want it, and we see eye to eye on everything." At the same time, a power in the production was saying: "We've got to weed out the adolescence—like giving the child away. That's an adolescent notion. If a woman gives her kid away, she's really got to be stoned, and if she's that stoned, she wouldn't care."

Dennis took over at the start of rehearsal. Rumors were that she might say, "This is rotten," and the director might say, "I never liked that anyway," and it would be something that he and Levi had worked on for a year or more. Levi was apparently confused and upset by what was going on, but it was his first time out, he was only in his middle twenties, and it took a while before he saw the total weakness of his position. "It wasn't till Boston that I realized the helplessness. She was the producer. She did the directing. During performances she came in with different ad libs. None of this was done maliciously; she was doing what she thought was right. Then she brought in a play doctor. I didn't want it, but it was in my contract; she had the right to bring in someone. My agent at the time told me it was standard on your first play. Naturally I wanted the play done, and Sandy wouldn't do it without that clause." (A note to future playwrights: having a play-doctor clause, first playwright or not, is under no conditions standard. Levi's agent at this time was Daniel Hollywood.)

Soon, Dennis was rewriting the play with scissors, literally, cutting out sections here, pasting them in there, making the script as she wanted it at that given moment. She was out of control, and no one could stop her. She did four versions of the play. The play never worked, but the feeling among people connected with the show was that it suffered damage from Boston on. Dennis was writing and Dennis was directing, and the production was enormously unpleasant. The play doctor had been dismissed, and there were rumors in New York that the play might close out of town in Baltimore. A friend of Dennis' talked about her and the way she was behaving: "There have always been two camps about Sandy; a lot of people never could stand the mannerisms, but I've always gone with her. Now I don't know. She's emasculated everyone around her. Off stage she's terribly lucid, and like a rock. But on stage she's created this vulnerable picture. I used to think success at any cost. Now I'm not so sure."

An actor who worked with her before she became famous said this. "She gets mad at the audience when they don't react the way she wants them to. Some actors try and work harder; they figure it's their fault, they're doing something wrong, and they'd better try like hell and fix it. Sandy figures it's the audience's fault, and she gets mad; it's incredible acting with her when you feel that anger and hatred coming out."

Whatever it may be like acting with her, watching her in *Daphne* proved one thing about Dennis: the fluttery, stuttery, I'll-never-get-the-words-out-straight style she uses on stage is completely fabricated. Toward the end of *Daphne* she had several long speeches to deliver, and she did them without pause, stammer or arm flail. She just stood there and said the words.

She opened *Daphne* in New York after all. The play ran for less than six weeks and lost $100,000. The broadcast notices were bad. Not only for the play but for the lady. One TV critic found her accomplished but annoying. Another said, "Miss Dennis stutters and sounds as if she is imitating Rocky Graziano." But the three New York papers saw it differently. The *News* critic found her "artful" and "adorable." The *Post* said she was "a brilliant dramatic actress." And the *Times*—the crucial notice—said she was giving "a memorable performance."

Clearly she was not.

That is a provable statement: if a performer of Dennis' magnitude appeared on the Broadway stage in a play in which she was "adorable," "brilliant" and "memorable," the show is simply not going to close after 41 performances. This is a girl who was on the cover of *Time* magazine a month before the show opened. This is a girl whose last Broadway performance was one of the personal triumphs of the decade. If Ingrid Bergman can run a stiff like *More Stately Mansions,* in which she did *not* get splendid personal notices, for 150 performances, then Sandy Dennis can run a stiff longer than 41. *If* she was what the daily papers said.

Writing in the Sunday *Times* about *Daphne,* Walter Kerr said the following: "I love Sandy Dennis and I'm going to love her a lot more the next time she completes a single sentence. She has developed a habit, just recently, of treating sentences as though they were poor crippled things that couldn't cross a street without making three false starts from the curb, breaking in mid-flight, shying back in terror, starting over bravely, hesitating in the middle of traffic. She's going to get herself killed one of these days if she doesn't get on with it . . . William Daniels, a fine actor always and one who *does* complete sentences even if it shortens the evening, remarks that Miss Dennis' seven-year-old son looks like her. Miss Dennis replies, 'No, that's not true.' Then, after a bit of semaphore with her liquid hands, she adds, 'That's not so.' Then, after compressing her lips while enlarging her eyes, she adds, 'He does not look like me.' In the end, it becomes impossible to know whether the line was written that way or whether the actress is just saying it that way, or whether you're just hearing it that way and need rest.

"Good actresses should first get good texts and then pronounce them."

I think that's unfair criticism on Kerr's part. At least the daily boys had the decency to stand by their creation. Kerr may have been accurate, but Dennis has *always* overdone the mannerisms he criticizes her for here. If anything, she flailed more in *Any Wednesday* than in *Daphne*. And I think that if these men were going to elevate freaks to positions of importance in the acting world, it's their duty to stand by them in time of need. (The answer, and this is conjecture, is that Kerr was *not* a daily critic when he panned Dennis. He had become a Sunday writer, and I think—and no one can ever prove me wrong—that if he had been the daily critic, he would have found kinder words.)

Being an overnight daily-paper critic is a club, an increasingly small one, and they love their darlings to the death. With one exception: the actress must always continue to exaggerate reality. When Tammy Grimes (Kerr had once called her "a genius") opened this year in *The Only Game in Town*, most Broadway people felt that it was the first fine, unmannered performance of her career. The critics panned her. They loved Geraldine Page when she was all fidgety mannerisms. The lady is an actress now, and the affair has cooled. Even wonderful Julie Harris has been chastened: after giving a stunning, real performance in *Marathon '33*, she awoke to less than her usual responses. The lesson is evident: critics' darlings can do whatever they want, but they must never ever under any conditions learn to be human on stage.

In the end, the creation of critics' darlings affects Broadway adversely in only two ways: (1) it celebrates a style of acting that is false and not necessarily as winning as the critics would have us think; (2) since all critics' darlings are women, it makes life even tougher for male actors than it might ordinarily be. And ordinarily, life for American actors on Broadway is nasty, mean, brutish and short.

John McMartin, a splendid American actor, who is currently playing the lead opposite Shirley MacLaine in the film of *Sweet*

Charity, said this: "It's probably not true, but it seems to me that nobody writes for men on Broadway now. Most of the main parts are for women. If a good male part comes along, it's usually in an English play, and they bring the actor over." Robert Redford, who became a star in the stage and screen versions of *Barefoot in the Park,* put it this way: "I didn't spend the years I spent in New York so I could end up acting in Hollywood. But in every script they've sent me, you could just feel the critics getting ready to roll over and play dead for the girl. All the guy ends up doing is looking at her with his hat in his hand and saying, 'You're wild and you're mad, and I love you.' " William Redfield, an actor, who wrote the wonderful book *Letters from an Actor,* about Burton's *Hamlet,* put it this way about critics' darlings: "The way Walter Kerr loves the way Betsy von Furstenberg moves her hips on her second-act entrance is enough to drive a professional actor up the wall."

Or to Southern California.

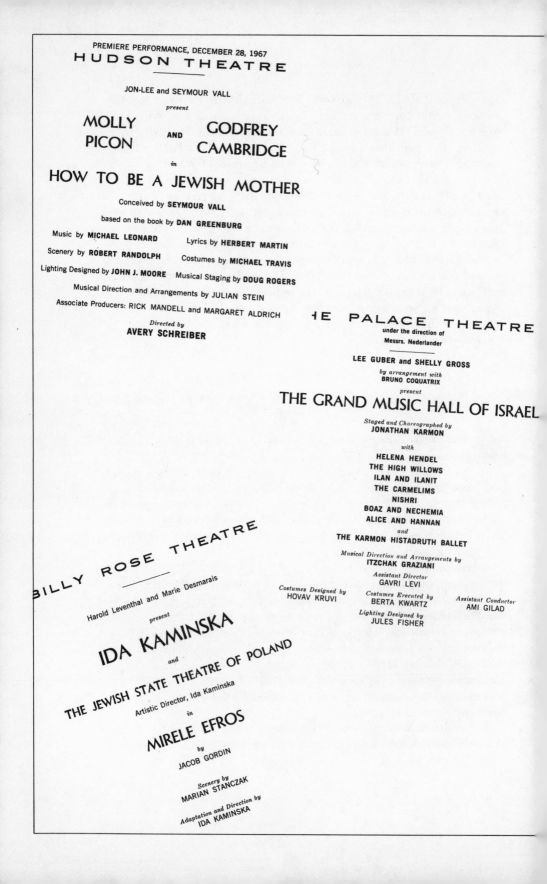

PREMIERE PERFORMANCE, DECEMBER 28, 1967
HUDSON THEATRE

JON-LEE and SEYMOUR VALL

present

MOLLY PICON   AND   GODFREY CAMBRIDGE

in

HOW TO BE A JEWISH MOTHER

Conceived by **SEYMOUR VALL**

based on the book by **DAN GREENBURG**

Music by **MICHAEL LEONARD**   Lyrics by **HERBERT MARTIN**

Scenery by **ROBERT RANDOLPH**   Costumes by **MICHAEL TRAVIS**

Lighting Designed by **JOHN J. MOORE**   Musical Staging by **DOUG ROGERS**

Musical Direction and Arrangements by **JULIAN STEIN**

Associate Producers: RICK MANDELL and MARGARET ALDRICH

Directed by
AVERY SCHREIBER

HE PALACE THEATRE

under the direction of
Messrs. Nederlander

LEE GUBER and SHELLY GROSS

by arrangement with
BRUNO COQUATRIX

present

THE GRAND MUSIC HALL OF ISRAEL

Staged and Choreographed by
JONATHAN KARMON

with

HELENA HENDEL
THE HIGH WILLOWS
ILAN AND ILANIT
THE CARMELIMS
NISHRI
BOAZ AND NECHEMIA
ALICE AND HANNAN
and
THE KARMON HISTADRUTH BALLET

Musical Direction and Arrangements by
ITZCHAK GRAZIANI

Assistant Director
GAVRI LEVI

Costumes Designed by
HOVAV KRUVI

Costumes Erecuted by
BERTA KWARTZ

Lighting Designed by
JULES FISHER

Assistant Conductor
AMI GILAD

BILLY ROSE THEATRE

Harold Leventhal and Marie Desmarais

present

IDA KAMINSKA

and

THE JEWISH STATE THEATRE OF POLAND

Artistic Director, Ida Kaminska

in

MIRELE EFROS

by
JACOB GORDIN

Scenery by
MARIAN STANCZAK

Adaptation and Direction by
IDA KAMINSKA

CHAPTER

10

Jews

There is no quicker way of realizing that Broadway is not our national theatre than by sitting through a season. If it reflects anything, Broadway reflects New York City, and really only a portion of that. New York has well over 1,000,000 Italian residents, and there was one Italian play this year, *Mike Downstairs,* starring Dane Clark, which closed quickly after harsh notices. But that is not the point. What is pertinent is that even before it opened, during previews, no one attended. It was just not pulling in an Italian audience.

There are over 1,000,000 Negroes in New York, 14% of the population, and although a spot check of 200 people entering the Negro *Hello, Dolly!* showed 11% of the audience to be Negro, that was by far the largest percentage for any show. At *Golden Rainbow,* for example, a sampling of 100 people entering the theatre revealed no Negroes at all. Two out of 100 were Negroes at *Portrait of a Queen,* and half that at *Here's Where I Belong.* There are hundreds of thousands Spanish-speaking New Yorkers, but the probability is strong that they constitute an even smaller part of the Broadway audience than do Negroes.

There are at least 750,000 Irish people living in New York, but this season there were no plays that were primarily Irish in feel. And even when there are Irish plays, they tend not to run. The longest-running Irish play in Broadway history, the beautiful *Philadelphia, Here I Come,* lasted only 326 performances. And a leading ticket broker said, "I loved it, but I just could not sell it to my customers."

He meant, of course, Jews.

The importance of Jewish people to American culture goes far beyond Broadway. For example, the week that the Broadway season officially began, at least one third of the top 20 books on the best-seller list in the Sunday *Times* book review section were either by or about Jews. The top novel was Chaim Potok's *The Chosen,* while the nonfiction leader was Stephen Birmingham's *Our Crowd: The Great Jewish Families of New York.*

Broadway sports an even higher percentage. Of the two dozen American plays to open during the season, at least half were written by Jews. (The percentage of English plays by Jews was considerably lower, Pinter being the only Jewish writer of note represented this season. Kenneth Tynan has been quoted as saying that "the English theatre has kept Jews out. It's anti-Semitic.") The Jews have not been kept out of Broadway: of the 30 members on the council of the Dramatists' Guild, at least two thirds are Jewish. There is, of course, no causal connection between having been born a Jew and writing of Jewish life: being a Jew means less to the writing life of Lillian Hellman than to, say, Arthur Miller. Neil Simon writes both Jewish and gentile; *The Odd Couple* is Jewish in feel, *Barefoot in the Park* non-Jewish. He says, "I'm aware when I'm writing Jewish or gentile. It's a matter of attitude. The Jewish is martyrdom and self-pity and 'everything terrible happens to me.' No, it's more than just attitude; the phraseology is different too." A list of other Jewish playwrights would include Odets and Behrman and Kaufman and Hart and Kingsley and Chayefsky and many, many more.

But the Jewish contribution to the straight play is minimal compared with the musical comedy. Rodgers is a Jew, and so was Hart, and Hammerstein was half Jewish, and Lerner is a Jew, ditto Loewe, ditto Gershwin and his brother, and Romberg and Kern and Berlin and Arlen and Harburg and Rome and Weill and Bernstein and Styne and Loesser and Bock and Harnick and Sondheim and Herman and Kander and Ebb. In the last half century, the only major gentile composer to come along was Cole Porter. Without Jews, there simply would have been no musical comedy to speak of in America. It is a remarkable contribution.

And if a lot of the creators for the theatre have been Jewish, so are a lot of people sitting inside. New York is, of course, the Jewish center of the world. There are more Jews in the immediate New York vicinity than there are in Israel. If Jews attended theatre only according to their population average, they would account for about one fourth of the seats sold to New Yorkers per year. But obviously, they account for a great deal more than that. No one can say definitely, but I think a conservative guess would be that Jews account for 50% of the attendance on Broadway.

And producers attempt to cash in on that percentage, especially as far as the musical theatre is concerned. The amount of ethnic pandering that goes on during a season is stupefying. Of the three "personality" evenings of the season, one was primarily intended for Jewish trade (Hackett and Fisher). Of the three revues, two were for Jews: *How to Be a Jewish Mother* and *The Grand Music Hall of Israel*. Of the standard-brand musical comedies, three out of ten were about Jews: *Golden Rainbow,* H*Y*M*A*N K*A*P*L*A*N and *I'm Solomon*. And counting the six long-running holdover musicals, two were primarily of interest to Jews: *Cabaret* and *Fiddler on the Roof*.

One final way to get at the importance of the Jewish audience is to compare the fates of the two Rolf Hochhuth dramas *Soldiers* and *The Deputy*. Comparing plays is always risky, but here it might be reasonably fair, since both were by the same author, came in on similar waves of controversy, and got similar mixed "money" notices. *The Deputy* was about Pope Pius XII's knowledge of the Nazi killing of the Jews; *Soldiers* dealt with Churchill's bombing of German cities during World War II, and had Churchill as the play's central character.

Soldiers lasted 21 performances. *The Deputy* lasted 15 times as long and closed as one of the ten longest-running serious dramas of the decade. You can only theorize about why one ran and one didn't, but my guess is simply this: *The Deputy* had a secret ingredient that *Soldiers* completely lacked: Jewish appeal.

Ethnic pandering is by no means unique to this season: last year saw *Hello, Solly!* and *Sing, Israel, Sing; Chu Chem,* a Zen Buddhist Jewish musical, closed out of town in Philadelphia.

There are those who feel that what is going on now—this Jewish vogue—is a result of the audience's love for *Fiddler,* and that it is running dry. But I'm not so sure. The following future productions have already been announced: a musical based on *The Rothschilds,* a musical based on *Our Crowd,* a musical based on the radio serial

"The Goldbergs," something based on *Everything but Money*, something else about anti-Semitism in the Soviet Union, still something else about a man who claims to be someone like Eichmann, plus a mystery with a rabbi hero who solves crimes by his knowledge of Talmudic law. Plus a musical version of Bruce Jay Friedman's classic Jewish mother-type novel, *A Mother's Kisses*.

The Grand Music Hall of Israel was a vaudeville extravaganza brought over to Broadway from the homeland. It was all unbelievably amateurish and filled with references to the then recent conflict against Egypt, the kind of show where someone would come out and say, "Here is a song in which I ask the people of the world to join hands in peace . . . and . . . I only hope it will be soon. . . ." The show looked like a put-on of the Moiseyev done by Brandeis University. It was almost unanimously praised. As a Jew, and as a man who loves the theatre, I was angry watching it. It seemed to me to cheapen damn near everything. They were selling Israeli Victory Commemoration medals in the lobby for five bucks a throw.

How to Be a Jewish Mother deserves but little more space, and this only because it did something that very few shows have ever done: it opened out of town as a two-character musical, plot and all, and in the course of getting to town, dropped the plot entirely and became a revue. Based on the best-selling non-book, it was adapted for the stage and produced by Seymour Vall, his first Broadway writing job, but hardly his first Broadway production.

For Vall is the founder of the biggest theatrical underwriting concern in the business. He gets paid for raising money for shows, and the first three he went into were *Advise and Consent, Carnival* and *How to Succeed in Business Without Really Trying*. Of the long-running shows still current, Vall has money in *Fiddler, Mame* and *Cabaret*. "We have most of the hits," he says. He is one of the canniest businessmen on Broadway. And what does he choose to get involved in for his initial attempt as a writer? A two-character Jewish musical. Obviously, somebody thinks Jews make up a significant proportion of the Broadway audience.

And they do. But that doesn't necessarily mean that they want to spend an evening looking at themselves. Of this season's musical shows with Jewish audiences chiefly in mind, four were set up to profit or lose in New York; the others were touring shows. And of the four, *How to Be a Jewish Mother* lost at least $110,000. H*Y*M*A*N K*A*P*L*A*N ran less than a month and lost $550,000. *I'm Solomon* lasted a week, and no one knows how much it ended up losing, but the published figure, undoubtedly low, was $750,000. *Golden Rainbow* is still running, and it will continue to limp along awhile, but the word is it will lose a ton before it closes. This is really the insane thing about the present glut of Jewish shows: most of them bomb.

I have little to say about the Jewish State Theatre of Poland. I do not speak Yiddish and feel completely unqualified to comment on what happened on stage. I can, however, say a few words about what went on in the audience. They had these gadgets—machines, translation things—I don't know what the proper name is. But you rented them in the lobby for, I think, a buck, and there was an earpiece that hooked over the top of your ear, thereby placing the tiny loudspeaker directly where you could hear the simultaneous translation.

That was the theory.

The show started, and you turned on your machine and there was nothing. Then you began hearing something. Not words. This long, staticky sound emanated from the thing hooked over your ear. Now naturally, this isn't ideal. But then, after a while, you can make out faintly someone trying to talk English. On stage it's Yiddish all the way, and the occasional English words you hear are simply not clarifying the action. So you turn the machine full blast, and what you hear is something like this: static . . . static . . . "Really? You don't say?" . . . static . . . static . . . "Actually" . . . static . . . "Turn that thing down. . . ." "I can't hear, will you take it easy with that thing?" "Not so loud with the machine, huh, buddy. . . ."

As you may have guessed, these last phrases are not translations of everybody's favorite, *Mirele Efros,* being done in Yiddish by the Jewish State Theatre of Poland. These last phrases are coming from the man behind you who happens to speak Yiddish, and your machine is now tuned on so loud that all he can hear is your static. Suddenly, as you mutter, "Sorry," you realize that all over the house, people are saying, *"Stop with the machines!"* Because none of them work, so everybody has them tuned up full volume, and the static is deafening in the theatre, disturbing everybody, both the ignorant and the linguists.

At intermission, the machine salesmen were doing a terrific exchange business. Two little men were reaching into an enormous box of translating machines, handing them out blindly to angry customers, while the boss stood behind his men saying, "Sorry, Miss.

Just one of those things." This he is saying loud. Softly, he is urging his hirelings to greater effort. The entire effect was like this: *"Sorry, Miss. Just one of those things* (hand 'em out, hand 'em out). *We understand your problem, Madam; please accept our apologies* (hand 'em out, hand 'em out). *They can't all be perfect, folks* (hand 'em out)."

An ethnic essay of this sort ought properly to end with a Jewish-mother story, and the best one I encountered all year occurred, not at *How to Be a Jewish Mother,* but rather at a performance by the Jewish State Theatre of Poland. A very uncomfortable young man is sitting beside his mother. He is maybe eighteen years old and clearly not overjoyed at the opportunity of catching *Mirele Efros* in the original. To his left, the inevitable mum; small, formidable, fifty-five or sixty, and good for years. She is clutching her son's left hand. From time to time he tries to extricate it, but she ignores this. They skirmish in silence. An usher appears, moving down the right-hand aisle. It is 8:30, and the usher, as she goes, calls out softly: "Whitney Korngold? Mr. Whitney Korngold, please come to the rear of the theatre." Receiving no reply, she continues on down the aisle to the front. "Whitney Korngold? Is Mr. Whitney Korngold here?" Now she is at the front and she turns, starting up the aisle, all the time saying, "Mr. Korngold? Is there a Mr. Whitney Korngold within the sound of my voice?" By now, the sound of her voice is a little bit louder. She continues on up the aisle, finally disappearing into the rear of the house.

The kid is still trying to free his hand. His mother has got it plonked down in the middle of her program, which is open, and she holds it tighter than ever as she reads away in silence. Then, louder: "Mr. Whitney Korngold. *Is Mr. Whitney Korngold here?"* It is the usher again moving down the other aisle. "Mr. Whitney Korngold! Whitney Korngold, if you are here, please come to the rear of the theatre immediately!" She moves to the front of the theatre again, turns and stops. *"Mr. Whitney Korngold! Please, Mr. Korngold, come to the back of the theatre."* By now the whole theatre is paying attention to her. "MR. WHITNEY KORNGOLD. IF YOU ARE HERE, MR. WHITNEY KORNGOLD, PLEASE COME TO THE REAR OF THE THEATRE." No one in the theatre budges. Clearly, Mr. Korngold is elsewhere at the moment. But the usher still stands firm, belting out her song: "MR.-WHITNEY-KORNGOLD-THERE-IS-A-MESSAGE-FOR-YOU-AT-THE-REAR-OF-THE-THE-ATRE-SO-PLEASE-COME-NOW-TO-THE-REAR-OF-THE-THE-ATE-ERR-MISTER-WHITNEY-KORNGOLD—"

The kid, fighting a desperate undercover action to free his hand, starts frantically to pull it away. But his mother will not release it. Finally, with the "WHITNEY KORNGOLD" at a peak, he whirls on her in frustration.

"God, that's stupid," the kid says to his mother.

She gives him a look. "What?"

"Repeating that name over and over."

"It's not stupid."

"Tell me the point of it then!"

"Well," she says, and she pauses a moment before thrusting home. "If she keeps on repeating it, maybe he'll think it's important."

The kid's hand went limp. The lights went down. The curtain went up. *Mirele Efros* in Yiddish.

Magic time.

PREMIERE PERFORMANCE, FEBRUARY 27, 1968

JOHN GOLDEN THEATRE

SAINT SUBBER

In Association with HAROLD LOEB

presents

CARRY ME BACK TO MORNINGSIDE HEIGHTS

A Comedy by
ROBERT ALAN AURTHUR

Starring

LOUIS GOSSETT   DAVID STEINBERG   CICELY TYSON

DIANE LADD   JOHNNY BROWN

Production Designed by
KERT LUNDELL

Directed by
SIDNEY POITIER

PREMIERE PERFORMANCE, NOVEMBER 7, 1967

BROOKS ATKINSON THEATRE

James Nederlander and Michael Myerberg, Owner-Managers

ALEXANDER H. COHEN

presents

ANTHONY QUAYLE   EILEEN HERLIE

in

PETER USTINOV'S
NEW COMEDY

HALFWAY UP THE TREE

with

HANNE BORK   SAM WATERSTON   MARGARET LINN
GRAHAM JARVIS   WILLIAM LARSEN   JOHN TILLINGER

Directed by
MR. USTINOV

Scenery and Lighting by
RALPH ALSWANG

Costumes by
JAMES HART STEARNS

Associate Producer
HILDY PARKS

Production Supervisor
JERRY ADLER

HELEN HAYES THEATRE

MICHAEL MYERBERG & DONALD FLAMM

present

PAUL FORD

"¿WHAT DID WE DO WRONG?"

HENRY DENKER'S NEW COMEDY

with

PHILIPPA BEVANS

LESLIE BARRETT   HUGH FRANKLIN
GREGORY ROZAKIS   HEIDI VAUGHN   ROY PROVIDENCE

and

RUSSELL HORTON

Directed by
SHERWOOD ARTHUR

Settings by
ALBERT JOHNSON

Costumes by
JACK EDWARDS

Lighting by
LEO B. MEYER

Music by
PAUL MARTIN

Executive Producer
PAUL JACOBSON

Special Guest Star
ENID MARKEY

PREMIERE PERFORMANCE, MARCH 13, 1968

BROADHURST THEAT

SAINT-SUBBER and LESTER OSTERMAN

present

JOHN FORSYTHE   ROSEMAR MURPHY

KIM HUNTER

in

GORE VIDAL'S WEEKEND

A New Comedy

with

MARCO ST. JOHN   STAATS COTSWORTH   ELEANOR WILSON
GRAHAM BROWN   ZAIDA COLES   JOHN MARRIOTT   GENE BLAKELY

and

CAROL COLE

Scenic Production by OLIVER SMITH
Costumes by THEONI V. ALDREDGE
Lighting by JEAN ROSENTHAL
Associate Producer SIMON L. SALTZMAN

Directed by
JOSEPH ANTHONY

The Way We Live Now

I have to explain for a moment how this book was written. How and when, really. In the spring of 1967, I began interviews, reading scripts, learning what I could about how things operate. This went on until the fall, when the new plays began opening, and I was able to compare what the people involved said they wanted with what they actually managed to get up on stage. I took notes continually all through the fall, winter and spring of '68.

In April, the actual writing began. The first draft of the present chapter, covering the way Broadway deals with the immediate world we live in, was written in May and scheduled by me for rewriting today, June 5, 1968, which is, of course, the day Robert Kennedy has been shot in California. As I sit here now, the news has just come over the television that he is at least still alive, out of the operation, but, according to CBS's Roger Mudd, the next 12 to 36 hours will be crucial.

I don't know that I could have written anything during these hours on a subject as inconsequential as the Broadway theatre if it weren't for the fact that I was planning to deal with Broadway and the contemporary world anyway. And this seems to indicate—this terrible possible murder in California—just how far removed

Broadway is, not just from what is happening in 1968, but from anywhere.

Broadway plays are too complicated to wrap and package to ever compete with the morning paper: improvisational actors can make up skits, but a playwright needs time. And I am not trying to suggest here that he ought to spend his time jotting down dramas about current events. I don't think Broadway need ever feel the obligation to be current in any "Stop the presses—extra!—extra!" way. Still, the shooting of Senator Kennedy immediately brings to mind two issues that have been tearing the nation apart during the past half-dozen years: the problem of young versus old, and the problem of black versus white. Of the some 40-odd plays that went into rehearsal this season, a total of two involved Negroes to any extent, considerably less than a flat percentage average of the national population. But if the Negroes were slighted, the hippies had no kicks coming: incredibly, one out of every seven plays dealt with hippies.

Even more incredibly, two of the hippie plays had the identical plot: Henry Denker's *What Did We Do Wrong?* and Peter Ustinov's *Halfway up the Tree*. Obviously, there were some differences: Ustinov's was somewhat more contemplative and deeper, if skin can be said to have depth.

Still, the similarities stupefy: both plays have as main characters middle-aged men of middling success, the one a British general about to retire, the other an American manufacturer of television antennas. Both men are confronted with a similar situation: their sons, both beatniks, hippies, etc., have got into trouble at college, the desire for social reform, in both cases, having motivated them. Both fathers, when confronting their progeny, are berated for being ignorant, out of tune, out of touch, done, used up, not "with it." Both fathers, after some private contemplation, decide to take action. Both fathers decide to take action in exactly the same way: they reappear after their scoldings dressed as their sons are dressed, in hippie clothing. Both sons are horrified that their fathers would behave in such a silly manner. Both fathers go out into the world dressed as hippies. Both fathers' actions are picked up by national television. Both become famous. Both sons, seeing the error of their ways now that their fathers have put the whole rebellion thing in perspective, immediately reform.

Sitting through one play with this plot is punishment enough for one season: sitting through two is enemy action. There is no thought of plagiarism here—my God, no one in his right mind would steal a plot like that. There were two plays with the same story because, like good news, bad ideas travel fast.

And what was so bad? Basically, the overpoweringly simple-minded solutions that the plays offer. At a time when students from Columbia to Paris are losing blood because, from where they are, the world looks rotten, it is simply false to suggest that if only a mirror were held up to them they would all quickly hop back into their Brooks Brothers costumes.

Clearly, what we are dealing with here is generational pandering: if the audience on Broadway were made up predominantly of people under twenty-five, instead of being middle-aged, I doubt whether the plays would ever have been produced. Something terrible and strange is going on today between the young and the old, and if poets are the unacknowledged legislators of the world, playwrights ought to be around at least to help define the geographical boundaries.

Because the turf is changing. A young Ivy League professor tells the following story: "This was pretty funny when it happened, but it shook me a little too. I was teaching a course in story writing one year; the kids were all around twenty and I was thirty-five. But I'm pretty immature, so it all seemed even enough; we communicated O.K. This one kid handed in a story that was an O. Henry-type thing; it all hinged on the last line. But it also hinged on the reader being familiar with an obscure kind of female contraceptive. I'd never even heard of the damn thing, and my wife had maybe heard of it once. When the class came back the next week, I read the story out loud to the group, and they commented on it some. But none of them said what I wanted them to say, so I said it. 'Listen,' I told them, 'if you're going to base a work of fiction on an obscure piece of information, what you'd better do is drop that piece of information somewhere into the body of the story so the reader will understand you at the end.' What was obscure? they wanted to know. Well, I'm a little embarrassed now, because this is a very serious bunch, and I just can't come out and say I'd never heard of this odd contraceptive device. So I fumble out, 'Well, the story just seemed to have several obscurities. Just as a minor example, how many of you understand the little mention of the contraceptive device?' Well, they all did! They'd not only heard of it; they knew more about contraceptive devices than my whole college graduating class put together. They were spouting safety percentages on the pill and God knows what else. I started reading another story as soon as I could, but all I kept thinking while I was reading it was, 'Hey, they really are different.' We were only 15 years apart, and I don't think I'd have that much trouble conversing with a man of fifty; we both speak the same English. But with the kids, I'm not sure; all I am sure of is that it's not even a whole new game, it's a different game altogether. It looks like they're still playing baseball, only there's no home plate. And I just wish somebody would please explain the rules to me."

Carry Me Back to Morningside Heights was one of the two plays this season that dealt with Negroes in any way at all. It opened and closed in one week with dreadful notices, but there is strong doubt that it ever would have got here at all if Sidney Poitier had not chosen to direct it.

The plot, simply enough, is that of a guilty Jew, who, to expiate his feelings, attaches himself to a young Negro, becoming the Negro's slave. That's it. The rest is all jokes based on the principle of reversal: jokes about carp being Jewish soul food, jokes about who has rhythm, etc. The country is blowing apart, and Broadway comes up with a one-joke show on slavery.

But flimsy as that joke may be—and God knows if it's nothing else, it is that—still, *Carry Me Back to Morningside Heights* is sturdier than the other play investigating the Negro problem: *Weekend*. *Weekend* is about a spoiled-rotten rich kid who fakes being engaged to a Negro girl in order to embarrass and blackmail his father into giving him money so that he may continue an existence that one can only assume is frivolous. The beauty part of *Weekend*'s plot was that the kid's father was not just any white Protestant millionaire; he was a white Protestant millionaire who was a U. S. Senator on the verge of announcing for the presidency of the United States. And if the stunner of *Morningside Heights* was that it was directed by Sidney Poitier, the thing you blinked at in *Weekend* was that it was written by Gore Vidal. "I got the notion for *Weekend* from the marriage of Dean Rusk's daughter. I was charmed by the hypocrisy of it all: Rusk offering to resign if it embarrassed the President, knowing full well it was the only real coup of the Johnson administration in some time. I got to thinking what this would do to a presidential candidate. I have a gift for the theatre, not a great one, but one that's pleasant for me to exercise. I like writing plays. I like writing novels too. I suppose I'm attracted to decadent forms."

Conceivably, there is some comic way of using this material, but Vidal sure didn't find it. Treating it all as a blackmail game between a spoiled-rotten child and his devious father, bringing on the parents of the Negro girl and making them turn out to be more conservative than most conservatives—it's just silly. You can make the problem of race comic if you possess sufficient skill, but you cannot make it silly.

And you can't make the generation problem disappear by dressing cute either. But how do you write a play—in other words, communicate—on the subject of not communicating without preaching? How can you bring to life dramatically the generation gap?

I think there are infinite ways, and the following plot suggestion is not offered as being necessarily first-rate but merely something capable of being dramatized. How about a play where the two main characters are a father and a son, and the son is off to Canada to avoid the draft? Now, even in a void, these two characters have things that they feel passionately about to go over. It doesn't matter who they are; that's up to the specific playwright and the story he wants to tell. Make the son a coward, it's one story. Make him sincere and pacifistic, it's another; but either way, the action holds. What about the father? He can be John Wayne, and it's one kind of play. He can be Dr. Spock, and it's another. Let him be Alger Hiss, and we've got still another action going, but at least it's action. And it deals with today. My God, how many hundreds of young men are in Canada now, how many more are going on trial to avoid the war on pacifistic grounds? Where will we set our play? If it is in the U.S. before the decision is made, fine; if it's in Canada and he's already crossed over, it's another situation. It can take place in both countries; that's up to the dramatist. But whatever he does, it's still interesting. And pertinent.

There's something going on today, and Broadway sure isn't talking about it. That's because, Broadway people tell you, there's no audience for serious plays: people want to be entertained. That may be, but around the time of the openings of the two Negro plays, Bantam Books brought out the President's riot report. In the first five days, 500,000 copies sold. Now this was a paperback book, so you can throw out the snob appeal. And it was nonfiction, and nonfiction traditionally does not sell that way in paper. In two weeks, sales went to 750,000 copies. Assuming that New York City accounts for 10% of a paperback's sales, that's 75,000 people who shelled out a $1.25 for a paperback book that was never meant to be easy reading. Which means there's got to be *some* interest in race.

Still, the Broadway people repeat, the public doesn't want to hear about anything somber; there just isn't any audience for it. Well, there sure wasn't any audience for these four plays either. *Morning-*

side Heights ran for seven performances, *Weekend* for 21, and their combined losses were $250,000. The duplicate hippie plays did only a little better. *What Did We Do Wrong?* lost $100,000, while the Ustinov play lasted eight weeks and was saved from financial disaster not by anybody wanting to see it but by a movie sale.

Just how does the audience feel about pertinent plays? According to the Theatregoers Study, the audience has clear-cut views of what it wants. Four desirable traits are listed by more than three quarters of the audience. In order, they are: entertaining, good theatre, funny and witty. Nothing surprising here. But ranking fifth in preference is this: people want theatre to be "enlightening." And close behind that comes the fact that people want theatre to be "socially aware." Fifty-nine per cent of New York theatregoers *want* the theatre to be enlightening, but only 20% think it is enlightening.

There's a gigantic gap existing right now—today—between what people want from Broadway and what they are getting from Broadway. And Broadway isn't doing a goddam thing to even try to fill it. And since this preference is indicated by New York theatregoers, it has increased potential importance, since they are the audience that attends the drama anyway. If out-of-towners were the ones responsible for the figures, forget it; they go to musicals. The drama audience is wildly dissatisfied with Broadway, or so they say. Clearly, the word enlightening means different things to different people. And possibly, New Yorkers are only saying they want the theatre to be enlightening or socially aware because they think it's something they ought to say.

But what if they mean it?

That's the frightener. Because no one can say for sure just how the Broadway audience would react to an honest play about race or a confrontation between the generations, written on an emotional level that was neither pap nor pandering. The plays are either not being written, or they are being written but not getting produced. Wouldn't it be funny if all those producers, who spend all that time moaning about how hard it is to make a decent living and then end up backing British trivia, could be successful if they put on something decent and valid and Now? No, it wouldn't be funny—nothing is funny—because someone just called and said they got the guy who shot him, and he's a Jordanian, and so what, because he's not responding to the operation as he should, and some brain surgeon just said he's going to die. Shit.

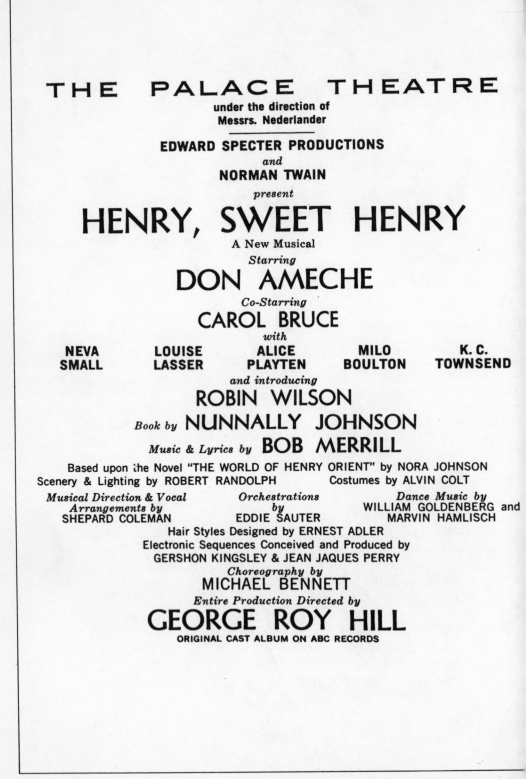

THE PALACE THEATRE

under the direction of
Messrs. Nederlander

EDWARD SPECTER PRODUCTIONS

and

NORMAN TWAIN

present

HENRY, SWEET HENRY

A New Musical

Starring

DON AMECHE

Co-Starring

CAROL BRUCE

with

| NEVA SMALL | LOUISE LASSER | ALICE PLAYTEN | MILO BOULTON | K. C. TOWNSEND |

and introducing

ROBIN WILSON

Book *by* NUNNALLY JOHNSON

Music & Lyrics by BOB MERRILL

Based upon the Novel "THE WORLD OF HENRY ORIENT" by NORA JOHNSON

Scenery & Lighting by ROBERT RANDOLPH   Costumes by ALVIN COLT

Musical Direction & Vocal Arrangements by
SHEPARD COLEMAN

Orchestrations by
EDDIE SAUTER

Dance Music by
WILLIAM GOLDENBERG and MARVIN HAMLISCH

Hair Styles Designed by ERNEST ADLER

Electronic Sequences Conceived and Produced by
GERSHON KINGSLEY & JEAN JAQUES PERRY

Choreography by
MICHAEL BENNETT

Entire Production Directed by

GEORGE ROY HILL

ORIGINAL CAST ALBUM ON ABC RECORDS

CHAPTER

12

It's Hard to Be Smart

Henry, Sweet Henry was the first musical comedy of the season.

It opened in Detroit to mixed notices. But business was good, and each week it got better, indicating a positive word of mouth, a strong audience show. The second stop was Philadelphia, and the notices there, for the most part, were the kind you'd write for yourself. One critic had reservations, but even he felt that the show was "already in the winner's circle." The other critics simply raved: ". . . swinging and tuneful . . . young talent ricochets all over the stage . . . hilarious . . . a kind of bawdy 'Bye, Bye Birdie.' " Even with the Philadelphia notices, the creative team continued to improve the show, pruning it, shaping it, so that it continually became more refined and sharp. As one member of the production put it: "We worked hard, the work was good; we figured the worst we could be was a hit."

They had sound reasons for their confidence: *Henry, Sweet Henry* had a lot going for it. It was based on the wonderful film "The World of Henry Orient," and the film's director, George Roy Hill, was returning to Broadway to do the musical. (Hill's first Broadway job had resulted in the Pulitzer prize-winning *Look Homeward Angel*.) The screenwriter also came along to do the musical, and he was uniquely fitted for the job: his name was Nunnally Johnson. And both the movie and the musical were based on a novel by Nora Johnson, who happened to be his daughter. For composer/lyricist, there was Bob Merrill, who had performed similar duties for *New Girl in Town, Take Me Along* and *Carnival,* and had supplied the lyrics for *Funny Girl.*

There were, as there always are, problems. The story, briefly, is about two young private-school girls who get an absurd crush on an egomaniac musician, Henry Orient, and follow him around relentlessly, ruining his love life. In the movie, Peter Sellers had played Orient, while two unknown actresses played the schoolgirls. They mopped up the floor with him. This is not universal knowledge, since the film was never commercially successful, but it is doubtful whether there exists anywhere in the English-speaking world a leading man who didn't damn well know that the girls—no matter who played them—were going to walk away with the show. This made casting very difficult. Tony Randall, who was offered the part and apparently liked the show, turned it down, saying, "I'd love to play it if only I were a fifteen-year-old girl."

The particular fifteen-year-old girl he meant was Val, the lead part. In the story she is rich and bright and lost, and she wears a ratty fur coat all the time. Casting Val was crucial to the success of *Henry, Sweet Henry.* One of the producers, Norman Twain, put it this way: "Every musical smash has to have that one incandescent performance." And there is truth to what he says. When you think of the long-running musicals, you think of Channing and *Dolly!,* Mostel and *Fiddler,* Kiley and *La Mancha,* Lansbury and *Mame,* Grey and *Cabaret.* (The one exception that immediately comes to mind, *West Side Story,* isn't an exception after all: Jerome Robbins gave the star performance there, as incandescent as any of the above.)

To play Val, a girl named Robin Wilson was chosen. She had had little stage experience, but she was signed anyway. Because of her voice. The director, George Hill, said: "It's a sensational voice. She's a little pudding of a girl with a big emotional sound. It's a voice that breaks your heart." (Hill had just finished directing "Thoroughly Modern Millie," so he was not unfamiliar with wonderful musical-comedy voices.) Merrill, the songwriter, said: "The girl's phenomenal. An original. One of the finest pop singers I've ever heard. It's a face and personality you just don't forget." (Merrill, remember, had done *Funny Girl,* so he knew a little about musical-comedy voices too.)

Henry, Sweet Henry opened in New York the night of October 23. Fifteen shows had already come in, but I think it is fair to say that, in spite of the earlier Pinter, the limited Dietrich engagement, the *Rosencrantz* triumph, in many ways this was the biggest opening of the year so far. Not because of Robin Wilson. And not because of Don Ameche in the title role. *Henry, Sweet Henry* was important to Broadway simply because of what it was: a musical comedy.

Should anybody not be aware of the importance of the musical to the present Broadway scene, a few statistics: (1) of all the money paid for tickets in the twelve months this book covers, from the beginning of June, 1967, to the end of May, 1968, close to 70% was paid to see musical shows of various kinds; (2) of all the spoken shows that played during that twelve-month period, counting the long runs like *Don't Drink the Water, You Know I Can't Hear You When the Water's Running* and *Cactus Flower,* plus the shows of this new season, *Rosencrantz, Girl in My Soup, More Stately Mansions* and *Plaza Suite*—taking all those 50-odd plays together, the amount of money they grossed in the twelve months totaled less than the total taken in by just four musicals, *Fiddler, Mame, Cabaret* and *Dolly!*

The pressures are greater on a musical opening. Because of the rewards. As far as money is concerned, today—right now—is the golden age of musical comedy. The runs of the great hit plays are becoming shorter (none of the top five opened in the past 20 years), while the runs of musicals are growing longer and longer. (Four of the top five are less than 20 years old, and two of them—*Dolly!* and *Fiddler*—are still running. And *Man of La Mancha* is still at capacity after well over 1,000 performances.)

And with the increased run comes the increased reward. The amount of money that it is possible for a composer or lyricist to make from one enormous success is almost obscene. Figure conservatively: 2% of $100,000 a week is about $100,000 a year. Let the show have two years like that and then taper off; we'll make it $250,000. Double that, because of the road company: $500,000 now. A big musical will have close to 20 productions going in foreign countries for several years, but this is peanuts; we won't even bother with it. A movie sale of $2,000,000 isn't wild any more (*My Fair Lady* went for over $5,000,000), and the composer gets 20% of the movie sale, so we're close to $1,000,000 now.

That's still nothing. The stock and amateur rights will go well into six figures, so divvy that up. And then get into the *real* money, the record business. The way the record business works, a song is paid two pennies per band on an LP. Take an original-cast album and figure it has a dozen songs; that makes a dozen bands. Of the 2¢, half goes to the music publisher, half to the songwriter. Let's say the album sells 1,000,000 copies. That's 1,000,000 times 12¢. It's eating money. (A really big original-cast album like *My Fair Lady* or *Sound of Music* will go many millions of albums.) Then there are the single songs picked from the show that go into other albums. Herb Alpert decides to pick a song from your show; it's just one number in his album, but his albums sell 1,000,000 copies, so that doesn't hurt.

And then there is the money earned when a song becomes a "standard." A standard might be called a song that still holds recording interest after it's maybe five years old. A music publisher explained to me that a composer might stand to make easily $250,-000 from one song such as "The Impossible Dream" from *Man of La Mancha*.

Now, since none of this financial data is secret information, it follows logically that an enormous number of skillful people are going to be working the musical field, hoping for the gusher. Yet in spite of all the skill that has gone into the making of the musicals of the sixties, the figures are kind of depressing. *Henry, Sweet Henry* was approximately the hundredth musical of the decade. Of these 100, perhaps 10% were so troubled that they closed out of town. Another 25% aroused such audience apathy that they couldn't even last one month. Maybe 50% more ran from a month to a year and still lost money. Around 20 showed a profit at the end of the New York run, but less than half that, perhaps seven, have made as much profit as $1,000,000. And since musicals tend to cost anywhere from one third to two thirds of $1,000,000, the percentage of return isn't really all that great.

So why aren't there more successful musicals?

One way of getting at the answer is to take one element of a musical—a song, any song—and try to explain why this one small part of the whole doesn't work. Perhaps if we can list some of the reasons for one little song not working, it might provide an insight into why it's hard to make an entire musical work.

Let's hypothesize that we're out of town with a musical, and it's opening night. And we're standing at the back of the theatre while the bodies file in. Now these are different bodies from the ones who saw the run-through back in town, if we had one. These people *paid*. Those of us standing in the back watching them come in are usually pretty talented people. One of us is the author of the book, probably a playwright part of the time, certainly a masochist all of the time. Because that's what book writers do: suffer. That's their job. If a show is bad, it's their fault, according to the critics, and if it's good, they don't get in the way of the score, according to the critics. They can get rich from a smash, but loved? Never. A musical-comedy book is about 60 minutes long, and a good deal of that 60 minutes is spent in leaden dialogue, the sole purpose of which is to cleanly lead into a song. The rest is plot, characterization slashed out in broad strokes, whatever jokes can be managed, all whipped together to make a bastard form that has, in almost all cases, no literary value whatsoever. And yet, with all this, the book of the musical is, many people feel, the single most crucial element in the mixture. It is not what makes a musical *good,* but it is what makes a musical *go.* No one comes out humming the book, but if the book is confused, no musical number is going to save things. It's the flour of a musical; it doesn't make the cake taste nice, but try baking without it.

Also at the back with us is the composer, who probably—but not necessarily—knows his music. (A lot of Broadway composers can't play the kazoo.)

And the lyricist. Of all of us, he is the quickest. He knows poetry, rhyme of all kinds, and if he's good, he has studied for years learning how to be clever. And if he's really good he has studied a few more years forgetting all about cleverness. Audiences don't care all that much about *uppity* rhyming with *cup of tea.* But almost without exception, lyricists love cleverness. They claim they don't; they disdainfully point out showy cleverness in their peers' work while denying it in their own, but secretly, shhh . . . they love little punny funnies . . . I think that of the three writers standing in the back, the lyricist comes closest to being an actor.

Also with us is the producer, who has the sweats just now, because he raised over half a mill for this effort, and if it stinks, it's going to be a lot harder doing that the next time.

Then there's the director, who's put it all together, and the choreographer, who's supposed to have done what the director told him, and all in all, we're a genuinely interested bunch of neurotics shuffling by the rear wall.

It might also be noted that the writers have probably put a good deal of time into the effort about to unfold. At least a year. Maybe up to eight. So there's a certain amount of blood involved.

Now for the bodies sitting down. There is a certain peculiar level of expectation on the audience's part for a musical. The whole event of a musical is different from any play. To begin with, when the lights dim, there's an orchestra playing. And there's a sense of bigness to the operation: the theatre is big, the sets are big, the actors' gestures are big. Everything possesses a size not present in a play. There is also a willingness on the audience's part to move into a world of familiar unreality. The audience concedes that the language they are hearing is not the language of the street.

The audience also—and this is crucial—gives the actor the right to deliver an *aside*. The aside is a dramatic device that has not been much in use in the past several hundred years. A poor jobless man discovers that his wife is about to have a child. In an aside, he would turn to the audience and perhaps mutter, "Pregnant? Ye gods. Who'll buy its gruel?" In a realistic play, he would probably talk to somebody in the play, perhaps a bartender. "Charley," he mutters across the bar, "my wife's gonna have a kid, and me without a job. Who's gonna feed the kid?" In a musical, the character simply walks to the front of the stage, plants his feet wide apart and belts the "Soliloquy" from *Carousel*. In other words, the character who takes stage is entitled to pour his guts out to the audience.

Not only does the audience give him that permission, the audience also believes, insists even, that what he tells it be taken at face value as truth. Very often, in this kind of song, it is a secret feeling, told in confidence. When Eliza sings of a room somewhere with lots of chocolate, and how loverly that would be, she is simply telling the audience what she feels: she is not pressuring her father to give her a larger allowance. O.K. So a strange reality is set up, but the audience accepts that, and what they want is to enjoy what's about to happen.

Start of overture. Coughing and rustle. End of overture. Lights out. Whisper, whisper. Curtain up. Blah blah blah, a few words, and then, *then* comes the magic moment: the first song.

And it dies.

We in the back commit a few mystic acts. We clap our hands over our ears, we kick the wall, we swear a little, all in an attempt to ward off evil spirits. But eventually, reality returns, and reality dictates that we face a fact which is very simple: a musical moment in our show doesn't work. All right. The number doesn't work. We make that note, and the rest of the show goes on, and eventually, either that night or the next morning, we all have a meeting about the show and how it went, and we all agree that the musical moment doesn't work.

Why doesn't it?

No one can ever state with mathematical precision just why a given song doesn't work. You can only guess, and with wisdom, experience and luck, you might come up with an answer. The following are some of the possibilities:

1. It doesn't work because the goddam soprano can't sing it. That's one of the commonest reasons put forward by songwriters. The material and the performer are simply not in harmony. Sometimes, for example, a performer can have difficulty phrasing a song properly, or the range is too great, and this brings on discomfort in rehearsal, which often turns to panic by the time the show is out of town. The performer is simply unhappy doing the song, and that's it.

2. Sometimes the director can't direct it.

3. Sometimes the choreographer can't put a "button" on it, a button being the closing moment that leads the audience happily into applause. Stephen Sondheim, lyricist for *West Side Story* and *Gypsy,* thinks this is the commonest reason for a number not working: lack of a button.

4. Sometimes songs don't fit the moment.

5. Sometimes the song tells us something we already know and don't want to hear again.

6. Sometimes a song can be in the wrong scene.

7. Sometimes a song can be in the right scene, but the wrong part of the right scene.

8. Sometimes an audience will disagree with what comes out of the character's mouth and simply refuse to believe what he's saying.

9. Sometimes the audience doesn't understand what leads up to the song—the reason for someone's singing.

10. Sometimes a song falls between two stools; the music is one thing, the lyrics another, and the effect becomes diluted, watery.

11. Sometimes an audience will not want to spend the amount of time required for a character to sing a song, especially if the character is an unimportant one. (This brings up the whole question of musical time, which will not be gone into except to say that musical time is compressed: three minutes of a song might be equivalent to ten or fifteen minutes of spoken dialogue.)

12. Sometimes a song can simply be wrong: wrong for the moment, wrong for the character, wrong for the show itself.

13. Sometimes a song can be programmed badly: a slow song following too closely upon another slow song. Two funny numbers back to back can sometimes damage one or both.

14. Sometimes a song can rip the fabric of a play. (Sometimes this happens and it works, as with "Ol' Man River." It's a specialty, a turn. Like a bar in the back of an automobile: it doesn't make the motor go, but it helps make the trip enjoyable.)

15. Sometimes a song can be a bad song. But this doesn't happen as often as one might think on Broadway, because most of the song-writers entrusted with half a million have a certain minimum proficiency. Besides, don't ask me to define what a bad song is; badness is more often a matter of personal bias than aesthetic judgment. In musicals, it is probably safe to say that songs often aren't as bad as they are wrong. Just to get a bit more complicated; sometimes the wrong song works. David Merrick was once turned down by a director for *Hello, Dolly!,* and the director sent a note wishing Merrick well and begging him, for God's sake, to get rid of the title number. The director was a fool, right? Does it change your mind if I say that the director was Hal Prince, who just might have the most astute musical-comedy mind in the business? Prince says this: "The 'Hello, Dolly!' number has nothing to do with Dolly Levi. She's a woman who has no money and scrounges around; she's never been to a place as fancy as the Harmonia Gardens, where the number happens. She's heard about it, and she goes there because she's heard about it and wants to have a good time. The way the number is now, you're talking about a woman who has lived her life at '21.' "

Prince is probably right, and just to carry the confusion about the "Hello, Dolly!" number—probably the great showstopper of the decade—one step further, you can say that not only sometimes does the wrong song work, but it wouldn't work if it were in a better show. For example, "Hello, Dolly!" wouldn't work in *South Pacific.* You could set it up just as well: Nellie Forbush has gone off to Guam for a while to get over her heartbreak caused by Ezio Pinza, and now she comes back, let's say to a fancy Oriental resort, and a community of nurses is waiting for her (and no one ever said before how popular she was). And as she comes down a ramp built especially for her entrance, all the nurses break into "Hello, Nellie, well hello, Nellie, it's so nice to see you back where you belong." You'd never buy the moment, never in a million years.

Now let's assume that we have decided why the number isn't working. The next decision is what to do about it. Should the number simply be cut—in other words, does the moment *need* music—or should it be replaced with a new number? It's easiest just to cut, but most of the time replacement is called for. O.K. We put in a new song. But what kind of a new song? Funnier than the old? Sadder? Faster, shorter, louder, or what? And should the same character sing it? Or should it be a different character? Or should it be the same character with maybe one new character added? Or maybe the whole chorus?

Let's assume we can answer all these questions. All we have to do is write a new song, right? Wrong. We have to write a new song that's better than the old song, which was the best we could do when we had time and no out-of-town pressure. Putting in a new song that's worse—it happens sometimes—demoralizes the hell out of everybody. But we've got one thing going for us: since we know who is going to sing the song, we know the limits of the performer's skill. Sheldon Harnick says, "Songs written on the road are often more effective because of your knowledge of the performer; I never think of myself as actually tailoring a song for somebody, but that's what happens."

All right, hang in there, because now we get to be creative. We hide out in our hotel room and write the song. That can take a couple of days. And it can take a week or two before we ever get to see it done on stage with an audience, because it has to be approved and choreographed and learned and orchestrated and rehearsed. But at last it goes in and it's an improvement, so we're done, right?

Wrong. Because this strange thing happens: with the substitution of the new number, some of what preceded it—at the very least the song lead-in—is different, and everything that follows it is in some way affected. So another number or scene that was working perfectly may suddenly, crankily, stop working. Or something following the old (bad) number, which seemed adequate, may, in the light of the new (good) number, turn rotten. So we've got to change that. And when you change *that,* everything else changes. Out of town, it's a constant wild race: changing, trying like hell to fix and patch and forget what you said the show was about back before rehearsal; under the gun you go with what works. And slowly, without anyone knowing it at first, the whole giant structure begins to change direction.

It's as if you want to go north, due north, that's the place, and off you start. But then there's a change and then another, and suddenly you're heading north by northeast, and that isn't quite the same any more, but what the hell, it's close enough, it's still north. And then one morning you wake up, and the sun's dead in your face, and you think, "East, huh?," and then you think, *"East?* I don't wanna go east, I'm a north man." And then you think, "Well, what the hell, at least I'm moving and—east, north,—motion's the thing; when you get right down to it, I'm a motion man more than anything." And on you go, leaving east behind now, moving more slowly but still moving, and you don't stop until the night you open in magic town, and Clive Barnes says he knew you were a bore as soon as he heard the overture. Which is what he said about *Henry, Sweet Henry*.

But the incandescent performance that all musical smashes need *Henry, Sweet Henry* had: ". . . stops the show . . ." the critics said; ". . . a miniature Ethel Merman, a real little star . . ." the critics said. And on the day following the opening, the *Times* devoted a three-column article to her, saying, among other nice things, that twenty-year-old Alice Playten "was a spectacular hit."

Those of you with keen memories might be a bit bothered by the fact that the *Times* was talking about Alice Playten, while the girl mentioned earlier by the creative people as being so spectacular was Robin Wilson. The logical assumption might be that there had been a cast replacement out of town. Not so. Robin Wilson still had the crucial part, and she got nice enough notices, but it was little Alice Playten in a supporting role that caught lightning in a bottle.

How could such gifted, experienced people have made such a mistake? First of all, Alice Playten's emergence was strictly a New York thing. "She never stopped anything out of town," someone with the show said. "Her numbers never went as well as on opening night. It needed a gathering of New York faggots to love her camp." Composer Merrill added this: "Robin Wilson's part didn't allow her to stop the show. And Alice Merman—that's a slip—Alice Playten is less than five feet tall and has one of the biggest voices in existence. It's a traditional theatre voice, a Broadway voice. . . ."

Second: whatever errors they made weren't done on purpose. But what probably happened was that they hired Robin Wilson, a twenty-year-old with a glorious soaring voice, to play a fifteen-year-old, but her twenty-year-old style was too mature for the part. So in order to make her come across as fifteen, she had to forgo her style. In other words, they hired a totally inexperienced actress to play the crucial part in a musical, hired her solely and entirely because of her voice, and then got rid of the voice and kept the girl.

I don't think it mattered much, because it turned out that Robin Wilson was a natural actress and performed well in the part, so her acting was in no way damaging. And her singing, even if not sensational, was good. As Merrill said, she didn't have songs to stop the show anyway. The show, by the way, before the critics got to it, was enormously pleasing for audiences. I saw it just before it opened with a theatre-party crowd, notoriously a rough house, and the reaction at the end of *Henry, Sweet Henry* was every bit as strong at the end as the reaction *Mame* gets. Only *Mame* got the notices. *Henry, Sweet Henry* didn't luck out; it closed in ten weeks. (No one knew it then, but the musical season was going to be so disastrous that even with a loss of $400,000, *Henry, Sweet Henry* was going to end up as one of the most successful musicals of the year.)

It's hard to be smart. Frank Loesser was asked once why musicals were so hard. Loesser, who did the scores for *Guys and Dolls* and *How to Succeed in Business* among others, is noted along the street for a marvelous musical-comedy mind. "Why are they hard?" Loesser said. "I don't know; maybe because people keep secrets from each other. Especially choreographers."

EUGENE O'NEILL THEATRE

Owned and operated by DAVID J. COGAN

CHERYL CRAWFORD and CARL SCHAEFFER

present

JEAN ARTHUR

in

THE FREAKING OUT OF STEPHANIE BLAKE

a new comedy

by

RICHARD CHANDLER

with

ALBERTA GRANT	STEVE CURRY	FRANKLIN COVER

WILLIAM DEVANE	ELLEN O'MARA

with

JAN MINER

and

SIDNEY LANIER

Sets and Lighting	*Costumes by*
BEN EDWARDS — JEAN ROSENTHAL	**JEANNE BUTTON**

Projection Photographs by	*Light Paintings by*
BRUCE W. STARK	JASON B. FISHBEIN

Music and Lyrics by **JEFF BARRY**

CHAPTER

13

The Dark Side of the Moon

From the New York *Times*, Friday, June 23:

The Eugene O'Neill . . . will receive . . . Richard Chandler's comedy, "The Freaking Out of Stephanie Blake." Jean Arthur will be starred in the Cheryl Crawford production.

From the New York *Daily News*, Monday, August 7:

New Partner
Theatrical attorney Carl Schaeffer has joined Cheryl Crawford as co-producer of "The Freaking Out of Stephanie Blake," the comedy by Richard Chandler in which Jean Arthur will return to Broadway, October 28, at the O'Neill Theatre.

From the New York *Daily News,* Wednesday, August 9:

Jean Arthur has arrived in town a month early, to take in the sights and sounds of Fun City, before going into rehearsal of "The Freaking Out of Stephanie Blake." . . . Miss Arthur's last Broadway show was "Peter Pan" 17 years ago.

From the New York *Daily News,* Friday, August 11:

John Hancock, who staged the black comedy version of Shakespeare's "A Midsummer Night's Dream," has been signed by Cheryl Crawford to direct "The Freaking Out of Stephanie Blake."

] 175 [

The above are four of the early releases on what was to become the one genuinely legendary production of the season. The word legendary applies to a certain kind of Broadway show that by virtue of its birth agonies and the resulting publicity achieves an immortality most productions never dare aspire to. *The Fifth Season* ran more than 650 performances, *Janie* a few less, but they are dead and forgotten, while *Buttrio Square* lives on. And so does *Portofino*. And *Breakfast at Tiffany's* will never die.

We are dealing in this chapter with sadism on Broadway. There is a lot of it. A lot of it. The majority of people not involved with any particular production generally wish the majority of those who are involved just enough pain to prove unbearable. Psychiatrists disagree about the reasons behind the high sadism level, but there is general head-nodding over the following famous dictum: "It's not enough for me to succeed. My best friend also has to fail."

Back to the four early releases now; nothing unusual in any of them, really. Announcement of the theatre: standard. Announcement of an additional producer: still standard, even though this usually means the show is having trouble raising the money. (Not so standard, and not stated in any of the four, is the fact that the author of the play was also the partner of the original producer, and supposedly responsible for a great deal of the money in the production.)

A few words about the play. It was a comedy about an Ohio spinster who comes to New York for a few days prior to a European trip. She finds that her beloved niece is involved with hippies in Greenwich Village, and the basic plot of the play concerns her going to the Village to bring her niece out. Now in a plot like this, there are only two things that can happen: either the niece leaves or she doesn't. If she does, there's no play. So she doesn't. So the spinster aunt stays down in the Village and tries to convince her further. Now, put a spinster aunt in with hippies, and only two things can happen: either she is influenced by them or she isn't. If she isn't, there's no play. So she is. So she puts on sweatshirts saying "Love is," and she talks hippie talk. All of this is predictable. This is the kind of play, then, that doesn't depend for its success on plot (that's worth maybe 15 seconds); it all works because of the fun along the way. And how much do we care about the lady we travel with?

The lady in this case was Jean Arthur. Wonderful Jean Arthur. Remember her in "Shane"? That was in the fifties. "Talk of the Town"? The forties. "Mr. Smith Goes to Washington"? Moving to the thirties now. She was there in the twenties too, making two-reelers as early as 1923. But this was '67, and a long trip back from exile. Whatever it was that she once had, did she have it any more? And would anyone remember? Or, more important, care? No way of knowing. But she was an experienced star.

The producer, Miss Crawford, matched her year for year, having been casting director for the Theatre Guild 40 years ago. She had been a founding member of the Group Theatre and the Actors' Studio and had produced *One Touch of Venus*, *Brigadoon* and *Sweet Bird of Youth*. But this last had been in '59, and in the sixties, failure followed failure.

Hancock, the director, was twenty-eight. He had spent time in Pittsburgh regional theatre, and the word was that he was talented. Now he was on Broadway. What did he think of the show he was to direct? "The play tries too hard to be commercial; Jean Arthur plays the drums, that kind of thing. It also cleans up the hippie world too much. You can't portray it in all its drug-infested reality, but you can't quite make it this prophylactic either." Strengths and weaknesses, gambles and worries. Nothing legendary.

Yet.

From *Variety,* Wednesday, August 30:
Ben Edwards and Jean Rosenthal will design the scenery and lighting for "The Freaking Out of Stephanie Blake," due October 26 at the Eugene O'Neill Theatre, N.Y. Robert Randolph withdrew from the design chores over artistic differences with the author, Richard Chandler.

From the New York *Daily News,* Thursday, August 31:
Freaking Delayed
"The Freaking Out of Stephanie Blake," the comedy starring Jean Arthur, will open at the Eugene O'Neill October 30 instead of October 26.

Indications. Little delays, little firings. Not quite so standard. On September 1, a friend of the production said that the author, Richard Chandler, had worked straight through the night before, that in addition to writing he was also helping with the producing, and that he was weary. "He's in no condition to talk to anybody." Not the best way for a writer to greet rehearsal period.

From the New York *Times,* Saturday, September 9:
Flower-People Play Makes Jean Arthur Bloom
Comedy Set for October 30 Casts Her as Turned-on Spinster

Actress, 50, Is Cheery About First Role in 16 Years
"Hello, everybody," Jean Arthur called from the stage of the Eugene
O'Neill Theatre yesterday, "here I am!"

The line, spoken in the husky-squeaky voice that has been familiar to
moviegoers since the advent of sound, marks Miss Arthur's entrance in
"The Freaking Out of Stephanie Blake."

The article went on, in 19 paragraphs, to talk of the first day of
rehearsal, of Miss Arthur's drum solo that would be on the antici-
pated recording of the play, of her life in Carmel, California where
she had lived quietly for years. It was a standard New York *Times*
first-day-of-rehearsal story. Nothing very interesting, nothing offensive; it reinforced what we already knew, and that was that.

Then the play went into rehearsal. As has been stated, this is the
quiet time; a show submerges, and in the underwater silence it is
more or less formed. There is usually nothing until the first public
performance, in this case, October 9.

From the New York *Times,* Monday, October 9:

The first preview of "The Freaking Out of Stephanie Blake" starring Jean
Arthur has been postponed from tonight to tomorrow night at the Eugene
O'Neill Theatre. It was announced that the stagehands and technicians
needed more time to install the complicated production . . .

It just didn't ring true. You don't postpone one night for technical reasons. Well, you might, if you were coming in from out of town
and had closed there on a Saturday and were racing to make it for
Monday evening. But for a show that hadn't gone out of town, a
show that was previewing here all along, it didn't wash. Trouble?
Had to be. Big trouble? No telling.

Yet.

From the New York *Times,* Wednesday, October 11:

John Hancock Leaves Play
John Hancock resigned yesterday as director of "The Freaking Out of
Stephanie Blake," attributing the step to a disagreement with the author,
Richard Chandler. Mr. Hancock said that he had requested his name be
omitted from the program of the play, which stars Jean Arthur. His suc-
cessor has not been named. Previews, which were scheduled for last night,
have been postponed to Saturday night at the Eugene O'Neill Theatre.
The première will be on October 30.

(Hancock: "The problem was the author. He was not only the producer but he also wanted to direct. Chandler was interested in the
casting of types and amateurs: he wanted real hippies and real
musicians. I love casting amateurs because they can sometimes give
you something wonderful, but only in one or two parts. What we
have is a group of non-actors, and it goes so slowly; they don't
know what they're doing, they won't remember what they did yesterday. . . .Getting canned, that came as no surprise to me. I
should have got out of it sooner. Your ambition betrays you, that's
the problem.")

From the New York *Times,* Thursday, October 12:

Producer to Direct Play

Cheryl Crawford, co-producer of "The Freaking Out of Stephanie Blake,"
has replaced John Hancock as director of the play. Mr. Hancock resigned
because of what he termed a disagreement with the author, Richard Chandler. Jean Arthur is starred in the production, which begins previews on
Saturday night and opens October 30th at the Eugene O'Neill Theatre.

The producer taking over the direction of a play is unusual, but
certainly not without precedent. Besides, Miss Crawford had directed on Broadway before, most recently in 1935.

From the New York *Times,* Friday, October 13:

The date for the première of "The Freaking Out of Stephanie Blake" has
now been settled—October 30th at the Eugene O'Neill Theatre. Michael
Kahn succeeds John Hancock as director.

Michael Kahn. Thirty. Was to have made his Broadway directing
debut later in the season. Mostly off-Broadway work. Well received.
The word on him was like the word on Hancock: talented. (Kahn:
"Why did I take over *Stephanie Blake?* I'll never take over another show again. I did it for sheer craft. I thought I could make
it charming and warm. And I thought *Here's Where I Belong*
would never get on. I was going crazy with nothing to do.")

From the New York *Times,* Friday, October 27:

Set "Freaking Out" Previews

"The Freaking Out of Stephanie Blake," which has delayed its opening,
will begin a week of previews Monday at the Eugene O'Neill Theatre, it

was announced yesterday. The comedy by Richard Chandler stars Jean
Arthur and is being produced by Cheryl Crawford and Carl Schaeffer.
Mariclare Costello has replaced Alberta Grant in the cast.

    Nothing out of the ordinary here. Except the cast replacement.
The two girls played the part of the niece, perhaps the largest part
in the play. Ordinarily, this might be a matter of great and genuine
concern. Here it's listed casually, after the names of the producers.
Hardly worth mentioning.
    To those hungry for suffering, the first preview was lip-smacking
good. At 8:33 the lights dimmed. At 8:34 they came back up again.
Miss Crawford, the producer, plodded down the aisle to the front
and faced the audience. The doom was thick enough to eat. Miss
Crawford began talking softly. At first, she was inaudible, but the
house hushed to her as she went on: ". . . we've got some new
scenes and a good many new lines. In the old days they used to have
a prompter's box in the middle of the stage. We haven't got that,
but we have our prompter here with us in the front row," and with
that she pointed to a girl in an orange suit. Then she stumped back
up the aisle, and the houselights dimmed again, this time on purpose.
    Rarely has sadistic expectation been so high. As a matter of statis-
tical record, two couples, who hadn't seen each other since the heav-
enly midweek closing of *Breakfast at Tiffany's*, ran into each other
at the first preview of *Stephanie Blake*. To people like that, *Stephanie Blake* had to be judged with the harshest critical standards. Because to fall so far you have to have a certain size, which is why most
of the legendary landmarks are musicals. When a one-set, three-
character job is bad, it's just bad. Now here was *Stephanie Blake*, a
straight play, challenging Valhalla. Would it make it?
    Was there ever any doubt? From the curtain rise, when two trem-
bling actors tried not to spill their martinis, there was that sigh of
contentment from the sadists: nothing could go right. Miss Arthur
entered at 8:42. It's a big moment. Jean Arthur returns. You want to
applaud. It wants to be a punctuated moment, set apart, clean.
There is a knock on the door, but no one goes to open it. This may
not seem like much, but if someone had gone to open it, they could
have made a gesture to Miss Arthur while she was still invisible to
the audience, and then stepped aside with the opening of the door
to take care of their actions, and Miss Arthur could then have had
the entrance moment. Clean. So we could clap. Well, she opened the
door for herself, and there she was with her back to us and then her

side, and she started talking as she entered, so the moment was never set apart. Clean. So what happened was that the audience started to applaud just as she started to talk, and then they became quiet to hear her. But by that time she was done with her opening line, so what you got was a few scattered claps and then nothing. Silence on Jean Arthur's Broadway return.

Things went like that all night. For the most part, it was just a matter of a bunch of actors moving through Jell-O, and it wasn't anybody's fault, really. The play was probably the only show in the history of the American theatre in which Everett McKinley Dirksen was the villain. (I know that doesn't make any sense, but in order for it to make sense the play would have to be explained in great detail, and that really wouldn't make any sense. Just take it as fact: everybody kept knocking poor Ev.)

It was over at 10:58 except for the curtain calls. At the first call, the curtain came down and almost hit Miss Arthur on the top of the head. She barely managed to jump back, and somebody said, "You should have let it hit you, Jean." Then the turntables (there were turntables) got stuck halfway through a turn, so the last thing you saw at the last curtain call was half of several sets, either two or four, and panicked actors trying to get the hell out of the way in case it all went mad and suddenly started whirling.

From Earl Wilson's column, Wednesday, November 1:
The Jean Arthur show, "The Freaking Out," etc., scheduled to open Saturday, will open November 9 instead. It played so well in previews, with songs, that composer Jeff Barry'll write some more.

From the New York *Post* (Earl Wilson), November 3:
Jean Arthur Ill
Tomorrow night's première of "The Freaking Out of Stephanie Blake" at the Eugene O'Neill Theatre was uncertain yesterday because of the illness of Jean Arthur, the star, who is suffering from exhaustion. . . . The comedy, by Richard Chandler, had been scheduled to open Monday, but it was postponed until tomorrow night and three previews were given. The trouble-plagued production, originally capitalized at $165,000, had an over-call of an additional 15 percent from the backers.

From the New York *Post* (Earl Wilson), November 3:
At a cost of about $50,000 to herself, Jean Arthur has been trying to make a brilliant Broadway comeback. . . .
But the chances that Miss Arthur will be able to resume and perform

at the opening now scheduled for next Thursday night are slim indeed. . . .

The crisis came at Wednesday's matinee preview when Miss Arthur, suffering extreme exhaustion, explained to the audience as she began the performance that she didn't feel up to it . . . "but I'm told I must go on and I'm going to because I believe in the show. But if something happens . . ."

From the New York *Times,* Saturday, November 4:
Illness of Jean Arthur Cancels Tonight's "Stephanie" Première
Tonight's Broadway première of "The Freaking Out of Stephanie Blake" was canceled after it became apparent that the star of the play, Jean Arthur, had taken ill. . . .

Miss Crawford said she had been unable to talk to Miss Arthur. Yesterday she sent the actress a telegram in which she said, "Your failure to appear at rehearsal this afternoon and at performances tonight and tomorrow will necessitate the closing of the play . . . with an estimated loss of $250,000."

From the New York *Post,* Tuesday, November 7:
"Stephanie Blake" Dead

The above statement is not true for the pure in heart.

PREMIERE PERFORMANCE, OCTOBER 31, 1967

BROADHURST THEATRE

ELLIOT MARTIN

(in association with CENTER THEATRE GROUP)

presents

INGRID BERGMAN

ARTHUR HILL COLLEEN DEWHURST

American Premiere

EUGENE O'NEILL'S

MORE STATELY MANSIONS

with

FRED STEWART	**HELEN CRAIG**		**LAWRENCE LINVILLE**
KERMIT MURDOCK	JOHN MARRIOTT	BARRY MACOLLUM	VINCENT DOWLING

Scenery by	*Costumes by*	*Lighting by*
BEN EDWARDS	JANE GREENWOOD	JOHN HARVEY

Directed by

JOSE QUINTERO

Production Associate
Marjorie Martin

Production by Arrangement with
Quinto Productions, Inc.

Your Goddamned Laughs: Stars

Eugene O'Neill's *More Stately Mansions* was the butt-numbing drama of the season. Ordinarily, when a soporific as overpowering as this opens, it gets blasted and closes on Saturday. *More Stately Mansions* got blasted as much as any O'Neill play is liable to get, but it ran for 150 well-attended performances and grossed over $1,000,000. I think the production did more harm to the cause of serious drama than any event in recent memory. God knows how many thousands of people left the Broadhurst Theatre thinking that if this was the number one dramatic event that Broadway could come up with, it was movies for them from now on.

Because of the presence of the famous Ingrid Bergman in one of the central roles, the production was "news" long before it reached New York. The *Times* covered Miss Bergman's arrival in America on its society pages, and when the play opened in Los Angeles, they practically reviewed it, headlining their article, COLLEEN DEWHURST OUTSHINES INGRID BERGMAN IN O'NEILL PLAY. Some magazines also reviewed the Los Angeles tryout, and soon Miss Bergman's face was shining out from the cover of *Life*, the front pages of newspapers, in television interviews, etc. The publicity kept building, as did the advance sale, in spite of the Los Angeles notices, and the producers claimed an advance of over $650,000, tremendous for a nonmusical, phenomenal for a drama—testimony to the fact that Broadway knew a star when it saw one.

But is Miss Bergman a Broadway star? And if she isn't, who is? In either case, what is a star anyway? Technically, there is a definition of a star, and once upon a time it meant something: a star was someone who got his name above the title. But that is nothing now, or if it is, then this year saw the Broadway debut of that famous star, Jordan Christopher.

Emotionally, what makes a star is something a long way from billing. No one really knows (people are always talking about "star quality" as if it were a specific instead of a euphemism), but in general, the single quality that all stars must have is this: insistence. There is something in their psyches that insists that while they are on stage *you watch them*. This quality of insistence is one of the reasons that stars can be so valuable or so damaging to a production: if a show calls for a star, if there is a part that is written for a star to take stage on entrance and hold stage, then you get a star, and you're home. But if you've got a play in which the parts are balanced, then you may come in big but you won't come in happy, because whatever play you had in mind will have long been thrown out the window by the star's destroying any semblance of balance.

Generally, stars can't help this. They don't intend to take stage, they have to. Something inside them insists on it, which is why you hear stories of stars demanding that they be given other character's funny lines, or songs, or whatever. Robert Preston tells a story that illustrates this peculiar psychological make-up: "A long time ago I was supporting a lady, I won't tell you who, it doesn't matter. We were rehearsing a play, and it went happily until opening night, when a scene we had together turned out to be funnier than she thought, and more than that, the laughs seemed to be coming on my lines. I always thought the scene was funny—I hoped it was anyway —so I was surprised when I found out the next day that the scene was being severely cut. Do I have to tell you I wasn't happy? And neither was the producer, who naturally wanted the scene to stay but didn't want his star quitting either. I went to see her, and we talked about the scene. I tried to tell her that although people were laughing on *my* lines, they were really laughing at *our* situation: it was both of us that they were enjoying. 'I don't care,' she said. 'I don't care what you say. I hate those lines—they're *your* goddamned laughs.' "

A performer obviously does not have to be an actual star to possess insistence. Angela Lansbury, certainly a star today, was just as certainly not one five years ago when she was billed after Lee Remick in the short-lived musical *Anyone Can Whistle.* All the same, prior to rehearsal, she suddenly called a meeting of the entire production department. She was disturbed, she said, about the script. Miss Lansbury is both a bright and articulate lady, and for over an hour she held forth on certain missing subtleties of characterization, a certain lack of warmth, a certain symbolic incompleteness in her role. Summing up her dissatisfactions, Miss Lansbury added, after a pause, "And besides, Lee Remick has five songs, and I have only four."

P.S. She got her fifth song.

Is Miss Bergman a Broadway star? Of course she is. And of course she isn't. Bergman was a star. Once upon a time. A movie star. From the years 1946 to 1948, she and Betty Grable were the two most popular female film stars in the world. After her affair with Rossellini, Bergman's career died. She came back with "Anastasia," but in the sixties it turned sour a second time. A leading film executive told me: "Having Bergman in a movie would offer no inducement to do the film."

Then why the advance sale in Manhattan? And why can Betty Grable hold her own month after month in *Hello, Dolly!* when she can't get arrested in California? Because there is a time lag. The movie audience is generally young, while the Broadway audience is middle-aged, and what the people at *More Stately Mansions* were there to see this year was Ingrid still as pretty as in "Notorious." On the night I saw *More Stately Mansions,* I noticed more people dozing than I had seen all season and more people with field glasses than I have ever seen in any season. Damn near all the people in the entire rear of the orchestra were focusing field glasses to see if they could spot any wrinkles.

Broadway rarely gets film stars of any consequence. Those movie people who do come are almost always anxious to get a film career going again. This season, there were only three performers on Broadway who might have been wanted for leading parts in film work: Sandy Dennis, Albert Finney and George C. Scott. As for the rest: a movie man said this to me of Steve Lawrence and Eydie Gorme, who drew the biggest advance this year: "There's like a curtain across the Rockies, and they're behind it; we don't know who they are out here. They're tremendous in New York. There are four places, really, where they're tremendous: New York, Las Vegas, the Catskills, Miami. But put them in Detroit, you'll hear an echo."

There are good reasons for film stars riding clear of Broadway. First of all, remember that a star wants to be watched by as many people as possible, insists on it. Then too, in the old days film jobs lacked the luster of working the boards. Not so any more, and when you remove prestige, Broadway simply has no way of competing.

A top Broadway name might get 10% of the weekly gross, $250,000 a year, in a hit. (In a musical you can double that, and there *are* still a few musical stars: Gwen Verdon, Zero Mostel.) But even for a musical sellout, that's only half a million a year, and film stars you don't even want command that much. Top movie names get $1,000,000 plus whatever percentage their agents can scrounge. A million dollars for maybe twelve weeks' work. Maybe even 15. And it's hard work too. But it isn't as wearing as 416 performances a year, over and over again.

Another thing: movies are better suited psychologically to the make-up of the star. I think that most stars' happiest life moment is the camera close-up: all that light, all that heat, all that concentration, all on you.

Heaven.

One final reason for movie stars avoiding Broadway: they're apt to be ignored. Here are some film stars who have appeared on Broadway in the sixties, together with the number of performances that their shows lasted: Charlton Heston (5); Rod Steiger (13); Jack Lemmon (36); Kirk Douglas (82); Maureen O'Hara (12). My guess would be that if Jack Lemmon returned to Broadway in 1980, when his movie fans had aged into theatregoers, he'd run a lot more than 36 performances, just as Miss Bergman did. For Bergman was an old-time film star, which made her worth one year on Broadway. But would she pull again? One leading theatre-party lady put it this way: "In a Neil Simon play, yes, but in a drama . . . well, it wouldn't be much fun trying to sell her again in a drama."

Well, who are the dramatic stars, the ones who work primarily in New York? Most of the old ones are, of course, gone. Helen Hayes is now acting with the APA repertory, but her last Broadway show died in 23 performances. The Lunts are retired; Cornell too.

And the new stars who took their places? Well, Jason Robards is a new star. And so is Anne Bancroft. But the two of them together in a show that got a wild rave from the *Times* didn't last 100 performances and lost close to $200,000. Geraldine Page can close out of town. Julie Harris works less and less on Broadway now, and Kim Stanley doesn't work at all; but I doubt that she ever had any personal following to speak of. Probably the biggest dramatic star left is Henry Fonda, but he hasn't had a smash in ten years. And that, *Two for the Seesaw,* was probably due as much to Anne Bancroft as to him.

The answer should be focusing now: there are no Broadway stars. Not in the sense that we meant when we used to say "star": people who drew, no matter what the vehicle, and more often than not toured after the Broadway run, cleaning up on the road. There are various combinations that will attract an advance sale and still some meaningful single names: Robbins, Champion, Simon, Nichols, Lerner, Rodgers. But these are the creative people. The perennial performers aren't pulling any more.

Broadway can still create stars. One millionaire manager said this: "Even today you can make it here faster than anywhere; look at Streisand, look at Uggams. Uggams had God knows how many years on the 'Mitch Miller Show,' and who cared? Then she comes in with a bomb like *Hallelujah, Baby!* and suddenly the networks can't wait to sign her up for specials. Look at Matthau—fine actor, around for years—nothing. Then *The Odd Couple,* and you can't touch him now. You can make it in movies alone, of course, and sometimes out of TV. But to make it big and make it fast, nothing beats Broadway."

Will there ever be Broadway stars again? I don't think so, at least not until the stage can find some way of competing with films. One active producer was irate that Albert Finney came to Broadway for only eleven weeks with *Joe Egg.* This is somewhat shortsighted; *Joe Egg* more than made its money back in the time Finney was here, and he would never have come if he'd been forced to sign for 18 months, or 24. The limited engagement is a promising thing. If major stars can be induced to play Broadway for ten or twelve weeks, I think it's the best that can be hoped for; the star doesn't lose too much money, he can exercise his theatrical muscles, and he won't go mad in a long run.

Of course, there will always be some film stars who return. Paul Newman acted here a few years back; perhaps he will again. And George C. Scott was here this past season. Scott is, as has been indicated, very much his own man. Many movie people simply don't understand him. One of them said, "Coming to New York for a year—it's crazy. I tell you, you don't know how much money it cost him doing the plays." Somebody once asked Scott why he had come to the theatre for the year instead of continuing with films. Scott mused for a while on moviemaking, on dealing with cameramen and make-up men and set designers and decorators and costume designers and producers and directors. "I came back," he said finally, "because I just got tired of having fourteen fucking neurotics between me and the people."

PREMIERE PERFORMANCE, NOVEMBER 5, 1967

ANTA THEATRE

GENE PERSSON
presents

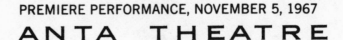

THE TRIAL OF
LEE HARVEY OSWALD

A NEW PLAY

by AMRAM DUCOVNY and LEON FRIEDMAN
based on an idea by HAROLD STEINBERG and AMRAM DUCOVNY

with

CLIFTON JAMES   RALPH WAITE

and

JOHN GERSTAD · GLENN KEZER · WILLIAM LEACH
DAN PRIEST · CHARLES RANDALL
GARRETT SAUNDERS · ANNE SHROPSHIRE
DOUG STARK · BARTON STONE · LOUISE STUBBS

and

PETER MASTERSON

as

LEE HARVEY OSWALD

Lighting designed by	Settings by	Costumes designed by
JULES FISHER	ROBIN WAGNER	THEONI V. ALDREDGE
Art Director	Associate Producer	Bruitage by
LEWIS ZACKS	JAY FUCHS	JOSEPH RAPOSO

Directed by TUNC YALMAN

La Vida

One has to be very precise about this: at seventeen seconds after two minutes after nine o'clock, on Sunday evening, November 5, 1967, on the stage of the ANTA Theatre in New York City, Peter Masterson began to speak. He was playing the title role in *The Trial of Lee Harvey Oswald*, and he had been seated on stage since 6:58, before the opening-night audience was allowed into the theatre. As they filed down the aisles, the curtain was up and Masterson sat alone on stage, quietly staring out at the people, looking very clearly like the alleged assassin of the late President. At 7:22 the houselights dimmed but a spot stayed on Masterson. A minute later, the play began. The first act ended at 8:17, and at 8:38 the second act started. Masterson was seated as before, silently listening as various actors playing witnesses made various statements and accusations from the far side of the stage. Then, finally, at 9:02:17, he stood up and delivered a 20-minute speech, as Oswald, explaining that man's actions around assassination day. By the time he stood to speak, he had been sitting there waiting for more than two hours.

The wait, of course, had been a good deal longer—ten years and then some longer. For it was sometime in 1957, during his senior year at Rice University, that Masterson, without ever having per-

formed in college or before, decided not to become a lawyer but to
come to New York instead and learn to act. Even today he doesn't
really know why he made the change; he just decided to do it. And
it took ten years before he got to say much in a Broadway theatre.

Before his watershed decision, Masterson had grown up mostly in
Angleton, Texas, 50 miles south of Houston. Angleton is a town of
3,000, and Masterson's father was mayor of the town and apparently
a pretty good country lawyer. He was offered a seat on the Texas
Supreme Court, which he turned down, because he liked it where he
was.

Masterson liked Angleton too, and still talks a lot about it; there
are very few things you can mention that didn't also happen in
Angleton. Sometimes the conversation will be going along on some
obscure subject—maybe dog sledding—and he will say, "There was
a dog-sledding contest one day in Angleton when I was a kid." Or,
"A couple of people from Angleton tried to swim the English Channel once; they practiced a lot down in the Gulf around Houston,
and they figured that they had the distance pretty well whipped.
But when they got to Bristol, they blew it, because they hadn't figured on how cold the Channel was." It is very difficult to know how
much of this to believe, or even how much of it he wants you to
believe, because Masterson is soft-spoken and deadpan and generally
doesn't kid much. This also makes it hard to tell when he is playing
devil's advocate, which he loves to do. "I was reading this book on
penology the other night," he will say, "and this expert who wrote it
thinks that torture should be restored, and I think he's got something." This kind of remark, tossed off, tends to start arguments,
and Masterson is good at that; he majored in history at Rice while
he was still planning a legal career. He had wanted to write since he
was twelve, and he won a college playwriting contest, and perhaps
that drew him toward the theatre some; he really doesn't know. His
chief exposure to acting was from television, the so-called golden-
years period. From all accounts, his growing up seemed normal
enough; he loved sports, and still does, and made high school all-
Conference in both football and basketball. He weighs the same
now as he did then, 155 pounds, and stands a little less than 5 feet 10
inches.

After graduation, he took a job for six months with Bob Mosbacher, a brilliant sailor and the younger brother of the defender of
the America's Cup. (Sailing is probably the thing Masterson does
best in this world: he crewed for Mosbacher in the Scandinavian

Gold Cup championships, and they won, the first Americans ever to do so. Masterson went back two more years, with another Houston sailor, and was on the winning boat both times. While he was living in New York, he borrowed a boat and won the prestigious Seawanhaka Cup races on Long Island. He has skippered or crewed on any number of winning boats in world class events.) He worked as a land scout for Mosbacher, who is in the oil business. Then he gave it up, and early in 1958 came to New York.

He studied with Stella Adler for two years, taking the first summer off to work at the Alley Theatre in Houston, where he acted not at all but managed to meet an absolutely marvelous girl, Carlin Glynn. She was young and bright and a scholarship student at Sophie Newcomb, but she left college to come to New York to act and then, in December, 1960, gave up acting to marry Masterson. She is tall and pretty in a high-fashion way; she looks, when she gets dressed up, "real chick" as the Texas ladies say. She can also be clumsy. Once, when they had friends over to dinner, there was a terrible crash in the kitchen, and the guests whirled, but Masterson didn't take notice except to explain, "Carlin's making dessert."

Masterson auditioned for the Actors' Studio, doing the part of Valentine Xavier from Williams' *Orpheus Descending*. He was accepted, and the Studio over the years has been his salvation. He works very hard there, and it has helped him to improve as an actor and also keep his sanity.

Because the jobs were not quick in coming. He took over the lead in an off-Broadway play for four months. He did a play in summer stock with Jane Fonda. He played the lead in *Of Mice and Men* in an Equity Library Theatre production. When the Actors' Studio did its productions of *Marathon '33* and James Baldwin's *Blues for Mister Charley*, Masterson played small walk-ons, and he went to London with the company, doing the lead in the Baldwin play there once or twice.

He and his wife lived in what can only be called a slum walk-up west of Broadway in the Forties. There were, inevitably, rats, but not many, and they were mostly small. Masterson has an uncle who is wealthy and keeps an enormous apartment in the famous Dakota apartments on Seventy-second Street. Sometimes Masterson and his wife would get to stay there. Then they would go back to Forty-seventh Street. They liked it better uptown.

But it took money to live that way, and the jobs just were not coming. He is a quiet person, Masterson, and never "on" the way most actors are, and never pushy. He has, as far as can be gathered, none of the ego drives that all actors not only have and thrive on but need. He is quiet, literate, well-read, and he likes that kind of life. For Christmas and birthdays and other occasions, he and his wife give each other books, probably because they can afford them, but then again, they probably would even if they could afford more.

His first daughter was born in 1963. As more and more actors moved to California, Masterson began contemplating doing the same. California was where the work was, theoretically, but he liked New York, and he and his wife used it well. They walked around it, visited it, went to the museums and the galleries as well as theatrical events. Nonetheless, early in '66 he moved to California. The Edward Everett Horton estate in Encino had several small houses on the grounds that rented at reasonable prices. Masterson took one that was available and sent for his family, which by now included a neurotic dog named Friendly, who on occasion gets hysterical pregnancies. The Horton estate was once beautiful, and it is still lovely. But the state of California built a freeway flush against the house, damaging the look of the property somewhat. To this day, the Horton house is probably one of the few mansions anywhere where you can jump out of a bedroom window and land in the middle of a superhighway.

In California, Masterson got to die in a couple of movies that died with him, "Ambush Bay" and "Counterpoint." He also did a little television. Mostly he just went around, constantly being "up for things," which either didn't happen or happened without his services. There was a West Coast version of the Actors' Studio, and he attended classes there as much as he could. But Jack Garfein was in charge of it there, and he is many things, none of them Lee Strasberg.

Then came the rumors of the Oswald part. Masterson never auditioned for the role. Gene Persson, the *Oswald* producer, was married to an actress, Shirley Knight, and she had worked with Masterson at the Studio back in New York. It was she who was really responsible for casting Masterson.

Finally, in February, 1967, he knew he had the part. What he didn't know, and what no one knew, was whether there was going to be a production to play it in. Money-raising was terribly hard, terribly slow, and for a while it looked as though the production simply would not get on. Doing nothing in California throughout the spring, Masterson waited. It was a hard time for everyone, wife, dog and two daughters now. The part, if the play happened, was so clearly a break that it made waiting particularly difficult. Then, in late summer, the production was set, and Masterson rented his house and packed up his family. On the drive to Texas both his kids came down with what looked like bronchial pneumonia. The family rested up in Houston, and Masterson took one day to go to Fort Worth and look up Lee Oswald's mother. He never told her why he was interested, but his interest was clearly genuine, and they chatted for a while about Lee.

Masterson arrived in New York and stayed with friends while looking for a place to rent. This is always difficult for itinerant actors, because they never know how long they are going to be employed. But one day he ran into a friend who had a friend who was going to California; Masterson rented the apartment and sent for his family. On September 21, the *Times* ran a little squib saying, MASTERSON TO PLAY OSWALD. The article, all of 37 words long, said that the play would open November 16 at a theatre to be announced later. This was obviously a bad sign: most plays have been booked into a theatre seven weeks before they open; the fact that this one didn't have a theatre yet meant they were still scrambling.

Eventually the ANTA was taken on what is called an interim booking. A play has the theatre booked, but until that time, the theatre is free to house another play. The difficult thing about this interim booking was that *Oswald* was due to open in the middle of November, and the permanent booking, *Spofford,* was due less than a month later, meaning that even if the Oswald play was a blockbuster, it would have to scrabble around for a new house on short notice.

Rehearsals began on October 4. The cast read through the play, and the director explained the complex use of projections and music that he wanted. "I think it might work very well," Masterson said after rehearsals. "Visually, it's going to be very nice with the sound." Then he paused: "The play needs something like that."

Rehearsals went along without particular incident. Masterson's wife, who had done some television commercials before leaving for California, went back to her old agency. She borrowed $300 from her parents and bought half a dozen co-ordinated outfits. It was the most complete wardrobe that she had ever had, and soon after she got it, she also got a commercial. The wardrobe mistress for the commercial stopped by the apartment they were renting, in an old building on upper West End Avenue, to check which clothes Masterson's wife should wear for the commercial.

"I'd forgotten how big the rooms are in these West Side places," the wardrobe mistress said as she walked in. (This is a standard New York insult if it comes from an East Sider.) Masterson's wife took the wardrobe mistress to look at her new clothes.

"Is this it?" the wardrobe mistress asked.

"Yes."

"How nice to be so unencumbered," the wardrobe mistress said.

It was a good clean knifing bitch remark. Masterson's wife did her best to look on the bright side: at least it had happened in New York.

Rehearsals continued to be primarily technical, necessitated by the complexity of the production. Nobody was working with the actors much, and Masterson was as quiet and laconic as usual, suffering with the football Giants when Tarkenton overscrambled, rejoicing when Homer Jones turned it on. One weekday he was sitting studying the sports page while his wife made arrangements with a baby-sitting agency. "I'll be back at midafternoon," his wife said. Then there was a pause. "I can't *be* any more specific," she answered, replying to an unheard but obvious question. There was another pause. Then, intimidated, she said, "I understand that you want to book your lady again but . . . oh, all right, I'll be back between three and four." She hung up and returned to cleaning the apartment while Masterson continued with the *Times*. When the phone rang again, his wife took it. "I don't understand," she said. "I told you between three or four; why are you calling me back?" She paused, listening. Then: "I can't tell you any more than I've told you, between three and four and—"

"*HANG UP THIS PHONE!*" Masterson screamed into the receiver, having grabbed it from his wife's hand, bellowing with all his might into the mouthpiece. "*JUST HANG IT UP!*" Then he slammed it down into its cradle. His wife said later that this was the first time the pressure of the play had shown.

For things were going terribly with the production. Previews were supposed to begin on Friday, October 27. They got pushed back until November 1. The opening was due on Thursday, November 9.

Just before previews were to begin, Masterson called up a friend, late. It was a Sunday, and he said, "Hey, did you see the game?" meaning the Giants.

"No," the friend said.

"I just wondered if you'd seen it or not," Masterson went on.

"No," the friend said, wondering why Masterson had called so late.

"They've moved up the opening," Masterson said then. "We're not opening on the ninth. We're opening the Sunday before."

"I wonder why they moved it up," the friend said, knowing it was because they had no money and that on a Sunday a play can open and close the same night if its reviews are bad.

"So we can close the same night if we don't get the *Times*."

"Ah."

"On top of that, my favorite uncle died."

"Well, the Giants won."

"That's right," Masterson said. "It could have really been a bad day."

The first preview of *The Trial of Lee Harvey Oswald* took place on November 1. Masterson was seated on stage as the audience entered, which was someone's literary notion, the point being that Oswald is always in our thoughts, so he should be there when the audience comes in and stay there during the intermission and still remain while the audience leaves after the show. It sounded logical enough, but it was miserable for the actor. Sitting and staring out at nothing for hours is hard enough, but doing it on a stool when you have a bad back is no help, and Masterson has a history of mild back trouble. But that wasn't what really made it hard: what really made it hard was the audience at intermission walking up to Masterson and talking to him and about him as he sat there, unable to acknowledge their presence. "How does he do it?" somebody wondered. "Lookit the poor guy," another said. "Hey, get him a lemonade somebody," a third announced.

Masterson sat impassively through it all. When he finally got to give his speech toward the end of the play, he was fine. After the performance he went out with some friends to a Chinese restaurant for ribs and egg rolls. It was Wednesday, four days before the Sunday opening. "I know I won't be able to watch the Giant game Sunday," Masterson said, "I know that."

What he did not know was that at that moment, in a restaurant across the street, four days before the opening, the producer was firing the director. Now, firing the director is a shattering blow to any company. Firing a director four days before the opening is impossible.

On Sunday, November 5, the drama section of the *Times* had a picture of Masterson and the play he was about to open in. This is a big moment in any actor's life. The caption in the *Times* listed his name as James Peterson.

Though there was no director, the cast rehearsed the day of the opening. After rehearsal, everyone went home. Masterson stayed in his dressing room with a friend, watching the Giants game on the friend's Sony. Mostly they concentrated very hard on the game, but every so often Masterson would go off on some tangent. He talked about two recent dreams. "I dreamed Pete Gogolak kicked a 50-yard field goal that won the game, but he hurt his back badly doing it." The other dream was longer: "I was at a yacht club, a strange one; I didn't know anybody, and I needed foul-weather gear. There was this blue sailboat, and I couldn't get to it [he had been offered a blue boat to sail in the coming Olympic trials]. I needed the gear but everyone was gone, and I couldn't get to the boat." It was quiet in his dressing room, quiet in the whole theatre, actually, except for the sounds of the football game. It was after four by this time, and the opening was set for 7:15. "Hey," he said to the friend, "what the hell do you think those dreams mean? I remember once in Angleton, I was in a football game, and I just knew if they gave me the ball I was going to score. *I just knew.* No way anybody could stop me. I'll never forget it."

"What happened?"

"They gave me the ball; I got creamed at the line of scrimmage. At Rice I was last man on the basketball team, and in this one game we were so far ahead that the coach figured there was no way I could change the outcome; so he put me in. I brought the ball up court, and all the fans—they knew how green I was—started shouting, 'Shoot! Shoot! There's no time, *shoot!*' I glanced around for the clock, but it was over my head where everyone could see it but the players, and now they were really screaming for me, 'Shoot! *Shoooooot!*' So I got to mid-court and let fly all I had, and then I found out there was a minute left to play. You don't know what dumb is until you've stood there at mid-court with your team a mile ahead and you're shooting the ball with a minute to go."

"What happened?"

"What do you mean?"

"To the shot."

"Oh. Yeah. It dropped in."

The Giants game ended, the Giants losing a heartbreaker, and as he started making up, the nerves came. He wore a dark toupee for the part. "It's hard to get the damn thing on," he said. "Opening night it is anyway. Is it on? Is it straight? Does it look like hair?"

At a few minutes before seven, he went out alone and took his place on stage. The play was doomed, and he probably knew it. The audience coughed throughout the first act. When the second act started, the coughing came again, and the sound of it wracked his wife. Then, as has been stated, at 9:02:17, he gave his speech and the coughing quieted and it went well, and there was a burst of applause for him at the curtain call at 9:29.

In his dressing room, there was the usual post-opening chatter. "Well done." "Goddam, Sam, but you are one fucking actor." "I was proud of you." "It was marvelous; really, it was."

"It was fun," Masterson said. "I hope we get a chance to do it again."

The party afterward was held in a sculpture studio on East Seventy-seventh Street. There were reflecting pools on the floor that looked like marble. People kept accidentally walking into them and getting their feet wet, Masterson's wife among them. Backers circulated through the several floors of the gallery, which had two television sets in one large room on the second floor. Masterson never entered that room, staying out in the large central room between the bar and the buffet, talking quietly to anyone who talked to him. The first review, at 10:30, was affirmative; it found the play interesting and worth seeing, and although it had doubts about most of the acting, it liked Masterson. The review was far from a rave, but one backer said, "That's the best review I ever heard from that sumbitch," and hurried out to the bar.

The next review was by Newman on NBC, and he said that the play had no force till Oswald took the stand, and he wished the dramatics had started sooner. "I consider that a very mild criticism from him," a backer said. Another backer turned: "It was *not* a good review, face it." "I didn't think it was so bad," the first backer said. The second backer looked at him: "How much worse could he get?"

Now Leonard Harris was on CBS. He liked it pretty well, but he particularly liked Masterson as Oswald, who, he thought, acted well and sympathetically. Masterson had met Harris earlier in the week when CBS had come to film a few moments of the play, and they had talked awhile. Harris is very bright, and Masterson very much wanted a decent notice from him. When he got it, he was clearly pleased.

Then the wait began for the *Times*. Of all theatrical traditions, this is the most painful, because if the *Times* review is good, you hear about it, but if it isn't, no one says anything; the party just goes on and on until eventually everybody realizes the *Times* must be terrible. Then the party splits and fragments slowly until there's no one left but drunks.

Masterson was told early that the *Times* review was indeed terrible, and so was spared the wait. He made his farewells, thanked whoever needed thanking, and then walked to Allen's on Seventy-third and Third with some friends—a writer, an editor and a director and their wives. They all had hamburgers and beer, and Masterson, knowing full well the production had closed, talked about it. He had played the title role in a Broadway play, just like Sandy Dennis, only, considering everything, it had probably got him little and cost him a good deal of money, traveling in with his family from California. But in spite of everything, he talked quietly and with remarkable coherence about the play—its faults and his— where the production had erred, which wrong turns taken had come back to haunt them all. It was a cogent discourse under any conditions, and under the prevailing ones, remarkable, and people listening must have thought that the mind doing the analysis would have worked well in the legal profession. But he was a professional actor instead, and a good one, and out of work again at thirty-three. There is a saying, "Everybody looks good with a hit." Had *Oswald* been a hit, Masterson would have been over the hump. But the reverse of the saying also holds: no one, but no one, looks good in a flop.

And the Oswald play was, of course, a flop. Not quite as total as Masterson thought that night: it managed to run one more week before closing after nine performances at a $100,000 loss. The following Sunday, Masterson watched the Giants on TV again. No trouble getting the wig on now. He hung around New York after the play was over. "You forget what year it is in California," he said once, and he was in no great hurry to get back. So he stayed, and he read for a couple of parts, but he didn't get them. He did get a part on "N.Y.P.D." playing a rapist. He was caught and jailed in 30 minutes. This was in the spring.

By early summer, he was making plans to go back to California.

PREMIERE PERFORMANCE, NOVEMBER 14, 1967

HENRY MILLER'S THEATRE

under the direction of
Messre. Nederlander

Helen Bonfils, Morton Gottlieb and Peter Bridge

present

EILEEN ATKINS
IAN McKELLEN
IAN McSHANE

in

THE PROMISE

by
ALEKSEI ARBUZOV

Translated by Ariadne Nicolaeff

Scenery by William Ritman

Lighting by Tharon Musser

Directed by
FRANK HAUSER

CHAPTER

16

The Enemy

Any Broadway show may be said
to fall into three phases:
1. The preparation of the script
2. Casting
3. Rehearsal and performance

Keep It in the Family, one of the plays mentioned in the chapter
on Murphy's Law, was probably destroyed during the first phase, the
script preparation. *Dr. Cook's Garden* and *Song of the Grasshopper*
both expired in the last phase—rehearsal and performance—when
communications broke down between the various creative personnel. Which one of the three phases is the most important is a matter
of opinion only. But this much can be said: more shows die because
of miscasting than for any other single reason.

How do you go about casting a play? If a producer is looking for
a star, he generally sends the script to the star's agent, who may or
may not send the script on to the star, who will undoubtedly reject
it. No one ever gets the star he really wants for a play. Don't think
for a minute they wanted Streisand for *Funny Girl* or Channing for
Dolly! or Harrison for *My Fair Lady.*

Generally, what you cast for is a quality. You decide what the
specific quality most basic to the part is, and then try and find an

actor who possesses it. But a problem arises: What is basic? Is a character the charming man who enters in Act I or the sadistic wife-killer he turns out to be just before the final curtain?

Whom would you cast in a light comedy about a successful Long Island financier? Cary Grant? Done and done. Now, whom would you cast in a detective story about a poor, tough, bitter private eye? Bogart. Easy. What if they switch roles? Would you believe Cary Grant as a poor, tough, bitter private eye? You would? You're crazy. How about Bogart in that comedy about the money man? No chance, right? Wrong. He played it, and wonderfully, in "Sabrina."

Meaning that Bogart is a better actor than Grant? Not remotely. If it means anything, it's just that Bogart's quality is capable of en-compassing a wider range of roles. Cary Grant, as he exists today, simply cannot hide the basic quality of being a wealthy, sophisti-cated, successful man. (He may not be any of those things in real life, but the quality that comes across on the screen insists that he is, and it is that quality you cast for.) Grant can tell us he's a poor dumb slob; he can swear it a thousand times over, but we'll just never believe him. Grant doesn't have to play comedy; his quality works in a thriller just as well, as anyone who saw the brilliant job he did, say, in "North by Northwest" will recall. But the successful intelligent man of the world must be incorporated into his role or the piece will end in failure.

The Promise ended in failure on Broadway. In London it had been well received and had run almost a year. The nicest thing the critics generally said of it here was that it was "worthwhile"—a fatal word—and *The Promise* expired in less than three weeks. The two different fates that the play met could easily be accounted for by the differing tastes of the two cities, but I think it was more than that. For *The Promise* was, to begin with, a Russian play, and no more native to one city than the other. It was a three-character play with two of the original actors. And it had the same director and almost the same set as in London. The only change was in leading ladies, and it was because of this miscasting that *The Promise* died.

Briefly, the play concerns the fates of two boys and a girl over a 17-year span. The first act takes place in 1942, when they meet dur-ing the siege of Leningrad. They are reunited four years later in the second act, and in the last act come together a final time, in 1959. They are teen-agers when we first meet them, likable and smart, with dreams. One of the boys wants to be a poet, one an architect of bridges; the girl wants to be a doctor, not just a general practitioner, but a specialist. And during the course of the play, both boys fall in love with the girl. She marries the would-be poet, and they live a long time together, unhappily, until finally, probably too late, he leaves her so that she can perhaps have a chance at something better with the other man.

One of the poignant things about the play is not that the trio don't get what they want, but that they do. The would-be poet, for example, becomes a published poet. But he is dry and academic, and no one reads him. The girl becomes a doctor, but not a specialist. And in the London production, in the last act, when the girl looked at her two loves and wondered where their promise went, it was a moment of inexpressible sadness. But the moment was nothing in New York, because by the time it came, the play had long since stopped making sense. How can the same script make sense in one play and not in another, especially when there are only three actors involved and two of them are the same?

Easy. Because *The Promise*—sprawling through time, with the two boys after the one girl, leaving, then returning, then leaving again, then back, both of them always going and coming and going —only worked because the girl in London had the single basic quality essential to the part. Whatever else the girl might be, *she has to be a mother*. Not a childbearer. *A mother*. She functions as both mother and lover to the two men who spin around her through time; they are orbiting sons, drawing close, moving away, constantly circling. The actress in London possessed that motherly quality, and that quality gave the play focus, made it make sense. In the audience you could feel the need of the two boy-men for her, and you knew why they kept coming back and back and back to her.

The actress who played the part in America—Eileen Atkins—had won best-actress polls for her performance in *The Killing of Sister George,* and God knows she deserved it. But the part she played in *Sister George* was that of a thirtyish Lesbian, weak and helpless, over whom two bull-like ladies struggled. Basically, the part in *Sister George* was that of a child. A child is what Eileen Atkins plays. It may not be what she is, but it's what comes across, and it will probably always be what comes across. A childlike quality has nothing to do with age: there are children of four who are already motherly and women of seventy who come across as children. Eileen Atkins can be a child in any period, any style, any occupation; but she must be allowed to let that childlike quality work for her.

It worked dead against her in *The Promise*. The producers and director had done their casting badly, and skillful as she was in the part, the play disintegrated. You never really knew what was going on, or why; the boys' leaving and returning seemed arbitrary and, in the end, silly.

It wasn't Miss Atkins' fault. The producers and director wanted her. Why did they make such a damaging decision? My guess is that they did it for any number of reasons. First of all, the producers had worked with Miss Atkins on *Sister George* and knew her enormous skill. Secondly, they'd probably gone to other people first: maybe the Harris girls—Julie, Barbara and Rosemary—whom everybody's after these days. Eventually, they had to make a choice: to use the best talent available. Whatever the reasons for their mistake, this much can be said: they didn't do it on purpose.

I went to see Kazan about casting.

Out of the theatre for several years now, he is still regarded as the great casting expert of our time. He has a small suite of offices in the Victoria Theatre building, and even though he was busy finishing the screenplay for "The Arrangement," he talked to me for a while. His secretary led me in from the reception room. Kazan's office is small, and so is he. At close to sixty, he still throws off a magnetism, a strength and virility that are astonishing. At least I think he throws them off. I can't be too objective about Kazan, because most of my early major theatrical experiences in both plays and films were because of him: *Streetcar, Salesman,* "Waterfront," "Zapata," on and on.

He sprawled on a couch and started talking. "As far as casting's concerned, begin with this: an actor can't be good in a lousy part. And unless the part is somewhere in the actor, you're never going to be able to fake 'em through it. That's why you've got to know what people really are, not their artificial egos.

"Actors get trapped in a personality that's partially their own invention. It made them a commodity, it made them salable. You've got to break through that barrier. You've got to find some way to smash the wall that makes you the merchant and them the merchandise. If you can do that, then you have a chance.

"I'm always looking for temperament. Do they have it? Or are they spayed? After actors audition for me and I tell them they're done, I watch them. Does something register? Anger? Frustration? Is there something they're not showing me? Many times I'd call them down then and talk to them. Maybe I'd say, 'You seemed a little upset at the end there; something bothering you? Something you did? Didn't do? What?' You'd be amazed how it comes pouring out of them; actors are like that. Then maybe you have a chance at finding out what their real qualities are, not what they're showing.

"The Actors' Studio helped me. I got to know a lot of actors there. And I used to be an actor myself, so I'm not afraid of them. I know that if they explode today, tomorrow they'll be quiet. A lot of directors mistrust actors; it's as if they're volatile goods whose behavior the director can't control. Women know children: I'm always amazed at their patience. I'd just say, 'Shut up, get out of here,' and there'd be tears. But a woman uses her knowledge, says something, does something, and the whole situation is resolved happily, the whole problem solved.

"Most actors have that false front. That's why I have drinks with them, walk around with them, talk, anything. None of this intuition crap. And I cast people I know. I think you inevitably do that. In 'The Arrangement' here—I've known Hume Cronyn for years—personal friends—I'm casting him for a part in 'The Arrangement' that most people would think I'm crazy to do. But I've watched him over the years. I know something about him that he's never shown before."

I said, "How do you know he'll show it now, since he's never wanted to up till now?"

Kazan looked at me. "I'm not sure. You're never sure. You take a chance. Always."

I thanked him, started to get up.

"Casting is a test of my knowledge of what people really are."

I nodded, starting to daydream now. In the daydream, Kazan was looking at me, then glancing at the open script of "The Arrangement." ". . . Goldman? . . ." he didn't say. ". . . Is this theatre book of yours a major project? . . ."

". . . I don't know . . ." I didn't answer. ". . . Why? . . ."

". . . No reason . . . but there just might be a part for you in 'The Arrangement.' . . ."

". . . For me? . . . I haven't acted since I played Friar Tuck in the third grade, and even then I didn't have lines. . . ."

". . . That's part of what I need . . . inexperience . . . I'm not saying it's a lead, understand . . . but it's a goddam good part, and I think you'd be fine. . . ."

". . . But I've never . . . I mean, I couldn't just jump smack

into movie work without training or anything . . . I'd make a fool
of myself. . . ."

". . . Look, you stupid bastard, why would I want to ruin my own
movie? Now I'm telling you: *you can play the part.* Do you believe
me? . . ."

". . . Yessir. . . ."

". . . Then are you going to continue that theatre book or follow
me? . . ."

". . . You. . . ."

". . . O.K. then, Goldman, get yourself an agent and be on the
Warner Brothers lot this summer. Good-bye. . . ."

". . . Good-bye . . . thank you. . . ."

"You're welcome," his secretary said. "Good-bye." Just before the
door closed I glanced back at some of the posters on the wall:
All My Sons and *Skin of Our Teeth, Cat on a Hot Tin Roof,
Tea and Sympathy,* and I realized that a great part of the casting
skill comes from the strength of the man himself, from the personality that perhaps he made, in part, himself, and perhaps he's trapped
in it now, but if that's what he's selling, I'm buying. Because I'm
thirty-six years old.

And he's Kazan.

Most people, however, are not Kazan, and most parts are not star
parts, and for a combination of the above reasons, most producers
hire casting directors. Casting directors are forced, by the nature of
their work, to see everything: on Broadway, off, off-off, Equity Library productions, etc. Many of them go to the theatre five or six
times a week. Often they won't see all of a show, but they'll stay
until they've seen all the actors. One of them told me, "Sometimes I
have to see nine things a week, and after seeing nine of them, you'd
call them 'things' too." Basically, the reason for hiring a casting director is kind of strange: most theatre people simply do not go to the
theatre. Oh, they see the hits, and if a friend is in something and it's
unavoidable, they see that too. But as a general rule, theatre people
go to theatre remarkably little: over the years, the simple act of attending has become too unpleasant for them.

Alan Shayne is a casting director, at first for Broadway, mostly for
television now. He used to be an actor, then bled into casting work.
He is doing some television producing now as well, and it is not
inconceivable that in a year or two the casting work will be entirely
behind him.

I asked him about his job. "If it's a male part," he said, smiling, "you always start with Laurence Olivier. Then you work down." Shayne is a thoughtful man, well-spoken. "It's really not complicated work. You read the play and you find out the producer's particular needs. Does he need stars for financing? Usually he does. Has he already offered it to stars? Does a star come with the package? There aren't any new leading men and women; we've been watching them for years, and I certainly can't come up with a new idea. If you're involved in trying to finance a play, you know as well as anyone who the leading actors in this country are.

"The point about casting directors is that it is possible, if you see everything, to know more about actors than the producer or director. And your taste, if you have it, is constantly being refined. You've seen the same actor eight times when he comes in to audition, and if he's been fine six of those eight, you know the director is wrong when he says, 'He's no good.' The actor *is* good, and sometimes that can be helpful in assisting the final selection of a cast. But most often, directors want it easy. They'll say, 'Get me X, I've worked with him, he's nice around the set, he remembers his lines and he won't make waves.' "

Shayne maintains an office in the David Susskind complex, Talent Associates (he cast "East Side, West Side" and "N.Y.P.D." among others), and the room is stuffed with files and pictures of performers. Like most casting directors, Shayne carefully keeps folders on which actors can play which types of roles. Following is a partial listing of types within just one category, "Character Actors, Male": Jewish, Hungarian, floorwalker, Spanish, spooks, English, nebbish, tough prisoners, cops, old doctors, accents, David Burns, fifties, forties, *schticks,* leads, classical, judges, old judges.

Shayne also keeps an insane file. Performers are always sending pictures to casting directors, and Shayne, having been an actor, is very sympathetic to what an actor goes through. But sometimes photographs come in that are so horrendous that if you thought about it seriously you'd cry. So, to keep his own sanity, Shayne maintains his insane file: a female impersonator with one breast slightly bulging; a girl blowing bubble gum with the bubble so big it totally obscures her face; 15 amateur cheesecake shots of a homely peroxide blonde; a topless dancer from Frisco with a note accompanying the picture saying she can "shoot, shout or shit"; a wrestler with an idea for an early-morning spot-reducing television show, the gimmick of the program being that every day the wrestler would bound on camera and battle ugly fat.

The day of our interview, there was a knock on his door, and an actor whom Shayne knew was standing there with a writer who worked for Susskind.

"Just thought I'd say 'hello,' " the actor said.

He and Shayne shook hands.

"I'm not really in town," the actor said. "I've just finished a movie, might be pretty good, and I'm heading back to California and the family. There's a couple of things out there and I have to pick one of them."

"Wonderful," Shayne said. "I'm glad it's all going so well."

"It is," the actor said, and as he started to go, he said casually, "Listen, if there's anything you can use me for, I'd stick around."

"There's nothing I'm casting just now," Shayne said.

"Right," the actor said, and then he was on his knees in front of Shayne, saying *Anything! Anything!,*" and he was laughing while he did it, while he put his hands into prayer position as he knelt there. It was all a terrific joke, and the writer friend laughed, and Shayne made a laugh too, only the actor was forty and out of a job. When everybody stopped laughing, the writer and the actor went away.

Shayne sat at his desk a long, long time and shook his head.

Michael Shurtleff has been a casting director for many plays and musicals—*Carnival, Any Wednesday, Odd Couple*—as well as films —"The Sound of Music," "The Graduate." "What my job is really all about is when some actor who's not known gets a role," he explains. "Anyone can make up lists."

Most roles, of course, are cast by the audition system. Usually, auditions are held during the day in some Broadway theatre or other. The creative staff of a play—writer, director, producer, etc.— gathers in the darkness of the orchestra, while up on stage an endless stream of panicked performers come out from the wings onto the dimly lit stage and read parts for a few minutes, usually with the stage manager, who cannot act at all. The director either waits till the reading is done or cuts the actor off at some point, thanks him, and while the actor smiles and exits, the creative staff discusses employment. This process goes on until eventually the parts are cast and the play can enter rehearsal.

There are simply no words to describe the barbarity inherent in the audition system. It is agony. It is also almost totally inefficient. An actor comes out, gives a terrific reading full of bounce and drive, and is hired; seven weeks later the play opens in New York, and he is giving exactly the same performance, only now it isn't so bouncy any more. Some actors audition like crazy and can't act for beans. Some simply cannot audition.

Shurtleff says this about casting: "It's all subjective, but people keep trying to operate as if it were not. In the end, it always comes down to this: I like him or I don't like him." Still, there are ways that an actor can help himself in an audition, and for that reason, Shurtleff gives a class in "How to Audition" at his studio on West Forty-eighth Street. The studio is a long rectangular room with a stage at the far end and half a dozen rows of wooden chairs facing it near the entrance door.

The morning of February 21, Shurtleff was to begin another audition series. Class was to start at 10:30, and at 10:15 a young girl walked in, the first to arrive, eyes tearing from the cold (it was 6° outside). She looked around and said, "It's a good thing there's a stage, y'know?" to a singer-type girl who came in behind her. The singer type almost didn't shrug as she took her place in the back row. The tearing girl, rebuffed, moved silently to the far side of the room and sat. A stunning girl came next, tall, dressed rich, with eyes of movie-star blue. Fourth, an old woman, grey hair in a tight bun. Then a man, beefy, a bartender type. He made his way to the rear corner and sat heavily. He took off his coat, looked around, saw the movie-star blue, and forced a conversation open. It was 10:20 now. Another girl, nondescript, in the doorway. The rebuffed first girl glances at the nondescript. For a moment they look at each other, and then, as the nondescript one enters the room, they begin like intimates suddenly on the same oasis.

Rebuffed: You were in what's-'is-name's acting class.

Nondescript: That's right.

Rebuffed: I remember, you did that thing. You finish? I quit.

Nondescript: Me too. He liked that indicated stuff.

Rebuffed (nodding): He did like hammy things.

Two girls enter together, both blonde, both cute, maybe ten feet tall together, maybe a total of thirty-five years old. Dancers.

First (as they sit): They want me to understudy the other part. You think I can look old enough to play twenty?

Second: Never.

First (coats off now): Well, let's see what's in the paper. (She opens Backstage, not the New York Times.)

Second: Anything exciting?

First: Hey, The Happy Time wants dancers. "Ten to twelve years old." You think I can look young enough to play ten to twelve?

Second: Never. (*They continue to read, seventeen and lovely, already too young and too old.*)

10:25, and the room is filling up. A stunning black girl in a brown pants suit. A boy. A girl. Several boys. More girls. 10:28, and the rebuffed girl stands. "Anyone see a cigarette machine?" she says. A boy offers her a Camel. "A Camel?" she says in amazement. "They still make those? They'd knock me down they're so strong. They're the worst things you can smoke." The boy shrugs, puts his pack of Camels away. "I'll have to go and get some cigarettes I guess," the rebuffed girl says. Actors have a word for what she was really doing; they call it "indicating." It is a term of derision for sloppy, exterior, unfelt work. The girl really was frightened because class was about to start, and so she began indicating about the cigarettes. Everybody indicates. You walk into a room filled with people and you're embarrassed, and you snap your fingers as if you've forgotten something, and turn and exit. When you snap your fingers, you're indicating. If you'd really forgotten something, something important, you'd just go get it. The rebuffed girl started for the door, then stopped and quickly took her seat, because it was 10:29 and Shurtleff was hurrying through the doorway. He pulls a stool over to the near wall and sits, about to begin, when an embarrassed girl runs in, saying, "I'm late, I'm sorry, but . . ." Shurtleff quiets her, saying, "You're in the nick of time," and the embarrassed girl says, "Nick. Nick of—I know him," trying for the joke, but it dies. Shurtleff starts to talk. He is blond and slight, and there is no telling how many hours he has spent in darkened theatres watching actors curdle.

"We're here," he says, "to try to bring into focus what happens to you in class with what happens to you in auditions. I don't think pleasing *them* is what you should concern yourself with; they don't know really what they want. For 'The Graduate' they said they wanted a young Jimmy Stewart type, and they ended up with Dustin Hoffman. Trying to find out what they want won't get you anywhere. *What they really want is you.* I can say this easily, but I know it's hard for you, because you want something." He pauses a moment. Then: "The term we use in this class for the people watching you out there is 'the Enemy.' *Acknowledge that!* That's how you feel about them. It is a war, and they are the enemy. And they tend to be rather humorless. But not as humorless as you tend to be."

A boy comes in late then, mumbling an excuse, and Shurtleff nods, "Hello, Nick," and is about to go on when the girl who tried to make the joke before comes out with, "Is that Nick?" Shurtleff turns toward her. So does everyone else. They're all staring at her now. "Nick," she manages. "You know, when I came in, you said I was 'just in the nick of time,' and I only wondered if that was the 'Nick' you were talking about, the 'in-the-nick-of-time Nick,' you know; you said . . ." But the joke won't play; it simply will not play, no matter how she tries breathing life into it. Scrunching up, she quiets.

"Your conduct at readings is terribly important," Shurtleff says now. "Directors know they're going to have hell with the star, and they don't want it from the rest of the cast. Don't come on apologizing about being late. As a general rule, you are late, but don't apologize. I don't know how many times I've heard, 'I had to take my mother to the hospital' or 'The cross-town bus broke down and I couldn't get a cab. . . .' If you do apologize, there's only one conceivable excuse. Say, 'I'm sorry, I had another audition.' That sets them to thinking about what else is casting and that you must be wanted, and if they ask what you auditioned for, just answer, 'I think it's bad luck to tell.' If they press you, stick with the bad luck. And please, when they say, 'How are you?,' don't tell them. You're always saying, 'Well, I've got this terrible cough, and I can't for the life of me shake it and . . .' The state of your health interests no one. Remember that. Be businesslike, be friendly—they're not incompatible—and get to it."

As he talks, Shurtleff gets a lot of laughs. These are professionals he is talking to, and they've all been late, talked about their coughs, all the rest. And they listen. Carefully. Some of what he says is simply common sense. "Wear the same dress each time you audition for the same role; it's identification, and I think you should carry it through. If you wear a purple dress the first time, wear it again when you're called back. I don't know how many times a director has said to me, 'I thought that girl in the purple dress was coming back,' and I say, 'She was back, she was in orange,' and he says, 'Of course. That's right. Well, she wasn't so good this time.'" And the class nods.

Sometimes they burst in with little stories of their own. A middle-aged woman tells, "I tried and tried to get through on the phone to this TV casting lady, and when I finally did, she said, 'Who's this?' When I told her, she said, 'I'm busy,' and slammed down the phone in my ear; then later she called and had a job for me, and she mentioned the slamming-down-of-the-phone incident, and I put on my sweetest voice and said, 'Oh, please don't apologize,' and she said, 'Shit, I wouldn't apologize to you.' "

It is all fascinating stuff, and there is a feeling of shared suffering in the room. Because they all hate auditions. They should. They're degrading, humiliating, ineffective—and the best system yet invented for casting a play. Unless you happen to know personally exactly whom you want for every part, and each of them loves the part you offer, and they are all available at the same time. There is a chance of this happening. And Mussolini is alive in Argentina.

I don't know if it's possible to indicate just why auditions are so horrid. But say you were a doctor—a surgeon—and you'd spent ten years of your life learning your craft. And then you were called into a room, and there on a table was a lump of clay and a butter knife, and someone out in the darkness said, "Make an incision," and you said, "What kind of incision?," and they said, "We're simply interested in whether you can cut or not," and you said, "Could I study the details, please?," and they said, "There's really no time for that, just pick up the butter knife; we're only interested in the quality of your work now." And you picked up the butter knife and dumbly made a cut, and after that they said, "Ah, that was certainly a very nice cut, yes, a splendid cut; thank you, we'll let you know if we want you to perform." And someone came out after that and led you away. If this happened to you over and over, you might feel that you hadn't quite had a chance to show the full range of your talents. Not only that, but after all the years of learning your craft, you find that no one really gives a damn about the full range of your talents. They just want to know if you can cut clay with a butter knife. Eventually, this might all prove frustrating. And eventually, the frustration might lead to a certain hostility.

"Hostility," Shurtleff said, warming to his central theme. "Recognize your hostility; this is crucial. You are hostile toward the whole audition system, and don't pretend you're not, or it will creep out and ruin you. So take your hostility out on anything except the enemy!

"You've got to remember that the enemy is a poor ulcer-ridden creature sitting in the dark. It's a constant war out there: the director against the author, and the costume man against the world, because he's convinced he's the only man with taste; and the set designer is fretting about whether the actors will get in the way of his masterpiece.

"I remember an actor who had auditioned half a dozen times for a lead opposite a star; it would have been the best part of his life. The seventh time they brought him back, he came out on stage, and the director saw him and said, 'Not yet. I don't want you yet.' The actor got off and waited, and then the stage manager brought him back out again, and this time when the director saw him, he said, 'Get off, I don't want to see you now!' And the actor left again and waited again, and later the stage manager brought him out a third time, and the director said the same thing to him again, 'What's the matter with you? I told you to get off, now get off!' The actor didn't say anything; he just left again, and he waited in the wings for a long long time and finally, when he came back out on stage and the director saw him, the director couldn't believe it, and he said, 'I don't want you. Get off! *Off!*' And the actor exploded. Right then. Right there. He started shouting and screaming at the director, the writers, telling them all just what he damn well thought of them at the top of his voice. And when he was done, he stormed out, and the director turned to me, bewildered, and said, 'I don't know what got into him, but he'll never work in the theatre again and—' "

"*WHO WAS THAT DIRECTOR?!!!*" somebody screamed, and the whole class whirled around—Shurtleff too—and there in the back corner of the room and out of his chair was the beefy bartender type, and underneath the fat you could tell now there was power and—

"Take it easy," from Shurtleff, quietly.

But the actor is beyond that now, and he cannot stop screaming. "WHO WAS IT? THAT DIRECTOR? TELL ME HIS NAME!"

"—sit down," Shurtleff says, still quietly.

"That pig prig—keeping a decent man from making a living—*who was he?*"

"—will you all please look at the hostility," Shurtleff tells the class.

"—I could kill him. I could." And he isn't being dramatic. No, he is being dramatic. But he means just what he's saying.

"—that's going to get you a lot of jobs, isn't it?" Shurtleff says. "Look at you. I wouldn't hire you. Now if you want to know the truth—"

"—what right does he have—"

"—the truth was—"

"—what right does any man have to say who's going to work and who isn't?—"

"—*the truth was*—" Shurtleff emphasizes, and he waits a minute, but he is not interrupted this time, so he goes on. "The director *wanted* the actor for the role. It was the author who didn't want the actor. The director was fighting the author, and the director had arranged for the star to come down and read with the actor, to try and change the author's mind, and the author didn't know this. But the star was late, and if anyone was wrong, it was the stage manager who kept bringing the actor out instead of letting him wait in the wings, but no one had *told* the stage manager what was going on."

Quietly, from the corner now, the beefy man stares at his big hands. "I think that director should be dead."

"Look," Shurtleff explains, "it's a war, but you can't win by fighting them, only by wooing them. I've never seen a situation where I thought an actor was more entitled to blow his top. And I *still* think it was a mistake. Of course people are rude to you in the theatre, but I haven't taken a subway ride in years when people weren't rude to me. Of course you're hostile toward the whole audition system. Don't pretend you're not. But never take it out on the enemy. You lose if you fight with the enemy. Save it for later. Kick a wall. Hit your mother. Shove a friend . . ."

I was watching auditions for a major play of the 1968–69 season. The author was there, and he was American; the director sat a row ahead, very English. The part they were casting was a fair supporting role, a sort of successful young merchant who becomes a friend of the main character, a wise old man.

Actor after actor came out. All of them attacked the part differently. Some were energetic, some suave; some moved around the stage, some stood still. Finally it was lunch time and, a little disappointed, the author said, "We just haven't hit on anybody."

"You wouldn't think it would be all that difficult, would you?" the director said.

"The incredible thing to me," the author said, "is that none of them has the least notion that the guy's a horse's ass."

"Horse's ass?" the English director said. "Does that mean something special here in America?"

"He's not smart," the author explained. "The character isn't smart."

"He's not smart?" the director said.

"He's a fool," the author emphasized.

And now the director, still proper and English as hell, is starting to bristle a bit. "Well, I hardly think he can be such a fool since he's worked his way up from being poor."

"You can be shrewd and be a horse's ass, y'know."

"—he certainly speaks rather well for someone who's so stupid—"

"—that's all put-on—"

"—*doesn't that mean he's smart?*" The director is on his feet now, a big man, bigger than the author, and before the author can answer, the director roars right on with, "I do not think he's stupid; if he were stupid, why in the world would our hero befriend him—tell me—"

"—I'll tell you—"

"—go on!—go on!"

Even the enemy has enemies.

PREMIERE PERFORMANCE, NOVEMBER 28, 1967

CORT THEATRE

King / Hyman / Wolsk / Azenberg

present

BOB DISHY   GABRIEL DELL

in

CARL REINER'S
SOMETHING DIFFERENT

A New Comedy

also starring

LINDA LAVIN

with

MAUREEN ARTHUR

HELENA CARROLL   VICTORIA ZUSSIN

and

CLAUDIA McNEIL

Scenery and lighting by   *Costumes by*
WILL STEVEN ARMSTRONG   **ANN ROTH**

Associate Producers
JACK EDREICH, DORIS KULLER, JANE COHEN

Production Supervisor
JOSE VEGA

Directed by
MR. REINER

17

In Trouble on the Road

Carl Reiner's comedy *Something Different* had its world première in New Haven on October 23. For the first quarter hour, all was quiet in the Shubert Theatre. Then the audience started to laugh. Nothing hysterical—just good solid laughter rolling in toward the stage. By the time the first act curtained, everything was going better than could have been expected.

It wasn't till Act II that genuine hysteria set in—huge laughs, blockbuster explosions coming fast—and by the time the second act was over, the audience was bubbling. Intermission talk was loud and complimentary, and everyone was heading back for the third act before they were officially requested to do so, obviously a good sign. At 10:47 a happy bunch of people sat quietly as the third act opened.

Thirty-five minutes later, stony-faced and angry, they hurried out of the Shubert Theatre, throwing their coats on as they made their muttering way, and the producers, watching them go, were aware that once again Broadway's classic situation was taking place: a show was in trouble on the road.

We all know what it's like: we've read the books and seen the movies. And we all also know that in spite of the fact that the situation is usually treated comically it really isn't funny.

More than anything else, the situation is bewildering. A playwright once likened the problems of being in trouble on the road with those of an inventor, but an inventor with a very specific set of difficulties:

1. The inventor has already made his invention and has discovered in front of God and everybody that it doesn't work.

2. Since what he invented doesn't work, and since he knew (or thought he knew) just what it was he was inventing, he now finds himself in this situation: he is an inventor, and he hasn't a clue any more as to what it is he is trying to invent.

3. Not only does he not know what he's trying to invent, but even if he did know, he wouldn't know how to make it work.

4. Even if he knew exactly how to make it work, he still wouldn't know if anybody wanted the damn thing or not.

Something Different, as it stood after opening night in New Haven, had one thing very much going for it: it was terribly funny. Most comedies are low on laughter; that's why gagmen are brought in out of town. *Something Different* had more than enough laughs to be a hit. (Walter Kerr was eventually to write in the Sunday *Times* that the play had the best laughs on Broadway. Almost all the laughs were already in the show.)

But there were two factors working against *Something Different.* The first stemmed from the simple fact that work on the road is exhausting and requires experience; and here, not only were the author and director both new, but they were the same man. Reiner was handling both jobs.

The second problem was related to the peculiar nature of the play itself, because *Something Different* was a craziness, and I don't think the plot can be summarized, at least not in English. But mostly, the play chronicled the attempts of a playwright to duplicate an enormous earlier success. By "duplicate" I mean duplicate: he literally re-creates the circumstances of his past life. The successful play was written while he was a bachelor living with his mother, writing in his mother's kitchen with his mother harassing him. So in the first scene of Reiner's play, the writer gets the old kitchen together. Except that now he is married and living in a fancy New York suburb with twin sons, one of whom is Negro. (I told you it was a craziness.) His wife is upset at the fact that her den is turned into a replica of her mother-in-law's kitchen, and she becomes more upset in the second scene when she is forced to try and become a duplicate of her mother-in-law, fright wig and all. But the wife is a failure as his mother, so the playwright calls an employment agency to see about renting a mother. In the meantime, he has ordered some cockroaches from a local exterminator because his mother's kitchen was loaded with them. The exterminator arrives with the cockroaches and almost immediately begins an affair with the playwright's wife. The exterminator isn't really an exterminator; he is actually in the pest-control business. He feeds the bugs, keeps them warm, and that way they don't bother anybody. He doesn't kill anything because he believes in the commandments of his mother, a famous religious leader. The playwright has never heard of her and wonders why he hasn't, if she was so famous, to which the exterminator answers that she had rotten public relations. "Give the old lady a chance; if she don't make it in 1,500 years, then start hollering fake."

The above is intended only to indicate the kind of play and kind of humor Reiner was trying to shape. The second act, the funniest, was taken up with the hiring of the mother. Eventually, the playwright chooses a Marilyn Monroe type to play the part. Jealousy is created between his wife, who is involved with the exterminator upstairs, and the playwright, who is involved with his "mother" in the kitchen. The madness builds, and in the frenzy, the playwright is able to begin creating again, and the new play is written.

The first two acts took place in the den/kitchen of the estate in the suburbs. The third act takes place in a theatre, with the playwright, his wife and the twin sons sitting in a box on stage and commenting on the play that the playwright has written. In other words, a play within a play. And this was where the trouble came. Because the character's play was supposed to be a titanic disaster, an *avant-garde*-type thing, serious and bad, while Carl Reiner's play was supposed to be funny and good. To complicate matters even more, both plays were called *Something Different*.

Everyone involved with the production knew going in that the third act was going to be where the trouble was, but no one knew how to go about fixing it, making it work. Now, with two acts loaded with laughs and a third act that brought forth only audience hostility, they had to try and come up with an answer. Reiner rewrote constantly in the days following the New Haven opening, and new sections of the third act were thrown in as quickly as they could be memorized, but they wouldn't come to life; they all just kept lying there. The Boston opening was just a few days off, and the Boston run was going to be disastrous financially if the notices were bad; there wasn't much advance, and if business for the three-week

Boston run was terrible, the show would be almost broke. The New York rumors were already out and winging: the show was set to shutter out of town. The third act—the third act was killing the show, and no one could figure out how to make it play.

So they cut it.

That may not sound like much, simply cutting an act entirely— whap! like that and it's gone—but when the news got back to Broadway, no one could believe it. Manny Azenberg, one of the producers, said, "People are stunned. I've been getting calls all day: '*How can you cut a whole third act?*' I have to explain to them that we're doing an entirely new thing; we don't rewrite, we just excise. In Boston we're going to cut the second act. We've scheduled a week of previews back in New York; that's when the first act goes. We're going to open with just a curtain. If we get the notices, we'll have a helluva chance."

They didn't get the notices in Boston, but they didn't get bombed either. All the critics, no matter how they felt about the play as a play, forgave it a lot for being so funny. Elliot Norton called Reiner a "nutcake" and said the play was plotless and planless and sometimes witless, but on its own terms often idiotically funny. And he loved the actors, who "maintain an unparalleled uproar during both of the two surviving acts." (News of the third-act excision had obviously preceded the play.) Audiences liked the show now. Business was good and kept getting better, proof—as much as anything ever can be in the theatre—that word of mouth was favorable and the people were leaving happy.

But the show was still in trouble. As one of the stagehands said, "There is no way to make it a solid play because it's not a play; it's just funny. If they say that, we'll be fine in New York." All the shows in Boston were in trouble at the time—*How Now, Dow Jones* and *How to Be a Jewish Mother* were trying out there too—and late one night, musicians and stagehands from the shows got together for an all-night poker game. They were commenting idly about the various difficulties their shows were in, when someone asked if any of them, in all their years of experience, had ever worked a show they knew was good when it was out of town. They all immediately said "no." I suppose the point is simply that out of town every show is in trouble. George Abbott, who has been involved with a flat 110 Broadway productions, was asked once if he had ever had a show that was solid from the start. "One," he said "a little comedy called *Kiss and Tell.*" One out of 110 is probably an accurate Broadway average.

Reiner seemed to be holding up remarkably well when we talked after a matinee in the middle of the Boston run. We walked back through the November cold to his suite at the Ritz. He is, from all accounts, a genuinely kind man, and for someone who is both a comic and an actor, surprisingly quiet. (He told his cast on the first day of rehearsal that he had only screamed twice in his life; he couldn't remember the first time, but the other was when he yelled at Shelley Winters. And, he said, any man who yells at Shelley Winters can't be all bad.) He looked well and his talk was full of spirit, a lot of it engendered by having the curse of that third act off his back. "It was such a relief to drop it; I wrote three different ones in New Haven. In the last one I just had the actors standing dead silent on stage for two minutes—you don't know how long two minutes is till you have your actors standing silent on stage that long—and then I had the curtain brought down, and the playwright says to his wife, 'Well, how do you like it so far?' The audience screamed at that, and then I brought the curtain up, and one of the actors coughed, and the playwright grabbed his wife and said, 'You hear that cough? I wrote that!' But the rest was murder. I was killing myself trying to make it work, and Joe Stein said, 'Drop it'; Joe Mankiewicz said the same thing—'Lose that third act'—because, he said, no one had ever successfully done what I was trying to do, intentionally and consciously write a bad play and have an audience like it. Did it feel good when it went."

.When we got to his suite, he relaxed in an overstuffed chair and talked quietly and calmly about what he was going through, almost as if he were on vacation. "I thought the script was done. Really. I did. I'd written it four or five times; it was done. Before rehearsal, I actually believed the script was in perfect condition, can you believe that? Was I wrong."

How did he feel about directing and writing both at once? "The directing doesn't bother me. We hired very creative actors, and they contribute a lot; we did that intentionally. 'Be creative,' I told them. 'I'll take credit for your work.'"

What about freezing up—which happens a lot to writers on the road—did that bother him? "That hasn't happened yet; I don't know that it will. Usually, if I start characters talking, I know someone will talk back. If someone says, 'Hello,' someone else will say, 'Hello' back, 'Get out of here,' something."

Reiner's daughter was coming up for dinner, so I wanted to give him time to rest. Not that he needed rest. It was extraordinary the way that this man, on his first time out, could not only write a comedy but also direct it and keep his sanity—all three at once. I muttered something to this effect and got up to go.

"I guess I'm holding up pretty well," Reiner said, and he started to see me to the door. "I believe that." He walked with me until we passed a large mirror. I continued past it, and he started to, but then he stopped and stuck out his tongue. He pulled it back in, then stuck it out again, and with it out advanced toward the mirror, studying intently. "Ever burn your tongue?" he asked me.

"You mean like after hot food?" I said. "Sure. On pizza all the time."

Reiner shook his head and studied his tongue again, more intently now. "I don't mean a burned tongue like your tongue is burned, or anything. Not like that. Not that kind of burned tongue. This is another kind. Actually, it's not really a burned tongue at all, it's a vitamin deficiency. You ever have that?"

I said I hadn't.

"It's really raw," Reiner muttered, his eyes nearly crossed now as he continued his tongue scrutiny, moving right up next to the mirror. "Every time I move, it feels as if I'm scraping my tongue, it's so burned. Only, like I said, it's got nothing to do with a real tongue burn; it's Vitamin A, the doctor said. I'm short on Vitamin A. Who would have thought you could have burned your tongue so that it hurts like this just by being a little low on Vitamin A?" I thanked him very much and left him with his tongue.

One way or another, the pressure shows.

On the last Thursday night in Boston, the production came together. Everything worked—the funny stuff was funnier than ever—giving the show such momentum that the stuff that didn't work didn't matter. But working in Boston and working in New York just aren't the same, and on November 20—the night of the first Broadway preview—everyone involved was nervous again. The audience laughed a lot, but opinion was in no way unanimous. I swear the following is true: after the first act, two people seated in different groups near me said at almost exactly the same time, "That's one of the best acts I've ever seen," and "There's no excuse for that; it's one of the worst things I've ever seen." Pacing behind the audience were the producers. "Suicide time," one of them said as the audience left for the night.

Saturday night, November 25, was three nights before the opening, but Clive Barnes of the *Times* came that night. It was a terrific performance. The audience—real paying people—laughed, and the actors were splendid; no one had told them Barnes was coming. In the darkness, along the sides of the house, the publicity staff and various managers and producers crept in silence, peering toward Barnes to see if he was enjoying himself. It was, as one of the producers told me afterward, "a fucking outrage—grown men with field glasses trying to see if one guy is laughing or not."

Opening night was Tuesday, the 28th, and the curtain that went up at 7:40 saw a much different show than the one that had started in New Haven five weeks before. Now the play was sort of about a lot of things but not really about much of anything. It still concerned a writer and his efforts to re-create his ideal working conditions, and he still hired his mother while his wife went wild upstairs with the pest-control man, so it was possible to make a certain amount of sense out of the proceedings. But actually, all the show was, was funny. Blockbuster funny. They had the laughs, but that was all. The laughs had sustained them in New Haven, had kept them breathing in Boston, seen them through the week of previews in New York. But the play wasn't long on character, or pith, or Aristotelian beauty.

Now, suddenly and horribly, on opening night, the laughs disappeared.

No one knew why. No one knows why yet. But for some cockamamie reason, after weeks of funny rehearsal and weeks of funny performing, the show wasn't funny. It had been funny all week in previews, so it wasn't that the show was too clutzy for the sophisticated New York audience. But whatever the reason—tonight, the night, the only night, the night it was all done for—it was done for. Titters they had. Mild amusements. Some laughter. But the blockbuster moments were gone. The play had always started slowly, and it wasn't until ten minutes into the first act that the first house shaker happened. Usually the moment was good for 15 seconds of showstopping laughter, sometimes 20. Tonight, it went for seven. And just as when the big moments go bigger than usual, they help the weaknesses, so when they don't go as well as usual, the weaknesses swell arthritically.

Curtain was at 9:29, and afterward there was a party at a restaurant on Lexington Avenue, Downing Square. The backers were there and friends of the production, and the actors also came, but gradually, as eleven o'clock approached, most of the powers in the play left for the Sardi building and the Blaine Thompson advertising office, where the traditional vigil is held on opening nights.

Several rooms of the offices were used, and there was champagne,

Chivas Regal Scotch, sandwiches, coffee and Danish. By a few minutes after eleven it was known that Channel 5 TV was a categorical
rave and the *Daily News* a categorical disaster. And from somewhere, though no one knew exactly where, came the rumor that the
Times wasn't good. Reiner waited for the next TV reviews, as did
Alan King, one of the producers. Twenty or thirty people moved
around the rooms—producers, wives, ad men, publicity men. "We
have to sweep the TV, that's all," somebody said. There were two
TV sets in different rooms, flicking to different stations. The three
reviews come on at no set time on the three channels, 2 and 4 the
most important, and 7.

Finally, Channel 2, with Leonard Harris saying: "I had hoped for
Something Different from Carl Reiner. It wasn't there."

Reiner, listening, muttered, "That's too bad."

"It's not the end of the world," someone told him.

"Oh no?" said Reiner.

Suddenly Edwin Newman was on Channel 4 with, "*Something
Different* is a play about a playwright who cannot write a play.
From the evidence tonight, neither can the man who wrote *Something Different.*" Newman went on to say that the show was "cheap
and vulgar" and that "each complication in the so-called plot makes
the heart sink."

In the room, Reiner turned to me and gestured to my notebook:
"Put in there, 'Shit goddam,' " he said. "Say, 'Shit'; the author said,
'Shit.' "

On the television, Newman was finishing his notice now. "I
should add that the people who produced *Something Different* put
on *The Impossible Years* a couple of seasons back. I thought that
was awful too, but it amused a lot of people. Edwin Newman, NBC
News."

After Newman's *Impossible Years* mention, the atmosphere in the
room, which had been despair-ridden, became unendurable. "He
had to give us a little extra," somebody said. Alan King, who had
starred in *The Impossible Years,* sat absolutely immobile. All of
those involved in *The Impossible Years* knew now what a dreadful
thing it had been; and they all had cared for the Reiner play. Getting this double blow, the bad notice *plus* the nasty remark from
Newman, crushed them all: none of them was prepared for the gra-
tuitous cruelty.

(Only it wasn't cruelty. At least Newman hadn't meant it that
way. He was aware that a lot of people were laughing—even on that

terrible opening night, the play had some laughter—and he was trying to tell his viewers that if they had liked *The Impossible Years*
they'd like *Something Different*. Newman was doing his best to be
fair, to be nice. He had no possible way of knowing that his remark
was going to bring tears.)

Now Channel 7 was on: "The funniest show to hit Broadway this
year."

"That man's a liar," Reiner said to the screen.

At 11:30 the news programs were done. "When do we get the
Times?" Reiner asked.

"Maybe ten minutes," an ad man told him.

Everybody tried to talk as they waited, grouped around the various phones in the various rooms, waiting for someone to phone in
from the *Times* building. At 11:37 the phone rang, and everybody
grabbed and listened, but it was a false alarm, not the *Times*. Now
the people didn't even bother talking. They just sat and stood, waiting, the silence deadly. At 11:46 the phone rang again, and everybody jumped and grabbed for receivers, and this wasn't the *Times*
either.

"Shit," somebody said.

It was all riding on the *Times* now. There might have been a
chance before to get by with a medium *Times* review plus the TV,
but now it was a rave or nothing. And probably it wasn't Barnes's
kind of show; but then, he had seen it on a good night, an honest
night, a night with real paying bodies in the house, not a theatre
full of professional press who got in for nothing. So you couldn't tell
about Barnes, not really, not for sure.

At 11:52 the Barnes review was known, and it was—as rumor had
had it—bad. The show was clearly doomed, which was a shame. I
saw the show a lot—all of it five times, some if it more—and it never
failed to make me laugh. And Reiner seemed a decent man and I
like the producers, so I will remember the show.

But what I will remember longer was the reading of the *Times*
notice over the phone. You must remember that the people listening
were all literate and brighter than most, and the actors were a
bright group too, and no one has ever accused Barnes of being
stupid; all these bright people had put all their bright effort into
this one show, and another man had written a review of it. I
don't know who was reading the review over the phone from the
Times building, but he was not literate, not remotely; he could
barely read at all—he kept stumbling, reading through commas and

periods, not making sense, then starting over and misreading yet again and going back, and as whoever he was read on, all these bright men were clutching the phones, trying desperately to make sense of it all, the jumble of it all, this final incoherence coming in over the phone, high in the night in the Sardi building. . . .

PREMIERE PERFORMANCE, NOVEMBER 29, 1967

THE PLYMOUTH THEATRE

THEATER 1968

RICHARD BARR   CLINTON WILDER

presents

BARBARA   BARRY   BEATRICE
BEL GEDDES   NELSON   STRAIGHT

in

EDWARD ALBEE'S
EVERYTHING IN THE GARDEN

from the play by GILES COOPER

with

ROBERT MOORE

TOM ALDREDGE	CHARLES BAXTER	WHITFIELD CONNOR

AUGUSTA DABNEY	M'EL DOWD	RICHARD THOMAS	MARY K. WELLS

Setting by
WILLIAM RITMAN

Lighting by
THARON MUSSER

Directed by
PETER GLENVILLE

18

Homosexuals

The use of money is the theme," said producer Richard Barr. Playwright-adapter Edward Albee said it was more than that: "This is a condemnation of upper-middle-class America. I want this to be a WASP indictment. The theme is morality." Is there a conflict here? And in any case, what is *Everything in the Garden,* Albee's Americanized version of Giles Cooper's English play, really about?

Act I: a suburban couple is having trouble. Money trouble. They smoke a brand of cigarettes they don't like so that they can save the coupons. Their young son is away at prep school. They bicker: Should she take a job? She says yes; he is dead set against it. A friendly neighbor, a bachelor, ambles in and addresses the audience. Are they going at it about money again? he wonders. It really is too bad. He himself is rich, having inherited money. An Englishwoman arrives and talks privately with the wife. The Englishwoman has heard that the wife might like a job. She takes out a lot of cash, offers it to the wife. Eventually, the wife realizes that the English-woman is a madam and wants her to whore two afternoons a week in New York City. The wife is furious. The Englishwoman-madam calmly starts to tear up the money. The wife stops her. The madam goes, leaving behind some of the money. The husband, who has been out buying inexpensive liquor, returns. In a while, the wife suggests they go to dinner somewhere expensive. Can they afford it? the husband wonders. The wife says she has been saving a little out of housekeeping expenses. The audience knows she intends to use the money the madam left and that she will indeed take up the madam's offer.

Second scene: six months later. A package arrives for the husband, no return address. The package contains 49 $100 bills. The husband is staggered: Who in the world could be sending him money? He tries to figure it out with his wife's help, but they come up with no one. The rich bachelor ambles in, sees the money. He suggests they give a party that night to celebrate, and the couple agrees. The bachelor leaves, the wife goes to invite people, and the husband, looking for cigarettes in his wife's purse, finds more money. He confronts the wife and finally she admits it: she has been whoring two afternoons a week. In the midst of the scene, their son comes home. They send him upstairs and their fight builds in violence. He calls her "whore" and "whore" again, but there is to be a party that night, their friends have been invited, and it's too late to stop them from coming; so the act ends with the upset husband helping to make party plans.

Act II: the party. Three couples come. They are anti-Negro, anti-Semitic. The young son of the host and hostess, filled with a liberal prep-school outlook, innocently makes remarks that go against the guests' beliefs. His father, angry, sends him upstairs. The madam arrives in the midst of festivities; she has problems with the law and must stop her New York activities. It turns out that all the wives at the party are whoring for her, and all the husbands know it. The wives are sent to the garden; the husbands and the madam decide to find a place in the suburbs to carry on. The wives return. The rich bachelor ambles in, drunk. He remembers the madam from London. He realizes that she is a madam and all the women are whores. He starts to leave, but the madam has him stopped because he'll talk. The husbands kill the bachelor, take him out to the garden and bury him near the cesspool line. The guests then leave. The husband and wife sit on a sofa and stare out. Curtain.

"The use of money is the theme," said producer Barr. Said playwright Albee, "The theme is morality." There is also something else at work here, something hidden, as it so often tends to be on Broadway. This play makes three central statements:

    1. All wives are whores.

2. All husbands are panderers.

3. The only wisdom lies with bachelors and young boys.

In other words, *Everything in the Garden* is as clear a statement of the homosexual mystique as one could hope to find.

Why or what homosexuals are is not to be taken up here. Is their problem—if problem it be—biological, or purely mental, or something else? This is something beyond any knowledge of mine, and, I think, everyone's. A militant Lesbian said recently: "Anything you say is all supposition: *the research has not been done.*"

This is a difficult chapter to write because of the necessity of being "hinty." It is perfectly all right for me to come out and say that Marcel Proust was a homosexual, but that is because he is dead. The living homosexuals, the ones who inhabit the world of the arts and, particularly for this discussion, Broadway, are not about to be named. Around the theatre, there is a general knowledge about most of the homosexual community, but so many are married, and so many of those who are married have children, that it's almost a case of "only their hairdresser knows for sure."

Generally, the homosexual doesn't have to hide quite as much as he once did. Like the lot of most minority groups, his is slowly improving. Not to the point where, for example, a performer or writer can come out flatly and admit it; but dissembling is on the decline. Perhaps this accounts for the opinion of those who feel that homosexuality is increasing. It may be, but another guess would be that it simply is more open now.

One of the reasons put forward for this is that Americans are gradually becoming a trifle less hypocritical, a trifle more sophisticated. Another reason is that various people of import, opinion makers if you will, enjoy the company of homosexuals. Princess Radziwill, for example, is rarely without a homosexual, and her sister, Jacqueline Kennedy, has her court homosexuals too. In a recent *Cosmopolitan* article naming the men around her, at least four of the men listed are internationally famous homosexuals.

Not only are the opinion makers helping the homosexuals; various national magazines and newspapers are involved also. You don't even bother to talk about *Vogue* and *Bazaar:* the proliferation of homosexuals on their staffs has been common knowledge in the magazine business for years. But that's to be expected, since they are in the fashion business, and fashion provides a homosexual sanctuary. (I think that homosexuals, like any minority, tend to cluster: it's easier for them; there is less resistance to them; the tensions are fewer.) What is interesting is a comparison of *Time* and *Newsweek* over the course of a year. This is strictly my own opinion, but *Newsweek* seems to be much more homosexually slanted than *Time*. Example: *Time* referred to Tiny Tim as "the most bizarre entertainer this side of Barnum & Bailey's sideshow," and the tone of their article was not reverent. *Newsweek* raved about him, and in a long article called him "a primitive-sophisticate whose singing is a perilously but perfectly balanced blend of poignant nostalgia and the razor-edged put-on." Another example, and one that probably is insidious: *Newsweek* ran an article on men's jewelry and asked the question whether the wearing of it was effeminate. The answer they printed came from a movie star who said "no," of course it was not effeminate, it was fine to wear it. But the movie star whom *Newsweek* chose to quote is an internationally known homosexual. If everybody in show business knows it, surely *Newsweek* must have known it, so quoting a homosexual as proof that the wearing of jewelry by men is a normal masculine act has to be called a bit suspect.

The Sunday entertainment section of the New York *Times* is also known to be homosexually oriented. Their most celebrated Sunday expert is a famous homosexual, and there has been, at least in the past year, an unusual number of flattering articles about homosexual favorites, many of the stories of no particular news value.

The confusion of roles between men and women is increasingly under discussion today, and with good reason. Several years ago, when a masculine-type photograph of Barbra Streisand, clad mostly in leather, appeared on a national magazine, the observation was made that the appeal of all the current international show-business sensations was based on sexual ambivalence: Streisand looked like a boy, the Beatles looked like girls, and who knew about Nureyev?

This was, of course, less than five years ago, but the two show-biz phenomena who emerged most prominently during the period of this book make Streisand seem as pure as Lombard, Nureyev as defined as Flynn. Tiny Tim, whose career was aided after a long, detailed, praising study of him appeared in the Sunday *Times* entertainment section, is a figure capable of scaring children. I have seen a six-year-old recoil from him on television. Now this may be a disturbed six-year-old, but I'll tell you something: Tiny Tim scares me too. (I think this is one of the most complex problems in trying to discuss homosexuals rationally—we all have feminine instincts and since so many homosexuals are undetectable, it gives us pause. It gives me pause, anyway.) The other communications hero(ine) of the season could only be the product of a homosexual's imagination, and that is Penelope Tree. There has been a move toward glorifying the unappetizing female over the past few years: "Baby" Jane Holzer, who streaked for a few moments through the Andy Warhol sky, was not the kind of creature calculated to set men's hearts pounding. Twiggy, of course, was built like a boy, but the face, when the best photographers in the world got through with it, possessed prettiness. Penelope Tree is really, like Tiny Tim, the ultimate put-on of the heterosexual world by the militant homosexual society. The joke of the Tree child is simply that the success achieved in glorifying homeliness and making "normal" society go along (out of fear of not being "with it") indicates to the militant homosexual just how intellectually impoverished the heterosexual society really is.

There are obviously a considerable number of homosexuals. How many? The *Times* magazine section estimated 4,000,000 men in America. Certain areas of employment have a higher percentage than others, and Broadway is one of those fields.

How many homosexual producers and directors were active on Broadway this past season? The figures about to be given are obviously inaccurate. They are based on talking with both heterosexual and homosexual theatre people, on gossip, on putting two and two together. They are, to repeat, totally unreliable. They are also conservative. The percentage is undoubtedly higher than reported here. (When the statement is made that a show has homosexuals active as producers, it does not mean that all producers are homosexuals. If one out of three was homosexual, it counted as one. If three out of three were, it counted as one.) This is simply an estimate about the number of productions that had homosexuals crucially involved in the upper echelons of power.

Of the 58 productions listed in *Variety*'s year-end survey as either "successes," "failures," "status not yet determined" or "closed during tryout or preview," at least 18, or 31%, were produced by homosexuals. Of the same 58 productions, at least 22, or 38%, were directed by homosexuals.

As I said, these figures are low. I think it would be safe to estimate that in any given Broadway season, anywhere from a third to a half of the producer-director talent is homosexual. The percentage among the playwrights seems somewhat less, but in general the more famous playwrights tend to be associated with homosexuality.

Arthur Miller is the only major American playwright since World War II who has not been associated with homosexuality. He is also the only Jew. He is more than made up for statistically by the large number of Jewish homosexuals who have been major influences on the Broadway scene.

In sheer numbers, then, the homosexual is an important part of Broadway. How important is he aesthetically? Let's put it this way: the homosexual contribution to Broadway simply cannot be over-rated. Many of the best plays of the past 20 years have been written by homosexuals. Most of the major musicals of the sixties have been directed by homosexuals, the songs from most of the hits of the sixties have been written by homosexuals, the dances created by homosexuals, the clothing designed by homosexuals. In musicals, particularly, the homosexual contribution is tremendous: of the ten longest-running musicals of the decade, two, at the most, were accomplished without homosexual contributions in the writer-pro-ducer-director echelons.

The quality of homosexual work, like the quality of heterosexual work, varies. Some producers do not like to work with homosexuals; some producers prefer, if possible, to work only with homosexuals. There are some homosexual directors who distort work and make it clearly homosexual; there are others who don't. There are some pieces of material that they are particularly good for; some they may damage. This is equally true of heterosexual talent.

In general, the homosexual on Broadway, especially the play-wright, has to dissemble: he writes boy-girl relationships when he really means boy-boy relationships; he understands boy-boy rela-tionships, but is forced to write them as boy-girl. It is terribly frus-trating to many of the writers. (Not all: many homosexual writers are not particularly interested in matters primarily sexual. But some are, and they are damaged by the necessity of writing falsely. They are the writers, I think, who eventually tend to become the most vicious of the practicing playwrights, their frustration building, as it naturally would have to.)

As everybody knows, homosexuals lead terribly difficult lives. One homosexual may complain that it is frustrating beyond measure when, returning from a long trip, he cannot embrace his "wife" at the airport, but must go through the frustrating hypocritical gesture of a handshake. This kind of talk may be upsetting to us (we don't like to think about "that kind of thing"), but it often sends homo-sexuals into genuine despair. They are mulattoes in an all-white neighborhood, and it isn't easy.

Look, I am a Jew and I am a novelist, and if a law were passed
that said Jewish novelists were now illegal, I would have to decide
whether I could switch careers or not. If I decided I couldn't, I
might change cities—going where no one knew me—so that when I
used a new name, no one would think anything of it. And I might
have a nose job. Now, all this might make me a better novelist: the
fear, the venom born of being forced to dissemble and live a terrible
and constant lie might bring out positive qualities in my work.

But then again, it might not. Speaking for myself, writing about
only gentiles (otherwise someone might suspect) would probably
affect my work not remotely. But what about Saul Bellow? Or Bernard Malamud? Think of them without Jewish themes, Jewish material, Jewish backgrounds. The work withers; it disappears. And if
they were forced to write only about gentiles, they would be writing
about material they were not particularly familiar with, material
they didn't really want to write about, material that was not crucial
to their psyches, material they were using only because society was
forcing them to alter their artistic life against their will.

Might make a man bitter.

Might make a playwright, if he is a homosexual and forced to
write about heterosexuals (otherwise someone might suspect), become a bit nasty, since the heterosexuals are the ones who loathe him,
harass him, who won't let him be. So he treats heterosexuals vi-
ciously. The married couples hate each other; the woman, with
whom the homosexual tends to identify, is either a gentle dreamer
destroyed by an insensitive man, or a destroyer herself. And the man
is either a stupid stud, hot for a quick roll in the hay, or a weak,
contemptible failure.

Now, since all marriages (heterosexual as well as homosexual)
stand a good chance of being less than perfect, the Broadway audience buys this venom as a reflection of reality. I don't know or care
what Tennessee Williams' sexual preferences are, but when in his
Seven Descents of Myrtle the crucial speech is spoken by a crude
animal male, and the gist of the speech is that nothing exists on this
whole kingdom of earth as good, as meaningful, as fine, as perfect, as
what can happen between a man and woman, I think, well, maybe
Williams is right: a good marriage is certainly a wonderful thing.
But Williams doesn't mean that: he has the character go on to spec-
ify that by what can "happen" between a man and a woman, he
doesn't mean the interplay of character, the growth of understanding, but simply the entrance of the male organ into the vagina. "Yes,
you could come home to a house like a shack, in blazing heat, and

look for water and find not a drop to drink, and look for food and find not a single crumb of it. But if on the bed you seen a woman waiting, maybe not very young or good-looking even, and she looked up at you and said, 'Daddy, I want it,' why then I say you got a square deal out of life, and whoever don't think so has just not had the right woman. . . ."

This may be true. It is certainly a limited world view, but if a man wants to hold to it, that is his right: nothing matters but the sex act with a woman. Fine. But Tennessee Williams is a fifty-seven-year-old bachelor. And he may have a sex life that makes Errol Flynn look like Holden Caulfield, but I have never read Williams' name in print in connection with any woman in any romantic way. I'm not saying he doesn't have them lining up down the block. All I'm saying is, I question his wisdom on this particular point. Stephen Crane wrote a war novel without the experience of combat, and I think writing is not a matter of putting down necessarily what you know but what you can make people believe. I'm not saying Williams is wrong and I'm not questioning his right to his own personal philosophy, but I sure have stopped believing what he tells me about sex.

As far as Broadway is concerned, the three leading experts on heterosexual married life during the past 20 years have been Williams, Albee and Inge, all of them—at least to my knowledge—bachelors, and I wonder if their knowledge of and attitude toward the subject might not be a little limited. And I wish they'd try some other subject matter sometime, because I'd like to see what they'd come out with, since they are obviously skillful, and in the case of Williams, a lot more than that.

All of which is why I think (hope) that one of the most important events of the Broadway season was the blockbuster success off-Broadway of Mart Crowley's terrific homosexual play, *The Boys in the Band*. It would be marvelous if this success started Broadway toward a sexual freedom it has never attained. After all, the homosexual is here, and he's not going anywhere.

It might be nice to know, at last, what's really on his mind.

PREMIERE PERFORMANCE, DECEMBER 7, 1967

LUNT-FONTANNE THEATRE

DAVID MERRICK
by arrangement with EDWIN H. MORRIS & CO., INC.

presents
A NEW MUSICAL COMEDY

HOW NOW, DOW JONES

starring

| ANTHONY | MARLYN | BRENDA |
| ROBERTS | MASON | VACCARO |

with

JAMES CONGDON   SAMMY SMITH   CHARLOTTE JONES   REX EVERHART
JENNIFER DARLING   ARTHUR HUGHES

with
BARNARD HUGHES

and

HIRAM SHERMAN

| *Book by* | *Lyrics by* | *Music by* |
| **MAX SHULMAN** | **CAROLYN LEIGH** | **ELMER BERNSTEIN** |

Based on an original idea by CAROLYN LEIGH

| *Scenic Production by* | *Costumes Designed by* | *Lighting by* |
| **OLIVER SMITH** | **ROBERT MACKINTOSH** | **MARTIN ARONSTEIN** |

*Musical Direction and
Dance and Vocal Arrangements by*
PETER HOWARD

Orchestrations by
PHILIP J. LANG

Dances and Musical Numbers Staged by
GILLIAN LYNNE

Associate Producer
SAMUEL LIFF
Original Cast Album by RCA VICTOR

Production Directed by

GEORGE ABBOTT

Theatre-Party Ladies

How Now, Dow Jones had perhaps the most maddening name of any show in recent years; it was the Ajax, the white tornado of musical-comedy titles.

It opened in December with an advance of approximately $500,-000, making it one of the biggest advance-sale shows of the year. Usually, when a show has a large advance, there is a predictable reason, and briefly, here are some of the other shows that had large advances and why. *Golden Rainbow* had the biggest for a musical, close to $1,500,000, because of the popularity of its two recording stars, Steve Lawrence and Eydie Gorme. The two straight plays with the largest advances were *More Stately Mansions,* with Miss Bergman accounting for the sale, and *Plaza Suite,* with George C. Scott and Maureen Stapleton buttressing what is probably the biggest portmanteau name in the business today: Simon/Nichols.

So now let's account for the advance of *How Now, Dow Jones.* David Merrick produced it, and that didn't hurt, but you don't spend your money to see David Merrick. The director was Arthur Penn, famous now for "Bonnie and Clyde," but this was before that broke. Penn had never begun with a musical (he had taken over *Golden Boy* on the road), and of his last three plays, only one—*Wait Until Dark*—was not a disaster. The book writer for the show was

Max Shulman, who had done one musical before, *Barefoot Boy with Cheek*, which failed 20 years ago. Carolyn Leigh wrote the lyrics, but lyricists don't matter much unless they're Alan Lerner. The composer, Elmer Bernstein, was a movie man who had never even tried a Broadway show before.

So it had to be the stars, right? If it's not the creative people, what else can it be but the performers? Well, *Dow Jones* had stars, three of them: the legendary Marlyn Mason, everybody's favorite, Anthony Roberts, not to mention that household word, Brenda Vaccaro.

Not only did it own that trio of luminaries, but *Dow Jones* also had a plot: a girl who announces the hourly Dow Jones average has a fiancé who says he'll marry her only when that average hits 1,000. The girl gets with child by another man. So what does she do? She announces the Dow Jones average is now over 1,000, a jump of maybe close to 100 points, just like that.

And everyone believes her.

Not one financial expert in all these 50 states thinks to himself, "Hmmm, a little odd; no sign of even a boomlet, and here's the biggest recorded stock increase in the history of the world. Perhaps I might just check that out." No. Everyone goes crazy and starts buying everything, and the country is on the verge of financial ruin.

With a plot like that, are you surprised there was a little trouble out of town? Director Arthur Penn was the first to go. I spoke to him after he'd been fired/resigned (pick one). He is a talented man, and people wondered why he had got involved with the thing in the first place. He said, "There were, as there always are, a multiplicity of motives. My purpose was to get money to make some low-budget movies—this was before 'Bonnie and Clyde'—and I couldn't think of a better way than doing a musical. I thought the show would be satirical about Wall Street, and I thought the absurd love story would only figure in a trivial way. I think the word pandering is not inappropriate to why I did the show. Whatever was venal in my motives was very well substantiated."

Merrick brought in George Abbott to do what he could with the show. What did Abbott think of the book? "It's a ridiculous premise," he said. A new choreographer was hired, new songwriters were sent out of town for tryouts, and various gagmen were also present on occasion.

The show, for all the effort, was not well received, but because of its advance sale, it ran; not long enough to make its money back, but it lasted the season. This show, with no names and a mediocre score and a premise beyond credulity, had a cool half million in the till the night it opened. Care to guess why?

(The title, that's why.)

That maddening title turned out to be the best money name of the season. It all makes sense—kind of. But in order for it to do so, there has to be a brief discussion of one of Broadway's unique phenomena: the theatre-party ladies.

The *Times* has said that the theatre-party ladies are ". . . agents, mostly women, who act as liaisons between major theatrical producers and the social, philanthropic and educational organizations that book performances as fund-raising benefits." In other words, you have a charity and you want to raise some money for it. So you go to a theatre-party lady, and she books you an evening, say, for *Plaza Suite*. Your charity then takes the tickets and sells them for more than the box-office price, the difference being a tax deduction for the purchaser. Your charity makes its money on the difference between the box-office price and the price you decided to sell your tickets for—$25.00, $35.00, $50.00, whatever. Obviously, from the charity's point of view—since the profit is made on selling tickets—you want to pick a show that's easy to sell. That is why certain shows will come in with enormous advances, while others have none. The shows with large advances are more salable: it is less work for the charity people to sell the seats for the highest possible price, thereby assuring the greatest profit for their charity.

The theatre-party lady makes her money, generally, from the producer of the show, who gives her a flat $7\frac{1}{2}\%$ of the total box-office ticket price of the seats sold. There are almost infinite variations on the producer–theatre-party-lady financial relationship (everything in the theatre is negotiable), but in general the $7\frac{1}{2}\%$ fee is standard. Translated into money, this means that if a party lady sells the orchestra of a theatre that has 800 seats, and, say, 50 seats are kept out as "house seats" (seats set aside nightly for the personal use of the theatre owner, producer, star, etc.), the total of 750 seats at $10.00 a seat is $7,500. The party lady's take will come to something over $550 for the night's work. (If the charity sells the seats for $25.00 each, their gross comes to nearly $19,000, their profit to something over $11,000, the box-office price of the seats having to be subtracted.)

There is an aesthetic reason for going into this mathematical business in such detail: well over 90% of the party lady's business is done *prior* to the opening of a show. Party ladies are, in other words, the single most crucial element in building an advance sale for a show. The reason for the bulk of theatre-party work being done prior to an opening is simply that if the show opens and is a hit, a producer doesn't want new parties because he doesn't want to lose that $7\frac{1}{2}\%$ of the gross. And if the show is a bomb, the charities don't want to book it, because they know they'll never be able to sell tickets at the prices they need to charge.

There is a certain amount of dispute among producers about the exact importance of an advance sale: in any case, it provides a hedge against disaster. Generally, producers feel that it takes from five to seven weeks for the public to forget bad reviews and to give the show a chance to run on word of mouth. "The Sound of Music," the most successful film of all time, would never have existed if the stage presentation hadn't had an enormous advance: the reviews were rotten and the early box-office reaction was terrible. But gradually word of mouth spread, and the show became the only book musical in history to survive terrible notices and run 1,000 performances. More recently, *The Impossible Years* opened to crippling reviews. But the party advance for Alan King enabled the show to run at capacity for a while. By the time the advance was used up, two things had happened: (1) the show had attained sufficient longevity for people to assume it must have something; (2) the word of mouth, for a certain segment of the theatre-going population, was excellent.

Alan King is a perfect example of the peculiar nature of the theatre-party business: when *The Impossible Years* was casting, no one knew really who he was other than that Catskill comic you sometimes saw on the "Ed Sullivan Show" bitching about crab grass. Now the great bulk of theatre-party business is Jewish, and King is a Jewish favorite. No one along the street knew it, so when the play got blasted out of town and still broke house records, everyone was flabbergasted. But King had put in years pleasing the folks on the borscht circuit and in Vegas and Miami—watering spots not unfamiliar to the tribe. When he came to Broadway, they followed. It would be my guess that the percentage of Jews in the theatre-party business is even greater than their over-all audience percentage. Jewish people tend to be (generalization time again) active in charity work, and this may account for their influence in the party business. (Paradoxically, the charities do not want Jewish shows particularly, because they know much of their selling will be to non-Jewish ticket buyers, and the more limited the appeal of the show, the harder the sell will have to be.)

It is undeniably true that most producers will do anything, a-n-y-t-h-i-n-g, to come in with a large advance. It is also true that most of the shows with the biggest advances turn out to be stiffs: *Golden Rainbow, Illya Darling, Mr. President, Breakfast at Tiffany's.* Hal Prince, Broadway's leading musical producer, feels there is a reason for this: "Historically and forever, the show with the big advance is the disaster of the season; I think it's good *not* to know what you're going to see in a theatre. Big-advance shows have a preconceived notion that eventually destroys them. If you've got one of those famous ladies as your star, and the show wants to go one way, against the lady, you're not going to be able to go with the show. You've got to give the public what they've paid all that money down in advance for or they'll hate you. People think that with a big advance they have the freedom to do a show properly, without all the money worries that usually happen out of town; actually, they don't have any freedom at all."

But while there may be disagreement over the importance of having an enormous advance, there is no disagreement whatsoever on the importance of the theatre-party ladies to Broadway. They will not release their annual figures, but the estimates of their total sale ranges from a low of $3,000,000 a season to a high of $10 million. (My own estimate, at least this season, would just about split the difference, $6,000,000 to $7,000,000.) Since Broadway itself grossed about $55 million this season, the percentage of party sales is obviously considerable.

Except it's more than that.

Because, out of that $55 million, approximately $35 million was grossed by holdover shows. And they have comparatively few parties. So the ladies' percentage isn't, say, $6,000,000 out of $55 million; it's closer to $6,000,000 out of $20 million. Almost a third. A terribly dangerous thing.

What's so dangerous? Just this: theatre-party ladies don't care if a show has quality or not; they are only interested in what will sell. This season, for example, I was present while some of them were pushing *Golden Rainbow* to some charity chairwomen, at the very moment that the producer of *Golden Rainbow* was firing writers, postponing openings, all the actions associated with a show clearly in trouble. And, of course, the charity chairwomen who buy from the party ladies don't care if a show is any good either. Their problem is identical to that of the party ladies: Can we sell it easily and quickly? Theatre-party ladies and charity chairwomen have really only two concerns: (1) a product should be immediately recognizable as commercial; (2) the product should be in its proper place at the proper time; cancellations and postponements kill both of them.

In other words, almost a third of the seats sold for new shows this entire season were sold by people who did not care even remotely about the quality of the product they were selling. (This coming season, for example, 1968–69, there are three musicals coming in that will have over $1,000,000 in advance sales, two of which are known to have desperate book trouble, while a third is known to have both an atrocious score and an inadequate director.)

The party ladies are, in general, a much-scorned group. One producer (who has done well with them) put it this way: "They're nothing but a bunch of independent whores—they'll sell anything. For chrissakes, they're practically all Jewish, and one of the shows they worked hardest for this season was about a known anti-Semite, and one of the big shows for next year is about a Nazi Lesbian."

How powerful are the party ladies really? They are in some disagreement themselves on this subject: one of them felt that the basic show selection was hers three quarters of the time, another estimated closer to half, while a third told me the final decision rested almost invariably with the charity people themselves. I think the last attitude is closest to what is functionally true. The party ladies can narrow down the selection; they can even damage a show's value to a charity by whispering of rumored trouble (this usually happens when the party lady is unable to get the date required from the production), but there is no way in this world for them to get a Hadassah group to swing for *The Trial of Lee Harvey Oswald*. And if a charity has its heart set on Ingrid Bergman, that's who they're going to see. This is only logical: all the ladies sell essentially the same service, and if one of them pushes a show to a charity that doesn't want it, and the show is a stiff, the charity is going to enlist the services of a different party lady next season. If there is skill in being a party lady—and there is—it comes in connecting the appropriate charity with the appropriate show, without becoming domineering. In other words, party ladies can help, they can hinder, but make or break, no.

Whatever their actual influence, the party ladies are constantly catered to. A famous director who began his career after World War II said: "When I started out, I don't think I ever met a theatre-party person. Not till the late fifties. Now you audition for them; they're institutionalized. This is terrible, because it presupposes that you have to sell a show to a certain audience with a certain culture, certain interests, certain requirements. Because of the theatre-party ladies, you have a kind of censorship operating in the theatre now."

All musical producers audition their scores for the theatre-party ladies. On June 15, 1967, nine months before it was to open, *George M!* was done for the party ladies in the Belasco Room at Sardi's. A number of charity chairwomen were present too. Joel Grey sat in the back of the room, while up at the front Mike Stewart, the book writer for the show, ran things. There was food and drink and trouble with the air-conditioning. Sweating heavily, Stewart began. "This will take 28 minutes, and I think I ought to tell you what we are that other musical comedies are not, and that is, we are funny and we are terribly musical." He talked for a bit more of how he came to do the show and then launched the musical section. He had a pianist and two singers helping him, a boy and a girl. (The girl was Alice Playten, who was to score such a success in *Henry, Sweet Henry.*)

Stewart led the audition along wonderfully well; he read little snippets from the book, set up songs quickly, moved along swiftly. He appeared to be enjoying himself, whereas, as he said afterward, he was smashed, and can only get through them when he is drunk enough. Still, he was charming, and as the Cohan songs continued, the ladies applauded the familiar numbers. Joel Grey noticed this and said, "These broads are creaming."

He may have been right, but still, after watching various auditions over the course of time, I am unable to shake the constant feeling of the emperor's new clothes. Because in the first place, it doesn't matter if they like a score or not; if Richard Rodgers wrote it, it'll sell, even if it's rotten, and if my three-year-old supplied the words and music, that would sell too, provided that Julie Andrews had contracted to appear in it. And in the second place, hearing a song in a room has nothing whatsoever to do with hearing it in a theatre. And more than that, more than anything, is this simple fact: no one, but no one, is capable of hearing a dozen songs one right after the other and maintaining any critical objectivity about the value of the score. A really educated musical-comedy mind might be able to maintain a valid critical judgment through maybe six songs. Conceivably eight. But after that, it's all buzzing around in your head, the songs all one musical lump, and trying to figure out if they are pretty or not pretty, valid or invalid, or any other damn thing, is out of the question. Still, if you're a producer, you invite the ladies up to the Belasco Room at Sardi's, or somewhere else comfortable, give them a little hot to eat, a little cold to drink, and try to charm them, all the while knowing it doesn't matter, because they can only sell what's salable, never mind what's good.

Stewart finished his *George M!* audition in 27 minutes—60 seconds less than the estimated time—and after it was over, he mingled with the party ladies, a charming guy, sweating more heavily now after the ordeal of the performance. He had done a first-rate job of selling the show, and he was tired but still in there, pushing the merchandise with all he had, when up walks a party lady and says to him, "I just saw the most marvelous audition."

"Thank you very much, I'm glad you liked it," Stewart says.

"Not you," the party lady answers. "Steve and Eydie—last night —in *Golden Rainbow*. They were, I'm telling you, sensational."

Now Stewart is a bright guy, sensitive enough to know when he's just been castrated. But he's dead game, so he hangs in there: "Wasn't I sensational?"

"You were wonderful. Listen, I've seen you do it already, so I know you. But Steve and Eydie—they were just so cute."

"I'm cute," Stewart says.

"Yes," the party lady says. "Of course you're cute. But you're not a performer, are you?"

Stewart nods, whipped, and the lady moves on. A couple walks up to Stewart, who is short, and tells him what a nice job he did of telling the story of Cohan, who was, of course, also short. "You know what they say," Stewart replies, unaware that he's about to deliver a Freudian. "Never hide your height under a bushel."

Party ladies are very much aware of the esteem in which Broadway holds them. Elsa Hoppenfeld, who was an adjuster at Macy's before she became a party agent, says: "We do a job, we really do, and no matter what they say, we want people to buy good plays. Everybody says things about us, I know, but how often does the average person buy a drama? Charities are no different; they're made up of people."

Lenore Tobin is thought by many to be the best of the party agents. She has been at her work a long time, and the work is hard. "I sell a service," she says. "I try to help the charities with how to sell a ticket. I try to keep the dialogue open. The public is informed— you'd be amazed how informed they are. But they have to sell tickets. This is the worst year we've had since I've been in the business. There's a change in the attitude of everybody; Broadway hasn't gotten there yet. It's the difference between Ed Sullivan and the Smothers Brothers, and Broadway just hasn't caught up. But it will. I hope it will. These are crazy times now. Do you know what's going on? I don't know what's going on. The theatre's in sad shape, yes, I agree, but am I responsible? I don't think I am. Nobody wants to suffer any more. Listen, wouldn't I like to sell dramas?" I think she probably would, but she ends up making her money from things like *How Now, Dow Jones*.

To summarize the reasons for its advance:

1. Women tend to make the selection of the show for their charity.

2. Men tend to pay for the tickets for the show that the women have selected.

3. *How Now, Dow Jones* was a musical, and musicals generally meet less sales resistance than straight plays.

4. That title indicated that the show was at least intended to be funny.

5. The title also indicated that the show was going to be about the stock market.

6. Men tend to be interested in the stock market.

7. Women tended to be reasonably sure their husbands wouldn't snarl at them for their selection. (This last is surprisingly important. As one party agent put it: "People don't want anyone getting mad at them. At least with a show like this, with a title like this, the wife could say, 'Well, how was I supposed to know it would turn out to be terrible? I thought it was going to be funny.' They buy an Arthur Miller, and their husbands turn on them and say, 'I don't suffer enough at the office? You've got to put me through it here too?' ")

In other words, the title proclaimed that the show was going to be a light, stock-market musical, and the party ladies could do business with it, regardless of its quality, because they could sell it to the charity ladies; the charity ladies could do business with it, regardless of its quality, because they could sell it to the people; the people took it, regardless of its quality, because it sounded like it might be "fun."

This is not good for Broadway. If enough people keep on choosing shows in advance for reasons having nothing to do with the quality of the show, there's got to be a reaction eventually.

I spoke to a charity chairwoman. "For us, 'best' means 'easiest to sell.' *Hot Spot,* with Judy Holliday, we had that one. *Jennie,* with Mary Martin, we had that too. The men got so angry. We just can't risk taking a Broadway show any more, so this year, we decided on 'Funny Girl,' the movie. Sometimes, if you pick even a good Broadway show, the star's out sick, but with the movie, at least we know that Barbra Streisand's going to be there every night. We always used to pick a Broadway show, but I'm very depressed about the whole thing. I don't know; if 'Funny Girl' is no good, next year our charity's going to have a fashion-show luncheon."

PREMIERE PERFORMANCE, DECEMBER 14, 1967

ANTA THEATRE

ZEV BUFMAN
presents
In association with JAMES RILEY

MELVYN DOUGLAS

AS

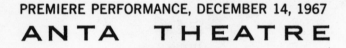

A New Comedy by
HERMAN SHUMLIN

Based on the novel, "Reuben, Reuben" by
PETER DeVRIES

with

BARBARA BRITTON

| JEROME | AUDRA | TRESA | ALAN |
| DEMPSEY | LINDLEY | HUGHES | NORTH |

and

PERT KELTON

Scenery and Lighting by   Costumes by
DONALD OENSLAGER   WINN MORTON

Directed by
MR. SHUMLIN

20

Crap Game

I saw *Spofford* at a late preview. Preview audiences often possess a certain behavioral honesty forever lost once the critics have told the public how to respond. *Spofford,* an adaptation of sections of a novel by punster Peter DeVries, concerns a Connecticut chicken farmer (Melvyn Douglas) whose niece is spurned by the son of a rich family. He decides to find out about the rich and in the course of his inquiries turns the town somewhat inside out.

On the night I saw it, the audience was groaning before the first act was half over. At intermission, a very unhappy man said to his wife, "I wish to hell I had some idea of what I'm going back in there for." For those who did go back in (a lot did not), the second act's biggest laugh came when an actress called an actor's coat "a dog-tooth jacket," and he said, "Houndstooth." There was a young couple involved in the plot, college-kid types, and when he said, "Marry me," she replied—and I am not making this up—"I've got to find out who I am first." The show did not end till 11:02, but by 10:55 the aisles were flooded. When the cast took its curtain calls, there was little applause for the third lead, less for the second lead, and when Melvyn Douglas came out for his well-earned solo curtain call, he was met with something very close to silence: there simply weren't enough people left to make much noise.

The first critic I heard was on the 10:30 TV news the night of December 14. He called it a tedious evening. Then I got Channel 7: he said, "It meanders around until you think it will never end." But Channel 2 liked it. And Channel 4 liked it a lot. Then the other counties were heard from. "The best new American comedy of the season." "A play full of warmth and humor." "A warmly amusing comedy." "Great fun." "A rich and warm American comedy." "Funny and droll." "A sparkling, literate and very funny Christmas gift to Broadway."

Spofford was home. Not a hit, perhaps, but at the very least it would run for the season. Someone who had been with the production all the way explained why it wasn't bigger: "We always knew that the problem with the play was: Was it too literary? It turned out it was, but the critics loved Douglas and forgave us. The play's too damn dull for raves. We got the best notices we could, and even though they were good, a certain seepage of dullness crept out. Face it; we were lucky."

Spofford is a perfect example of what makes Broadway such a crap game. It was a bore, but it had a nice job by Douglas, so there were at least two possible reactions. You could have said, "A nice job by Douglas can't save *Spofford* from being a bore"; or you could have said, as the critics tended to, "Douglas makes *Spofford* a gentle, pleasant evening in the theatre." These freak things happen. Paul Ford has been Paul Ford for a million years, always the same, always wonderful. But on the night that *Never Too Late* opened, the critics decided not to give the usual Paul Ford notice: "Mr. Ford struggles nobly with his material, but it is a losing battle." That night it's hats in the air and a 1,000-performance run and fortunes for everybody. There is simply no conceivable way of knowing when this contagion will strike the boys on the aisle. But one of the reasons that so many inconceivable plays get to Broadway is that when they're dying out of town they dream of the *Never Too Late*s and come on in.

A general rule of thumb made up by me is this: 5% of the shows that open each season are of such impressive quality they have to get good notices. About 35% are so unendurable that there is no way they can survive. The remaining 60% are in the hands of the gods. Most shows *could* run: they're neither so demeaning to the human spirit nor so uplifting that their fate is set prior to opening. And some of these—such as *Spofford*—do run; some of them die, as *Johnny No-Trump* did. It is a major Broadway crap game.

Another crap game is not *which* shows run but *where* they run—at what theatre. For there are "good" theatres and "bad" theatres, and which constitutes which is one of the better examples on Broadway of prehistoric mythmaking.

The "best" (most-sought-after) straight-play house on Broadway is the Plymouth, where Neil Simon's *Plaza Suite* is housed. Assuming it runs until 1970, which is a reasonable guess, the Plymouth Theatre will then have housed three plays on regular bookings in five years, and two on interim bookings. The three regular bookings were the three Simon comedies, *Odd Couple, Star Spangled Girl* and *Plaza Suite.* The two interim jobs were the short-lived *Keep It in the Family,* followed by *Everything in the Garden.* What this means is that for a period of some five years the Plymouth Theatre was not only housing hits but it was housing *something.* This is important, because the overriding problem facing a man who owns a theatre is having a play inside.

A little arithmetic. It might cost $3,000 a week to run a theatre with nothing inside it. This lumpy object is going to set you back $125,000, maybe $150,000, a year if it's dark, so keeping a theatre lit with any attraction is the name of the game for theatre owners.

All right, the Plymouth is a good theatre. What's a bad theatre? The Longacre will do. In a period equivalent to that mentioned in connection with the Plymouth, the Longacre has had some doozies, not all of which are common knowledge to the masses. *Peterpat:* that lasted 21 performances. *The Sign in Sidney Brustein's Window:* 99 performances, and close to the Longacre's top. Hal Holbrook played there awhile as Mark Twain, and he did business, but the run was legitimately limited. *Slapstick Tragedy* lasted a week. That was 1965–66. The 1966–67 season was a bad one. The Longacre had *A Hand Is on the Gate* for 20 performances. Gilbert Becaud, the French singer, made it through 19. *My Sweet Charlie,* the year's champeen, bit the dust after 31, leaving the rest of the season for the one performance of *The Natural Look.* This year the Longacre has bounced back. Sandy Dennis was Daphne there briefly, and then Robert Anderson's *I Never Sang for My Father* brought home the bacon 124 times.

Now why is the Plymouth so much better than the Longacre? Well, first of all, obviously the Plymouth can do more business, right? Wrong. *Plaza Suite* can do $54,000 a week at capacity; *I Never Sang for My Father* could have done $56,000. Well, if it isn't size, what else? The second balcony. The Longacre has a second balcony, and second-balcony seats don't sell; so you don't want a theatre with a second balcony if you want a long run. The St. James has a second balcony: *Hello, Dolly!* has played the St. James for five years now.

If you really want to know the difference between the Plymouth and the Longacre, it's location. The Plymouth is on Forty-fifth Street, see, and in the theatre business, Forty-fifth Street is it. Forty-fifth Street has the most theatres, and the most theatres means the most people walking by, and you just don't want to be anywhere except Forty-fifth Street. This thinking is based on the following truth: come theatre time, Forty-fifth Street is loaded with last-minute shoppers looking for a theatre to get into. Saul Lancourt of Leblang's Ticket Agency gets enthusiastic describing it: "At 7:15 the subways exploded! Out they'd pour—all the people—coming to see what they could see."

Lancourt, of course, was talking about 40 years ago, and that is what is wrong with the last-minute shopping or "walk-in" business theory: it is an old truth, very old, and one that no longer washes. (Broadway is filled with them: "A smash helps the whole theatre," meaning that when there's a smash, business goes up for everybody. *Plaza Suite* was a smash and nothing happened. As a matter of fact, after *Plaza Suite* opened and people were desperate to get tickets but unable to, two shows opened at the Golden Theatre right down the block: *Carry Me Back to Morningside Heights* and *The Exercise*. They both died bouncing on the first Saturday they could. As far as I can determine, nobody knows what people do when they can't get into *Plaza Suite*. They probably go to a movie.) There used to be such a thing as walk-in business. But no more.

You say this to a Broadway pro, and his answer will be logical: there are seven theatres between Seventh and Eighth Avenues on Forty-fifth Street where the Plymouth is. There is one theatre on Forty-eighth Street where the Longacre is. So there's got to be a little bit more walk-in business on Forty-fifth. O.K., you agree, there is a little bit more. O.K., he says, now that "little bit" is liable to be the difference between running or closing on a marginal show that is just scraping by, which is why Forty-fifth Street is so important. Those walk-in pennies.

Then you say, "If you're so worried about pennies, why don't you cancel your Monday-evening performance, which dies, and substitute a Sunday-matinee performance, which everyone agrees will take in more money?" The Broadway pro answers thus: "Granted Sunday mat is better than Monday night, *but not on a smash,* so that's why you keep the Monday night, in case you have a smash and can sell the higher-priced tickets."

We are now, as you probably have guessed, in the Orwellian world of doublethink. The Forty-fifth Street location is crucial, because we're thinking of the marginal show, and to hell with the "hit-or-bomb" psychology. But we keep the Monday-night performance because of the hit-or-bomb psychology, and to hell with the marginal show.

These are tobacco men, not medicine men; they are pros, hard Broadway businessmen, and they believe what they are saying. They don't just think the Longacre is worse than the Plymouth; they've got proof: look at the record. And it's unquestionably true that shows at the Plymouth run longer than shows at the Longacre. But that has nothing to do with the theatres; it's because the Plymouth gets more commercial shows. *Plaza Suite* was the most-sought-after play this year. And if Simon's show had opened at the Longacre, the lines would have been just as long, the money just as big. The reason that the Longacre gets weak shows is because the owners of the Longacre can only get dreck to play there. Dreck has a way of not sticking around. Therefore the shows at the Longacre close. It's circular thinking: a bad show is put into a bad house and it closes. Proof.

I should guess that less than 2% of the passionate theatregoing public can name the theatres that their favorite shows were in. It simply doesn't matter. But the battling and knifing that go on each year is the reason Broadway runs red at booking time.

The same lunacy holds true for musical houses. Location is crucial. You've got to be on Forty-fifth Street or Forty-fourth Street, and that's it. If you've really got a strong show, that's where you've got to be. *My Fair Lady* played the Hellinger all alone way up on Fifty-first Street. Location didn't seem to hurt it, at least not fatally.

The Broadway Theatre—the biggest of the legitimate houses— is too big. Everybody in the business knows that. You simply cannot fill the Broadway; there are too many seats, and you can't get it sold out enough to make the tickets scarce and "hot." It seats 1,788 people, and that is simply too many. The best musical house— the most fiercely fought for—is the Majestic. *Fiddler on the Roof* is at the Majestic. Know what? The Majestic is the *second* biggest theatre in town and it seats 1,655 people, just 133 fewer than the too big Broadway. This is madness. More madness: the Majestic used to be the *worst* house in town. No one would touch it. *South*

Pacific opened at the Majestic. Since then, it has been the number one musical showcase, and as one jaundiced Broadwayite observed of the Majestic: "It hasn't moved."

Spofford played the ANTA Theatre. The ANTA is somewhere in the middle, as far as theatre desirability is concerned; it is flexible though, because—with 1,214 seats—it can be booked for either a straight play or a musical. The booker for the ANTA is Norman Twain, thirty-eight, and terribly energetic ("I move ten times faster than anybody; that's not always good, but I do it"). He has booked the ANTA through four seasons, and he has done well for three of the years. He understands his position in the theatre hierarchy: "Doc Simon just isn't going to give me his next show, and neither is Hal Prince. They go to the top houses. I've got to make up my mind about what's left." And his position is really a crap game, because if he guesses and guesses wrong, his theatre is liable to be empty for the remainder of the season.

"It costs $130,000 a year to run the ANTA. Dark. That's a skeleton crew—cleaning staff, any box-office people, insurance, the rest of it. Holmes protection costs a hundred a week. With a show running, it costs $7,000 a week. That includes front and back doormen, ticket takers, ushers, four musicians, four stagehands, everything. It's a good investment if you have a smash. When *A Man for All Seasons* played here, I think they were clearing $6,000 a week.

"Next year I don't know whether I'll have a straight play or a musical. With a musical the house can gross $85,000 a week, and the theatre gets a quarter of that, over $22,000. With a straight play, we can gross maybe $65,000, but the percentage is a little higher."

Twain's first show in the ANTA was the charming comedy *The Owl and the Pussycat,* which ran a year. In his second season, he had *The Royal Hunt of the Sun* for more than 250 performances.

His third year was disastrous. He had hoped for *Dinner at Eight* and in trying to get it, lost out on *Philadelphia, Here I Come,* which lasted over 300 performances at another house. Twain lost *Dinner at Eight* and spent the season scrambling. In September he had a company of flamenco dancers, and they lasted four weeks. After that, things went downhill. All in all, he said, the theatre was lit eleven weeks, which means it was dark for 41, and that's not retirement money.

This year he booked *Spofford* and considered himself fortunate. It ran from December into June. He also booked two interim shows, *Song of the Grasshopper* and *The Trial of Lee Harvey Oswald,* and picked up four more weeks of booking time. He guessed on *Spofford*, because after he read it and knew that Melvyn Douglas was going to play the lead, he simply could not imagine anything less than raves for the star, which he hoped would insure a run. There were a number of other shows he could have had and turned down, he said. Among them: *New Faces, Something Different, The Promise, Everything in the Garden, The Only Game in Town* and *Joe Egg*. He was frightened of *Joe Egg* because Albert Finney had only an eleven-week contract. Among his possible choices for the season then, he guessed right.

When I talked to him last, he was desperately trying to figure out which show to take for next season. He had all of them on various lists, strengths here, weaknesses there, imponderables someplace else. He had it narrowed down to two musicals and three plays. But what really had him sweating was that he had just heard a strong rumor that a Famous Theatrical Figure was considering the ANTA for next winter. Twain was sweating because he was frightened that the Famous Theatrical Figure might go to another house, right? Wrong. Twain was having fits because he was frightened that the Famous Theatrical Figure might *not* go to another house. Why? Because, if the Famous Theatrical Figure really wanted the ANTA, Twain would obviously have to give it to him, and that was Twain's problem. For the Famous Theatrical Figure is known throughout the trade as being totally unreliable when it comes to schedules, so Twain was in the position of having to give his theatre to a man who was not going to bring in a play, thereby opening Twain up to another dizzying season of flamenco dancers.

I left him at his desk, waiting for the phone not to ring.

ETHEL BARRYMORE THEATRE

SAINT-SUBBER and
KATZKA-BERNE PRODUCTIONS

present

MARGARET LEIGHTON   E. G. MARSHALL

GERALDINE CHAPLIN   FELICIA MONTEALEGRE

SCOTT McKAY   RICHARD A. DYSART

AUSTIN PENDLETON   BEAH RICHARDS

LIAM SULLIVAN   ANDRE WOMBLE

in

LILLIAN HELLMAN'S

THE LITTLE FOXES

Directed by

MIKE NICHOLS

Setting and Lighting Designed by
HOWARD BAY

Costumes by
PATRICIA ZIPPRODT

Hair Styles by Ernest Adler

Production originally presented Vivian Beaumont Theater
by
The Repertory Theatre of Lincoln Center Under the direction of Jules Irving

CHAPTER

21

Culture Hero

Mike Nichols' production of *The Little Foxes* opened in October at Lincoln Center, where it was ecstatically received. Walter Kerr, writing in the Sunday *Times,* called it "American theatre at its best." It was another triumph in a string of triumphs for Nichols, and one could leave it at that. Except that *The Little Foxes* was different, for with the reception of this work, Mike Nichols became something rare in American life: a culture hero. Broadway had not produced anyone comparable since Kazan almost ten years before.

Many theatre people compared Nichols' production with a particular success of Kazan's, Archibald MacLeish's Pulitzer prize-winning verse drama, *J.B.* For in both cases, simply the name of the director was enough to transform an evening of absolute mediocrity into a triumph. Obviously, there were differences. Kazan's mystique had taken a pretentious, soporific play, and with the help of a brilliant production, forced it into being a success. Nichols' mystique was, if anything, more remarkable: he had taken an excellent melodrama, given it an execrable production, and triumphed nonetheless.

There is no way that someone writing a book like this can prove that a past production was good or bad: the production that won the reviews is as dead now as Burbage's *Macbeth.* But perhaps one illustration of the way the material was handled in *The Little Foxes* will indicate what it was that so many found wrong with the production. (Almost everyone I talked to felt that the work was atrocious: obviously, much of this is simple envy. But some of the criticism, coming from theatre people close to Nichols' own success level, must have some basis in something.)

Lillian Hellman's play revolves around a southern family's getting together sufficient funds to make a business deal with a Chicago tycoon. In the opening scene the family is entertaining the tycoon at dinner. They traipse on stage individually, so that each character can get entrance applause and destroy any possible chance of the audience's concentrating on the play. Nichols loves to do this, by the way: create little moments that call attention to things other than the play—characters walking off stage while talking, or talking to other characters who are off stage. It's very catchy, and you find yourself saying to your neighbor, "Gee, that's clever" (which is what you're supposed to do). But the minute you say that to your neighbor, you're not thinking about the play but about how clever the director is. So, in essence, the audience's mind shifts from the work itself to the staging of it. This is self-serving direction, and no one is better at it than Nichols.

Back to the opening scene. All the family has entered and all the audience has applauded all the entrances. The "bad guys" in the play are the Hubbard brothers and their sister, Regina. One of the brothers is married to a lush, Birdie, who plays the piano. The Chicago tycoon has asked to hear Birdie play. So she does. And while she is playing, Nichols has the Hubbard family do an amazing thing: they don't even bother to conceal their irritation at the Chicago tycoon whom they are trying so desperately to impress. They grunt and glower and stomp and look at their watches, all of this in front of their crucially important visitor. Now, it would be fine, if they were angry, to have them show their anger to each other and to us, all the time veiling it from the visitor. But they don't even do that: not only is their action rude, but it is wildly out of character with what they are trying to do—impress the visitor.

In other words, what Nichols did throughout this production was have the characters behave as if their subconscious were common knowledge. Now this is simply not what people do. Most rotten guys try like hell for cover. If Iago comes on snarling, Othello's pretty much of a moron for trusting him. If the Hubbards come on evil, how can anything they do surprise each other, much less us? Later they begin to double-cross each other. Nichols has directed them to do it like triumphant Cheshire cats, and it is inconceivable that anyone could believe any of the subterfuges they attempt against each other.

One more thing. Nichols chose to have the Negro maid serve as—you should pardon the expression—a symbol, never mind of what. The play opened with her walking out front, staring dead at the audience, going, "Ech, ech, ech," and gesturing with her head back to the Hubbards talking off stage at dinner. Then, as if that weren't enough of a suggestion for us, she walked to one side of the stage, went, "Ech, ech, ech" again and gestured with her head back to the off-stage eaters. Then she crossed the stage for her third "Ech, ech, ech" and ensuing head toss. By this time we got it: they were mortal fools and she was wisdom. I kept expecting each laughing "ech, ech, ech" to be followed by her saying, "The weed of crime bears bitter fruit; crime does not pay. The Shadow knows, ech, ech, ech, ech, ech."

Anyway, the theatre had produced a new culture hero, and probably no one in the art world has moved so far as fast as Nichols in five Octobers. October 13, 1962, was a Saturday night, and Elaine May's play, *A Matter of Position*, closed out of town in Philadelphia. Closed violently. Audiences hated the play. This marked the end of a second career for Nichols, who was the star of the play. The first career—the night-club and record act with Miss May—was ending by then. Both Nichols and May are immensely glib people, but they were beginning to double back on themselves. The play would have been a marvelous out, two new careers at once. But it didn't work, and so, in October, 1962, Nichols found himself among the unemployed. He made the jump to culture hero in five years flat. His Broadway work prior to *The Little Foxes* consisted of three comedies, *Barefoot in the Park, Luv* and *The Odd Couple*—all gigantic successes—plus one musical, *The Apple Tree*, which was a considerable financial failure, and which Nichols had terrible trouble directing, finally having to call in help out of town. But even with *The Apple Tree* his notices were impeccable. (Nichols had also done one off-Broadway comedy, *The Knack*, and the film direction of "Virginia Woolf," immensely successful.)

Kazan became a culture hero with *J.B.* He had been famous long before, but the ultimate jump into the culture-hero category was not until the MacLeish play. There is no intention here of comparing Nichols and Kazan. They are both greatly gifted, and they do different kinds of plays.

But it would be worthwhile to consider briefly Kazan's career before it established sufficient momentum to enable him to take the ultimate career step. Kazan was also a performer first, having spent half a dozen years in the thirties with the Group Theatre. Among other Broadway productions that Kazan directed prior to *J.B.: The Skin of Our Teeth, One Touch of Venus, Jacobowsky and the Colonel, Deep Are the Roots, All My Sons, A Streetcar Named Desire, Death of a Salesman, Tea and Sympathy, Cat on a Hot Tin Roof.* Kazan had also done some films. Among them were: "A Tree Grows in Brooklyn," "Boomerang," "Panic in the Streets," "A Streetcar Named Desire," "Viva Zapata," "On the Waterfront" and "East of Eden."

The point of the above is this simple truth: you can tell a lot about the spirit of a time by its heroes. It took Kazan 20 years before his name was enough to guarantee success. It took Nichols five. And the kind of work Kazan did must also be noted: there are very few distinguished plays in the forties and fifties that he did *not* direct. And the film work was, if not equally impressive, pretty damn good. His work is passionate, serious, significant. Nichols' work is frivolous —charming, light and titanically inconsequential.

It is interesting to note that after *J.B.* Kazan had one more success on Broadway, *Sweet Bird of Youth,* before his stumbling *After the Fall,* his painful *The Changeling.*

Nichols' phenomenal notices for *The Little Foxes* were the *low* point of his year. After that came *Plaza Suite* on Broadway, "The Graduate" on film. It's not just success that is increasing for Nichols —it's everything. He is not a director any more: he is a star. When the New York Film Critics Awards were given this year, it was Nichols who appeared on the cover of the tabloid *Post,* chatting with Ingrid Bergman. Sidney Poitier was there, but Nichols was on the cover. He is, while still in his middle thirties, becoming legend. And legends are not allowed flaws.

Example: when *The New York Review of Books* was critical of *The Little Foxes,* a blasting letter was sent in. From whom? From a *New Yorker* film critic, Miss Gilliatt, who, in her phrase, is a "loved friend" of Nichols'. While we're on *The New Yorker,* another example: in their weekly capsule review of "The Graduate" they said, "Mike Nichols has directed (and appears to have written much of) this energetic and very funny account . . ." and it goes on from there. Now here's the thing: Nichols didn't write "much of" "The Graduate." How do I know? Easy. I've read Charles Webb's novel, which the movie was based on. All you have to do is glance through the book to see what an enormous percentage of the fine dialogue is straight from the printed page, as several film critics recognized when they reviewed "The Graduate." Now remember, Nichols' "loved friend" is a movie critic for *The New Yorker*, but so what? It's just not enough for *The New Yorker* that Nichols *only* directed one of the most successful films in history; he had to write "much of" it too. All you can gather from this is that when Nichols' announced film version of "Catch-22" opens, *The New Yorker* will comment that "Mike Nichols has directed (from his own energetic and very funny novel) this cinematic version of . . ."

And to be perfectly blunt, Nichols does not do much to hide the flawless side of his nature. When he accepted the New York Critics Award, *Variety* quoted some of his acceptance remarks on the *"auteur* theory" of direction. The *auteur* theory, by the way, is a bit of madness perpetrated by some French movie intellectuals (who think Jerry Lewis is a major artist), who say that great films can only be created when there is an *auteur*—an author—of a film, when, in other words, the film is the work of one man. Here is what Nichols said: ". . . at risk of demolishing the *auteur* theory of direction, this film was made by a group of people. Photographer Robert Surtees, art director Richard Sylbert and film editor Sam O'Steen worked with me as a team. I can't really tell you who did what. I hope I did some of it."

I hope I did some of it. There is an actor's term for this called "shit kicking," and it means false modesty. It would have been one thing for Nichols to say, "The following men were crucial in the making of 'The Graduate,' " and then name them. That's a reasonable, believable, grateful thing to say. But put what Nichols did say into another context: Joe Namath at a sports banquet accepting a trophy after a championship game in which he threw the crucial touchdown pass. How would it sound if Namath said this: "I had fantastic blocking in the line and great protection from my backs, and the move that the end put on that defensive guy was beautiful. I sure am glad we scored that winning touchdown. But to tell you the truth, we work as such a team that I don't really know any more who did what. I hope I did some of it."

Now obviously the quarterback is crucial to the success of a touchdown pass. Sure, the blocking has to be there. But it's up to the quarterback on a long pass: he's got to wait until the last possible second, no matter what pressure he is under, and with no chance for error throw the ball 50, maybe 60, yards in the air in order for it to get to his receiver in such a way that the receiver can catch it without breaking stride and go on in to score. The quarterback is the man. And so is the film director. And everybody knows it. Nichols' saying, "No, I'm not, folks, I'm just a member of the team," does two things: (1) he castrates the genuine value of the men he mentions, thereby elevating himself alone to the highest position; (2) at the very time he is doing the castrating, his words seem to indicate that he is doing the opposite.

After he picked up the New York Film Critics directing honor, Nichols received the Tony for best direction for *Plaza Suite* and the Academy Award for directing "The Graduate." Remarkable. To win them both in one year. Even more remarkable, though, is this: no one else got beans from either production. No actress won anything, no actor, no writer, nobody. Last year, when Peter Hall won the Tony for directing *The Homecoming,* it was named best play, and the male star of the play also got the best-acting award. Similarly, in movies the year before, when Fred Zinnemann won the Academy Oscar for directing, both the picture he directed, "A Man for All Seasons," and its star, Paul Scofield, won awards.

But Nichols wins alone. This doesn't really matter. What counts is that there is a new culture hero in the land. And we have made him. He reflects us: our time, our taste, our needs, our wants. And what we want is Nichols. And what Nichols is, is brilliant. Brilliant and trivial and self-serving and frigid. And all ours.

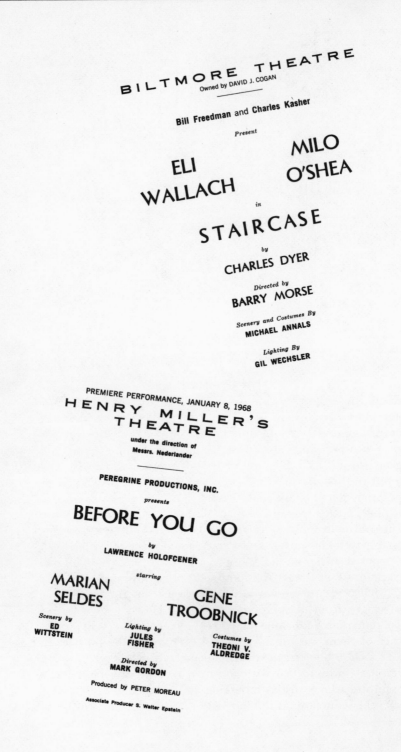

BILTMORE THEATRE
Owned by DAVID J. COGAN

Bill Freedman and Charles Kasher

Present

ELI WALLACH   MILO O'SHEA

in

STAIRCASE

by

CHARLES DYER

Directed by

BARRY MORSE

Scenery and Costumes By

MICHAEL ANNALS

Lighting By

GIL WECHSLER

PREMIERE PERFORMANCE, JANUARY 8, 1968

HENRY MILLER'S THEATRE

under the direction of
Messrs. Nederlander

PEREGRINE PRODUCTIONS, INC.

presents

BEFORE YOU GO

by

LAWRENCE HOLOFCENER

starring

MARIAN SELDES   GENE TROOBNICK

Scenery by
ED WITTSTEIN

Lighting by
JULES FISHER

Costumes by
THEONI V. ALDREDGE

Directed by
MARK GORDON

Produced by PETER MOREAU

Associate Producer S. Walter Epstein

CHAPTER

22

The Three Theatres

Staircase and *Before You Go*
opened on consecutive nights in January. They were both two-
character plays. They were both about love. They were both sad
comedies. There were obvious differences: *Staircase* was English, *Before You Go* American; *Before You Go* dealt with the meeting and
mating of two misfits, a boy and girl; *Staircase* also dealt with two
misfits, but in this case they had been together, more or less, for 20
years, and they were homosexual.

Both plays failed. *Staircase,* which *Variety* gave six out of seven
favorable overnight reviews, starred Eli Wallach. With good notices,
a reasonably well-known star and a sensational piece of subject matter, it aroused little public interest and died in less than two
months. *Before You Go* arrived to mixed notices, aroused no public
interest whatsoever (it grossed less in five weeks on Broadway than
Fiddler on the Roof does on Saturday), and closed with a loss of
$150,000, remarkable for a one-set, two-character play.

Neither of them was an unsuccessful evening in the theatre. In
Before You Go a bookkeeper caught in the rain while walking her
dog eventually goes to bed with the man who gives her shelter, a
phony sculptor who is just as miserable and lost as she is. The play
chronicles the seduction; as the lost lady who has delusions of being

an actress, Marian Seldes made the cliché of the homely culture vulture fresh and new all over again. It was a beautiful piece of acting, and it is because of her, I think, that the play failed so miserably. The following is an attempt to make some sense of that statement.

People tend to speak of the Broadway theatre as if it were a single organism. It seems to me that actually there are three theatres in existence simultaneously on Broadway, each with its own specialists.

First and most famous and most prosperous is the Musical Theatre. Definition: that's when they sing. The most famous participants of the musical theatre in the sixties are both directors: Jerome Robbins and Gower Champion. Champion has been the more active, directing five musicals through the end of this season, and since, as I write this, the fate of the fifth is still hanging, I can only say that his first four were successful. The greatest of his hits, of course, is *Hello, Dolly!*

Robbins directing a musical is, for me, the one world-class talent operating on Broadway today. The trouble is that he isn't operating very often any more. His most recent show was *Fiddler on the Roof* in the fall of '64. He has, however, been "helpful," as they say, in two other musicals this decade: *Funny Girl* and *A Funny Thing Happened on the Way to the Forum.* And if Champion's first four shows were successful and averaged over 1,000 performances each, and if that is incredible—which it is—what can you say of Robbins, whose three musicals have averaged over a three-year run?

Now, in March, 1963, within five days of each other, both had plays open. Not musicals. Plays. Champion's was by Lillian Hellman, and it lasted 17 performances before expiring to the loss of $175,000. Robbins tripled Champion's run: his production of Brecht's *Mother Courage* ran 52 times, and lost only $150,000. But in their other play-directing attempts, Champion has bested Robbins: he brought in a Paul Ford comedy, which ran 33 times before it lost its $100,000 investment. Robbins' other straight-play attempt, *The Office,* starring Elaine May, closed before it opened.

Totaling it up then between the two of them (and not counting this year's Champion musical *Happy Time,* which is still running), they have been involved in seven musicals this decade, which have run for more than 8,000 performances so far, and have all been profitable into the uncounted millions of dollars.

Their four straight-play attempts have lost over $500,000 and averaged 34 performances. Many reasons have been put forward why these men, so obviously gifted in one field, should be so disastrously inept in another. An associate of theirs says this: "In a musical they start with a total picture in their minds and then all they do is put in the puppets. In a play they have to work with actors; they have to draw out, not put in, and neither of them can do that. Only puppetsville."

Before You Go belonged to the second category, to which I have given the really rotten name, the Popular Theatre. It's an inept name because it has nothing to do with people going to see it; there is nothing necessarily popular about Popular Theatre. Still, it's the best name I could come up with. Whatever you call it, the thing that characterizes Popular Theatre is this: it wants to tell us either a truth that we already know or a falsehood we want to believe in.

Popular Theatre *re-enforces*.

Now this is all very simple-minded, but *Before You Go,* which is about two unhappy misfits meeting and touching, says something we already know: love will find a way. What we are being told may not be true, and we may consciously know that, but we still want to be told it anyway. I cannot believe, for example, in light of our divorce statistics, that Americans actually believe any longer that love really will find a way, that Cary Grant is just around the corner. But they want to believe it. It's appealing to think so. The Popular Theatre then, whatever else it may be, *can never be unsettling.*

Before You Go told the story of a lost homely girl who finds a lost, homely guy and perhaps happiness after the curtain comes down. To repeat: love will find a way. And Marian Seldes was so touching, so sad, so vulnerable as the homely girl that she made the whole thing true.

But she's *homely*.

She is a tall, gawky, graceless thing and she is playing a tall, gawky, graceless thing, which would seem to be terrific casting; and it would be, but not in the Popular Theatre. If you want to do a comedy about a homely girl in the Popular Theatre, you've got to cast Lauren Bacall as the homely girl, which is what they did in *Cactus Flower* and one of the reasons why it ran for more than 1,000 performances. When they say that Bacall is a dog in *Cactus Flower,* we know that they're wrong. My God, how can she be a dog? She was a movie star when she was barely out of her teens. Gorgeous? No. But never unattractive. And the fact that she was really glamorous Lauren Bacall frees us to enjoy the laughter in *Cactus Flower,* whereas the laughter in *Before You Go,* much of it caused by Miss Seldes' brilliant performance, never came easily or wholeheartedly because it was too true, and because it was true, too painful. Conclusion: if you're going to do a piece of Popular Theatre, there are certain requirements that must be met. Since Popular Theatre must never be unsettling, the minute you unsettle us you're dead. There are hundreds of casting examples to further illustrate this point, but two will do.

Any Wednesday has a premise that might prove touching: a mistress turning thirty. It's really kind of sad if you think about it; turning thirty is traumatic enough for any woman, or so the poets tell us, and a mistress on such a day might logically have cause for reflection and just as logically not like the picture she sees. And if she becomes unhappy, which she assuredly must, so will we. But *Any Wednesday* is Popular Theatre. Love will find a way, and so they didn't cast someone turning thirty; they cast Sandy Dennis, who was probably around twenty-seven, but who looked twenty-two and acted eighteen. She said she was turning thirty, but we never had to face the reality of believing her, so the pain of the play was, happily, not there for us.

A Majority of One, the popular comedy of 1959, starred the late Gertrude Berg as an American lady who gets involved with a Japanese man. Well, in Popular Theatre, if you had cast Sessue Hayakawa, you would have closed before you'd opened. The management of the play had the sense to cast that famous Nipponese star Sir Cedric Hardwicke in the role. So we knew, sitting happily out there in the dark, that that wasn't really any Pearl Harbor sneak up there on stage pawing our Molly Goldberg.

Staircase tells very little story. It concerns two aging homosexuals —barbers by trade—one sarcastic, one motherly, neither particularly effeminate. They are existing in a moment of some tension, because the sarcastic one has been arrested for dressing in female attire and has been summoned to appear in magistrate's court. The two men belabor each other verbally throughout the evening, and in the end, after all the battling, find that they need each other.

Now if *Before You Go* tells us that love will find a way, *Staircase* gives us an entirely different truth, one that the bulk of the heterosexual audience does not want to hear or believe: homosexuals are human. No matter how unsettling we may find them, no matter how low they may stand on any of our value scales, they are human, they are people; they are, in other words, just like us.

This is a difficult and unpleasant truth, and that is why *Staircase* does not belong in the badly named Popular Theatre, but in the third theatre, which, in a stroke of blind luck, I realized could best be called the Third Theatre. The Third Theatre wants to tell us something that we don't want to know. Homosexuals are human, *Staircase* tells us, and the management that imported this homosexual romance did what must have seemed logical: they made damn sure everyone in the audience knew that everyone on stage was as straight as Robert Mitchum.

I can remember no other Playbill notes that went on as much or as incessantly about the married life of its creative people, in this case four: the two actors, the writer and the director. Of Eli Wallach, who played the sarcastic homosexual, the Playbill notes began: "ELI WALLACH (Charles Dyer) has illuminated the New York stage since the late 1940's when he appeared in the American Repertory Theatre presentations of *Henry VIII, Yellow Jack, Alice in Wonderland* and *Androcles and the Lion.* He and his wife, Anne Jackson, first acted together in an ELT production of Tennessee Williams' *This Property Is Condemned,* previous to their marriage. They have since shared the stage on Broadway in the Charles Laughton production of Shaw's *Major Barbara* and in *Rhinoceros* and *Luv,* and off-Broadway in the ANTA matinee *Brecht on Brecht* and Murray Schisgal's *The Typists* and *The Tiger.*" At the end of the résumé, in case we weren't sure Wallach was straight, it added: "The Wallachs reside in Manhattan and have three children."

Milo O'Shea, who plays the motherly homosexual, didn't get straightened away till halfway through his credentials: "In 1958 he was spotted by Sir John Gielgud and brought to London where he played with Dame Sybil Thorndyke and Sir Louis Casson in *Treasure Hunt,* which ran eighteen months. During this period he met Maureen Toal who was also playing in the West End. When *Treasure Hunt* closed, the couple returned to Dublin where they married and set off on a three-month tour of America with the Dublin Players."

The name of the author was Charles Dyer (the same name as Wallach's character in the play), and he had an obscure biography. Dyer didn't much want to put down anything about himself since he felt, perhaps rightly, that what the writer really is like rarely concerns an audience. At the end of his biography, however, there was a final sentence which clearly relieved all pressure: "For the record, Dyer is happily married with three children; and has been thirty-seven for many years."

Barry Morse, the costar of "The Fugitive" series on TV, directed the production, and he was heterosexual too, which was indicated halfway through his Playbill note: "In 1951 his wife decided to spend the summer in Montreal with their two children, visiting relatives."

In other words, the message was: "Don't worry, folks; we're only pretending." And the message indicated by the program was carried through the entire production. I think this is what killed *Staircase*. Because it was not Popular Theatre but Third Theatre, and it meant to unsettle. As *The Boys in the Band* proved, there was obviously a tremendous market for a play about homosexuals. Now if there was a market, and *Staircase* got the notices and had a star, why didn't it run? It didn't run because, basically, it pleased nobody. The Popular Theatre audience clearly was unhappy because the play was essentially unsettling. But the Third Theatre audience wasn't satisfied either, because by putting on a homosexual play as if it were *Mary, Mary,* the production managed to alienate that segment of the audience too. *Staircase* satisfied no one.

The three theatres, then, exist concurrently on Broadway today, each with its own specialists, each with its own audience. One final note: the difference between Popular Theatre and Third Theatre is *not* the difference between entertainment and art. Popular Theatre can be art, and most Third Theatre is dull. The only point is that no matter which one you do, you must understand the kind of play you are attempting to bring to life and go in that direction. To put a genuinely homely woman in *Cactus Flower* would have been just as crippling to that play as it was to *Before You Go,* and *Staircase* was dead the minute they decided to style the production as if it were a charade performed by happily married daddies.

HELEN HAYES
THEATRE

ROBERT WHITEHEAD *presents*

in association with

ROBERT W. DOWLING

THE PRIME OF MISS JEAN BRODIE

A New Play By
JAY ALLEN

Adapted from the Novel By
MURIEL SPARK

Starring

ZOE CALDWELL

With

LENNOX MILNE   ROY COOPER   AMY TAUBIN

JOSEPH MAHER   DIANA DAVILA   DENISE HUOT   CATHERINE BURNS

And

DOUGLAS WATSON

Scenery & Lighting Designed by
JO MIELZINER

Costumes by
JANE GREENWOOD

Incidental Music Composed and Arranged by
JOHN COOK

Directed by
MICHAEL LANGHAM

New Girl In Town

Most long-running successes on Broadway fall into one of two groups: the musical or the light comedy. Occasionally, a serious play will crash through. There is a fourth group that every so often surprises, and this is that more or less bastard form, the comedy-drama, which is hard to define except to say that it has Chekhov for a father.

Member of the Wedding was such a success, and more recently, *Two for the Seesaw*. This kind of hit usually has three common elements: (1) good notices; (2) good word of mouth; (3) a new girl in town, a new star, like Julie Harris in *Member of the Wedding* or Anne Bancroft in *Two for the Seesaw*.

The Prime of Miss Jean Brodie was such a show. Based on Muriel Spark's wispy novella of the same name, it moves in and out of time, telling a 1930's story of an Edinburgh schoolteacher who is, among other things, a romantic fascist, and who selects various girls to be her pets in "the Brodie set." Brodie is a pile-driving force in the children's lives, not necessarily for their betterment. But her power cannot be denied. She says, "Give me a girl at an impressionable age, and she is mine for life." Eventually, one of the children battles Brodie and, through various plot machinations, destroys her.

None of this is much dramatized in the sensitive Spark piece. But

Jay Allen, an ex-actress from Texas, managed to shape a play that was done with enormous success first in London. Rewritten and improved, it opened in New York in January and was well received. None of the important critics was negative, and Kerr, in the Sunday *Times,* was tremendously enthusiastic. So the first smash comedy-drama requirement—good notices—was more than met. Word of mouth, the second, is the hardest to prove, but the feeling along the street was that *Brodie*'s was terrific. Audiences were enthusiastic: New Yorkers told New Yorkers.

But nothing really makes a show like a new girl in town, and *Brodie* had Zoe Caldwell. The critics said: "Superb," "Memorable," "A new magic personality in the theatre." She became *the* actress of the season, a fact confirmed by her winning the Tony for the best starring performance.

When an enormous hit opens, if it has a large advance sale, it sells out immediately. If not, then it builds, usually achieving sell-out status by about the end of a month, and staying there for an indefinite period of time. The general expectation immediately after *Brodie*'s opening was that the show would sell out for at least the first six months, taper off somewhat during the summer, then run through the remainder of the following season—a year and a half by conservative estimates—and money in the bank for all.

It never happened.

It never came close to selling out, and only once in its first 20 weeks did it do over 80% of capacity. It was a small hit, it ended up in the black, but of all the shows this season, *Brodie* was the one that most baffled the pros. Why wasn't it a smash? All kinds of suggestions were put forward, ranging from an erratic star to a set better suited to *Medea* than a sad comedy about love and the loss of love.

The *Brodie* staff worked hard to try and put the play across. Briefly, they split their publicity efforts into pushing both the play and the star, since both had been so well received. Zoe Caldwell was almost totally unknown when she opened in January; there had been no attempt to build her up while the show was on the road. This is generally held to be sound thinking on the part of publicists. One of them said to me, "Never tell an audience you've got a new star coming in. They resent it. Let *them* discover her."

This was the philosophy that was followed with *Brodie.* Seymour Krawitz, who handled the publicity for the show, explained: "We kept quiet for any number of reasons: the part was taxing for Zoe; she had to work hard on it all the way through. Then too, some actresses can shift gears easily; the publicity work comes almost as a relief from the acting, the one balancing the other. Zoe can't do that; she's very intense about her work. And also, publicity just isn't as meaningful to her personally as it is to some others. But after the opening, we wanted to bracket in all the crucial interviews fast: *Everywhere you turn you see Zoe Caldwell;* that was the impression we wanted to create." Here is a partial schedule that Miss Caldwell followed in the days around the opening:

> January 15 — interview with *Time*
> January 15 — interview with Toronto *Telegram*
> January 17 — interview with New York *Times*
> January 18 — interview with Toronto *Star*
> January 20 — interview with New York Sunday *News*
> January 22 — interview with New York Sunday *Times*
> January 23 — interview with *Newsweek*
> January 24 — interview with Reuters
> January 24 — interview with *Newsday*
> January 26 — interview with AP
> January 26 — interview with *The New Yorker*

There were also, of course, television appearances of a local variety mostly, and several talks and picture sessions with representatives of the press from her country—Australia—and later, other magazines. If *Everywhere you turn you see Zoe Caldwell* was the publicists' objective, New Yorkers could only agree that they were successful.

The operative words in that last sentence are "New Yorkers."

The Center for Research in Marketing, in its Theatregoers Study, came up with another possibility why *Brodie* disappointed at the box office. To understand it, it is necessary to know just where people come from who attend Broadway theatre, and the effect that their point of origin has on their theatrical taste.

Briefly, "local" people, people who live in New York City itself or the surrounding areas—Long Island, Connecticut, New Jersey, etc. —make up approximately two thirds of the entire Broadway audience. Out-of-towners—"tourists"—constitute the remaining third. And the tastes of the "locals" and the tastes of the "tourists" vary enormously. To give an example of that difference, here are the five favorite recent films of the two groups:

New York Area Theatregoer	Out-of-Town Theatregoer
1. "Bonnie and Clyde"	1. "To Sir, with Love"
2. "The Graduate"	2. "The Graduate"
3. "Guess Who's Coming to Dinner"	3. "Thoroughly Modern Millie"
4. "A Man and a Woman"	4. "Camelot"
5. "In the Heat of the Night"	5. "Bonnie and Clyde"

There is no reason to assume that such a preference difference exists only in films, and indeed it does not. Out-of-towners form a far greater proportion of the audience at musicals than they do in the theatre in general: one third of the total audience, one half of the musical audience. And correspondingly, they are much less interested in comedy and particularly uninterested in drama. The same third of the audience accounts for about a quarter of the comedy house, less than one seventh of the straight-play theatregoers. It is difficult to know in just which of the last two categories *Brodie* belongs, but put it where you will, the point is this: unimportant as it may be to the straight play, the out-of-town audience was the reason *Brodie* never took off.

The Theatregoers Study selected four straight plays that opened between January 16 and February 14; they are in order of appearance: *The Prime of Miss Jean Brodie, Joe Egg, The Price, Plaza Suite*. Since *Brodie* was the first to open, it had the longest time to make its presence known to the out-of-towner. Also, it had been a famous play for well over two years because of its London triumph.

But of the four plays, fewer out-of-towners had heard of it than any of the others, and of those who had heard of it, even fewer wanted to see *Brodie* than any of the others.

Over 20% of the out-of-town audience had heard of and wanted to see *Joe Egg*.

Over 30% wanted to see *The Price,* in spite of the fact that it was a heavy drama, which out-of-towners ordinarily avoid almost entirely.

Almost 50% of the out-of-town audience wanted to see *Plaza Suite*.

Only 8% of the out-of-town audience wanted to see *Brodie,* and only 15% had ever even heard of it, a smaller percentage than for any of the other plays mentioned here.

There are any number of other statistics available, but they only reinforce the above percentages, which indicate that as far as the out-of-town third of the audience was concerned, *Brodie* didn't exist in any practical, box-office way. If, for example, *Brodie* had had the appeal that a drama like *The Price* had, it might have hit capacity early on. And once a show hits capacity—once there are no tickets available—you're almost home. The herd instinct takes over in theatregoers: when something is impossible to see, everyone has to see it.

So Brodie, with all the ingredients for a smash and having been a smash once already, failed to repeat because the tourists didn't come running. The bulk of the publicity that Miss Caldwell received was what might be called in the "over-kill" category: it was Zoe Caldwell, Zoe Caldwell, Zoe Caldwell everywhere you looked in New York, but we knew that already. The Theatregoers Study shows that among New Yorkers approximately the same percentage wanted to see *Brodie, Joe Egg* and *The Price*. So all those New York interviews, all those endless articles entitled "The Prime of Zoe Caldwell," or "Zoe Caldwell's Prime," or "Zoe in Her Prime," or "The Prime of Zoe," or "Zoe Caldwell's Having a Prime Time" only made us want to say, "All right already, what else is new?"

The geographical difference in audience taste and the possible effect it can have on Broadway is important and will be gone into in some detail in the concluding chapter. As for poor *Miss Brodie,* this much can be said here: it wasn't one of her little girls that ruined her; it was that old lady from Dubuque that done her in.

PREMIERE PERFORMANCE, JANUARY 18, 1968

BROADWAY THEATRE

DAVID MERRICK

presents

ROBERT GOULET · DAVID WAYNE

in

THE HAPPY TIME

A NEW MUSICAL

Book By
N. RICHARD NASH

Suggested by the Characters in the Stories by
ROBERT L. FONTAINE

Music By
JOHN KANDER

Lyrics By
FRED EBB

with

GEORGE S. IRVING

JEANNE ARNOLD

JUNE SQUIBB

JULIE GREGG
CHARLES DURNING

MIKE RUPERT

Lighting By
JEAN ROSENTHAL

Settings By
PETER WEXLER

Costumes By
FREDDY WITTOP

Film Technical Direction By
BARRY O. GORDON

Film Sequences Created By
CHRISTOPHER CHAPMAN

*Musical Direction And
Vocal Arrangements By*
OSCAR KOSARIN

Associate Choreographer
KEVIN CARLISLE

Orchestrations By
DON WALKER

Production Manager
MICHAEL THOMA

Dance and Incidental Music Arrangements by
MARVIN LAIRD

Directed, Filmed and Choreographed By

GOWER CHAMPION

Original Cast Album by RCA Victor

NATIONAL THEATRE
LOUIS A. LOTITO . . . . MANAGING DIRECTOR

DAVID MERRICK

presents

MARISA MELL · PERNELL ROBERTS

in

MATA HARI

A NEW MUSICAL

Book by
JEROME COOPERSMITH

Lyrics by
MARTIN CHARNIN

Music by
EDWARD THOMAS

with

JAKE HOLMES

W. B. BRYDON
NADINE LEWIS

MARK DEMPSEY
BLYTHE DANNER

GEORGE MARCY
DOMINIC CHIANESE

and

MARTHA SCHLAMME

Scenery and Lighting Designed by
JO MIELZINER

Costumes Designed by
IRENE SHARAFF

Orchestrations by
ROBERT RUSSELL BENNETT

Musical Direction by
COLIN ROMOFF

Dance Music Arranged by
ROGER ADAMS

Associate Producer
SAMUEL LIFF

Original Cast Album on RCA Victor

Dances and Musical Numbers Staged by
JACK COLE

Directed by
VINCENTE MINNELLI

CHAPTER

24

The Muscle

The fates of two major musicals, *Mata Hari* and *The Happy Time,* bring into relief the importance of the Muscle to any production. The Muscle of a show—and every show has one—is that person who is in charge at Armageddon. The Muscle is chiefly responsible for what finally does or does not get on stage. Sometimes the Muscle can be a star, viz. Sandy Dennis. Sometimes it is the director. It can be the writer, if the writer is Arthur Miller (without Kazan) or Neil Simon (without Nichols). There are occasions, almost always disastrous, when the general manager or even the set designer can be the person who shapes things. If the Muscle is properly placed, the show has a chance for success: if not, not.

Mata Hari was the one genuinely ambitious musical of the year. With the spy-spoof fad at the flood, with Bonds and Flints and U.N.C.L.E. operatives all around us, the writers of *Mata Hari* had the really extraordinary notion of doing a musical play about the most famous female spy of them all. And doing it straight. *Mata Hari* was a serious antiwar show. In fact, Mata Hari was not really the central character. The fictional character LaFarge was, and it was his job in the story to track down the truth about the woman, to find out if she was or was not a spy, and if she was, destroy her. In the course of his search, he found out that she was indeed a spy, fell in love with her, and had her shot. The book, with no attempt for laughs, was the work of Jerome Coopersmith, and on paper, it seemed exceptionally capable.

The lyricist of the show was Martin Charnin. "Six years ago I had the idea for a musical on Mata Hari, and I went to a couple of producers, who all said, 'Hey, what a terrific part for Martha Raye.' They saw it as camp. I forgot about it after that." Eventually, he and Coopersmith and Edward Thomas, the composer, got together and wrote the show. Charnin was in great part responsible for a subplot thread, that of a young soldier who is first seen as a civilian, gets drafted, goes to fight and eventually becomes an enthusiast of the war.

This is a lyric sung by the young soldier. It is a letter written from the front, to his mother, Maman. It indicates, as well as anything, the kind of show the authors were trying for and the skill of the people involved in the attempt.

> I am safe, Maman,
> I am fine,
> We are deep, Maman,
> at the line.
> There are sounds, Maman,
> of the war,
> Rifles crack, Maman,
> cannons roar.
> I have fear, Maman,
> I'm afraid,
> Not of bombs, Maman,
> nor grenade,
> There's a voice, Maman,
> I can't still,
> And it says, Maman,
> "Can you kill?"
> and it says, Maman,
> "Can you kill?"
>
> It is cold, Maman,
> it is black,
> With the dawn, Maman,
> we attack.
> There's a hill, Maman,

we must take,
Can you tell, Maman,
that I shake?
I may die, Maman,
I may die,
This may be, Maman,
my good-bye.
It is time, Maman,
there's the sun,
Will I fight, Maman,
will I run?
Will I fight, Maman,
will I run?

He was young, Maman,
he was small,
I was trapped, Maman,
by a wall.
Then he lunged, Maman,
and I spun,
Face to face, Maman,
gun to gun.
Then and there, Maman,
I could see,
He was me, Maman,
he was me.
Just a boy, Maman,
not a man,
Can I kill, Maman?
Yes I can.
Can I kill, Maman?
Yes, I can.

When enough of the show was written to show to a producer, the three writers took it to David Merrick. Why? One of them said: "David gets them on; it's as simple as that." Merrick agreed to produce the show, and at Merrick's suggestion, Vincente Minnelli was given the chance to direct it, and accepted.

This is probably always *the* step in the making of a musical: a director has got to get it up there. It's his baby, in a sense, and you have to go with him as long as you can, with his suggestions, his "feel"; if you don't, then you're involved in a mutinous situation, and it's hard enough getting a musical done without a mutiny going on.

Minnelli is a very famous film director, but he had not worked on Broadway for a quarter of a century. He spent the interim mostly at Metro-Goldwyn-Mayer mostly on musicals. "Meet Me in St. Louis" was a Minnelli-directed musical. So was "The Band Wagon." And "An American in Paris." And "Gigi" won him the Academy Award. He was in the front rank of Hollywood directors.

Once.

Lately, it's been rough. They really don't come back to Broadway for any other reason. Not after they're set out there for any period of time. Not a quarter century of time. Here are Minnelli's last five films, all of them critical fiascos. How many have you heard of? How many have you seen? How many have you liked?

1. "The Sandpiper"
2. "Goodbye, Charlie"
3. "The Courtship of Eddie's Father"
4. "The Four Horsemen of the Apocalypse"
5. "Two Weeks in Another Town"

Marisa Mell, the one genuine stunner to sign for a Broadway show this entire season, was given *Mata Hari*'s title role: Pernell Roberts, late of "Bonanza," was chosen to play LaFarge. Rehearsals began. At first the show simply seemed undirected, misdirected. But by the time of the first-act run-through, Merrick was approached to do something about Minnelli. He refused. Mr. Minnelli's vision of the war, whatever it was, was going to open in Washington for try-outs.

Basically, Minnelli's contribution to the show was to make it Mata Hari's story. The original title of the show was *Ballad for a Firing Squad,* and it was a romance, and passionate. That was what it was meant to be. Minnelli made it sexless. He had taken a deadly serious antiwar effort and directed it as if it were a Nelson Eddy–Jeanette MacDonald movie.

The first Washington preview, done for the Women's National Democratic Club, with Senators and Cabinet members and Lynda Bird Johnson among others present, was a case of instant legend. Murphy's Law went into overdrive: wigs fell off, sets collapsed, dancers tripped over each other, and the audience wouldn't stop laughing in the wrong places. The culminating event occurred at the end when Mata Hari, shot dead by the firing squad and lying there breathing heavily in full view of the audience, raised her hand to her forehead. The next day, one Washington society column was headlined MATA HARI HILARIOUS.

The show opened there a few days later and got bombed. Again, and consistently, Merrick was requested to bring in a new director. Again, and consistently, Merrick refused. Merrick was definitely the Muscle here, and if the show was to be saved before it got to New York, Minnelli clearly was not the man to direct it. His work was so helpless, so inept, that he had the bulk of the action taking place upstage at a distance far removed from the audience, making the show, in a musical-comedy sense, all but invisible. Most musicals need to be brightly lit and played as close to the footlights as possible so that the audience can see and hear them.

An example of the deadening effect of having the show going on toward the rear of the stage can be given by the following story, which happened near the end of the Washington run. Three Theatre Guild-type ladies were walking up the aisle after it was over. "Well, it's not as bad as they say," the first said. The second said, "I liked that patriotic number a lot." A man walking out ahead of them turned and said, "May I tell you why you liked that number?" The ladies nodded.

"Because it was done down by the footlights. You could see it."

"*Yes!*" all three ladies said, and they all but jumped up in the air on the word.

Since I was the man walking out ahead of them, I can swear to the veracity of the anecdote. All three did cry out "Yes" simultaneously because it was that clear a thing: Minnelli had directed the show in such a way that it took place, for practical purposes, out of sight of the audience.

When I saw *Mata Hari*, I talked to a couple of ushers—one tall, one short—before the curtain. Doing my best to be reportorial, I began by saying, "They're having trouble, is that right?"

The tall usher gave me a look: "I was here for that first preview, if that's what you mean."

"Was it that bad?"

The girl exploded. "She's shot! Mata Hari's shot! And she's dressed all in black, except that she's got white hands—gloves, I guess—and she moves the hand close to the audience and rubs her nose! ANY AMATEUR KNOWS YOU DON'T MOVE WHEN YOU'VE BEEN PRONOUNCED DEAD." She paused a moment. "It's better now. They cut the firing-squad scene. I think she panted too heavily. The whole show's better now."

"They laughed last night," the short usher said.

"Yeah," the tall girl agreed. "But not in the serious parts." Then she turned to me. "Whatever anybody says, Pernell Roberts is marvelous."

She was right. He was.

Not that it mattered, since the show closed in Washington. How much it lost is conjecture: guesses range from $500,000 to $800,000. Even when I saw it, much of the potential quality of the work was evident. At intermission people kept saying, "It's better than they said," or, "It's really not so bad." Could it have been saved? A lot of people think not. One reporter told me: "It could never have worked. Mata Hari is by nature a sexy dame. There wasn't a laugh all night. No fun. The whole show was on the wrong trail." There were many suggestions to try and make it all a spoof. My own guess is that although I have no idea whether the show could have worked, the spoof necessity is nonsense. *Gypsy* was about Gypsy Rose Lee, who was the most famous stripper of them all, and there isn't a mention of stripping in that whole long brilliant first act, and no one ever complained. Because the director, in that case Robbins, showed the audience where to look and what to expect.

In this case, Minnelli was helpless to do anything except just what he did. The show was complicated by as damaging a job of costuming (by Irene Sharaff) as anything I've ever seen. Marisa Mell is a beauty. By Hollywood standards. By Broadway standards, she's Garbo. Sharaff managed to make her look plain or else, by the use of gigantic hats, to hide her face entirely. The blame for this must rest with Minnelli too, just as much as his approving sets that put the action in left field.

The only prayer the show had was to get rid of Minnelli, but Merrick would have none of this. Merrick was the Muscle and he stood pat. Why? He is as astute a showman as Broadway offers at the moment, and the best guess is that he was under heavy pressure at the time. He had three musicals dying on the road then and he probably felt that the other two were more fixable. God knows he worked to salvage *Dow Jones,* bringing in an entirely new creative team. But *Dow Jones* was a show you could hemstitch: raise the pocket a little, take off the cuffs, maybe it'll fit. *Mata Hari* was a musical with a concept, and good or bad, you had to buy it from the start. Unified shows like *Mata Hari* are always hardest to fix out of town because they have a texture peculiarly their own. A show like *Mame* can always be jazzed up: add more brass, write more gags, shove in some up-tempo numbers. *Mame* isn't meant to make sense, really; it's just meant to entertain people on the lowest, broadest level. Besides, *Mata Hari* didn't have much of an advance in New York compared with the other musicals that Merrick had in trouble. Perhaps if it had, he might have made a stab at saving it. But he didn't. A man can only do so much, and Merrick closed *Mata Hari* on the road. It was his decision. He was the Muscle.

The Happy Time was another Merrick musical, but in this case he wasn't even close to being the Muscle: Gower Champion was. And if Vincente Minnelli distorted *Mata Hari*, Gower Champion was at least as responsible for changing *The Happy Time*. The idea of doing something with *The Happy Time* material had been with Merrick since before the straight-play hit opened in 1950. The original stories on which the play was based appealed to Merrick, and he tried to get the rights then, but failed. "What I liked about it was the French Canadians on the North American continent trying to keep their language and nationality while surrounded by English people. I thought they were fighting an interesting battle. Years later I bought the play. But we're not using it."

The reason that they didn't use the play is explained by Richard Nash, who was to do the *Happy Time* libretto. "When David first offered me *The Happy Time*, I turned it down. I thought the story was too sentimental and it was about a teen-ager doing things I thought a teen-ager had a perfect right to do. Then I went to London to live for a year, and one night while David was over we were walking and he brought it up again. I said, 'No, I don't want to do that, but I have got an idea for an original about a small-town Midwestern photographer who comes home every four or five years and wrecks the family. And finally his father makes him tell the truth about the 'glamorous' life he's been leading—that he's a liar and a failure and has never found himself and is always living on the edge of dishonesty.' I made him a photographer because I wanted to find an artist who could go either way, towards art or commercialism. The original concept that I had came from three words: pictures; images; fantasies.

"Anyway, Merrick said, 'Why do they have to be Western—you're always doing Westerns—why don't you make them a French-Canadian family?' And I said, 'Why?' And he said, 'Because I own *The Happy Time*, and I've got to put it to use.' "

So the story evolved about a charming photographer who returns to his family in a small Canadian town filled with stories of travels and awards, which only his father knows are false. The third central character was the photographer's nephew, crossing into manhood, who adores the photographer and finds his own hard-working father stuffy and a bore. Eventually, when the pressures on the boy build and he wants to go and follow the photographer, the old grandfather makes the photographer tell the boy the truth: that it is all false, that his life is tawdry and dreary and worth nothing at all. Ideal casting for Jacques, the photographer, might have been Robert Preston or, if you wanted a French actor, Yves Montand; someone, in other words, with mileage. Nash explained: "I wanted a man who ought to have been a father by now, a man who has lost his chances, and to whom the nephew means everything, so that when he tells the truth and gives him up, he's really giving up something. *Reality versus romance is my only theme.*"

For the score's composers, Merrick hired John Kander and Fred Ebb, fresh from their success with *Cabaret*. On June 21 they played the score for a bunch of friends in Ebb's apartment on Seventy-second Street. As previously stated, a score played in a living room and a score played on a stage have almost no resemblance to each other, but certain things could be said of the *Happy Time* songs after one hearing: they were lyric, they were quiet, they were small. Nash and Kander and Ebb had written a "little" show that was intensely personal; they had written what might almost be called a chamber musical, and possibly it would have played well in a small straight-play theatre with a small orchestra and no chorus to speak of—just the characters in the family.

Gower Champion was signed to be the director. Apparently what appealed to Champion in *The Happy Time* was the notion of the photographer. Somehow during discussion the suggestion arose that the pictures taken by Jacques during the play should be simultaneously visible to the audience, projected onto a gigantic screen. As one of the creative people put it: "Gower took the projections notion and ran with it; the show became a memory piece with the whole stage a photographer's studio—no sets—everything is seen in terms of photographs, in terms of the photographer's own memory. He's like the stage manager in *Our Town,* except that it will be his own life he'll be telling. More than that even, the pictures that the audience will see projected on the screen are the pictures in his head, but not necessarily what happened: sometimes he'll try to make the pictures conform to what he wants to be true. There's a song, 'I Don't Remember You,' that he'll sing to a girl, and while he sings we'll see the two of them together. In other words, his mind is remembering something different from what he says is true and even thinks is true: he can lie to himself too."

It was a stunning visual notion, but it presented certain problems. First of all, no one had the least idea if the projections would work. Merrick said, "I don't understand the projections. It's a big gamble; we have little scenery now. But Gower on the visual side is sensational, and I'm trusting that judgment." Champion *is* sensational on the visual side; anyone who has seen *Dolly!* has to be impressed with the look of it. Champion says, "When I'm considering a show, I usually get a visual picture of something in my mind. In *Dolly!* it was the wrap around the orchestra." In addition to trusting Champion's visual judgment, Merrick leaves Champion alone. There is a story about *Dolly!* when it was in such legendary trouble in Detroit. Someone called Champion and said, "He's here," meaning Merrick. Champion sat over the phone for five minutes before calling back and saying, "I'm not coming in today and I'm not coming back till he's gone." He then rented a car and went driving through the Michigan countryside. That night, when he got back to Detroit, Merrick was gone. Champion has said he has had two bleeding ulcers, and enough's enough.

Champion was in total control of *Happy Time*. Casting the crucial role of Jacques was terribly difficult. Champion suggested Robert Goulet, who was young, pretty, and had no mileage on him. Everybody else was against the notion. An observer of the Broadway scene said this: "The second I heard the Goulet rumor, I knew it would be Goulet. You've got to understand Champion to understand why. Champion is always asking himself, 'Am I really God?' His answer is, 'Yes.' Goulet fits right in with that. Everybody has always called Goulet an eight-by-ten glossy. Champion asks himself, 'How can I, Gower Champion, prove I'm God this time? I'll make Robert Goulet a star.' No one else wanted Goulet, and look who got the part." Champion wanted the show to rehearse in California, so the show rehearsed in California. Everything he wanted, he got.

But the problem that remained unanswered was the problem of the projected photographs, and Champion was completely aware of it. "The gimmick of the show is the projections," he said, "and they must not overpower the show." Technically, the projections presented enormous problems: since so much of the production depended on photographs flashed on an enormous screen that provided the backdrop for the show, the photographs had to be taken early. Champion said, "The show is a bitch: we rehearse first only the situations involving the photographs. After the pictures, I'm nailed to those actors. I don't want to have to shoot all those things over again," something that he eventually had to do, since two of the four central actors were replaced.

Rehearsals were, in spite of Champion's extraordinary skill at preparation, a bit strange. Nash, the book writer, was in the East, working on *Keep It in the Family*. Goulet, the star, had night-club commitments that kept him away for a while. This meant that there was no way to work on book scenes, because Goulet, who was the narrator of the story, was in every book scene. So what you had was a major Broadway musical rehearsing in Southern California for which all actors and costumes had to be set at the start, if possible, in order to expedite the working of a technical device.

Then the sets came, and they didn't work.

When I say they didn't work, I don't mean there were a few pesky little problems that needed attending to. I mean that all the scenery in front of the gigantic projection screen had to be whizzed in and out via turntables.

Well, the turntables didn't turn so hot.

How much this little item set back *The Happy Time* in terms of dollars is a matter of conjecture, but it did force a two-week postponement so that sets could be built that would work. So there they were, 3,000 miles from home, with God knows how many thousands of dollars of sets that wouldn't work, and rumors of disaster working overtime, and then Champion did this great thing. "Everybody thought we were in trouble," somebody said, "which of course we were, but Gower thought it would look good if it came out in the papers that he was so confident of the show that he gave everybody a week off. So, with proper publicity, he gave everybody a week off."

Finally, on Sunday, November 19, the show opened in Los Angeles. Champion had already decided that the musicians would not be in the orchestra pit but backstage and that the actors would sing without seeing the conductor, who would be back with his musicians conducting via closed-circuit TV. Well, it turned out that the screen for the projections did not allow sound to come through, so the orchestra sounded as if it were playing in Pasadena. (Eventually, when the show reached New York, Champion had the musicians back in the pit.)

The Los Angeles opening was a social triumph. Natalie Wood was there. And Carol Channing. And Julie Andrews and Henry Fonda and Bob Hope, Gregory Peck, Walter Matthau, Fred Astaire, Lee Remick, George Burns, on and on. Everyone was there.

Everyone was there except the characters in *The Happy Time*. Because the projections simply overpowered the small size and feel of the show. It was as if a boy and a girl were put in front of a Cinerama screen; they would be dwarfed even when the Cinerama screen was blank. Put a picture on the screen, and who'd look at the boy and girl?

This was the problem with *The Happy Time*. It began as a small family show with an abrasive script filled with legitimate family argument about a failure who didn't get the girl. The problem really was similar in kind to the problem that Champion faced out of town with *Hello, Dolly!* "The razzmatazz style of the piece was out of balance with Thornton Wilder's play," Champion said. "And with Carol, the big numbers were what was working. So it was a matter of bringing the rest of the show up to that pitch."

In a sense, what Champion tried with *Happy Time* was to recreate the *Dolly!* experience. The projections—the razzmatazz part of the show—stayed, because that was the part of the show that was working. And the part that wasn't working—the part involving characters—Champion tried to brighten up, to make lighter, to give the audience, in other words, a "happy time."

There had been, as stated, a certain abrasive quality to Nash's script; the people, after all, had good reason for being at each other. The abrasive quality was scrubbed out, leaving what Nash had been afraid of in the very beginning when he originally turned down the show: a residue of treacle. The show got soft, gooey, marshmallow-cored.

The Goulet character originally had no girl in the show. There was a girl in the town—a woman really, not young—who was the local schoolteacher. But she and Goulet did not end up together. That changed. First it was decided to make the girl younger, and cast replacements began. Then, finally, after an incredible amount of hesitation on the part of Champion, the version that opened in New York had Goulet announce to the audience that he has married the girl.

The final change was the most important: Jacques, the phony photographer, the failure, the man who made up stories about his successful life around the world, was changed into an actual success. Now this presents a certain problem: it tears the guts out of the show. Whereas before Jacques had told his nephew that his life was all a lie, now what he tells him is yes, yes, it is true, he is famous and celebrated and everybody knows him, but nobody *really* knows him. His life, in other words, is glamorous and gay but superficial. Well, team, this ain't the same as its being a lie.

Most important, that change—making the unsuccessful man who dreamed of success and lived on unreality into an internationally successful photographer—completely negates any value that Richard Nash brings to a show as a writer. Nash's theme in *Happy Time,* as in *The Rainmaker,* is reality versus romance. That's what the man writes about. By making Jacques a success, the "romance" was gone.

At any rate, these were Champion's decisions, and the show began to change. Fred Ebb, the laconic and skillful lyricist of the show, said of it at this point: "If you really listened to what the people said up on stage you couldn't stand it, it would be so confusing. If you have ever thought that an audience pays attention to the libretto of a musical, what's going on out here now would very quickly disabuse you of that notion. We're playing part of one show, part of another, and the audience walks out smiling, saying, 'I didn't know that Robert Goulet sweated.' "

Merrick was helpless to do anything. In any struggle for power, the Muscle wins, and in a Champion show, Champion is the Muscle. He has earned that power by making many people rich, including Merrick. Merrick was not pleased with the show that he was producing: it was a long way from the French-Canadian family fighting for their identity against an encroaching English-speaking society. Champion as much as possible avoided confrontations with Merrick, who, when he couldn't find his director, would go around calling him a "Presbyterian Hitler."

Champion had warned everybody that Merrick would try and get them to do what he, Merrick, wanted by dividing and conquering, which, of course, Merrick is famous for. The kind of thing he's apt to do, for example, is to call someone on the phone and say, "This is David Merrick, and what we've got up there is a monumental disaster; I'm closing the show rather than humiliate us all." Or, if he's talking to a librettist, he might say that the book is getting ruined by the songs. In a very real sense, Merrick tries to almost panic people into changing a show to fit his vision of it. This is not remotely meant as criticism of the man; it's how he works and it's been successful, and many creative people respond to it. One successful man who has worked for Merrick said, "He scares me to death.

He literally scares me to death. But he gets the best work out of me by doing it." But all Merrick's efforts failed in this case, because Champion had told everybody exactly how Merrick would act and what he would say before he said it. When Merrick finally did act, the effect was much the same as that of any *déjà vu:* arresting, but not permanent.

The Happy Time came to New York and extended its previews while Champion continued to change the show. When the audience enters the theatre for the show, there is no curtain: what the audience sees is what eventually turns into the photographer's studio. All theatres have curtains, of course; it's a fire law. But the fact that *The Happy Time*'s curtain was up all the time proved particularly painful to Fred Ebb, the lyricist, who sneaked hopefully into an early preview. The Broadway Theatre is large, and this night it was not anywhere near full. Ebb, praying that the show might somehow at last work, sat hunched toward the rear of the orchestra, waiting for the lights to dim. Some people sat near him and looked around.

"I told you it was a bomb," one of them said. "It was a stiff in Los Angeles, and it's gonna be a stiff here. New Yorkers can smell a stinker. Look, the place is empty."

Ebb hunched down deeper into his seat.

"For chrissakes," another of them said, gesturing toward the stage, "ten bucks a seat and the rotten show doesn't even have a curtain."

"Of course it doesn't have a curtain," somebody else said. "It would only be throwing good money after bad."

Ebb watched the rest of the show from the distant rear corner, alone. . . .

The Happy Time opened January 18 without Clive Barnes, who was late, as has been explained, lecturing in Pittsburgh. And as has also been said, many of the notices for *Happy Time* were surprisingly venomous. But everybody loved Gower Champion's work. Here is a typical quote: "Another of Gower Champion's virtuoso staging and choreographic jobs doesn't succeed in giving sufficient substance and vitality to 'The Happy Time.' . . ." When it came time to give the Tony awards, Champion won two, for choreography and direction. He deserved his awards. But he also deserved to get blasted for the sentimental book and the unnerving vast feel of the show. Yes, he made it good, and yes, he made it bad.

There are few things more irritating to a theatre professional than reading a review that says something like, "Mary Martin did what she could to give life to 'such and such' last night at the Biltmore

Theatre . . ." That's not fair. "Such and such" *only exists* because Mary Martin wanted to do it. And every bit of its present form is as close to her pleasure as money and skill can make it. The Muscle gives a show its final form. If it's a Hal Prince show, he is the Muscle, and if you like *Cabaret*, praise him. But if you don't, blame him. Hal Prince is the Muscle always, unless Jerome Robbins is his director. Jerome Robbins is *always* the Muscle. So is Champion. So is Nichols. And so they will be until their productions start to lose money.

Being the Muscle is the most prized status you can have on Broadway, because it is the only way you can possibly achieve total satisfaction. Productions—all productions—are literally struggles for power, little wars, if you will, and the battle isn't waged over real estate or wealth, but over whose vision gets up there. Someone *has* to dominate. Theatre is a group endeavor, and every member of that group sees something in his head, and he wants that "something" translated to the stage. But only the Muscle has a chance to be fulfilled; the others may end up rich, but they'll also end up frustrated. Everybody else's vision dies somewhere along the way.

And that is why it is probably not too dramatic a thing to say that each and every Broadway show is in reality a little battle to the death.

BROOKS ATKINSON THEATRE

James Nederlander and Michael Myerberg, Owner-Managers

Joseph Cates and Henry Fownes

Michael Medwin (for Memorial Ltd.)

present

ALBERT FINNEY

in

A DAY IN THE DEATH OF JOE EGG

A New Comedy by
PETER NICHOLS

with

ZENA WALKER	**JOHN CARSON**
ELIZABETH HUBBARD	**SUSAN ALPERN**

AND

JOAN HICKSON

Directed by
MICHAEL BLAKEMORE

Designed by	*Music by*	*Lighting Design &* *Set Supervision by*
ROBIN PIDCOCK	**ANDY PARK**	**LLOYD BURLINGAME**

As Originally produced by The Glasgow Citizens' Theatre

Doing Our Thing

The purpose of this chapter is to tell you why I can't tell you about *A Day in the Death of Joe Egg*, which was, for me, the best thing to hit Broadway in years.

It is a play about a couple with a ten-year-old incurably spastic daughter whom they refer to as Joe Egg. "A drama," you said. No. A comedy. "Ahhh," you say, "a black comedy, one of those." No. A warm comedy. A warm, tender, moving, wrackingly funny, laugh-out-loud comedy. "Impossible," you say, but then, if you're exceptionally quick, you realize how they manage to do it: "They only talk about the child," you say, "but we in the audience never have to see her."

If you got that, my hat would be off to your wisdom, but you would still be wrong. They do bring the child on stage. The child spends perhaps a third of the play on stage, a vegetable in a wheelchair. Sometimes she has little fits, sometimes big ones; her pants get wet; she needs changing. Her father tells her mother at the start of Act II that he's killed her, and he uses a sofa pillow to demonstrate just how he did it. It's all a lie, of course; he doesn't try to kill her until the end of Act II. But the doctors manage to save Joe, so her father simply walks out, leaves, without a word to her mother. The curtain comes down on that moment, with the father gone, the

mother ignorant that she has been deserted, left forever with a vegetable child.

There is no way that *Joe Egg* can be warm and funny, which is
why, since it is warm and funny, its achievement is so great. Personally, I didn't believe that such a play was possible; it expanded my
view of the world.

Part of the reason why the play works is the special way it's done:
the parents, Sheila and Bri(an), talk to the audience, telling the audience what it had been like to find out that their daughter was ill,
trying to get her cured, failing. They play little scenes for us in
almost a vaudevillian way, and there is a small combo on the side of
the stage that adds to the vaudeville feel. And as Sheil and Bri make
us laugh out loud with their lunatic adventures with lunatic doctors
and their constant terribly funny banter and joking with one another, we come to realize that it is only their laughter that has kept
them sane through their anguish.

Albert Finney played Bri, and Zena Walker, who was incredible,
played Sheila.

Two moments now from *Joe Egg:* in the first, Sheila and Bri are
playing a scene for us, doing a "bit," in which Zena Walker is still
playing Sheila, but Albert Finney is Bri being the doctor Sheila is
talking to about Joe. He is a mad doctor, out of some Transylvanian
medical school, with a terribly thick German accent. The "doctor"
has just explained to Sheila that Joe will always be a "wegetable."

SHEILA
*V*egetable

BRI
Vegetable.

SHEILA
But why? If her brain is physically sound, why doesn't it work?

BRI
(*Sighs, looks at her, thinks*)
Imagine a svitchboard—a telephone svitchboard. Ja?

SHEILA
I worked as a switchboard operator once.

BRI
Das ist wunderbar. Vell, imagine you're sitting zere now, facing ze board.
So?

SHEILA
So.

BRI
Some lines tied up, some vaiting to be used—suddenly—brr-brr, brr-brr—

SHEILA

Incoming call?

BRI

Exactly! You plug in.

SHEILA

(*Mimes it—assuming a bright telephone voice*)
Universal Shafting.

BRI

(*Coming out of character*)
What?

SHEILA

That was the firm I worked for.

BRI

You've never put that in before.

SHEILA

(*Shrugs*)
I thought I would this time.

BRI

Universal Shafting? Story of your life.

Now when her "Universal Shafting" line throws him, when he is startled into sudden laughter by her saying a new line, the reality of the moment is so, I'm sorry, *real*, it stuns. Is Albert Finney startled? Or the mad doctor? Or Bri? And who said the line, Zena Walker or Sheila? Suddenly everything is sent spinning, and you don't know quite where you are any more, or what's going on, but whoever it is that's up there on stage, whatever it is they want, boy, do you hope they win.

The second moment comes at the first-act curtain. Sheila is alone on stage. Bri has wheeled poor Joe to bed. And Sheila tells us a long story about how once, just for a moment, she thought Joe was going to be all right because she seemed to have pulled down a bunch of blocks *voluntarily*. And after that, Sheila tries and tries to get Joe to repeat it, make it happen again, but Joe is still Joe, a helpless, incurable, spastic child, and there's the end of it. And during the speech, against her will, but because she just can't help it, Sheila cries. Then, back in control, she talks to us a bit about Bri and his constant joking about Joe, and she says, "I wish he'd talk more seriously about her. I wonder if he ever imagines what she'd be like if her brain worked. I do. And Bri's mother always says, 'Wouldn't she be lovely if she was running about?,' which makes Bri hoot with laughter. But I think of it too. Perhaps it's being a woman." And on those words comes lightning and thunder, though the lightning's only a brighter stage light and the thunder's only drums, but you've never seen anything as bright or heard as loud a noise, because there she is, poor Joe, and she's skipping rope like any other goddamned ten-year-old. And her entrance comes as such a shock, such a heart-stopping surprise, that—I don't know, but son of a bitch—that's what it's all about, right there.

Flashback: 1951. It is the summer after my junior year at Oberlin, and I am back home in Illinois learning how to type. I am going to be a writer, and writers should know how to type, so I decide to teach myself. Besides, there's Korea, and if you can type, maybe they'll let you be a clerk and not send you where you'll be killed.

Hot, dull days outside Chicago. Hours of "a s d f j k l; a s d f j k l." Every so often, to break the boredom, I would sprawl on the couch and turn on the TV; the Cubs were playing the Giants. I hate the Cubs. All through grammar school, a friend of mine, Peter Zischke, and I were the only two White Sox fans in town. The Cubs were good, the Sox always second division, so we took our share of punishment, Peter Zischke and I.

So there I am, an incipient draft dodger, learning to type, with index fingers aching from the reach, and this rookie drives in a run against the Cubs. I go back to my typing; a little later I'm back on the couch, and there's a catch made that robs the Cubs, and this same rookie has done it. Back to the typing. But now I am anxious to return to the game, because even though I haven't heard of this rookie, anybody who dents the Cubbies can't be all bad. I fall on the couch just in time.

He parks one. I mean, he powders it. *Splat!* And the thing is bouncing in the bleachers. I watch him circle the bases, and he has made my day. The game ends soon after, with the Giants winning. The next day I am typing again, and again the Cubs are on the tube, only this afternoon I am on the couch by game time. Nothing much happens until this rookie rockets one again. From the heels and gone. The kid is a hitter, but so was Dino Restelli till the pitchers learned he couldn't hit the curve. I quickly type "a s d f" a few times, then decide to quit kidding myself and finesse the typing till after. I flop back down on the sofa, and in no time some Cub belts one out, a shot to dead center, gone. This is painful to me, because I really hate the Cubs and I hate the Cub fans too, and the minute the guy creams the ball, they all start screaming and shrieking.

But this rookie, this stupid Giant rookie, this stupid, green, moron rookie is so dumb he doesn't even know it's out of the park. He takes off after the ball, and he can fly, but what the hell's the point, the ball's gone, it's practically out of there now, only the rookie goes into overdrive; his hat flies off and he's chasing with all he's got, and the ball's in the air and he's on the ground but he's gaining on it all the same. And then the center-field fence moves into the picture, vine-covered and immobile, and if it wasn't for the fence, this kid might have a shot at the ball, but not with the fence there. And suddenly you know he's so stop-the-fight stupid that he doesn't even realize the wall's there slamming in on him. Now there are just the three of them in the picture, the ball, the wall and this rookie, and he a dead man, except that suddenly you know no wall is going to give this kid trouble. Because the gloved hand flies up, the ball drops in, and he spins off the wall, the throw back to the infield completed almost before the ball is even caught.

It was Willie Mays, obviously, and I fell in love with him that afternoon and have never wavered since. I'm sure he's had better series than that one, but every time I looked up he was rocketing one, or charging like an infielder to take a ball off his shoe tops, or starting before the bat crack to where the ball was eventually going to land. And watching him then, I realized unconsciously that it was about time he arrived on my horizon, because during all those years of being bored by baseball, of sitting in bleacher seats for pitchers' battles, or dying with the heat while the manager brought in some slow reliever, I'd been waiting for Willie.

He was what it was all about. Those skills of his—the speed of the turn and throw *after* the catch, the instinctive start to where the ball was going to land almost before the ball had been hit—those skills were only for baseball. Oh, he probably could have played halfback, and I'm sure if you'd take a day to teach him tennis, he'd whip you soon enough. But it wouldn't have been the same. He was the reason I watched all those terrible years. I was waiting for Willie because in my head there was a notion of the way things ought to happen but never quite do. Not until Willie came along and did his demonstration and I could finally sit there and say to myself, "Oh sure, *that's* it." Mays is peculiar to baseball.

Joe Egg is peculiar to the stage. There is no way that it can ever be as good in any other form. You can make a movie out of it, and if the writing and acting are sound, it'll play. And you can make a novel out of it, too, and go inside the people if you like, and the situation would probably still hold. But not as well. And it won't work as well as a symphony or a ballet or a painting or any other goddam thing. And it won't work as well on the printed page either, just as talking about Willie's hat flying off isn't the same as seeing it go, because when you only talk about the hat, you miss seeing the way the body works underneath it.

I've been waiting a long time for *Joe Egg* too. It's the reason I've sat through all those stiffs, bolted all those rotten Times Square dinners, battled crowds to get through the lobby before the play, fought for taxis after. I've been waiting all this time for *Joe Egg* to come along and do its demonstration, so that I could sit back and say to myself, "Oh sure, *that's* it." *Joe Egg* is what it's all been for: it's the theatre's special "thing," and no other art form can steal it away. It is, in the true and non-phony sense of the word, "theatrical," and that's why nobody can ever *tell* you about *Joe Egg*.

You gotta be there.

SAM S. SHUBERT THEATRE

JOSEPH P. HARRIS and IRA BERNSTEIN

present

STEVE LAWRENCE   EYDIE GORME

in

GOLDEN RAINBOW

A NEW MUSICAL

Book by
ERNEST KINOY

Music & Lyrics by
WALTER MARKS

Based on a Play by **ARNOLD SCHULMAN**

Dances & Musical Numbers Staged by
RONALD FIELD

with **JOSEPH SIROLA**

SID RAYMOND	**WILL HUSSUNG**	**HOWARD MANN**	**FAY SAPPINGTON**
ALAN KASS	**SAM KRESSEN**	**DIANA SAUNDERS**	**MARILYN COOPER**

and **SCOTT JACOBY**

Scenery & Lighting by **ROBERT RANDOLPH**   Costumes by **ALVIN COLT**
Musical Direction & Vocal Arrangements by **ELLIOT LAWRENCE**
Orchestrations by **PAT WILLIAMS** and **JACK ANDREWS**
Dance Music Arranged by **MARVIN HAMLISCH**
Hair Styles by **ERNEST ADLER**   Production Stage Manager **TERENCE LITTLE**
Original Broadway Cast Album Recorded by **CALENDAR RECORDS**

Entire Production Directed by
ARTHUR STORCH

A DIPLOMAT PRODUCTION

Washing Garbage

The chief points of interest about *Golden Rainbow:* first, it was the one "rilly big shew" of the season; because of its stars, Steve and Eydie, it was the only show all year to have an advance of over $1,000,000. The second main point to be made about *Golden Rainbow* is this: it could never have been any good.

Any explanation why should begin with a remark made years ago by Sheldon Harnick. Harnick, a gentle soul, was out of town with a musical, and there was trouble. One particular book scene was causing untold agony; it was short and stupefyingly dull, but it couldn't be cut entirely because it tied up a mass of plot complications. Nothing the writer could do seemed to help. A dozen different approaches to the scene were tried, and each managed to be worse than the preceding one. Still, the plot had to be taken care of, so the writer kept at it, and one morning the actors were reading his latest version out loud from the stage when Harnick wandered into the theatre. Harnick listened to the newest version. After it was done, the writer walked over to him. "It's better, wouldn't you say?" the writer asked.

"Oh, yes," Harnick managed.

"But it still isn't any good, is it?"

Harnick shook his head sadly and said, "The trouble with washing garbage is that when you're done, it's still garbage."

That was the story of *Golden Rainbow,* as we shall see. The plot came from Arnold Schulman's sweet 1957 play, *A Hole in the Head.* The main character, a man of forty, is trying to run a resort hotel in Miami. A widower, he lives with his son of twelve, and the boy's future is the main concern of the play. The boy's father, needing money quickly, phones his successful older brother in New York and asks him to send $5,300 because the boy is sick and needs care. The kicker, of course, is that the older brother and his wife don't send the money; they fly down instead, and are appalled at the way the boy is being brought up. They have the finances as well as the time to bring the boy up right. Will they take the boy away or will he stay with his father, who can't really bring him up with much of anything but affection? (There is a terrific small part of a widow whom the father has a blind date with in the hopes that he'll settle down, but the match doesn't come to anything.)

In other words, the comedy hinges on what will happen to the boy. This is all handled realistically and with kindness; there are no villains in the play. The father, clearly a failure at running a hotel, is good for only one thing: making a living by selling on the road. But if he does that, who will take care of the child? Obviously the older brother and his wife, who have money, security and the experience of having raised two sons of their own.

It was composer-lyricist Walter Marks's idea to make a musical of *Hole in the Head.* Marks was intrigued by the simple story and the Miami locale. He wrote a few songs for the play and eventually contacted the author of *Hole in the Head,* Arnold Schulman.

Schulman at first apparently didn't want to make a musical of his play. He had gone through a ghastly experience with *Jennie,* the Mary Martin disaster of a few years before, and the notion of returning to the theatre, particularly the musical theatre, was uninviting. Then Schulman was told that Steve Lawrence was interested in playing the lead. Lawrence, a record name, had achieved considerable personal success playing the title role in the musical version of *What Makes Sammy Run?* The show lost a lot of money, but it ran a long time, and the length of the run was attributed to Lawrence's popularity. At this point, Schulman must have begun to get sucked in. He has been quoted as saying: "I found myself caught up in it again, just as with Mary Martin: big stars, guaranteed-for-a-year run, all that crap."

Lawrence was perhaps a little young to play a man with a twelve-year-old son, but he had the talent to pull it off. And the lovely secondary role of the widow seemed a natural for Eydie Gorme, who had never acted before.

Only she didn't want to play a secondary role. Even a good secondary one. She wanted a star part, an equivalent star part. The trouble was that there wasn't one in the story. So Lawrence and Gorme began attacking the part of the older brother in the play; they felt he had all the laughs, all the good lines.

In a moment of madness, someone—probably Schulman—suggested making Gorme the older brother. It would take a little reworking, obviously, changing the part originally played by David Burns—that of an ultraconservative Jewish businessman in his fifties—to something that Miss Gorme could handle. But Schulman set about trying to do it.

There was never any doubt who the director would be: Arthur Storch. This was Lawrence's decision and kind of interesting in that Storch had been the original director of *What Makes Sammy Run?* before he was fired in Philadelphia. It was Storch's idea to change the Miami locale to Las Vegas. "I felt that what Florida once meant —a jumping boom town, an unstable atmosphere to bring up a kid in—was what Vegas now had."

For choreographer, Lawrence hired Ronald Field, who had won a Tony the preceding year for his brilliant work on *Cabaret*. For producers, Lawrence secured the services of Joe Harris and Ira Bernstein, two of the best general managers on Broadway, although they had never produced before. The original billing of the show listed Harris and Bernstein as coproducers with Diplomat Productions, Lawrence and Gorme's company. It should be clear by now that the Muscle in this production belonged to Lawrence. The show was set to open November 8.

Schulman's version of the script had Miss Gorme as the sister of Lawrence's dead wife. She comes *with her mother* to Las Vegas, having received a wire that money is needed for Lawrence's child. Appalled at the way the child is being brought up, she determines to take him back to New York, where she lives with her mother, while she pursues her career as a buyer for Lord & Taylor.

Lawrence, when he received Schulman's first act, called Schulman in delight over the work, and at practically the same time began looking for someone else to take over the writing of the show. Secretly, the producers dispatched the choreographer to France where

Mike Stewart was living. Stewart, a name totally unknown to the general public, had at this time written the books for three Broadway musicals: *Bye, Bye Birdie, Carnival,* and *Hello, Dolly!* Stewart read the book and thought it was terrible, which was what everyone expected. He then listened to a demonstration record of the score and thought *that* was terrible too. Nothing was settled one way or the other, and the choreographer flew back to the States. Then the producers sent the composer to France to see Stewart. Rumor has it that Stewart said that 75% of the score had to go. This did not sit well with the composer, but still nothing was settled definitely because Stewart was, after all, the most successful book writer in the business. By this time, things were a little tense.

Because the advance sale just wouldn't stop mounting.

Steve and Eydie had done an audition for the theatre-party ladies, and the ladies all agreed: it was *the* show. So, except for the fact that the score was no good and nobody liked the book, everything was terrific. Except that Arnold Schulman had to be got rid of, and since he owned the original property, that wasn't as easy as it might have been.

But financial arrangements were made, and on July 28 the *Times* carried the story headlined, AUTHOR LEAVES OWN MUSICAL. Three days later the *Times* carried another story which said that the possible cancellation of the whole show would not happen, that arrangements with a new writer were being concluded but that the show would likely have to be postponed from its scheduled November 8 opening. Now postponing a show is bad under any conditions, but for *Golden Rainbow* it was particularly damaging because all those post-opening tickets had already been sold to parties. And that meant all those cancellations. And angry charities. And stung theatre-party ladies. Still, what had to be done was done, and on August 2 *Variety* printed an article that said that Mike Stewart was now rewriting the book for *Golden Rainbow*. This was a reasonable story —Stewart was back in America now—only it wasn't true. Whatever happened when Stewart finally met with the powers of the production is a matter of some dispute, but clearly there was not a meeting of minds. Stewart was out. But then, he had never been in.

Every day, more thousands in theatre parties. And no book.

Finally, Ernest Kinoy was hired. Kinoy, a television writer, is quick and craftsmanlike, and all concerned wished him well. (But secretly, all that was wanted was that he come up with a book that made sense, never mind the laughs, because—supersecretly—*Golden*

Rainbow had this incredible ultimate weapon: Neil Simon was going to take over out of town. This was much whispered. "Doc'll do it. Doc'll save us. Doc'll give us gags.") So with a new book writer and a new opening date, January 4, the biggest show of the season went into rehearsal. The agony was over.

The hard part was about to come.

The plot now had Lawrence wiring for money and Miss Gorme arriving, *alone*. It was almost as if all the other parts had to be dispensed with and all the extra lines added to Miss Gorme's part in order to make it as big as her husband's. Miss Gorme played the sister of Lawrence's late wife. She is appalled at the life her nephew is leading. It also turns out, folks, that she dated Lawrence back in the old days; they were almost a "thing" until her sister entered the picture. One of the items that crippled this story was its blinding predictability. You knew what was going to happen before it happened, and you were hardly ever wrong: Steve and Eydie, watching a desert sunrise, would eventually discover true love.

But the other thing, the fatal thing, the thing that made the show a true example of washing garbage was this: the threat was gone.

If you're walking down the street with the Kohinoor diamond, and someone sticks a pistol at your head and says, "Hand it over," you hand it over; no one would ever quibble with you. But if you're walking down the street with the Kohinoor diamond, and someone sticks his pinkie at your head and says, "Hand it over," it isn't the same. It's just not believable that you would give up the most valuable thing in the world to you because of a little finger. You'd scream, fight, run, shout for help, but you'd keep the diamond. There's no reason not to: remove the pistol and you remove the threat.

Get this plot now: the widower father of a child is taking care of the child, granted, a bit bizarrely. Comes along his sister-in-law, who lives alone and works all day for Lord & Taylor, and she says, "I'm taking your kid 'cause you can't take care of him properly."

The answer's gotta be, *"You're* gonna do it better?" A woman alone? A woman with a full-time job? A woman who's never had any experience raising a child? A judge is going to take a child away from its God-given father and ship him off to a spinster aunt who won't even be there to take care of the kid?

No way.

The run-through of *Golden Rainbow* was not, apparently, a triumph. A dancer at the run-through said: "I knew right then that

Eydie was going to have laryngitis for the Philly opening; that way she couldn't lose. Just getting through the opening night would be a triumph. Don't you know opening night in Philly she can hardly talk. And don't you know ten days after that she was already rewriting the lyrics."

The show received what is called "mixed" notices, but business was marvelous. Still, the show was in terrible trouble. Every day Doc Simon's name was whispered again (apparently Simon never had the least notion of doing *Golden Rainbow;* it was already December, and *Plaza Suite* was very much on the horizon), and every day more and more people—friends of the stars—began bearing down on Philadelphia. Lawrence was taking over the show more and more. His career had undergone a terrible battering a few years back when his own television show, over which he did not have control, had been a disaster. Since then he has wanted complete charge of anything he has done. If it mattered any more, and sadly enough it doesn't, I think Lawrence could be the biggest musical star on Broadway. He can sing, he can move, he has presence, he has style, and he can act when he has to.

Whether he could also handle the advertising I'm not so sure, but that was the rumor that swept the street as the Philadelphia run neared its end. Lawrence wanted it all, and the producers simply didn't bother to fight him. They are canny men, and my guess would be that they knew the show would run at least a while because of its gigantic advance, and perhaps the length of its run would depend on how happy the stars were in their parts. So no matter what the cost, the stars were made happy.

Phony "breakups" were put in for Miss Gorme. This is a loathsome television *schtick* used extensively by people like Sammy Davis, who are laughing hysterically at one moment and then serious the next, and you know suddenly it is all false, the laughter, all put on. Eydie could giggle—her television experience had taught her that—so twice in the show she does her breakup: she seems to laugh suddenly, out of control, and Lawrence stops and grins and waits for her to get control, and the audience is delighted at seeing the two of them so loose and having such fun up there on stage. They also let Eydie play drunk because it helped her get through a scene she had trouble acting straight. They did what they could.

But they were still in trouble, and they knew it.

So they fired their choreographer and brought in a new one to redo some numbers, and they postponed their opening again. Statistics are not kept on most previews before opening, but *Golden Rainbow* was to have a grand total of 43, which may be the high for the decade, unless *Hot Spot* edged it out. On and on they worked; new songwriters were brought in to suggest new numbers, new book writers, friends of friends, anybody.

But they could never make it good. They had removed the threat and destroyed the plot, and what they probably should have done is jettisoned the damn thing entirely and just let the stars do their night-club act. But they clung to enough of the old plot to hang themselves.

On Sunday, February 4, they finally opened. The critics were surprisingly gentle. They weren't nice, but they weren't nasty either: just sort of bad. The show ran, of course. With an advance like that you have to run, at least a while.

Oh yes. Doc Simon finally did come. He saw a Wednesday mat in Philly, made a few suggestions, then beat it back to town. He didn't get where he got by being dumb.

PREMIERE PERFORMANCE, FEBRUARY 14, 1968

THE PLYMOUTH THEATRE

SAINT-SUBBER

presents

GEORGE C. SCOTT   MAUREEN STAPLETON

in

NEIL SIMON'S

New Comedy

PLAZA SUITE

with

CLAUDETTE NEVINS	BOB BALABAN	JOSE OCASIO

Scenic Production by	*Lighting by*	*Costumes by*
OLIVER SMITH	JEAN ROSENTHAL	PATRICIA ZIPPRODT

Hairstyles by ERNEST ADLER

Directed by

MIKE NICHOLS

Sunny Boy

At 9:50 A.M. there were 43 people standing in line at the box office of the Plymouth Theatre. At 9:55 there were 50. A digger—someone who buys large numbers of seats in advance for himself or, more usually, an illegal broker—was at the head of the line, buying a ton of seats, slowing things up. Finally, he left, and the next man in line asked for two seats for a Saturday night. "April 13 is the next Saturday night I have open," the box-office man said. He was speaking on the morning of February 15.

At 11:25 there were 150 people in line. Now understand, this isn't Radio City Music Hall. You don't get in for the next show; there's no instant gratification involved here. These people were standing there knowing that they would have to be content with the future.

At 11:30 a man bought two tickets and left the Plymouth lobby. He had waited in line 90 minutes to make the purchase. But the line was only 50 people long when he started; now it was triple that. At 1:15 there were still 150 people in line. (There was only one box-office window open during this period. There are two box-office windows in theatres, but if you open them both, you can obviously handle the crowd twice as fast, and the line will disappear in half the time. And since that's exactly what you don't want—the line to disappear—you keep only one window open.)

It was a sunny February afternoon, and the people in line didn't seem to care how long it might take to get up to the box-office window; three hours, maybe five. They were well dressed, most of them —men with briefcases, women with children in strollers—and they were perfectly content to stand there, waiting their turn to buy tickets for the first real blockbuster play to hit Broadway in 798 days.

Neil Simon was back in town.

Everyone knows that Neil Simon is a popular playwright, but not everyone knows just how popular a playwright Neil Simon is. This is just counting shows that have opened on Broadway in the sixties. Simon has had about the same number of productions as Edward Albee. But Simon has had more performances than Albee. Tennessee Williams has had about the same number of productions too. But Simon has had more performances than Williams. As a matter of fact, Simon has had more performances than Albee and Williams put together. William Inge? He's had a bad time of it this decade, but you can lump in his plays, and Simon has had more performances than Albee and Williams and Inge put together. Add Arthur Miller. That's not really fair, because in the sixties Miller has worked mostly with the Lincoln Center Repertory, but even adding those in, Simon has still had more performances than Albee and Williams and Inge and Miller all put together. The English: Harold Pinter. Harold Pinter or John Osborne. What about Harold Pinter *and* John Osborne? Simon has had more performances than Albee and Williams and Inge and Miller and Pinter and Osborne all put together. Throw in Richard Rodgers? Done. Throw in Richard Rodgers. Simon has had more performances than Albee and Williams and Inge and Miller and Pinter and Osborne and Rodgers all put together.

Why?

There is a story, probably apocryphal, concerning Stan Musial in his prime. A sportswriter approached Musial and asked whether he worried about slumps, and Musial thought a moment before saying that he didn't much, "because if I get to going badly, I can always hit to left," the point being, I suppose, that instead of trying to pull the ball out of the park for a home run, he would be content just to go with it where it was pitched, settling for singles until he was back in form. In other words, he could always hit.

So it is with Simon: he can always be funny. Actually, to "be funny" isn't Simon's gift. "I don't consider myself a funny person. I can say funny things sometimes, mostly as a defense. But with my family, I'm still like a kid: I'm polite, and I sit down and try not to mess up the room too much."

What Simon is able to do, to use his own phrase, is "write funny." "I started to make a living writing funny when I was nineteen. When I was in my teens, my brother wanted to write humor, so we bought a couple of joke books. Then in the army I saw Sid [Caesar] in, what was it, 'Tars and Spars'? I'd never seen anything like that." Eventually, Simon went to work for Caesar, and he loved it: "Mike Stewart would sit at the typewriter and correlate, and Sid would sit in a big chair facing him, and the rest of us would sit around them and I never laughed so much in my life. Everybody would throw out suggestions or funny lines; I was new, and I don't have the kind of personality to jump up and say, 'This is what's got to happen!' So sometimes I'd whisper to Carl Reiner and Carl would say, 'Doc's got it! Doc's got what ought to happen.' It was a marvelous thing when I went to work for Sid."

Eventually, of course, he stopped writing for television and started Broadway work. *Come Blow Your Horn* opened in 1961, and in the seven years since, Simon has become perhaps the highest-paid writer in the world.

Plaza Suite was originally four short plays, all occurring in the same suite at the Plaza Hotel. The first, virtually a monologue for George C. Scott, the male star, was cut during rehearsal, not because it wasn't funny—it may have been the funniest of the four—but because it didn't fit with the rest of the show, which didn't need any more laughs as it was and was also running long.

The last of the three plays that opened in New York, "Visitor from Forest Hills," generally got the best notices. Simon calls it an "entertainment piece," and it is easily the funniest of the remaining plays. It revolves around the situation of Scott and Maureen Stapleton, man and wife, who are trying to get their daughter the hell out of the bathroom where she has locked herself in instead of going downstairs to get married.

The middle play, "Visitor from Hollywood," has Scott and Stapleton enacting a seduction scene in which he is a big-deal-type Hollywood producer and she is his old true love from Tenafly, New Jersey. The piece is short, probably not completely thought out, and worth mentioning only because it is Simon's first attempt at writing sex comedy.

The first play, "Visitor from Mamaroneck," has Scott and Stapleton as a married couple in trouble. She has taken the particular suite to celebrate the anniversary of their wedding night, spent there 24 years before, only it turns out that she probably has the wrong suite and they've probably been married only 23 years. And Scott is probably having an affair. During the course of the action, the "probably" turns out to be truth, and the play ends with Scott leaving Stapleton and going off to see his mistress, his return enigmatically left up in the air. "Mamaroneck," the longest of the trio, is not only the best of the three and the best thing Simon has yet written, it is also, I think, the watershed play of his career.

For me, Simon is the most skillful playwright to have surfaced in the sixties. Not the best. The most skillful. What keeps him from being the best is that with all his skill he is trivial: you don't even remember what *Barefoot in the Park* was about when you're applauding the curtain calls. He is almost afraid to let a moment pass without laughter. A friend of his says: "Doc's never really relaxed unless a joke has just paid off or he's got one building." But friends also say that in real life he isn't like that; it isn't always happy-ending time with lots of laughs before the fade-out clinch. He is a bright man with a good mind and a fine supply of bile.

Only he can't quite tap it yet.

"Mamaroneck," for example, was originally going to be a full-length play, and the version that is playing now was the first act. "But after I finished what I've got now, I thought, 'That's really the end of it.' I couldn't think of an ending. In order to go on with it I would have had to write a happy ending: the second act would have shown him living with this young girl, maybe, and the third act would just be getting together again with his wife."

But aren't there other possibilities? Scott could have been happy living with the young girl; or Stapleton could have ended up happy, to her own surprise, now that she was done with a rotten marriage; or Scott could have been happy living with the young girl, but the young girl might have found him too old for her, too predictable, too dull. There are any number of other possibilities, all of them conceivable, all of them valid.

All of them a little on the dark side.

But Simon writes sunny. That, I think, is the main reason why he is so beyond-words successful; there is a sunny quality to his work, and you feel good when it's over. Not smarter; not cleansed; just good. And even though his thoughts are filled with shadows, his writing landscape is always bright. Now this would be fine, if he saw the world that way, but he doesn't. In other words, the fact that he says he would have had to *write* a happy ending is true, but he doesn't *feel* that a happy ending would ever have happened. He says: "I don't think the guy ever comes back to his wife. So many people around fifty have left their wives and married their secretaries; it's sort of a horrible thing."

But the "horrible thing" is more than he can put down now. That's why I think "Mamaroneck" is so crucial to his development; the man can go on doing "entertainment pieces" till the world looks level. The question is, will he? Or will he continue in the same direction as the first tentative step taken in "Mamaroneck"? God knows it is tentative; it was all he could do to end the play enigmatically, without some kind of contrived happy ending.

My personal feeling is that Simon might possibly be like Philip Barry, only better. Barry wrote wonderful comedies—*The Philadelphia Story, Holiday*—and less successful serious plays that never quite came off—*Hotel Universe, Here Come the Clowns.* I think that Simon, if he wants to, can do what Barry never managed: put it all together under one roof, into one play.

Will he? If the reception of "Mamaroneck" gives him sufficient confidence, maybe. Some critics didn't care much for it: Barnes said in the *Times* that "Simon is at his worst when he is at his most serious."

The morning after *Plaza Suite* opened, I was down at the theatre trying to look casual while moronically counting the number of people in line, when a camel-coated figure in sunglasses walked quietly by the crowd and headed for the stage door of the Plymouth. It was Simon, and I made some terrifically funny remark to him about how it was too bad, his having his first real bomb. No one noticed him as we stood there in front of the theatre, more and more people queuing up as we talked. I wondered if the line was the biggest he'd ever had for one of his plays. He took off his sunglasses and watched the people a moment. "I think *Odd Couple*. It's like *Odd Couple*."

I asked him how the opening had gone and he said, "We stood backstage after that first one ["we" being Simon and Mike Nichols, who had done such a fine, unmannered job of directing the "Mamaroneck" play], and we said we just couldn't hope for a better reaction. The best it ever got."

We shook hands and said good-bye, and he started into the Plymouth. Then he stopped. "Barnes didn't like the first one," he said. (Get this now: here is a man who, with the opening of the night before, has earned anywhere between $1,000,000 and $4,000,000, who had brought in the third blockbuster of a seven-year career in a decade when no other active writer has had more than one. If ever a Broadway figure had the world by the short hairs, this is the man, and what's on his mind and genuinely troubling him is that the most important critic in the city found his first attempt at a serious work a failure.)

"Most of my friends like the first one best. Barnes didn't like it though." We said good-bye again, and he slipped unnoticed into the theatre.

If Barnes had been less than kind about one of the three plays, some of the magazine writers were venomous toward the entire evening. *The New Yorker* critic felt that all three plays were full of disfiguring mechanical gags and that *Plaza Suite* marked a long step backwards for Simon.

The *Newsweek* (super)critic was so incoherently vitriolic that *Variety* even mentioned it later, wondering in their February 28 issue, "What could have been bugging Jack Kroll when he wrote that hysterical pan of 'Plaza Suite' in *Newsweek?*"

I think what was bugging him as well as the other critics and theatre intellectuals who worked up a considerable antagonism for the plays was this: in his earlier works, Simon was working on such a superficial level that so what if he's successful, he's just a TV gagman, right? But with the "Mamaroneck" part of *Plaza Suite,* he was giving the first indications of possibly working the other side of the street, and this they could not have.

Articles about Simon published after *Plaza Suite* opened indicated that the exhilaration was gone for him now. He is so successful, so wealthy, that many of the basic drives are sated. If this is true, it isn't particularly unusual. But something else, I think, is adding to the despondency: Simon went into *Plaza Suite* convinced he could still stand or fall on his own, that he had freedom. Before *Plaza Suite* left town, he said, "The position I'm in now only affords me an advance sale. The curtain goes up and I'm on my own; they don't give you anything free."

But reports kept coming in while *Plaza Suite* was out of town that audiences simply would not stop laughing, whether they were supposed to or not. It was Neil Simon, goddammit, and they were gonna laugh. After *Plaza Suite* had opened, he was asked about this. "It's true. Night after night we took out laugh after laugh. It got so insane: there was a moment in 'Mamaroneck' where George said something to Maureen, gestured, turned and walked to the door, and they laughed. We cut the line out altogether; he just gestured, walked to the door. They wouldn't stop laughing. Finally we had him go straight to the door, and they laughed at that. I don't know; Kazan and Robbins, they don't work Broadway any more. It's so crazy: I hate it when they knock me, and I hate it when they say 'Fantastic.' "

On May 8, in the Belasco Room at Sardi's, Simon received the Sam S. Shubert Foundation Award. I don't know what the award is given for, probably not much of anything except making the Shuberts richer. This year it was Simon's turn, and some Shubert mouthpiece got up and said they were giving the award to Simon because he makes people laugh at a time when the world is filled with fear. Then Simon was given this box with a medal in it, and pictures were taken, and he stood there while the room applauded. It was an impressive assemblage: Merrick and Prince were there, and Cohen and Chayefsky and Robert Goulet and Maureen Stapleton and lots of old theatre pros. It was a room filled, as someone remarked, with men who had spent years knifing each other; grudge mingled with hate over the cannelloni. But when the award was handed out, the applause was prolonged and genuine, for Simon's most remarkable achievement is this: in an envy-ridden racket, no one ever says anything unkind about him. He is not only the best comedy writer, he is somehow undespised. Until you've spent a year talking with these people about these people, you can't realize what an ultimate achievement that is.

When the applause finally stopped, Simon looked at the medal in the box. He started to talk. "I haven't had a turnout like this since my *bar mizvah*," he began. Laugh. "This award means a lot to me, and it especially means a lot winning it here in the Belasco Room, because this is where the opening-night party was held for my first play, *Come Blow Your Horn;* I remember that night because, well, it was my first opening, my first time out on Broadway, and they wouldn't let me in to the party. There was a man outside and he said, 'Who? Who are you?' and I said, 'I'm the author; just let me hear my reviews,' and he said, 'Nobody gets in.' " Simon talked a little more about the award that he had won for making people laugh. That's a great thing, making people laugh, and I wish Broadway had half a dozen pros as good as Simon turning them out every year. But it was also true, at least for me, that the award, coming from people like the Shuberts—the perfect representatives of Business on Broadway—meant that making people laugh was not just a part of the game, but its goal too. Now what happened next means nothing, and besides, I'm always looking for symbols. Still, it must be reported that Simon dropped the medal on the floor. It was probably an accident, and he quickly picked it up.

But I hope he drops a lot more medals like that before he's through.

BILLY ROSE THEATRE

MITCH MILLER presents

PAUL ROGERS NANCY WICKWIRE
in

"HERE'S WHERE I BELONG"

A NEW MUSICAL based upon the novel
EAST OF EDEN by JOHN STEINBECK

Book by | Music by | Lyrics by
Terrence McNally | Robert Waldman | Alfred Uhry

James Coco   with   Ken Kercheval

Heather Mac Rae

Bette Henritze   Dena Dietrich   Patricia Kelly   Casper Roos

—and—
WALTER McGINN

Scenery by
Ming Cho Lee

Costumes by
Ruth Morley

Lighting by
Jules Fisher

Dances and Musical Staging by TONY MORDENTE

Musical Direction & Vocal Arrangements by
Theodore Saidenberg

Orchestrations by
Glenn Osser   Norman Leyden   Jonathan Tunick

Entire Production Directed by MICHAEL KAHN

PRODUCED IN ASSOCIATION WITH UNITED ARTISTS
ORIGINAL CAST ALBUM BY UNITED ARTISTS RECORDS

Paul Rogers is a member of The Royal Shakespeare Company

HUDSON THEATRE

NOEL WEISS
Presents

ZIA MOHYEDDIN
in

THE GUIDE

by

HARVEY BREIT and PATRICIA RINEHART

Based upon the novel by R. K. NARAYAN

also starring

TITOS VANDIS   and   MICHAEL KERMOYAN

with JERRY RAM
and CHANDRIKA

Directed by
SHIRLEY BUTLER

Lighting by
MARTIN ARONSTEIN

Production Designed by
WILLIAM PITKIN

Temple Dance Staged by MATTEO

Music Supervised by
RAVI SHANKAR

Exclusive World Pacific Recording Artist

28

The Business

OPENING A SHOW

*H*ere's Where I Belong, a musical based on John Steinbeck's novel *East of Eden* opened on Broadway in March, 1968. It was produced by Mitch Miller.

Briefly, the plot concerned Cal and Aron Trask, twin brothers. Cal is bad, a troublemaker (but bright), a whorer arounder. Aron is good. Their father, Adam, favors the good son and is constantly berating the bad. The family moves to Salinas, California, shortly before the First World War. The boys' mother is dead. Or so they are told by their father. Actually, she is alive and well in Salinas, running a whorehouse. Now Aron, the good son, falls in love with Abra, a good girl, who—it turns out—becomes secretly attracted to the bad son, Cal. Adam, the father, visits Kate, the madam-mother, and gets her to sign a piece of paper that has something to do with his getting the money to send his good son to Stanford. The Trasks, father and sons, get involved in shipping lettuce by train, refrigerated, to New York City. The train gets stopped by a snowslide and they are ruined. This is the first-act story. The second act is less complicated. World War I has started, and Aron, the good son, is away at Stanford. Cal, the bad son (who knows by now about his mother), goes into the bean-growing business and in a few weeks (he is perhaps eighteen) makes $15,000, enough to pay back all the money that his father lost in the lettuce venture. He has also begun an affair with Abra, the good girl friend of his good brother. Come Thanksgiving dinner, Cal gives his father the money, but his father refuses to take it because Cal's bean growing has benefited the British and is immoral money, earned by war profiteering. Cal, shattered, takes his brother for a walk to his mother's whorehouse and forces a confrontation. Aron, shattered, runs away; Adam, shattered, has a heart attack. Lee, their Chinese servant (who has as large a role as anyone in the play except Cal), pleads with a crippled and stricken Adam to forgive his son, which Adam quietly does. The curtain comes down on Cal playing a deer-foot whistle that his father had whittled for him years before.

Many people remarked that this story is more fitting for grand opera than a Broadway musical, and that may be true. But unless a story is clear, it isn't fit for anything. And that was the terrible problem with *Here's Where I Belong*. What was *the* story? Was it Cal? Or Cal and his father? Or Cal and his brother? Or Cal and his brother and their relationship with their father? Or Cal stealing his brother's girl? And what about the mother in her whorehouse? It is an enormously complex piece of narrative to try and bring to life, complex and desperately serious. As one of the creative people said, "We didn't go into this to make a quick buck."

But the buck, whether quick or slow in coming, is an inescapable part of any musical today and one of the sources of great concern along Broadway. The buck. The costs. The fortune it takes to get it up there. And it is a fortune now. It requires maybe twice as much money today to do a musical as it did ten years ago.

Why does it cost so much to bring in a musical? Whenever questions about costs come up, general managers are the men to give the answers. Briefly, a general manager speaks for the producer in all matters of business. He negotiates contracts for actors and theatres, sets, costumes, etc. General managers—good ones—are enormously important to the financial well-being of a show, and they often tend to speak their own language. The following is a transcription of some general managers in conversation:

"I don't want the Belasco."

"What's wrong with the Belasco?"

"It's a hemp house."

"So?"

"So I need a counterweight. A counterweight house I'm fine."

"Sometimes a hemp house is better."

"Give me a sometimes."

"I can't come up with one right off, but you know I'm right."

"All right, you're right; I still gotta have a counterweight."

"Give a hemp house a little consideration and maybe . . ."

"Willya stop it! If I get a counterweight, I got a flyman can han-dle it all. Everything. A hemp house I gotta put on extras."

"Everything's flown in your show?"

"What do you think I've been talking about?"

"O.K., O.K., then you don't want the Belasco."

Max Allentuck, a slender, young-looking man of fifty-seven, was the general manager for *Here's Where I Belong*. Allentuck has been a general manager for a quarter of a century, and among the shows he has managed are *Death of a Salesman, Diary of Anne Frank* and *The Music Man*. There is a contemplative air about Allentuck; he speaks slowly, constantly smokes a pipe. "You have to allow for a musical to lose $150,000 out of town," Allentuck says. "You may not lose it, but you've got to allow for it if you're going to be budgeted properly." We were talking before *Here's Where I Belong* went on the road. "To do a musical without built-in insurance you have to be very brave."

"Built-in insurance" means something salable to the general pub-lic and the theatre-party ladies. *Here's Where I Belong* had nothing to sell: the authors and director were new or unknown; none of the leading performers had any sizable personal following. Everyone went into rehearsal with the full knowledge that unless they got rave notices, they were dead.

The money for the show—approximately $500,000—came from United Artists. This is standard today—a movie or a record com-pany putting up an enormous portion or all of the costs. Years ago, when a show could be done for $250,000, the money could be raised by selling small units to individuals. (It can still be done, of course, but it's miserably hard; one musical this year succeeded, but it took over 16 months.)

Here is where that $500,000 for *Here's Where I Belong* went. (All figures are, of course, approximate. They're reasonably accurate, but not to the penny.)

Advances to the authors:	$ 14,000	
Scenery:	$ 87,000	(This is high, but as Allentuck says, "Every show has its own structure. This one had twelve realistic sets, like the leaves for the willow tree—the first-act-curtain set. Those *leaves alone* cost $4,000.")

Props:	$ 15,000	
Costumes:	$ 48,500	(Including both advance to the designer and executing the costumes, plus any purchases that had to be made for the execution.)
Electrical and Sound:	$ 11,000	(This included an advance to the lighting designer, renting electrical and sound equipment, plus any equipment that had to be purchased.)
Directors and Assistants:	$ 19,150	(This included advances to the director, the choreographer, the vocal arranger and the dance-music arranger.)
Rehearsals:	$ 68,440	(This included salaries for the company. There were 42 people in all, and their salaries totaled $36,590. The crew cost $7,500, and $2,000 went for wardrobe and dresser personnel, $1,500 to the production secretary. The pianists were paid $2,500, while the conductor and musicians received $10,500. Stage managers were paid $6,000, the company manager $1,850.)
Advertising and Publicity:	$ 28,000	(The press agent got $3,000, including salary and expenses. Newspaper advertising came to $20,000. Printing and photos and signs totaled $5,000.)
Other:	$117,300	(This includes an enormous jumble of things: theatre rental, getting the scripts mimeographed, casting fees, flying people in to read, office expenses, legal expenses, payroll taxes, insurance, welfare and hospitalization, and $25,000 for musical arranging, copying, box-office expenses out of town, living expenses out of town, getting the sets up out of town, taking them down out of town, bringing them back to New York, getting them up in New York. And more.)
Bonds, Advances and Deposits:	$ 65,200	(This is, in a sense, returnable money, but it is still money that must be put up in advance and not touched until the show closes. It includes $25,000 to the theatre, $30,000 to Actors' Equity—the equivalent of two weeks' salary for the cast. Actors used to get stranded a lot. By insisting on the two weeks' salary in case of bankruptcy, Equity has overcome this hazard. Advances to other unions cover the rest.)

This comes, so far, to a total cost of $473,590. Since the musical was financed at $500,000, that leaves a total reserve of approximately $26,000. Obviously, in order for *Here's Where I Belong* not to be in serious financial trouble, it had to do business out of town.

The first newspaper advertising appeared on Sunday, December 3, prior to the January 15 opening. There were follow-up ads after that, and by the time the opening had arrived, 813 mail orders had been filled. Rule of thumb on an out-of-town mail order might be $15.00 per letter, meaning that approximately $12,000 had come in by mail. On January 8, the box office opened in Philadelphia. On Monday, they took in $1,750 over the window. ("Wrapped" is the theatre term.) The total for the week over the window was $7,550. (A hit show can wrap $15,000 a day.)

They played the Shubert Theatre in Philadelphia for three weeks, and capacity would have been about $290,000 for the run. To break even, $150,000 was needed. As indicated above, they had less than $20,000 in mail orders and box-office advance. But they did have Theatre Guild and Show of the Month subscriptions, and this may have accounted for between $75,000 and $90,000 in advance sales. Helpful. Life-giving almost. But still not enough. If they were not to take a terrible financial beating in Philadelphia, they needed good reviews.

The reviews were dreadful. The day after they opened, there were 44 pieces of mail. Seven days after that, there were 24. The week after that, there were none. Box-office sales fell off terribly. During the second week, they wrapped an average of $1,000 a day over the window. In the last week, the daily average dropped to less than $400.

Here's Where I Belong grossed a total of $114,000 in its three weeks in Philadelphia. The losses amounted to $56,000, and they still had to play previews in New York and then open. And they were already over their budget. The budget did not provide for overcall, and the show either had to close out of town or come up with some more money.

Producer Mitch Miller came up with the money himself. Out of his own pocket. Well over $100,000. Obviously, the man believed in the property. He had not set out to do a *Mame* or a *Dolly!* He had a serious musical play on his hands, and he cared for it and wanted it to have a chance to breathe.

Here's Where I Belong came quietly back to the city and opened for previews on Thursday, February 8. It played half a week, grossed a little over $7,000, lost a little over $16,000. By this time it was clear that the show would not be ready for its announced February 20 opening. There was too much to do—new dances, new writers, new songs. Miller decided to postpone the opening until the show was ready. March 3 was the date decided on.

They played their first full week of previews in New York and lost $31,000. The next week they lost $34,000. The final week of previews was worse. New musical arrangements, new costumes were needed, overtime had to be paid, and their total previewing loss was $116,- 000. A month later Allentuck was going over the figures in his office in the Palace Theatre building. "It was bad enough in Philadelphia —the costs—but at least we were doing some business. Out of town, if the director wants moving scenery, if he wants an actual presentation of how the show will look moving from scene to scene, then all stagehands are required. They have a four-hour minimum call, and that doesn't include performance. That's 30 men at, figure, $4.00 an hour, so it's $1,560 per time. And the cost for an orchestra rehearsal averages about $500 an hour, and they have their minimum call too. But these are expected costs and all part of the normal process of putting a show together; you don't expect to freeze your show opening night on the road. But back in New York, that's when it got sticky. We were absorbing all the total expenses during previews. Every time any money was needed, the show had to go into its own pocket to get it. That's where you get killed."

They opened March 3. They needed the notices. They didn't get them. Some of the pans were cruel. I don't know why. The show wanted to move you, it never insulted, and it had several musical moments—"Good Boy," "Waking Up the Sun"—that were as fine as anything heard on Broadway all season.

Can musical costs come down? None of the general managers that I spoke to thought so. Carl Fisher, manager of *Fiddler on the Roof* and *Cabaret,* said that "$500,000 to $750,000 is what you have to capitalize a show for now. If you don't do business out of town, the costs become incredible. It happened with us on *Superman.* I don't think costs will get less. I don't see how they can. I don't know how much more ticket prices can go up either." He sat in his office in Rockefeller Center and shook his head. "I don't know what's going to happen."

Allentuck doesn't know either. "It costs $600,000 to bring in a musical now, and unless you hang on to the big sources of funds— the record companies, the movie people—you're in terrible trouble. You need the fat cats, but the way this year has gone I don't know how much longer they're going to be around. What worries me is the audience—the unions have been outrageous for years, but we've lost the in-between audience; we've lost the young people and we've been losing them for a long time."

They sure didn't come to *Here's Where I Belong*. It closed the night it opened at a loss of $604,000, making it the most expensive one-night stand in Broadway history.

CLOSING A SHOW

Shows open for any number of reasons. Generally they close for only one: the cupboard is bare. Occasionally, very occasionally, a play will have an honest limited engagement and close while making money, as *Marat/Sade* did a few seasons back. But generally the term limited engagement is an advertising ploy on the part of the management to get people down to the box office *now*. This season, at one point, for example, Merrick advertised *Rosencrantz and Guildenstern Are Dead* as a limited engagement.

Often, the decision to close a play is made on the eighth floor of the Sardi building in the offices of Blaine Thompson, Broadway's leading advertising agency.

The Guide opened on March 6, and the next morning, the various powers of the production began to gather in the Blaine Thompson office. The meeting was set for 11:00, and a few minutes before that a young woman sat quietly in the office lobby; she was the sister of *The Guide*'s producer, Noel Weiss. On the walls around her were the posters of the current Blaine Thompson shows: *Fiddler* and *Dolly!* and *Cabaret* and *La Mancha* and *Plaza Suite* and all the rest.

At 11:05 Weiss's sister was shown into Fred Golden's office. Golden is one of the heads of the agency, and he was out for a moment. The only person in the office was the show's press agent, Harvey Sabinson. Sabinson is pretty much considered to be the best press agent on Broadway. He is articulate and serious and teaches at Yale. As the sister entered, he was reading *The Guide*'s review in the New York *Post*. Weiss's sister sat in a corner and after a moment, when Sabinson seemed to be done reading, asked, "How is it?"

"Not good," Sabinson told her. "He says it's dignified but dull."

Golden hurries into the office, then sees Sabinson with the *Post* notice. "He says it's respectful but not good," Golden tells Sabinson. Sabinson nods.

Then he and Golden stare at the notices quietly. This is a mournful time. The show has already run up expenses of $130,000—$30,000 more than the original budget—and they are tactful men.

Rather than prattling on meaninglessly, they wait quietly for Weiss to arrive and decide the fate of the show.

Quietly, Weiss's sister asks, "Can I see that, please?" And she indicates the *Post* review.

She is so sweet and polite that Sabinson almost laughs in surprise. He hurries around a desk and hands her the notice, saying, "This is America; we have conscription and race riots, and you're free to read what they're free to write."

Weiss's sister reads the notice, and again there is a terrible silence as Sabinson and Golden stand in their proper places, waiting.

"Which of the newspapers is the most important?" Weiss's sister asks.

Ninety-nine percent of the time, if that question were asked along the street, the answer would be, "The Suffolk *Sun,* what the hell do you think?" But now the question has been asked with such interest and dignity that Sabinson can only quietly reply, "Most people think the *Times.* The *Times."*

"Is TV so important?" she asks.

"Most people feel it is," Sabinson says.

"Why is that, do you think?"

Sabinson says, "Because all those millions of people are exposed all at once in that half hour, and you know they're listening, paying attention; you don't know who reads the reviews in the papers." ·

Golden starts talking. "I'll tell you something: they're getting more important all the time, the TV reviews. I think there'll soon come a day when, if we get good from the papers and bad TV, we'll close on Saturday."

On those final words, producer Noel Weiss enters. This has been his first Broadway attempt, a serious play about an Indian con artist who is mistaken for a holy man. Weiss kisses his sister, sits, and is handed a bunch of notices—radio, TV, various newspapers. He looks at them a moment. "They didn't like the play," he says then. "None of them."

"Um-hum," Sabinson says.

Golden says it too. "Um-hum." They have both been through this many times.

Then Weiss's general manager asks, "Well, what do you think, Noel? What do you want to do? Close the play, try and run it, what?"

This is the ultimate question on any show, and now it has been spoken. Eventually it catches them all: *Oklahoma!* faced it; *Fair*

Lady too; *Dolly!* and *Fiddler* will have to in their turn. Expenses are this and income is that, and when never the twain shall meet again, it's Katie bar the door, good-bye.

Stephen Sondheim made the splashiest debut of any lyricist in the fifties with his words for *West Side Story.* The show was in all ways a triumph, and when it closed, someone sent Sondheim a wire: "Better luck next time." Sondheim thought the wire was funny. Only really, he didn't. Nobody does. Anything that you can do to keep a show running you do. No matter how feebly it staggers along, at least it's alive. At least there's a conceivable chance for a movie sale, an English production, some freakish jump in business.

It all comes down to finances. It always does. To run *The Guide,* a one-set show with approximately 15 actors, cost $24,000 a week. That is the weekly operating cost; if you gross that much, you break even for the week. If you take in more, you show a profit. If you take in less, it's a loss, but not dollar for dollar: if you take in $14,000, you don't lose $10,000, because various people are on a percentage, and the amount of the percentage will vary with the gross.

The weekly $24,000 for *The Guide* breaks down approximately this way: $6,500 guarantee to the theatre; about $7,000 in cast and stage managers' salaries; about $3,200 in royalties to authors and director; about $2,500 in weekly advertising costs. This is approximately $19,000. The other $5,000 goes for incidentals: general managers, company managers, wardrobe people, four stagehands at $300 a week each, insurance, press agents, a payroll tax of 10%.

To try and cut down, you can possibly get certain concessions. Maybe the theatre would take a cut in their guarantee, from $6,500 to $5,000. Maybe you could get the authors to waive their royalties. Thus you might get the weekly costs down from $24,000 to $19,000. But this can't be done for the first three weeks: no cuts are legally allowed until then.

So *The Guide*'s problem was this: it had to take in a total of $72,000 for three weeks, just to break even. After that, things might get just a bit easier.

On the day they opened, their advance sale amounted to $1,200. And no one was in line at the box office. And the brokers weren't calling. Twelve hundred dollars accounted for. Seventy-two thousand dollars needed just to last three weeks.

"I think we'll close Saturday," Weiss says.

"Who'll we play to until then?" the general manager asks.

Weiss says, "Ask a few people."

The general manager dials his office to get his assistants to start drumming up "freebee" people for the rest of the week.

"Call some of the drama schools," Sabinson says. "After all, it isn't the kind of play anyone can't profit from by seeing." He says this to the room at large.

Weiss riffles the notices. "They just didn't like it at all," he says.

"What about the ad space you reserved?" someone asks him. "You want to cancel?"

"Keep the ad space," Weiss replies. "Use it for the actors. Quotes about them."

"What about saying, 'Go see *The Guide*'?" Weiss's sister says.

An ad assistant shakes his head. "You can't drive people to go see it."

Then half a dozen men cluster around the *Times* review, which was the best. For a few minutes they debate quotes. Then an ad assistant says, "This is the whole thing right there," and he reads aloud: "The magnificent Pakistani actor Zia Mohyeddin gives a beautifully judged account of the title role—funny, cynical, rueful and, in the conclusion, poignant. This performance by itself would be worth seeing. . . ."

"You wanna give Titos a nod?" someone asks, meaning Titos Vandis, who gave a lovely performance in the second lead, as the con man's friend.

"If we can," Weiss says.

"You can louse yourself up with too many quotes," the ad assistant says.

"Maybe just a quote on Zia then," Weiss says. "No one could be angry about that." Then he stops, perhaps because it is already Thursday, the show will be shut in 48 hours, and no one will really have enough time to get angry. "What about 'Go see *The Guide*' and then the quote on Zia?" Weiss says.

"Yes, sure," everyone else says, because that's it, it's all over.

Weiss goes back to his sister. "Go see *The Guide*," he says. "You were right."

She smiles, stands.

Someone asks, "Do you want to put in 'Last three performances'?"

Someone else says, "Let's say, 'Final performance Saturday night'; that will make them think we've been around awhile."

Sabinson says, "Noel, do you want me to send out a press release?"

"I think so," Weiss answers, but he clearly is thinking of something else. He looks at his sister: "That quote on Zia—'This performance by itself,' it says. Doesn't that imply there are other good performances?" She indicates that it does, and this clearly pleases him. He has put at least $30,000 of his own into the production, but there will be time to think about that later.

Golden gives an assistant the final copy of the ad that is to run, and then he and Sabinson chat with Weiss about the business. "Quote ads don't propel business on mixed notices," Golden says. "We've found that out."

"Press-agentry is the most inexact science next to medicine," Sabinson says. (Everything is tapering off quietly now.) Someone wonders about the proposed use of computers to get people theatre seats, thereby possibly cutting down on illegal ticket speculation. Would that make any difference to the theatre? "I don't see why," Sabinson says. "We've created dishonest people; we'll create dishonest computers."

Weiss laughs. He and his sister go to the door. Good-byes are exchanged. As Weiss and his sister start down the hall, Sabinson calls after them: "Noel, when they make the movie of your life, Teresa Wright will have to play your sister." It was a sweet compliment, sincerely intended and taken.

Sabinson and Golden sit back down for a moment. *The Guide* has been the 36th straight play this season, the eighth to close in a week or less; losses for the year are already rumored at close to $5,000,000. There have been bad theatre seasons before, but this one has them both a little frightened. They look at each other.

"Let's go to work," Sabinson says then, "or whatever it is."

BILTMORE THEATRE

Owned by DAVID J. COGAN

LOSAL PRODUCTIONS Inc.

by arrangement with

OSCAR LEWENSTEIN and MICHAEL WHITE

presents

GEORGE ROSE in

'LOOT'

by JOE ORTON

Directed by

DEREK GOLDBY

Co-starring

CAROLE SHELLEY

with

KENNETH CRANHAM · JAMES HUNTER

and

LIAM REDMOND

Scenery and Lighting by
WILLIAM RITMAN

Costumes by
PATTON CAMPBELL

Corruption in the Theatre

Loot, a black farce by the late Joe Orton, was imported to New York after a lengthy London run. It received wildly mixed notices and did practically no business whatsoever. In an attempt to hypo ticket sales, the management allowed American Express cards to be accepted at the box office in lieu of cash. One columnist reported that this was the first time a play had allowed for a credit-card system of payment. The results of the experiment were closely watched along the street but proved nothing since no one went to see *Loot* anyway. But the possible use of credit cards brings up the entire subject of servicing the public, and on Broadway, when you talk about servicing the public, you mean corruption.

Corruption in the theatre is generally split into two categories: (1) ticket corruption; (2) everything else. I have covered as much of "everything else" as I intend to in the chapter on producers; there's more, obviously, but this is not a muckraking book and enough's enough.

Ticket corruption, however, is such an integral part of the Broadway scene that it must be at least touched on. But before I get into it, I want to go on record as saying that I don't think there is any more corruption in the theatre than there is in any other cash business. An old detective once said to a young man, "Sonny, where there's cash, there's corruption." No one expects Las Vegas to be honest or taxi drivers not to steal.

A distinguished architect was building a movie theatre that was to be very small, less than 200 seats. When asked why it did not have a larger capacity, he explained that the owners had discovered that in such a small movie house the ticket seller could handle everything alone, and to steal in a movie theatre requires two people: the ticket seller and the ticket taker. On a given signal, the ticket taker gives the customer a torn half-ticket back, but not the same ticket that the customer had handed over. This the ticket taker keeps intact, and eventually returns it to the ticket seller, who pushes it over the counter to some ensuing customer. The ticket taker and the ticket seller split what they can steal over the course of a day, week, decade.

Probably, corruption should not be limited just to cash businesses. We are, as we admit when pressed, a money country, and corrupt: the extent of corruption going on between the steel-producing companies of this land and the men who purchase their products for automobile manufacture makes any theatre-ticket corruption a joke. But, of course, ticket corruption, or "ice" as it is most commonly called, is not a joke.

John Wharton, probably Broadway's most distinguished theatrical lawyer and an expert on illegal ticket practices, says this: "The worst thing about ice is that it creates a moral climate: when you can make more dishonestly than you can honestly, you're in trouble. Like pawnbroking, it's a lousy business, and it attracts a bad grade of people."

Many historians feel that ice began with Jenny Lind back in 1850, and it has been a thriving fungus ever since. Wharton has a special definition of ice: simply put, it is the extra amount of money that the illegal ticket broker pays to get the ticket, and *not* what the ticket eventually sells for. If, for example, the box-office price of a ticket is $10.00, and the illegal broker pays $5.00 extra to get his hands on it and then turns around and sells the seat to a customer for $30.00, the ice involved in the transaction is $5.00. The $15.00 that the broker pockets might be called his "net speculative profit" not counting taxes. And, as Wharton takes great pains to point out, whether ice is paid or not in no way affects the final customer. If a broker sends some cousin of his to the box office to stand in line and buy the $10.00 ticket (a "digger"), the final price is still going to be

$30.00. No broker ever breathed who said to a customer, "Look, I didn't have to bribe anybody to get this ticket, so I'm passing my savings on to you." Much of Mr. Wharton's efforts over the years to rid the ticket business of corruption have been simply to eliminate ice by passing it on to those creative people who actually deserve the money and not to make all tickets sell at the printed box-office price.

There is, logically, absolutely no reason whatsoever why a ticket should sell for the printed price: the printed price is meaningless. Nobody wanted to see *Loot;* everybody wants to see *Plaza Suite,* so clearly the printed value of $7.50 on seats for both shows is of little value. To put it in perspective, let's shift to a different art: painting. A painter staggers along, and no one wants his stuff. Then he gets hot, and everybody wants his stuff. Would anyone amongst us not commit the painter to Bedlam if he didn't up his price a little after he was hot? Theatre tickets are limited. When a James Bond movie erupts, the management arranges to play the flick straight through the night to take care of the extra crowds. You can't do that on Broadway: no one had better suggest to George C. Scott that he add a midnight show each week night plus a 2:00 A.M. special on Saturdays.

In all the arts an article legitimately goes up in price when there is a limitation of supply coupled with demand. If you want to buy Durrell's "Alexandria Quartet," buy it, and if somebody charges you more than the list price, call the cops. But if you want to buy a first edition of "The Alexandria Quartet," then you're going to pay more than the list price, and you not only know it, you expect it. If someone gave it to you for list price, you'd probably be a little suspicious that it was phony, and you might not even buy it at all. In other words, we are talking of supply and demand, and it's not allowed to operate on Broadway. Legally. And so there's ice.

Ice is one of the two things theatre people don't talk about (the other is homosexuality). How much ice is there? Any answer has got to be inaccurate, since nobody knows. It's crime, and you can't ask, "How much does grand larceny gross a year?" and expect to find out either. One ticket man said this: "There is ice on every show every night. You probably think that's crazy! Why should someone pay extra for *Spofford* when he can just walk up to the window and buy seats? It's like this: if I'm your ticket man, and you're always after me for *La Mancha* or *Plaza Suite,* it costs me; maybe not so much in money but in time, in energy, in grief. Now if I find out you're only using me for the hard shows and using the box office for the simple ones, I'm not going to break my tail for you, am I? I mean, you've got to give me a break too sometimes; *Spofford*'s easy; I need that kind of work. I'll help you. But you've got to help me too."

Estimates about the total number of seats sold illegally vary. One guess was 150 seats a night per successful show. Another was 250. The most educated guess perhaps was this: 70% of all orchestra seats to hit shows and 70% of all shows on weekends are sold by brokers. If only half this number of seats are sold illegally, then you can say approximately that a third of all weekend seats are illegally obtained.

How much money does this come to? Impossible to answer. A leading columnist said in print that *Plaza Suite* was selling for $60.00 a pair. The highest price that I heard of paid for tickets this season was also for *Plaza Suite*. A lobbyist in Washington contacted a theatre person and said that he needed eight very good seats for Saturday night. The theatre person went to a box-office treasurer he knew—*not* the treasurer of the Plymouth—and told him what he needed. The treasurer made one quick phone call, then said, "You got 'em." The total cost was $560: $70.00 per seat.

On June 8, 1967, the *Times* ran an article about the treasurer of *Man of La Mancha*. The treasurer was accused of accepting a total of $200,000 in excess theatre payments since January of the preceding year. He was also accused of "demanding and taking the illegal payments, falsifying records to conceal financial information from others associated with the production, and failing to keep complete records on box-office receipts." Clearly, the figure of $200,000 has to be low: I mean, that's all the attorney general thought he could prove. Unless the man was stupid beyond all telling, he must have got away with something.

The business of ice today has been likened to the gold market: never has there been such a difference between what someone says something is worth and what someone else is willing to buy and sell it for. One of the reasons for the increase in ice has been the increase in what is called the "house seat." Originally, the house seat was what its name implied: the house, or theatre, would save a seat or pair of seats for last-minute emergencies—celebrities, catastrophes, etc. Saul Lancourt, the manager of Leblang's Ticket Agency got into the theatre in the late twenties. It is his recollection that at that time a show kept two house seats. In 1945, when he worked for *Harvey*, there were a total of 28 house seats, and *Harvey* was well above average. Today a musical will have 100 house seats a night. The director will have house seats, the producer, the writers, the stars, the various designers, the choreographers: everybody who can possibly muscle his way into the right to house seats will do so. (The theatre owner will have approximately one third to one half of the grand total.) The number and location of house seats are, of course, negotiable items. A powerful star can demand more than a second-rate choreographer can.

What's the point to all this scrabbling? A house seat has to be paid for, of course, but until approximately a day before the performance, it may not be sold to the public. So if you are the writer of a show and a friend calls you up, you can be assured of his having an excellent seat for your show. You can pay for it yourself or you can let him pay for it. The house seat isn't free; it's simply an enormous convenience. And a lot of people use their seats for that purpose and that purpose only. But after a recent hit opened, the agent of a composer was called by a stranger who turned out to be an ice broker offering a flat $5.00 a ticket for the composer's house seats for the run of the show. In this case, the composer, a sweet man with an enormous sense of personal guilt ("I'm not a Jew for nothing" was the way he put it), rejected the offer for moral reasons. A more jaundiced view was that he was right in his action but wrong in his reasoning: he should have said "no" because $5.00 was a rotten offer. Lately, the attorney general has made it mandatory for each person possessing house seats to keep accurate track of just where they go. This has cut down a little on the ease of disposing of house seats. But only a little.

A man who has dealt a lot with ice people talked about the operation: "When everybody gets paid off right down the line, there's no trouble. The ticket commissioner, the guy who gives out licenses, the theatre owners, the producers—all the people involved need their piece.

"If a seat sells for $10.00 the treasurer might sell it for $13.00 to an ice man who might get a call from a second ice man who needs it for that night, so he'll resell it for $16.00, and the second guy might turn around and sell it to a third ice man for $20.00. All this depends on which ice man needs the seats for that night. Of course, they're all making a profit. And the ticket usually stays right in the rack at the box office.

"It would take, I bet, $100,000 to go into the business. Some of them buy seats six months in advance and wait; you can't just go in and outbid everybody, because it's all kind of a family business. They're cousins, brothers, the box-office people and the brokers. Ask the attorney general's office; it's tough to break a racket when everyone's related.

"The only guy I know who *always* can get anything is the fire lieutenant. He gets what he wants from the box office or he closes the place down on infractions, only he never closes the place down. Whatever he asks for is his, free. I once heard a box-office treasurer say: 'Four for the fire lieutenant. He always gets his man.'"

For the individual house-seat owner, the money can mount up. A famous singing star who was in a Broadway success recently had three pairs of house seats per performance. Six seats. He made a deal with a broker for $8.00 a seat. For simplicity, let's say that that comes to $50.00 a performance. That's an annual total of slightly over $20,000, much less than the star's annual salary. But the money is tax free. Twenty thousand dollars in cash annually for the run of the show. All told, the star made an estimated *tax-free* $50,000 in cash from the run.

Ice is rampant on Broadway. And it is not simply the result of scheming box-office treasurers, although, according to John Wharton, for 20 years their union never demanded a raise. It's too simple to blame them. The general feeling along the street is that ice is the result of three people: the treasurer, the producer and the theatre owner.

The box-office man, of course, is in the most advantageous position to operate: I mean, the seats are right there, within arm's reach as he spends his days in his cage. His job, obviously, is to sell seats to people who come to the window. At least that's his job in theory. In practice, particularly if his theatre is housing a successful show, he *hates* selling tickets to people who come to the window. If it is even a halfway decent seat, selling it for the box-office price costs him money. No ice. And if his theatre has a bomb (unless it's late in the season), he still hates selling to the public: the fewer seats he sells, the less money grossed; the sooner the show closes, the sooner a new show will come in, and that new show might not be a bomb, and he'll be back in the money again. I have friends who have called up shows that were doing less than 10% of their capacity and were told by the box-office people that there were no seats available for six months. This is not abnormal box-office behavior. These are people who genuinely hate their work, and logically it must somehow affect Broadway adversely. If every time you went to a shoe store you were told that they wouldn't have any shoes till next summer, you might eventually switch shoe stores. Shoes, of course, are a necessity; Broadway is anything but.

I should guess that I bought 99% of all the tickets for all the shows I saw this season, and at least 90% of those directly from the box office. And because I was doing research for this book, I knew approximately what kind of business a show was doing. So you go up on a rainy Monday night and ask for an orchestra pair to a stiff, and the best you get from the box-office man is the 20th row on the side. That's because he's saving all those center seats in the first ten rows for this tidal wave of business that's going to materialize magically between 8:15 and 8:40. It's madness. One of the things that becomes irritating over the course of a season of dealing with box-office people is not their corruption but their stupidity. Eventually, you get tired of getting poor seats, especially when you are suspicious that there are better seats available, a suspicion proved when you walk into a relatively empty theatre. As a general rule then, box-office personnel, however charming they may be—and many of them are—are thieves.

But obviously they can't get away with it *all*. Think of the theatre owner: he has a piece of real estate, and it costs him over $100,000 a year empty, and the simple law of averages says it's going to be empty over one third of the year. When he gets a hit, it behooves him as an intellectual and a man of finance to grab all he can. It would be committable stupidity for him not to, especially since he knows the box-office staff is down there this very minute stealing like crazy, and *he* hired the box-office staff.

Theatre owners are not much beloved along the street. As has been said of them before this: "They have no creative ability and the money to prove it." The Shuberts own slightly more than half of the 34 Broadway houses in operation this year, and they grossed over 60% of Broadway's business. Anything uncomplimentary said of theatre owners in general goes more than double for the Shuberts. Many theatre people feel that if there is a villain in the Broadway situation today, it is the Shuberts. Stories of the Shuberts' financial wizardry are legend along the street. One successful theatre man put it this way: "They're the most powerful single element in the theatre and because they are, they're in a position to help the theatre, and they just don't. There is a 'screw 'em all' attitude that emanates from their organization, and eventually it pollutes the whole business." Whether the Shuberts are involved with ice, I have no way of knowing, but they're crazy if they're not.

And so is the producer if he doesn't go along. I think I mean that.

Of all the theatre thieves, the producer is the only one who has some valid claim to having lost a little blood in a production. Neither the theatre owner nor the box-office man does a damn thing to help a show succeed. But the producer was there from the beginning, and it may take him years to have another hit; if anyone is entitled to steal, he's the one.

The moral problem of the artist in the ice situation is the most complex. If I had worked for two years—more likely three—on a musical, and it came in (which would make it statistically unusual) and was a smash (which would make it more unusual still), I don't know what I'd do about the ice. If there is going to be illegal money made, some of it ought to go to me in lieu of a box-office treasurer or a theatre owner. If a seat that I have the right to costs $10.00 and is going to sell eventually for $30.00, whether I take any part of the money or not is of no consequence to the final transaction. If I, as the artist, don't take the money, so much the better for the treasurer, the producer and the theatre owner. In other words, I, as the artist, am faced with the dilemma of taking the illegal money or letting it go to someone who has infinitely less right to it than I have. Ideally, of course, I'd like to be sure that my tickets got to the public at the regular price, but there is no way I can guarantee that. I can call up and say, "My seats are for So-and-So," or I can release my seats, but I cannot call up and say, "I want my seats sold at box-office price to the next man in line." I could probably go to the theatre eight times a week, pay for my seats, and resell them at the same price to someone waiting. This would, of course, be a considerable waste of my time and an enormous inconvenience. It would also be illegal: ordinary citizens are not allowed to stand around theatre lobbies selling tickets. So what do I, as the artist, do? If there is a hit, certainly I am in part responsible. If there is a hit, certainly I will have house seats to dispose of. And they are going to go for more than the printed value, and I can't stop it. Ideally, of course, I would simply turn my back on the whole situation and be content with the legitimate money the hit would bring. Would I? Beats the hell outta me.

Not all ticket brokers are illegal. The Broadway Piccadilly is an honest house. Was, really. They were founded in 1916 and shuttered in 1968 because they simply could not satisfy their customers. They could not get decent seats from the theatres honestly. Why should a show deal with them for no profit when they could deal with an ice broker for enormous amounts? (It is usually simple to tell who the dishonest brokers are: they often close early and are ordinarily very small and located on the side streets in the theatre district. Figure it out: even though the space is small, the rents in those locations are whopping, and brokers have to salary their personnel. How can they stay alive charging the legal limit of $1.50 a seat? One of their most irritating problems, incidentally, is trying to sell enough tickets legally; they have to show sufficient gross sales so that the government won't get suspicious. It would seem a little loony for a man who reported eight tickets a day to keep on paying that rent. Sometimes ice brokers actually pay taxes on tickets they haven't sold, just to make their business look profitable.)

One of the very few brokerage houses with an honest reputation is Leblang's on West Forty-fifth Street, between Seventh and Eighth. Leblang's is managed by Saul Lancourt, who is retiring in June of this year, which is too bad. The man is a pleasure. Leblang's recently moved from their long-time Forty-seventh Street location, and they are still not completely settled. They are probably the biggest single agency under one roof. Basically, they are like any other service business. They have over 1,500 charge customers (a business counts as one charge; so does an individual), and the customers pay a fee of $15.00 a year for the service that Leblang's offers. Basically, the service consists of supplying theatre tickets for a given night at the legal price of $1.50 a seat. If you want the seat delivered to the theatre, there is a 50¢ delivery charge to any box office in town. If you want to pick the seats up yourself, Leblang's is open till theatre time.

Leblang's employs a total staff of around 20 people, perhaps half of whom are involved in selling. The bulk of the selling is done by a quartet of ladies who sit behind a counter all day long answering the phone. Annie, at the switchboard, has been with Leblang's for over a quarter of a century and has the reputation of being able to recognize the voices of almost all the customers and remembering which selling lady each customer deals with. The selling ladies have among them well over a century of experience working there. Goldie has been there so long she won't say, but the feeling is that it's close to 40 years. Unlike box-office personnel, who don't want to sell tickets, the Leblang ladies sell like crazy. Once they get someone on the phone, they try just as hard as they can to make some kind of arrangement for something, whether it is the show of first preference or not. (Lancourt says that 80% of their calls on any given day are for the hot ticket in town, whatever it happens to be. This shifts constantly: for a while this season *Cabaret* was the hottest seat, then

Man of La Mancha took over for a while, then *Mame* got solid when Lansbury's leaving became imminent, then *Plaza Suite* took over, which is unusual in that the number-one ticket is almost always a musical. Probably the number-one ticket now is *Hair*.)

The phones are going constantly, the conversation along with them. "*Plaza Suite* . . . for when? . . . no, I can't, but *Mame* . . . you've seen *Mame?* How about two lovely seats for *La Mancha?* . . . Fine . . . I'll have them at the theatre . . . yes, darling. . . . Tuesday night, *Man of La Mancha,* good-bye darling . . ." "*Plaza Suite* for tonight? . . . No . . . You'll take *Spofford?* I'd give you *Spofford* but they don't play tonight; they canceled the Monday night for a Sunday matinee. . . . *Fiddler? New Faces? . . . New Faces,* that's a revue that just opened; some of the critics liked it quite a lot . . . well, sometimes I don't feel like revues either. What about *Dolly!?* . . . If you want a drama there's *Jean Brodie,* there's *The Price* . . . I think I have a good pair left for that tonight . . . well, what can I tell you? It's Arthur Miller; how bad can it be? . . ." "*Plaza Suite* I haven't got, but I've got *Dow Jones*. Fine, two for tonight for *Dow Jones* . . . my pleasure . . ."

While this goes on in the front of the store, Lancourt busily attends to whatever the managers of honest brokerage houses attend to. "Go ahead and ask questions," he says, "please. Never mind if I look busy. I make it a practice always to do at least two things at once; it gives me an excuse for doing them all badly." Was this an average day? He shakes his head. "Quiet. A quiet Monday. Mondays are usually frantic: secretaries setting their bosses' plans for the week perhaps." Like everybody else, Lancourt is worried about the state of Broadway. "People are so accustomed to tickets being tough that they ask in advance; they have to prepare. Going to the theatre is a *schmere* now; it's a left-over from World War II when everything sold out. I remember when I started out at Grey's—you know about Grey's? They were a famous last-minute cut-rate broker; they had two men—*two*—with brooms to sweep up the change from the floor and put it in buckets to be carted off and counted. Now, if people haven't got their tickets, they're not coming downtown."

When the Broadway ice scandals broke in the early sixties, Lancourt formed the New York Theatre Ticket Brokers Association. "It was my naïve notion that we were a homogeneous group. Then I found out that there are the legitimate brokers and there are the gyp brokers, the ice men. They are the biggest part of the brokerage business in terms of dollars, though I think they sell fewer tickets than the legitimate brokers. Because of the scandals, I went to London and looked at their brokerage operations. They don't have ice over there, not the way we do. There may be an occasional digger standing in front of a hit, but that's all. What ice there is comes from Americans who insist on it. The English have a certain respect for money, and they're perfectly willing to wait. There is an utter disregard for the value of the dollar that is basic to the American character. No one disregards money as we do. And as for the English not having ice, I think there's another reason: I think they're better people than we are.

"I don't think the theatre is distinct from any retail operation. Around the country today, retail spending is way off. I think the theatre reflects the economic health and the psychological malaise of the country. Business is terrible during the week. A good season isn't Saturday night; it's Monday through Thursday. And I think that the ordinary middle-class, middle-aged couple is so fatigued by the state of events in the world today that to go to the theatre on a weeknight is insupportable. You could shoot a cannon off in the Hellinger on Monday through Thursday and not inconvenience a soul except an usher."

Out in the front of the store, a woman came in from the street. "Have you got anything for *Plaza Suite?*" she asked one of the selling ladies. "I'm sorry, I don't." The woman left, and the selling lady turned. *"Plaza Suite.* Everyone asks for *Plaza Suite.* I'll tell you the truth, if I had a pair for *Plaza Suite,* I wouldn't sell them to someone who walked in. I've got customers, customers I've had for years, asking for *Plaza Suite.* I've got to take care of them." She turned again as another selling lady asked her about a theatre. (They never refer in Leblang's to the name of a show: it is always, "Anything left at the Longacre?" and not, "Anything for *I Never Sang for My Father?*" And the shading of the colors of the tickets, indistinguishable to an untutored eye, has meaning for them. They get to know that the white ticket of one theatre will be a slightly different shade from the white of another.)

Most of Leblang's sales are done with and by women—secretaries, wives. Women are much harder to please. "They're accustomed to shopping," Lancourt says. "It's part of the fabric of their lives. In general, any show in town except *Plaza Suite* and *Hair,* any customer can see this week. Over the course of a season, you'll see everything. The only power we have is our sales power; we never unsell a show. Sometimes, when a show gets the notices, our switchboard lights up at 10:00 and never stops. With other shows"—and he shrugs—"it didn't open."

Most people do not get tickets for the shows they want most to see. But most people end up seeing something. Leblang's seats are sometimes good—"F Centers," Lancourt calls them—sometimes not so good. (An ice man had explained to me: "Leblang's and Mackey's are two honest agencies: I'm not saying that every single person who ever worked for them was, but the agencies are straight. And don't you think they get the worst tickets? The box offices don't like dealing with them. Who wants to do business with someone when there's no kickback?") Lancourt himself thinks Leblang's and Mackey's and any other honest brokers are alive for one reason and one reason only: "The ice business needs a front. All kinds of accounts no longer buy theatre tickets. *Everybody* isn't corrupt. There are businesses that tell their personnel: 'Take a client to dinner, a night club, whatever he wants—but no theatre.' They simply won't put up with the illegal machinations. I'm getting out of the business now, and I'll tell you, if I were just starting out, I'd never get into it: I'd go into movies."

It is late in the afternoon now, and gradually the selling ladies take off the comfortable shoes that they work in and get ready to go home. The long room seems somehow eerie being quiet.

Another woman has come to work now, a bookkeeper who totals up the transactions of the day. Lancourt walks to the front of the agency and locks the door. "Broadway is still not yet a business. The production setup, the promotion setup, the financial setup—this simply doesn't square with Harvard Business School." The bookkeeper continues adding up totals. Leblang's sells between 2,500 and 5,000 tickets a week. The bookkeeper is in a hurry because she is planning to stand at Carnegie Hall for a concert that night.

Somehow, that seemed to sum up a great deal of the madness of the theatre. A broker employee going off to stand at a concert; no F Centers; standing room. There is a knock at the front of the store, and Lancourt—the selling ladies gone—handles it. It is a couple wanting a pair for *Plaza Suite*. He shakes his head, smiles, tells them he's sorry, relocks the door.

Leblang's stays open till theatre time, "mostly to take care of busts," Lancourt says (people who come on the wrong night, other possible mix-ups). They used to keep the doors unlocked. Then, a few weeks before, on a Monday like this one, two men held up the store. They had pistols and cuffed Lancourt and another employee to a pipe in the bathroom. Eventually, Lancourt's calls were heard, but since then the front door remains locked after six, and Lancourt usually opens it only for people he knows. Theatre box offices are being held up constantly. Some female box-office personnel refuse to work their shifts until the theatre doorman comes and stands in the lobby. Box offices are easy to rob because, except for the few successes, lobbies are often empty. A man can run in, make his hit, and be gone before anyone can do anything. The theatre district isn't safe any more.

Lancourt gets set to go for the night. Forty years on the street, a few more days, and retirement. He points to the front of the store. "That door being locked. Terrible. This area simply isn't what it was. What is? Is anything? My daughter is getting her Ph.D in sociology. After we were robbed, when she heard about it, she was, of course, very concerned about my being all right. But once she knew I was, she said, 'Well, you created the society, Daddy.' "

And what of the corruption the theatre has created? An ice man says, "The producers and the theatre owners oriented themselves toward the brokers, and it's got to the point where it's too late. The public has had it." Corruption is all but total in the theatre. There isn't a totally clean box office on Broadway or a totally clean production either. There probably hasn't been one since Jenny Lind started it all, 118 years ago.

I doubt that ice can ever be eliminated. Too many people are making too much money out of the theatre just the way it is to change it. And it's not just the theatre people alone: most influential Americans like it the way it is too. This is a money country and money means privilege, and many—if not most—of the famous and wealthy Americans who go to Broadway get their tickets from ice brokers.

Oh, there's talk of reform, of changing the inept and stupid laws that refuse to allow supply and demand to operate, of letting it all work by computer. It would be a wonderful thing if you could eliminate corruption on Broadway.

But I think, finally, that the reason corruption will never be eradicated is because there is a certain mystique to being able to get theatre tickets. It's a way of reinforcing our own importance, I suppose, that has really nothing to do with money. You pick up the phone and say, "Four for *Plaza Suite*," and that makes you somebody.

I was once talking to a fancy-saloon owner, and he pointed out the window of his place to a "No Parking" sign and the car parked smack in front of it. The car was, naturally, a Cadillac, and, naturally, his. "Nobody goes near that car," he told me. "Every cop knows that car. They take care of me, I take care of them, and we all get along fine. I'm the only guy around who parks like that. You know what it costs me?" He named a price.

Across the street and down the block just a bit was a garage. I knew their prices, and I said he could have parked in the garage for less than half his present costs.

I will never forget the way he looked at me. "Who wants to park in a garage?" he said.

CHAPTER

30

The Hardest Month

On Broadway, April is the hard-
est month. February and March bring the second flood of productions; you can get through May on nervous energy, since the end of
the season's in sight. But April? As one critic told me, "You don't
know what hard is till you've sat through junk in April."

There is simply no way to tell someone how bad a bad Broadway
show can be. Usually, the listener substitutes the worst movie he's
seen lately and figures he's approximating the experience. But bad
shows, really bad ones, are a long way from "How to Stuff a Wild
Bikini."

In the first place, shows take place in legitimate theatres, so there
is an inevitable feeling of expectation. But more important, those
are real actors suffering up there, and their anguish is such that you
can't mock them; you can make wisecracks at the screen knowing
full well you're not going to hurt Annette Funicello's feelings.

Mike Downstairs was the best of April's plays: a Spinoza-spouting
Italian gets upset when the Authorities insist on holding an air-raid
drill in preparation for when the Bomb drops, and he is beaten or
killed and dragged off stage while all his friends roll around on the
floor as the curtain comes down. (The play was a comedy.)

New Faces of 1968 was a revue; the best seat cost $11.00 and the
freshest skit was a satire on the Miss America contest.

The Exercise was a two-character play about two actors who search for truth through improvisations, such as one where the actress improvises having a baby while the actor improvises being the baby; this cuts too close to the bone for her, psychologically speaking, so she has to terminate the exercise before its proper ending and are you already bored reading about this play? I bet you are, because I'm already bored writing about it. I think that maybe the reason is this: Who really cares about actors anyway? Actors are like toys for us; they take our mind off things while nurse prepares our bath, but we, dear God, do not want to know how they work. All that interests us about actors is their sex lives, and then only after they've become movie stars.

Leda Had a Little Swan closed after its final preview, but not before earning the reputation along the street of being the hardest show of the season to sit through. It was a comedy about bestiality, set in the future when educators give children animals as substitute sex objects to ease them through puberty.

The play was 80 pages long, approximately 80 minutes of stage time. It took 180 minutes to perform, which should give some indication of the pace imposed on it by director Andre Gregory, who was helped in his pacing by Michael J. Pollard of "Bonnie and Clyde" fame, and Severn Darden; they were not on stage together much. Until near the end.

Then came the climactic scene. Pollard simply would not say his lines, and Darden simply did not know his, and the scene they were attempting was a philosophical diatribe anyway, involving the morality of sodomy—Darden against, Pollard for—and it kept going on and on and on, with the most remarkable pauses from Pollard that I have ever witnessed. Finally, as the scene kept peristalsing along, nothing getting accomplished, the end clearly nowhere in view, I became obsessed with the thought that I was actually going to die right there in the Cort Theatre, dulled to death by Darden and Pollard. I said to my wife, "I think I'm going to die," and she said, "*I'm* having trouble breathing," so we fled.

I know the general manager of the play, Bob Kamlot, and I ran smack into him outside on the sidewalk. I said, "I'm sorry, I just can't stay inside any more," and he said, "Listen, forget it; walkouts don't bother me. You should have seen the walkouts we had when *Luv* was previewing. Some nights you just couldn't believe it." As he talked about walkouts and *Luv* and how nothing bothered him any more, these streams of people began flooding out of the theatre with the play obviously still going on inside, Pollard and Darden locked in permanent debate. Kamlot is a pro, and he did his damnedest to ignore the crowds all but running from the Cort, but finally even he was overcome. "My God!" he cried. "What's going on in there?" And he disappeared back into the wreckage.

This was at an early preview but word on *Leda* spread. A few days later, a young, industrious member of the *Leda* staff was out touring the ticket brokers, checking to see if they had posters for the show visible in their windows. The first ones he came to did, but when he came to one that didn't he walked inside.

The broker on duty looked up. "Vell?" He was a little old man, and he spoke with a very heavy middle-European accent.

"Just checking to see if you've got our poster."

"Vot show?"

"Leda."

"No poster!" Suddenly the old man was violent. "Dot show I vouldn't sell to my customers. From vut I hear about dot show . . . *ech!*" and he made a terrible shrugging gesture and turned away.

The young *Leda* man left quietly. But his troubles were not over. A few nights later he was on duty during the show, standing in the lobby with an usherette. It is his recollection that the philosophical-debate scene between Pollard and Darden was on. This is what he says happened:

"These two couples stormed out, clearly apoplectic. Naturally, I started edging away across the lobby, but the usherette went up to them and said, 'Is something wrong? Possibly he can help you,' and she pointed to me.

"Then one of the men started for me, and so help me, he grabbed me with both hands by the shoulders and started to shake me. He was just a guy who works somewhere, just an ordinary guy who likes the theatre, and he kept on shaking me and talking. 'I want you to know,' he said, 'that my wife and I go to the theatre all the time, and we've been to almost everything in the past few years, and I'll do whatever is in my power to stop this show from opening.'

" 'You're certainly welcome to your opinion, sir,' I said, 'but . . .'

" 'I'll come down here opening night and tell everybody not to go inside . . . I'll do anything . . . this show must never open. . . .'

" 'Sir,' I said, 'there are a lot of people inside trying to listen, so . . .'

" '*I'll get a court order if I have to!*' He kept on shaking me and shaking me. Finally, his wife came up and talked to him softly. He stopped shaking me after a while, and she led him away."

They never did *that* at "How to Stuff a Wild Bikini."

ALVIN THEATRE

ANDRÉ GOULSTON / JACK FARREN
AND STEPHEN MELLOW

present

TOM BOSLEY

in

THE EDUCATION OF

H*Y*M*A*N K*A*P*L*A*N

A New Musical

Book by **BENJAMIN BERNARD ZAVIN**
Music & Lyrics by **PAUL NASSAU & OSCAR BRAND**
Based Upon The Stories by **LEO ROSTEN**

with

BARBARA MINKUS

NATHANIEL FREY   GARY KRAWFORD

HONEY SANDERS • DICK LATESSA • BERYL TOWBIN

DAVID GOLD • DONNA McKECHNIE • NANCY HAYWOOD and MIMI SLOAN

RUFUS SMITH • DOROTHY EMMERSON • STEPHEN BOLSTER

WALLY ENGELHARDT • DICK ENSSLEN • DAVID ELLIN • SUSAN CAMBER

and HAL LINDEN

Settings Designed by **WILLIAM & JEAN ECKART**

Costumes by **WINN MORTON**   Lighting by **MARTIN ARONSTEIN**

Musical Direction and Vocal Arrangements by **JULIAN STEIN**

Orchestrations by **LARRY WILCOX**   Dance Music Arranged by **LEE HOLDRIDGE**

Production Stage Manager **EDWARD PRESTON**

Associate Producer **DAVID W. SAMPLINER**   Assistant to the Producers **VIVIAN FARREN**

Dances and Musical Numbers Staged by **JAIME ROGERS**

Production Directed by
GEORGE ABBOTT

31

And How Are Things in the Teachers' Room Tonight?

There is one particular line in the first act of the musical *The Education of H*Y*M*A*N K*A*P*L*A*N* that needs a little expanding: a scene has just ended in a black-out, and as one set rolls off and another rolls on, there is *almost* a moment in which the audience doesn't know where it is. Almost, but not quite. Because an instant after the black-out, a spotlight picks up a pretty young girl crossing toward where the new set is going to be but isn't yet, and as she makes her cross, she says to another girl who is standing on the far side of the stage, "And how are things in the teachers' room tonight?"

This is a line that could happen only in a George Abbott musical. Because once the words are spoken, the audience relaxes; it knows that eventually all the rolling on of sets and flying in of drops are going to create a teachers' room. All confusion vanishes; no one has ever been confused when Mr. Abbott is around.

Whatever it is that he is, he is the last of it. In his own way, he is the ultimate superlative. He has probably brought in more blockbusters than anyone else in the century. *H*Y*M*A*N K*A*P*L*A*N* was the 85th Broadway show that he directed, which means that he has averaged over two a year since he took up directing back in 1926. But he was acting professionally a decade before that, in 1913. Helen Hayes is ending a tremendously long and glorious career on the American stage now, and Abbott directed the show that made her a star, *Coquette*.

This was in the twenties, when he was known primarily as a melodrama man. In the thirties, with the success of *Boy Meets Girl, Brother Rat, Room Service,* etc., he became the leading American director of comedies.

In the forties he turned more to musicals—*On the Town, High Button Shoes, Where's Charley?,* among others. He was sixty-two when the decade ended, and for directing a Broadway show of any kind, that is old; for a musical, it is frightening. There are those who attribute Abbott's longevity in part to the fact that he has, whenever possible, worked with young people. The line about the "teachers' room" is really applicable to him too: of the 19 Tony award-winning composers and lyricists, eight had either their first show or their first hit with Abbott.

He directed 15 Broadway shows during the fifties. He also directed two major Hollywood films and took time out to act in an all-star revival of *The Skin of Our Teeth.* The 15 shows he directed averaged over a year's run, including such smashes as *Call Me Madam, Wonderful Town, Pajama Game, Damn Yankees* and *Fiorello!*

In the early sixties, he improved on his previous average. *Never Too Late,* which he brought in, in 1962, was his first straight play to run 1,000 performances. He was seventy-five years old and the hottest thing in the business, as he had been, on and off, for almost 40 years.

Then it all turned sour. *Fade Out-Fade In* lost a fortune. So did *Flora, the Red Menace. Anya* was an unqualified musical disaster, dying in two weeks. Last season he directed two dim-witted comedies that lasted a fat total of 25 performances. This season began with his taking over *How Now, Dow Jones* on the road. When he was asked why he had taken a salvaging job, he could have given any number of reasons, such as long-standing friendships with those involved, a desire to test himself in a difficult situation, etc. His answer was typical Abbott: "Listen, I had a couple of flops last year, and I was kinda glad to get something."

The Education of H*Y*M*A*N K*A*P*L*A*N was his from the beginning. Abbott was interviewed one morning before rehearsals. He shares a suite of offices in Rockefeller Center with Hal Prince. Abbott's own office is like Abbott: spare and functional. The most surprising thing about Abbott upon first meeting him is his size: most men who thrive late in life tend, for some reason, to be short; Abbott is tall, well over six feet, and broad and muscular. And always sun-tanned: he is a golf addict now, having given up tennis sometime in his seventies, and he lives a lot in Florida, for the golf. He was asked how rehearsals were going, and he said he didn't know. "You can tell that certain scenes will play, certain dances are effective, certain acting is good. But you don't really know much without an audience: you have to get hot bodies out there to be able to tell." Abbott is known in the business for not doing a great deal of homework. Once, when a new scene was about to be blocked, he called to the stage manager, "Where are the doors?" That was really all he wanted to know. "I do less than anybody, I think," he said. "I shock everybody with how little I do to prepare. I could make designs of actors' crossings, but if I did, I wouldn't use them, so I don't bother. Blocking's unimportant anyway; just so you get things to look natural."

He was rehearsing that morning in the ballroom of the Woodstock Hotel. Abbott is the kind of man who, if he's late, you figure there's been an accident. Rehearsals were due to start at eleven, and at 10:59 he walked in and said, "Let's go," to his actors. A stage is more or less marked off with chairs indicating the boundaries and the exits. Abbott sits slumped in a wooden-backed chair. An actress doesn't know the new scene that they are to rehearse, and Abbott says quietly, "We'll prompt you." The stage manager tells him that one of the actors is late. Abbott says quietly, "We'll jump around." Nothing ruffles him. He just sits there, a sun-tanned octogenarian, wearing grey slacks and a yellow turtle-neck sweater. Another actress comes up to him: "I haven't been able to sleep in two weeks," she says. Abbott answers quietly, "I've slept but I feel terrible." It is now 11:04. Abbott looks at the stage manager and says very softly, "All right," and immediately rehearsal starts.

An actress has a line, "Our whole class is dressed up." She says it just that way: "Our whole class is dressed up."

"Our whole *class* is dressed up," Abbott corrects. "You're proud."

"Our whole *class* is dressed up," the actress says, and she glances at Abbott for some kind of comment. He says nothing and is already working on the next little section. That is a trademark of his: if he likes something, he is silent; if he wants a change, he says so. Actors have gone through entire rehearsal periods afraid that he hated their work, because after they did their scenes he only said, "All right, next." They were his favorites, it turned out, but he rarely takes time to praise or blame. Time is the enemy of all productions, and he knows that; his concentration is constant, and standard theatrical trivialities—"Darling, that was just, well, I mean *soo-per*"—are not Abbott's bag.

"Turn around and look at the girl," he says to an actor now. "You're happy and you want her to hear about it, and it'll get you facing the audience."

Later, an actress' line is, "I hope I didn't interrupt."

Abbott turns to one of the authors. "Can we have an ending on that? 'I hope I didn't interrupt something' or 'nothing.' "

"Nothing," the author says.

Abbott says to the actress, "Your line is now 'I hope I didn't interrupt nothing.' "

"I hope I didn't interrupt nothing," the actress says.

Abbott glances at the author.

"Can't we cut the line entirely?" the author asks.

Abbott nods. "Cut it."

H*Y*M*A*N   K*A*P*L*A*N is a show about immigrants, most of them Jewish, and the actors speak with heavy accents. An actor is making an exit now, his last words being an odd Jewish name.

Abbott tells him, "Say that with less accent. It's a strange sound and it's got to be clear; the gentiles won't know that name." (Abbott is Scottish.)

The actor jokes, "How do you know any gentiles will come?"

Abbott does not joke back. "You only know the words you've heard before," he tells the actor. "Slow it down there. Make sure you get it out cleanly."

The actor gets it out cleanly.

Then another actor, the one who is late, comes rushing in. Abbott glances up from his chair and says quietly, "You're the villain in the show; don't be one to us."

"I'm sorry," the actor begins, "I'm terribly—"

Abbott points to a spot on the floor. It is the tardy actor's starting position in the scene. The lateness is already forgotten. They do the scene again. "Run it three or four times till they have it," Abbott tells the stage manager. Then he gets up from his chair to go downstairs where the dancers are working. He has staged a five-minute scene. It has taken him 15 minutes to do it.

This was February 20, and a week later H*Y*M*A*N K*A*P*L*A*N had its first gypsy run-through before going to

Philadelphia. Abbott doesn't trust the reactions of run-through audiences. Not only are they friends and fellow performers and therefore overly enthusiastic, but run-throughs are done on a bare stage, and as he puts it, "They can imagine more than you can possibly give them."

This run-through was at the Alvin Theatre at 2:00 and began, as is customary, a little late. Usually the director of the production gives a little speech to start with, welcoming the people in the audience, thanking them for coming and, if possible, throwing in a few jokes to warm up the house a bit. Abbott's speech to the house was, again, typical Abbott. He walked out from the wings almost in mid-sentence: "I'll tell you what the sets are supposed to be like." Here he was unavoidably interrupted by applause. Then he went on. "The scene is the East Side in the nineteen twenties. There are a lot of school scenes, and we'll stop dead after each one to get the chairs off. Tom Bosley has a cold, so his voice cracks. Anything else? All right, take your places and we'll go—no—hold it a second. Folks—you're all sitting too far back; we'll take a second for you to move down. O.K., now we'll go."

The run-through then went. Clearly, the show had quality; clearly, it had charm. Tom Bosley was marvelous as Kaplan. But some of the songs didn't work well, and much of the first act dragged. There was a lot of work to be done. Abbott seemed unperturbed.

A writer who has been on the road with Abbott said this: "There are two things that you worship him for out of town, and remember, this is not a very warm man. One of them is his strength. I remember this show I did opened in New Haven, and they didn't bravo us too much at curtain calls. Bobby Griffith was alive then, and he and Hal Prince were the producers. I was upset at the way things had gone and they said, 'Don't be. We'll meet with George, and you'll feel a lot better.' Bobby Griffith had been with Abbott as stage manager since before the flood, and Hal had been with him awhile too; they knew the show stunk, but they knew Mr. Abbott would fix it. They were the only two who called him George; with the rest of us, of course, it was always 'Mr. Abbott.' Except Bobby used to pronounce it 'Jawge,' and Hal couldn't quite say it without a little catch in his throat: 'Uh-George.' So we met with Abbott and we all sat down, and Bobby said, 'Well, what do you think, Jawge?' And Mr. Abbott said, 'I think the audience hates us, and I don't know how to fix it.' I'm telling you, you could hear the jaws dropping all over

New Haven. If there's one thing Hal can do it's talk pretty good, but he wasn't getting much out right then. And Bobby said later that it was the only time he'd ever heard Abbott say anything like that. Later in the day someone came up with an idea about how to fix the thing, but for a while it was like God had taken a header. You rely on Abbott's strength so much, you take it so for granted, that when it isn't there, it paralyzes you.

"The other thing about him is this: the man is without ego. Not only does he not have it, he can't take it in others. One day the star of the show, who, I might add, was stinking up the joint, called a top-level meeting—Bobby and Hal and Mr. Abbott and the song-writers. And when he had them all together, the star began sounding off about this was wrong and so was that. Now we all knew that what he was so upset about was that *he* was wrong, and not only that, he knew it. But you can't expect anyone to admit that, least of all an actor, so the company is waiting on stage while the star blasts on.

"*Then suddenly Abbott stands up!* This is a big man, remember, and he towers over everybody, and the star stops, and Abbott says, 'I'm sorry, I cannot be bothered with this: I have a company of actors waiting, and you'll have to work this out among yourselves.' *And he goes.* Well, you just don't walk out on your star like that, but Abbott did. And later he got to talking, and I'll never forget what he said: 'I've got to dominate,' he said. 'If I don't, there's not enough time.' And that's why, I think, he always likes to work with young talent. So he can dominate.

"Abbott thinks only about the show. He never thinks, 'Shall I put in a little something flashy so the critics will know I'm around?' It's the show. And you can say anything to him about the show; you can make any suggestion. *Once.* I mean, if you were rehearsing a show about poor people in Oklahoma, and you walked up to him and said, 'I think we ought to set the whole thing in Shanghai,' he wouldn't get upset. What he'd do is think about it seriously, because he'd know you meant it that way. And then he'd say something like, 'I don't think it would work because I don't think there are enough poor Oklahomans living there; we'd have to write in a lot of stuff explaining why there were so many of them there, and I don't think it would help much, moving it to Shanghai.' But don't say it to him twice! Don't come back the next day with something like, 'Listen, about that Shanghai business—' because he will take your head off softly. *Because now you're wasting his time.*

"Lemme give you a last incident about his lack of ego. There was supposed to be a first-act-curtain speech, and I really stunk up the place. I tried to write it the best I could, and each time I had a new version, we'd all get together, Abbott and Bobby and Hal. Now there was a procedure in these meetings: Abbott would read what I'd written, and then there'd be this silence, and finally Bobby would say—it was always Bobby who'd break the silence—something like, 'Maybe it's a little better, what do you say, Jawge?' And Abbott would say, 'Nope. Try it again.' So off I'd go and try it again, and then we'd have another meeting. Now when Abbott reads *your* stuff out loud, he has this thing he does: he reads the punctuation. Say you've written a line like: 'What's the point? I mean, what's the point of even trying? Somebody tell me.' And you give that to Abbott. He'll look at it a sec, and then out will come something like this: ' "What's the mean point?" No, no, I've got that wrong. It's "What's the point? What's the point of even trying somebody? Trying somebody"; does that make sense? Oh, wait, now I see; I'm forgetting to put in a question mark. Yes, I'll get it. Now: "What's the point of meaning?" That seems a trifle philosophical, doesn't it? Wait, this speech is full of question marks, and I've missed another. I'm sorry, here's how it should go.' And then he'd read it right, and then there'd be that silence, and finally Bobby would say, 'Think it might be a little better, Jawge?'

"I didn't know it then, but Abbott is famous for misreading your stuff. Anyway, I never did get the speech, so finally Abbott said, with as close to pique as he ever gets, 'Oh, I'll write it; you do something else.'

"That night he wrote the speech. I want to tell you, he stayed up half the damn night getting it down. The next morning we're all together, Bobby and Hal and Abbott and me, and Bobby says, knowing the answer, 'Jawge, you happen to get that speech done?' Abbott nods, and out comes this piece of paper, and he starts to read. Well, you've never heard emotion like that. I mean, Maurice Schwartz underplayed in comparison. He read that speech full and he acted it full, standing up, sitting down, waving his arms, his voice building and building as the speech went on. Finally, he finished it and sat back.

"Now the thing was, his speech was really raunchy. But Abbott had worked his tail off on it, and everybody knew that. So first of all, after he's done, there's the standard silence. Then after a while, all eyes turn to Bobby Griffith, because he's the one who we all know is going to say something.

"Only he can't. He just can't bring himself to say it's good, because he knows it isn't, and he can't bring himself to say it's bad, because not only has Mr. Abbott slaved over the thing, but what the hell, he's Mr. Abbott. Hal got busy doing those various little mannerisms that he's famous for, and he's not about to talk. And I'm sure as hell not. To this day I have never been in so long a silence. Finally, and I really mean finally, Mr. Abbott picks up his speech again and stares at it. Then he says it. 'Boy, does that stink,' he says, and he throws it into the wastebasket. Then he sits back in his chair and says, 'Well, that scene is now in the hands of the music department. Have them write a song.' They did, and it turned out to be probably the biggest moment in the show."

H*Y*M*A*N K*A*P*L*A*N never really had any "biggest" moments. It was a small show about an immigrant in night school trying to become a citizen; he falls in love with the smartest girl in class, but she is betrothed to another. It's just a tiny triangle. But charming. Charm is the key word here. There are lots of charm shows, and when they become hits, as *My Fair Lady* did, they can run forever. But they have little power, and if the critics aren't in the mood for charm that night, they're dead.

The out-of-town critics found H*Y*M*A*N K*A*P*L*A*N anything but charming. Business was terrible, and the three-week tryout was reduced to two. Abbott said they lost $90,000 out of town. "We had a big opening number; we looked just like a conventional Broadway show. It was all misleading, all wrong. You show an audience how to take a show in the opening scenes." He was not terribly perturbed when things went badly. Actually, that isn't quite true. He was perturbed; he is frequently, but he keeps it to himself. "You wake up with headaches, but you can't contaminate the cast," he says.

After the Philadelphia opening they went to work, making changes. Does he like changing from the start and working through the show? "I think I do. Yes." The work they did was lovely: the weaknesses at the run-through were either excised or covered over; the strengths were enlarged, made better. It was still a charm show though. No power. It needed raves to get by. "Pleasant." "Gently ingratiating." Those were the New York reviews they got in general. And they weren't enough. If Zero Mostel had been in the title role, I think the show would have gone a good two years. With Tom Bosley giving the performance of his career, it lasted 29 times and lost over $500,000.

Abbott left for Florida on the day after the opening. Seven flops in a row; not a real blockbuster since 1962. His career was down, but he was working on a comedy for the fall, and he had been down before. Besides, he was still young and full of energy.

An old pro who worked with Abbott for the first time this season spoke about him once in a hotel lobby after Abbott walked past. "I love that old son of a bitch," he said. Someone questioned him on the use of the verb: Abbott is not noted for warmth. "I'll tell you why," the old pro said. "He's something special in this miserable business: when he says 'Good Morning' to you, you don't have to spend the rest of the day trying to figure out what he meant."

THE PALACE THEATRE

under the direction of
Messrs. Nederlander

DAVID BLACK   KONRAD MATTHAEI
AND
LORIN E. PRICE
PRESENT

JOEL GREY

IN

GEORGE M!

A
NEW
MUSICAL

MUSIC AND LYRICS BY
GEORGE M. COHAN

BOOK BY MICHAEL STEWART
AND JOHN AND FRAN PASCAL

LYRIC AND MUSICAL REVISIONS BY MARY COHAN

MUSICAL SUPERVISION BY LAURENCE ROSENTHAL

WITH

BETTY ANN GROVE

JILL O'HARA   BERNADETTE PETERS   JAMIE DONNELLY
JACQUELINE ALLOWAY   HARVEY EVANS   DANNY CARROLL   GENE CASTLE

JERRY DODGE

SCENERY BY   COSTUMES BY   LIGHTING BY
TOM JOHN   FREDDY WITTOP   MARTIN ARONSTEIN

MUSICAL DIRECTION AND   ORCHESTRATIONS   PRODUCTION
VOCAL ARRANGEMENTS BY   BY   SUPERVISOR
JAY BLACKTON   PHILIP J. LANG   JOSÉ VEGA

ORIGINAL CAST ALBUM ON COLUMBIA RECORDS

ENTIRE PRODUCTION DIRECTED AND CHOREOGRAPHED BY

JOE LAYTON

32

Heartbreaker

Would it ever happen?

A musical comedy for the public *and* the critics. The public clearly was anxious for *George M!:* close to $750,000 in advance-sale tickets had been sold because of the combination of talent involved. The songs, of course, were by the great Cohan. Cohan was Joel Grey, fresh from his sensational *Cabaret* performance. The book writer was Mike Stewart, the most successful musical man of the sixties, with three straight smashes behind him, most notably *Dolly!* And the director/choreographer was the enormously talented Joe Layton, who had won Emmys for the Streisand TV specials, a Tony for *No Strings.* And in this biography of Cohan, Layton had outdone himself, coming up with perhaps his most inventive work, using a small cast, an exceptionally young cast, in continually clever musical ways.

Clearly, there had been war between the musical people and the critics from the gun this season. Clive Barnes had sounded the cry in his first musical review when he criticized the songs for the following reason: "They could have been written any time in the last 20 or 30 years and take no account of the enormous changes in popular music, even of the last five." Broadway musicals were "old-fashioned"; they "did not reflect today"; they were weary, stale, flat, and because of this kind of critical opinion, unprofitable.

Until *George M!,* a show that—at last—the critics went for.

George M!, which deals with the life of Cohan, was basically in the tradition of the "show-biz saga." We have always had that kind of story in books and films as well as on the stage, but it might be of some interest here to talk briefly about just what the "old-style" musical is that bored the critics so much. The following is an excerpt from an old-style musical. The setting is just before the first-act curtain, and the characters are a couple of vaudevillians, a son and his father. The son, maybe twenty-two or so, is getting his first big break. The father, who has been a failure in vaudeville, comes upon his boy just before the boy is supposed to go on stage. The father senses that something is wrong because the son, ordinarily brash and energetic, is subdued. Here is their dialogue:

FATHER
. . . Kid, kid, are you all right?

SON
No, Pop, I'm not. I want this so much, Pop . . .
(*It's hard for him to say it*)
. . . and I'm scared.

FATHER
Thank God, kid! Thank God.
(*Holding him*)
. . . I can quit worrying about you now.

SON
Pop, wait!
(*The father has started off, stops*)
. . . One more thing, Pop. You've been in this business thirty-five years. How do you know?

FATHER
Know what, kid?

SON
If it's good! It's not the applause, they're friends out there; they'll cheer no matter what. . . . How do you know if it's really good?

FATHER
It's hard to explain, kid, but there is something that happens. Suddenly, well, suddenly the whole stage is brighter! You know those lights are the same as you set them in rehearsal, but they suddenly seem brighter and stronger, and the orchestra's playing louder and faster . . . and kid, that whole stage just shines!
(*A pause*)
. . . Don't worry. You'll know it if it happens. Let's go, son. We're on.

Now don't you know that when the son goes out there and does his solo number, the whole stage lights up? I mean, was there ever any doubt? As the script put it, "And sure enough, somewhere through the song it begins to happen. The LIGHTS get brighter, the orchestra louder, the whole stage just shines the way his father said it would. . . ."

Can you believe that scene? The question really should be: When could you have believed it? Do you think you could have believed it in an early-fifties-type Doris Day movie? Do you think it might have washed in the late thirties if you'd given the lines to Garland and Rooney?

The snapper, kiddies, is just this: that scene is from *George M!*, the musical the critics went for. The dialogue is identical, except that instead of Father and Son they are called George and Jerry and refer to each other sometimes like that. But for the rest, it is verbatim. And not only is it *a* scene, it is the crucial first-act-curtain scene.

And not only is it less than Shakespearean, it is phony, and for an example of why it is phony, an Actors' Studio story. Some years ago, two new actor members, a boy and a girl, did their first scene in front of the entire group. They had heard, as haven't we all, of the Studio's supposed insistence on torn-T-shirt realism. So they did a scene, this boy and this girl, in which she was in the bedroom talking to him while he was in the bathroom. And when I say he was in the bathroom, I mean in the bathroom. (This is all indicated, you understand; they're both on a bare area more or less surrounded on three sides by other actors.) So they do this scene, she talking to him and he talking to her, and all the time he's on the squat. Pants down, drawers down, sitting there. He was covered by his shirttail, but just the same, this was realism.

After the scene was over, a couple of the older Studio members were blind mad. Because that's just the kind of image the Studio has been hung with for years, and they hate it, most of them. But there was another reason why these old members were mad, and when Lee Strasberg opened the meeting for discussion, one of the old members started talking. "It was phony," he said to the boy who had done the "defecating." "The whole thing was phony, and if you're gonna do it, *do it!* If you play a scene where you go to the bathroom in front of us, goddammit, when you're done, *you better wipe yourself!*" The old actor was right, of course; his logic was perfect. The whole bathroom bit was a stunt, phony.

And so is that scene from *George M!* I mean, the father is a failure. He's never been able to do better than scrounge out a two-bit boarding-house existence until he grabbed his kid's coattails. So how in the world would he ever, under any conditions, know when it was "really good"? If you're going to go to the bathroom, wipe yourself; if you're going to ask someone what it's like when it's "really good," ask someone who might have been "really good" once in his life.

People in the Broadway business, the skilled people, can tell within reason just how strong or weak their show is before it opens. Robert Whitehead, the producer of *The Price* and *Jean Brodie,* puts it this way: "You know pretty well what your troubles are. I usually know when something isn't working. I don't need to have someone come to see the show and say to me, 'You know, that isn't working.' He gets to go away afterwards. We've got to stay and try and make it work." Every time a show is about to open, word goes along the street: small chance; good chance; no chance.

Everybody knew how bad *George M!* was, in spite of Layton's directing work. The show had had its share of troubles on the road. Everybody knew how disappointing Joel Grey was too. He is a cold actor, and it worked for him in *Cabaret,* in which he was playing an emotionless thing. But in *George M!* the problem all along was to try to warm up the central figure. Grey is such a cold performer that the only two times he is required to show emotion in the show—the first-act-curtain moment quoted before and later in the second act when he hears of a death in his family—Layton has him play both moments *with his back to the audience.* One of the times Grey has a costume change to take care of, but my guess is that even without that, Layton would have had him face away from the people. As a performer Grey is gifted and bouncy and cute, and chilly.

" 'George M!' can have a personal Tony Award from me, and Joel Grey can have a couple," Clive Barnes said. "Brilliant," Watts said. "Fabulous," said Chapman. "Electric," said the UPI, while the AP topped that by saying that Grey ". . . performs with mercurial magnificence."

George M! was one of the two most painful productions of the season as far as most of the skilled theatre professionals were concerned. Both it and *The Little Foxes* were patently rotten and got away with it. No one begrudged anything to *Plaza Suite.* People weren't upset over the success of *Rosencrantz.* But *George M!* and *The Little Foxes* sent a brooding chill around midtown. Part of it, of course, may have been envy. But part of it was something else. Most serious theatre people like to know what's successful critically so that they can compare it with what, according to their taste, should be successful critically. When the two coincide, fine; when the split becomes as wide as it did for *Little Foxes* and *George M!*, it gets nervous-making. A lot of bright, caring people are trying to earn a decent living on Broadway, and when crap sells, panic sets in. The serious pros didn't smile a lot after *George M!* opened.

But miracle of miracles, neither did the public. With its large advance and with those money notices, a two-year run was a reasonable expectation, three years not unduly optimistic. Whatever the final results, the show *had* to sell out at least for the first six months. Only it didn't. From the first performances on, people were taking off during the second act. They didn't like the show. By the third week, *George M!* stopped selling out. John Q. wasn't having any.

Sometimes there's God so quickly.

GEORGE ABBOTT THEATRE

THE THEATRE GUILD and JOEL SCHENKER
present

VINCENT PRICE

PATRICIA ROUTLEDGE

In A New Musical

DARLING OF THE DAY

Music by
JULE STYNE

E. Y. HARBURG
Lyrics by

(Based on Arnold Bennett's "Buried Alive")

also starring

BRENDA FORBES *and* **PETER WOODTHORPE**

with
TEDDY GREEN

MICHAEL LEWIS   MITCHELL JASON   CHARLES WELCH   MARC JORDAN
JOY NICHOLS   LEO LEYDEN   CAMILA ASHLAND

Scenery Designed by
OLIVER SMITH

Costumes Designed by
RAOUL PENE duBOIS

Lighting Designed by
PEGGY CLARK

Musical Director and Vocal Arrangements by
BUSTER DAVIS

Dance Music by
TRUDE RITTMAN

Hair Styles by
D. RUSTY BONACCORSO

Orchestrations by
RALPH BURNS

Assistant to the Director
FRED HEBERT

Choreography by **LEE THEODORE**

Directed by
NOEL WILLMAN

MARK HELLINGER THEATRE

ZVI KOLITZ, SOLOMON SAGALL, ABE MARGOLIES
present

DICK SHAWN

in

I'M SOLOMON

A New Musical
also starring

CARMEN MATHEWS   **KAREN MORROW**

with
FRED PINKARD   PAUL REED   BARBARA WEBB   MARY BARNETT
and
SALOME JENS

WITH A CAST OF 60

Lyrics by
ANNE CROSWELL

Book by
ANNE CROSWELL and DAN ALMAGOR

Music by
ERNEST GOLD

Based On An Original Play
"KING SOLOMON AND THE COBBLER" by SAMMY GRONEMANN
American Adaptation in Collaboration with ZVI KOLITZ

Settings by
ROUBEN TER-ARUTUNIAN

Musical Direction and Vocal Arrangements by
GERSHON KINGSLEY

Lighting by
MARTIN ARONSTEIN

Dance Arrangements by
DOROTHEA FREITAG

Costumes by
JANE GREENWOOD

Orchestrations by
HERSHY KAY

Dances and Musical Numbers Staged by
KALMAN GINZBURG

Associate Producers: PHILIP TURK, KALMAN GINZBURG

Dances and Musical Numbers Staged by
DONALD McKAYLE

Entire Production Directed and Supervised by
MICHAEL BENTHALL

Where Has All the Flower Gone?

Darling of the Day and *I'm Solomon* were the two biggest musical disasters ever to open and close in a single season. Their combined losses are reputed to be around $1,500,000.

Darling of the Day may eventually end up in possession of a certain mystique, since certain newspaper critics liked it. In fact, all four main newspaper critics liked it: Barnes and Kerr, Chapman and Watts. But it still closed after 31 performances. The reasons that the newspaper notices did not save the show are:

1. Barnes did not review it at its opening; the second-string *Times* critic did, and he panned the show. Barnes gave his opinion later in a ballet column.

2. The show stunk.

It was so bad that the night I saw it a man connected with the show looked at me (this was at a preview) and said, "Deadly," before moving on. As he moved on, he was met by someone else, who said to him, "My God, talk about dying." Heads nodded in agreement all around. The audience reaction, except for a genuine affection for Patricia Routledge as the female lead, was mute.

What the newspaper critics saw I cannot imagine, but the television people were less jovial. One of them said, " 'Darling of the Day'

was based on a novel called *Buried Alive*. It should have been."
Leonard Harris was, I think, the first critic to use the adjective
abysmal about any musical performer's singing voice this season
when he accurately summed up the sound of Vincent Price in song.

This was a Kiss of Death production from the start. As early as
August, well before the show went into rehearsal, rumors were
strong that the director was going to be fired. The rumors turned
out to be not so much wrong as premature: the director went in
December. The librettist also left along the way, and the show
opened in New York with no one getting credit for the book, never a
happy sign. The creative people knew it was a disaster before it
opened; one of them advised a friend, "Don't come." Another said,
before the show even left for out of town, "I look forward to nothing
beyond the Toronto opening; anything after that is velvet."

I'm Solomon was even worse than *Darling of the Day*. The plot
concerned King Solomon and a peddler, who looked like each other
and changed places for one day. One critic felt that "not even Charlton Heston has ever had to wade through as much Biblical bubble
gum." The show advertised itself as "A New Musical with a Cast of
60." That's got to tell you something. I mean, when movies have
made "a cast of thousands" a cliché, what's "a cast of 60" supposed
to do to your pulse? One peek at the program indicated more
trouble: the set designer had a box around his name, and when the
outstanding billing for a show goes to the set designer, you just
know you're in for a bumpy crossing.

Going into detail about either show is unnecessary and cruel: the
people involved suffered enough without additional reminders. But
by the time *I'm Solomon* shuttered after seven performances, ten
musicals had gone into the record book for the season. Of the ten,
How Now, Dow Jones, Happy Time, Golden Rainbow and *George
M!* were still alive, so a final fate could not be predicted, though
an optimistic guess had the four of them losing at least $1,250,000
on their Broadway runs.

Henry, Sweet Henry	loss: $400,000
Mata Hari	loss: $500,000 to $800,000
Here's Where I Belong	loss: $604,000
H*Y*M*A*N K*A*P*L*A*N	loss: $550,000
Darling of the Day	loss: $700,000 to $750,000
I'm Solomon	loss: $700,000 to $800,000

Conservatively, that is $3,500,000 down the drain on just six shows,
close to $5,000,000 on all ten, and these failures more than ever

whipped up the cry that had been building all season long: What's gone wrong with American musical comedy?

Musical comedy has always had book trouble.

The first famous one, which historians always point to as the start of it all, was *The Black Crook* in 1866, and that phenomenon (it ran for 40 years in various companies around the country) only came into existence because of book trouble. A producer was stuck with a stiff of a melodrama. In order to hypo audience interest, he hired a stranded French ballet company and shoved the ballet elements right into the melodrama story wherever possible. On this somewhat dubious note, American musical comedy was born.

Cut to 1943. *Oklahoma!* A whole new ball game. What was so new? Well, there is this terrific opening song, called "Oklahoma!" and it is fast and loud and sung by nearly all the cast, and it tells us where we are and what it's like there; it sets the scene, more or less. Only *Oklahoma!* doesn't begin with "Oklahoma!" It begins with a woman churning butter while this cowboy ambles on stage and sings a slow, pretty number entitled, "Oh What a Beautiful Morning." Before *Oklahoma!* came along, a show about Oklahoma would have begun with "Oklahoma!" In other words, less emphasis was put on the standard brassy-type Broadway stuff and more was placed on the people.

Oklahoma! stressed more than ever before the importance of the book of a musical comedy. And this was bad for musical comedy. Because there aren't any brilliant musical-comedy book writers. There weren't then, there aren't now, and there never will be. Just as there won't ever be any brilliant cesspool diggers. There may be skillful cesspool diggers, just like there may be skillful musical-comedy book writers, but brilliant? No way. Why? Because the job does not summon forth the man. If you actually think of yourself as a writer, writing a musical-comedy book is degrading. It is constantly put at the bottom of any list of important elements in a show: if a book scene works but a song is a little off, the book scene is altered to accommodate the song, which is only right and proper. But book scenes are also at the mercy of performers, designers (set, costume and lighting), producers, wives, anybody. And there's no time. No time for delicacy of character, mood, anything. You've got to get in there, slash it out, then beat it before the production number. Neil Simon puts it this way: "You can say tiny things in a play; in a musical, everything's in quotation marks." You're just not going to find writers of genuine talent making a career in this field. But book writers are not the reason the musical is in trouble today, because they were *never* any good.

Clive Barnes has gone on record endlessly this season as believing that musical comedy is in trouble because it does not reflect the music of its time. That is, I think, bullshit. Musical comedy is under no more obligation to reflect the music of its time than Mr. Balanchine is to put the New York City Ballet through an evening of the Frug. There is no reason under this or any other sun why an audience of teen- and pre-teen-age children, the popular-record audience, should force the middle-aged men and women who make up the Broadway audience to listen to its sound. Any more than middle-aged people should be given the right to insist that ten-year-olds spend their hard-earned cash on Welk and Lombardo instead of Simon and Garfunkel. (This is an aside but a cruel one: Barnes, who is *nothing* without the *Times,* has so frightened the creative people along the street that one very famous and honored composer, who was out of town with a period musical, called up a collaborator and said in fear and seriousness, "Is there any way we can work a couple of rock numbers into the show for Barnes?" If I haven't made myself clear, the musical he was working on was set in a time long *before* the existence of rock music. The composer, no fool, knew this. But that is the power of the *Times.*)

In the opening decade of this century, Cohan and Kern, among others, began working in the Broadway musical theatre. The next decade saw Irving Berlin's debut, and Friml and Romberg, and Cole Porter and Gershwin, although Porter and Gershwin didn't really flower till the twenties. The twenties also brought us Vincent Youmans. And Rodgers and Hart. And all these men, Kern, Gershwin, Friml, Romberg, Berlin, Youmans, Porter, Rodgers and Hart, moved into the thirties. Kurt Weill started writing for our stage in the thirties. So did Harold Arlen.

Then 1943, and Rodgers and Hammerstein. Within half a dozen years after *Oklahoma!* Lerner and Loewe were going strong. So was Leonard Bernstein. And Frank Loesser. And Jule Styne. Bock and Harnick started in the fifties. And Stephen Sondheim's lyrics were first heard in *West Side Story* and *Gypsy.*

But the sixties are ending now, and the flower is gone. Hazlitt, the English essayist, said that "one who does a thing better than anybody else assumes a place in history that is sorely missed when he can no longer perform." And our marvelous older songwriters—

Rodgers, Loesser, Loewe, Berlin—just aren't performing as they did once upon a time.

And coupled with that is this sad fact: the younger ones can't cut it either. For the first time in this century, our supply of composers has run dry. Jerry Herman is the most successful new figure of the sixties, and that's not cause for rejoicing. Kander and Ebb did *Cabaret,* and they may well be the best team to emerge in the sixties, but their work simply does not stack up to Bock and Harnick, the best new team of the fifties, and their work does not stack up to Rodgers and Hammerstein, the best new team of the forties.

Musical comedy is in trouble today because the songwriters aren't there. The old men are dead or doddering, the young ones mostly dull. "Sorely missed," Hazlitt said, and right he was.

Sad, sad, sad.

CHEETAH

MICHAEL BUTLER

presents

The New York Shakespeare Festival Public Theater Production of

HAIR

The American Tribal Love-Rock Musical

produced by **JOSEPH PAPP**

Music by
GALT MacDERMOT

Book and Lyrics by
GEROME RAGNI & JAMES RADO

Directed by
GERALD FREEDMAN

Lighting by
LAWRENCE METZLER

Costumes by
THEONI V. ALDREDGE

Scenery by
MING CHO LEE

Musical Director
JOHN MORRIS

Associate Producer
BERNARD GERSTEN

Associate Scenic Designer
JOAN LARKEY

with

SUSAN ANSPACH   ED CROWLEY   STEVE CURRY   WALKER DANIELS
STEVEN DEAN   GALE DIXON   SALLY EATON
ALTOVISE GORE   MARIJANE MARICLE   ARNOLD WILKERSON

and

Warren Burton   Thommie Bush   Linda Compton   William Herter
Paul Jabara   B. J. Johnson   Jane Levin   Edward Murphy, Jr.
Suzannah Norstand   Alma Robinson   Gwynne Tomlan
and Band   Steve Gillette   Jimmy Lewis   Leonard Seed
Patti Bown   Greg Ferrara

Original cast album by RCA Victor

BILTMORE THEATRE

MICHAEL BUTLER

presents

The Natoma Production of

HAIR

The American Tribal Love-Rock Musical

Book and Lyrics by
GEROME RAGNI & JAMES RADO

Executive Producer
BERTRAND CASTELLI

Music by
GALT MacDERMOT

Dance Director
JULIE ARENAL

Directed by
TOM O'HORGAN

Costumes by
NANCY POTTS

Scenery by
ROBIN WAGNER

Musical Director
GALT MacDERMOT

Lighting by
JULES FISHER

Sound by
ROBERT KIERNAN

STEVE CURRY

with

LYNN KELLOGG   JONATHAN KRAMER   SALLY EATON   PAUL JABARA
JAMES RADO   MELBA MOORE   SHELLEY PLIMPTON
RONALD DYSON
GEROME RAGNI   LAMONT WASHINGTON

Donnie Burks
Walter Harris   Lorri Davis   *and*
Marjorie LiPari   Leata Galloway   Steve Gamet
Suzannah Norstrand   Diane Keaton
                          Emmaretta Marks   Hiram Keller
                                              Natalie Mosco
                          Robert I. Rubinsky

CHAPTER

34

Brave New World

Hair, the American tribal love-rock musical, opened in the fall for a limited run off-Broadway. The show received notices that any uptown show would have envied. The plot concerned a bunch of hippies, one of whom, Claude, had been sent his draft notice, and the characters ambled around with him as he more or less said good-bye to his hippie existence. At the end, symbolically, he cuts off his hair and goes off to war. If this summary seems confusing and vague, it is only because *Hair'*s plot echoed those adjectives. The book scenes, as much as anything else, served simply to launch musical numbers that indicated the hippies' youthful dissatisfaction with much of the world around them, particularly Vietnam.

But since the show was set for only a limited run, it either had to close or move. And since it was such an off-Broadway success, the question really wasn't whether to move it, but where.

Someone thought of Cheetah.

It was probably as astute an idea as anyone had come up with all year. Cheetah, a leading Broadway discotheque, was a perfect place to unite this show about kids and their troubles with kids who have troubles. Not only that, but the kids were in a sense getting to see the show free. *Variety* explained that the "price of admission will

382 [THE SEASON

cover the show plus post-performance terping and psychedelic light displays, which are the stock in trade of the club." It was obviously going to be a bonanza.

It bombed.

As someone close to the show explained: "We thought that taking it to Cheetah would open up another whole arena of theatregoing: we couldn't have been more wrong. The show wasn't as effective at Cheetah; the acoustics were terrible. The step was not significant enough to get space in the papers, and there was no chance to accumulate promotional material. So it was not re-reviewed. Those who did come liked it less than before, so they said nothing. We thought Cheetah was the 'in' thing for kids. We thought we could combine the discotheque-goers and the theatregoers, but the two groups never became a union. They had a lower-middle-class group going there. How can I put it to you? There were few visiting Caucasians."

Hair, as it was done at Cheetah, with the audience on three sides of a platform, was a very loose experience: the actors wandered around almost, it seemed, at will. (Actually, they were following the brilliant direction of Gerald Freedman, who had done the show off-Broadway originally and restaged it for the Cheetah presentation.) There was no fourth-wall feeling whatever, and the sense of participation that was allowed the audience was wonderful. I talked briefly to one of the actors.

"You like walking in and around the audience?" I asked.

"Yeah. It's nice. Keeps you from getting bored, you know?"

"Anybody ever get upset with the way it's done?"

"Not so far."

"The antiwar business: anyone ever blow up over that, yell back at you, maybe?"

"Wouldn't that be terrific if they did? 'Scuse me, I'm on."

I suppose the last remark ought to be explained: this conversation, dull as it is, is reprinted here because it took place during performance and not backstage. The specifics were simply that I was standing at the back. The actor—what his name was I don't know—was just waiting around for his next cue. He looked as if he wanted to talk so I started talking, and we must have gone on for maybe three or four minutes, chatting away. Mostly we talked about why there was nobody there. The house, enormous, was maybe one-tenth full. Anyway, the point of this is that you can't really dislike a show much when you feel loose enough to talk to the actors while they're working. And that freedom was one of the nicest things about *Hair.*

And the directing. Example: Know how *Hair* ended? Four, maybe

six, toy tanks were on stage—all the kids were gone now—and the
tanks were wound up and moving, slowly, slowly, and firing at each
other, toy tanks blasting away as the lights died. I don't know what
you think, but I think that's an eloquent way of stating the folly of
war. *Hair* was full of things like that. And the young cast helped.
There was an obvious but undeniable poignance in the juxtaposi-
tion of the twenty-year-old-looking kids and the war, which was then
—in December—tearing the country apart.

Hair was also, of course, amateurish in most respects. The lyrics
were unintelligible, the dialogue inept. But it had youth and nice
tunes and a terribly strong antiwar sentiment, and you didn't care
(I didn't) that it was repetitive and silly. It was, for me, beyond
criticism: I expect it is about the best theatre I'll ever see in a discotheque. But you don't impose the same dramatic criteria on *Hair*
that you do on *Happy Time*. One glories in its amateurishness, the
other in its professionalism. One tried to tell a coherent story with
character, plot, motivation and whatever else you want to include.
The other just rambled along, and when it got into trouble, the
actors started to jump around energetically and asked for your
forbearance. I gave it gladly.

Then the decision was made to bring *Hair* to Broadway where,
after terrible difficulty, it arrived on April 29. It had a much
augmented score, a much shortened book. The book, in fact, was
all but nonexistent now. But that was not the only change that
had happened to *Hair*. The theatre into which it moved was a
standard Broadway house, so that when the actors came into the
aisles, you were very much aware of a certain falseness, an attempted
theatricality. A new director, Tom O'Horgan, had been hired, and
he had changed the show in many ways, one of which was adding a
very strong whiff of campy homosexuality. Example: in the earlier
version, a young man is about to leave home, and his mother grabs
him and shoves his head into her bosom, saying with deadly serious
and therefore comic effect, "This is where it's at, baby, not out
there." When the moment took place in O'Horgan's Broadway version, the mother, instead of being played by a middle-aged subur-
ban-type woman, was played by a young male actor dressed in drag.

But if O'Horgan had damaged the show, a lot of the damage was
beyond anyone's control. When *Hair* opened off-Broadway, Johnson
was going to be President forever, hippies were still a conceivable
subject for drama, and the Vietnam war was very much as it had
been for years: unendurable and unending.

When *Hair* opened on Broadway, Johnson was no longer a subject for satirical venom: the man had announced his retirement and was going, going, gone. The whole hippie thing was going, going, gone, too: *Time* had an article a few days after *Hair* opened describing a garbage-ridden, drunk-filled homosexual slum and then said that this was what the Haight-Ashbury section of San Francisco, "once the citadel of hippiedom and symbol of flower-power love," looked like now. Hippies were still in existence, but the "movement" wasn't what it had been. And besides, when *Hair* had opened off-Broadway, New York had not yet seen the almost dozen shows that dealt with the same subject. It wasn't *Hair*'s fault, but hippies were a bore now. And even *Hair*'s most moving material, the Vietnam war, was somewhat nullified. There was a light, however dim, at the end of the tunnel: peace talks were starting in Paris. This obviously wasn't *Hair*'s fault either.

But recasting the crucial lead role of Claude was. The boy I saw at Cheetah was young and coltish, and one felt that it was a shame he was going to be drafted and maybe killed. In his place was put author-lyricist James Rado. Now I mean this: I think Rado is one of the most talented American actors under thirty-five. I have seen him easily hold stage with an actress who was giving what Walter Kerr called one of the dozen best performances of his theatregoing lifetime. Rado is big and good-looking, and he has power and technique as well as feeling. He has everything.

Except youth.

I don't know exactly how old he is, but I bet he won't see thirty again. And if he will, his physical size on stage and the maturity he projects make it seem as if he won't see thirty again. And there he is, playing the role of this kid who just got his draft notice. I kept expecting the obligatory scene in which the butler explains to the maid how the master was ill as a child and didn't get started in school until late and after college had taken two master's degrees plus a doctorate, which was why someone as long in the tooth as he was, was about to be drafted. So there it was, poor *Hair*, redirected and badly, recast and damagingly, with its pertinence gone.

Obviously, it had to be the musical smash of the season.

It was a triumph for the power of the television critics, all of whom loved it. As a matter of fact, the television notices were so good that in an early ad *Hair* didn't even bother to use the Channel 2 review that only said it was the "best musical of the year." Eventually, *Hair* got around to honoring the Channel 2 quote, but they had other wares to sell first. The two main quotes they used in their early ad campaign were ones that said that *Hair* "makes *Marat/Sade* look like *Peter Pan*" and another that called it "the frankest show in town."

These quotes are both, of course, saying the same thing: "Come see the penises!" That was the gimmick *Hair* pushed first: the little old penis. Now all shows have a penis or two around, but they are usually hidden by clothing. *Marat/Sade* had an actor walking naked on stage with his back to the audience. In other words, all those Scarsdale ladies got to look at a strange man's bottom. *Hair* turned the strange man around, reproduced several of him, and lo, at the first-act curtain, you in the audience got to see several penises. Apparently, they eventually dimmed the lights a bit to increase the aesthetic of the moment, but when I saw the Broadway *Hair* at a preview, I detected no dimming. The moment was there in all its Da Vincian glory: there were these dancers, a little edgy, standing there, limp penises and all. (There were also some bare boobs around, but this is the twentieth century, and bare boobs are nothing nowadays.) But a *penis!* Suddenly you knew what art was all about.

Then the moment died. Horribly.

Because the act ended in a black-out. Only you really can't ever get a total black-out on stage because there are always lights in the wings so that the actors and stagehands don't get killed in the rush. And during the black-out, what you saw were all these little naked gypsies, horrendously embarrassed, throwing their little hands across their fronts as they scurried madly off stage toward sanctuary. Now, of course, no one was shocked. None of the critics and no one in the audience. They all said, "How freeee! Isn't it divine?"

I was shocked.

Partially, I suppose, because I am a prude. But I like to think there was another reason. In "The Silence" Ingmar Bergman has Ingrid Thulin masturbate, and it is as unshocking and relevant as anything else you can think of that has artistic validity. The act of self-abuse only strengthens and clarifies what we know about the character. Masturbation is a perfectly legitimate form of human endeavor indulged in by a majority of the animal kingdom. I doubt that it accomplishes much in contributing to the dignity of man, but it is grist for the artist if he chooses to use it. Bergman did, and watching Miss Thulin was not even remotely shocking: it was painful and sad.

But a girl-scout type jerking off on camera: that's shocking. And so was the penis baring in *Hair*. It added nothing to the show, no matter how much the creative hierarchy pleaded artistic purity, as they tried to do. It was, as one admiring public-relations man said, "a terrific job of titillation. It's really what drew attention to the show." After the show was established, as indicated, they started using the "best-musical" quote.

As can be imagined, the LSD-endorsing, draft-card-burning aspects of *Hair* got to some of the Establishment critics: "The most dismaying low of 1967–68 is the Broadway version of an off-Broadway rock musical, 'Hair,' which has found a certain type of audience and may run for a little while. It is vulgar, perverted, tasteless, cheap, cynical, offensive and generally lousy, and everybody connected with it should be washed in strong soap and hung up to dry in the sun," wrote John Chapman in the *Daily News*.

" 'Hair' is a tangled mad-mod musical whose ultimate obscenities are not shocking though execrably tasteless, whose cast with two exceptions looks permanently bathless, whose points are not irreverent but sacrilegious; its hymns of 'love' are evilly hateful . . ." This was the opening of Jack O'Brian's notice in the New York *Daily Column*.

But if you think those notices are bad, catch this: " 'Hair' makes me sick . . . up there on a stage for 2½ hours is an ersatz tribe of loving, rocking, musical, hairy, quasi-hip people . . . they sing of 'Hashish' and 'Sodomy' and drag in a 'Colored Spade' (the play is just that imprecisely redundant), and whisper, 'I believe in love.' Showstopper: 'I Got Life.' . . . If you have never seen a nude boy before—from the front!—and you don't mind bringing a flashlight (suddenly the stage gets very, very dark), then go. . . . 'Hair' is mildly funny, like remembering when you thought people did it by using wires; both experiences are invalid, but you can still hallucinate on them, right?"

If this last notice seems to you to be a slightly different kind of negative notice, then you are very astute, because it does not come from an Establishment source at all: it is the review of *Hair* printed in the *East Village Other*, which is the hippies' own paper and obviously a source that understands its subject matter reasonably well.

Now a bit more from the *East Village Other*'s blast on *Hair*, because the critic is getting to a very solid point: "Unfortunately, the sellout audiences insist, it seems (including the critics who have also sold out), on watching the play as though it is a reflection of the Reality of Their Kids and tells them the answers. . . . Perhaps the most condemning comment to make about 'Hair' is remembering that at 2:30 A.M. I got a call asking me to go up to Columbia when the cops were out. The same night of the play . . . And to remember that the kid who called me was supposedly a member of the same kind of fun-loving tribal rockettes as those young Americans onstage . . . I wondered for a while if I would have been sickened by 'Hair' if the kids up there were Australian or French: Yes. *No one has the right to remove another's validity as a joke; it's too dangerous for both of them* [italics mine]."

And this is, of course, the ultimate truth about *Hair:* it is every bit as real, *and no more real,* than *The Desert Song.* A backer of the show told me, and this was before the opening, "I think I'll make a fortune. All the tourists want to see what hippies look like, but no one wants to go all the way down to the Village: it's too much trouble and it might be dangerous. Here we've got them all nice and safe and bottled for view on Forty-seventh Street."

And actually, all the damage that *Hair* had undergone in the change from its autumn opening was, in reality, a blessing. The lack of a burning Vietnam issue removed that reality: the audience didn't have to worry about Claude *really* being killed. And O'Horgan's camp-fag directing helped even more to direct the attention away from the original antiwar statement that the show wanted to make. And, of course, the greatest blessing was the miscasting of James Rado in the lead. It's just like casting Sandy Dennis in *Any Wednesday:* we secretly know she's *really* too young to be thirty, just as we secretly know Rado's *really* too old to be drafted. And all that those kids want is just affection anyway. And if Grayson Kirk had only been more loving, Columbia University wouldn't have gone.

Many of the critics who had embraced *Hair* downtown expressed disappointment with the Broadway version, but many more were convinced that *Hair* signaled the start of something new. I put this to an astute Broadway businessman. "Will *Hair* change things?" he answered. "You see those lines they had this morning? You better believe *Hair*'s gonna change things." He paused before saying it: "There will now be a spate of shitty rock musicals."

CHAPTER

35

What Kind of Day Has It Been?

Variety, in June, began its an-
nual theatre summation by saying: "The Broadway season of 1967–
68 was in most respects the best in several years. Financially, it set
new records. . . ." *Variety's* figures disclose that Broadway grossed
close to $59 million, an all-time high, beating the previous season,
which had been the best up to then, and had grossed a total of just
over $55 million. This is a jump of slightly more than 7%, which
indicates a healthy industry.

Only it doesn't.

If the industry were healthy, the jump would have been a great
deal more than just 7% because that amount doesn't indicate any
growth in anything except ticket prices. Example: when the season
began, in June, 1967, *Hello, Dolly!* could take in, at capacity, over
$82,000. A year later, in the same theatre, capacity was over $90,000,
a jump of close to 10%. As a matter of fact, taking just those musical
houses that had productions in both June, 1967, and June, 1968, the
total capacity has also gone up more than 7%. Several major musicals for the coming season have already announced a top ticket price
of $15.00. Next year will undoubtedly be record breaking too. As
long as they keep jacking up the ticket prices, *all* future seasons are
going to be record breaking.

But this is the greatest period of affluence in our history: there are more people with more money to spend than ever before, but they're sure not spending it on Broadway. Broadway's total gross has approximately doubled in the last 20 years. But the amount of money spent on *all* recreation has more than tripled in a similar period. The purchase of books and maps has quadrupled, etc.

As a matter of fact, I think the Broadway audience has been shrinking during these years. Twenty years ago, for example, *Oklahoma!* could take in approximately $31,000 a week at the St. James Theatre. Today, at the same theatre *Hello, Dolly!* now can gross over $90,000 a week at capacity. If the 34 Broadway houses had all played to capacity for 52 weeks this season, they could have grossed a total of almost $119 million; these 34 theatres actually did gross about $56 million. (*Variety* includes non-Broadway theatres in its totals, such as Lincoln Center and City Center.) An industry that is running at less than half of capacity and is not increasing its share of the potential market cannot be called healthy, no matter how record breaking its figures may be.

Financially, there were some optimistic signs: only three shows closed before they opened, the smallest number of any season this decade (the average for the seven preceding seasons had been seven). And the percentage of shows turning a profit was probably one of the two highest in the sixties: 22% made money—better than one in five—which makes it a relatively good year for the investors, right?

When you say that, smile.

Understand the following figures now: they pertain only to shows that opened during the 1967–68 season. They do *not* include any profits made by *Dolly!* or *Fiddler,* because those shows were not open for investment this year. There were, according to *Variety*'s year-end review, 58 shows that either are, were or will be hits or flops; touring shows that landed here a while are not included. These 58 were the ones possibly open to investment, and it is only these that are being discussed.

DRAMA (TOTAL: 25)

Smash hits	0	
Popular hits	2	(*The Price* and *Jean Brodie*)
Unpopular hits	1	(*More Stately Mansions*)
Snob hits	1	(*Rosencrantz*)
Movie sale hits	1	(*Seven Descents of Myrtle*)
Total hits:	5	

The 20 failures *lost* approximately $2,000,000. If you had backed all 25 shows, you would have ended up *losing* $1,000,000 on drama, at least.

COMEDY (TOTAL: 19)

Smash hits	1 (*Plaza Suite*)
Popular hits	2 (*Joe Egg* and *Girl in My Soup*)
Movie sale hits	2 (*Everything in the Garden* and *Only Game in Town*)

Total hits: 5

The 14 failures *lost* approximately $1,500,000. If you had backed all 19 shows, you would have ended up *losing* $500,000, at least.

MUSICALS (TOTAL: 14)

Smash hits probable	1 (*Hair*)
Personal hits	1 (*Dietrich*)

Total hits: 2

The 12 failures *lost* approximately $5,000,000. If you had backed all 14 shows, you would have ended up *losing* $3,500,000, at least.

Total: If you had invested all the money in all the Broadway shows this season, you would have lost, at a wildly conservative guess, $5,000,000.

Probably no season ever lost more, but I don't know that any of the above should be either surprising or disheartening (all of this is still looking at the season from a financial point of view). The theatre is a high-risk business, and it always has been. And more than that, unlike many businesses, the downside risk in the theatre is greater than almost anywhere else: in other industries you don't stand quite so great a chance of being wiped out completely. But in this decade, if a little over 21% of the productions show a profit, then a little under 78% show a loss. And most of the shows that do end up being profitable do so only in a small way. *More Stately Mansions,* for example, ended up with a profit of approximately $40,000 for all its gigantic advance sale and $1,000,000 gross. And most shows that lose, lose it all.

Some seasons, at a guess, do end up showing a total profit, which is incredible when you consider the odds against this. In those seasons several smashes cluster, and this probably turns the trick. I should guess that the 1965–66 season ended up in the black, primarily because of *Cactus Flower, Mame* and *Man of La Mancha,* plus half a dozen other successful shows, including *The Impossible Years, Marat/Sade, Sweet Charity,* etc.

And like any high-risk field, Broadway investment returns can be quick and considerable. If, for example, you had put money into *The Odd Couple,* you would have had a 350% profit in two years.

Barefoot in the Park has returned over 500% profit so far, and more will continue to come in, though its great earning days are obviously over.

For the investor, Broadway is not all that gloomy. A successful investor talked about it, and told how he had managed to show a profit in ten of the twelve years he has followed his system. "I suppose it is a system. It works for me. I think it could work for anybody, provided they have the same advantage I have—the ability to get to scripts. I think just trying to guess from backers' auditions or circulars would end up disastrously. But getting hold of scripts isn't all that hard anyway, especially if somebody wants your money.

"Anyway, here's how I figure . . . this is all approximate, understand. Say there are 50 shows a year. Half of them aren't worth discussing: amateurish. Either that or they have managements that are notorious for producing shows that run a long time and lose money. If you're in the business, you know who they are; if you're not, all you have to do is look at the producers' records. They have to list profit and loss for their shows in their offering circulars now. So you throw out half; that leaves 25 that you might possibly want to invest in. But you have to throw out maybe ten of those, because they aren't open to the public. You can't invest in Merrick any more, he's got some kind of deal with RCA, I think. And Hal Prince probably has all the investors he needs.

"So you're left with 15 shows. I invest in five of those 15. I invest the same amount in each of the five. If two of the five are profitable, I figure I'll come out ahead, and it's worked ten times in twelve years. One of the years I had a minor loss when I invested in some shows because of personal reasons: some friends were involved and I had to go along. The other year I lost was the season after I had both *Dolly!* and *Barefoot in the Park*. I went crazy and deserted my system and plunged erratically.

"The other ten years I've done anywhere from profitably to damn well. I think anybody can. The main thing is to avoid those shows that have no chance whatsoever, that first 25 I threw out. There's good money to be made in investing. My God, they were begging for money during the previews of *You Know I Can't Hear You When the Water's Running*. I don't know how many shares were available, but enough to have made a lot of money.

"When I am finally down to the, let's say, 15 possible shows, I make my final selection based on a combination of things: the star, the director, the management, nothing surprising. I think the management's the most important strictly from an investor's point of view; there's no profit to you when the show runs a year and loses everything.

"And if you're going to print this, I've got to add something in good conscience: over the last dozen or so years, I have cooled a little on the theatre as an investment. Because of the tremendous costs involved in production today, the payoff time has extended itself. Today, a musical, even a well-produced one, has to run six months at absolute capacity to break even, and how many musicals in history have done that? Still, I think Broadway is a reasonable place to invest your money. With intelligence. And caution."

Artistically, the season was schizoid. As the *Variety* article accurately sums it up: "The 1967–68 season was exceptionally good, by modern standards for straight plays. It was the worst in many years for musicals."

I think that musicals were so terrible not because there weren't any really good ones and not because the bad ones were as bad as they were—the season of five years ago, for example, brought us, among other worthies, *Sophie, Mr. President, Hot Spot* and *Nowhere to Go but Up.* It was the overpowering mediocrity that made the season so atrocious. When *How Now, Dow Jones* seems to be a good idea for a show, then you're in trouble. In other words, the average level of what Broadway people were content with was what made the year so deadening.

For straight plays it was comparatively a golden age. You could practically pick a list of ten best plays from American straight plays that appeared on Broadway. In the past couple of years, the *Best Plays* editor has had to scramble a bit: in 1966–67 two out of the ten best were American Broadway plays; the other eight were either musicals or imports or off-Broadway. The season before that, there were three natives on the list. This season at least the following ten had adherents: *Plaza Suite, Jean Brodie, The Price, The Only Game in Town, Something Different, Johnny No-Trump, Spofford, More Stately Mansions, Before You Go, I Never Sang for My Father.* Add some imports: *Joe Egg, Loot, Staircase, Rosencrantz, Birthday Party,* etc., and you've clearly had a Broadway season that will be looked back on with awe in years to come. I mean, we look back on the *bad* seasons with awe nowadays, with things getting worse each year, so what will a good one seem like?

But are the seasons getting worse? What kind of shape is Broadway really in, and what guesses can be made about its future?

Trying to be orderly about it, the theatre can be divided into four main groups: (1) the creative people; (2) the critical people; (3) the business people; (4) the paying people—the audience. These four groups have to somehow all mesh properly; they are all dependent on each other, to a greater or lesser degree, and the theatre needs all four working in some kind of decent order to operate anywhere near its peak.

Starting briefly with the critical people, because they are the easiest to peg. The television critics, particularly the two most important ones, Edwin Newman and Leonard Harris, are both good and becoming more important all the time. This can't happen quickly enough to help Broadway, because not in generations have the daily newspaper critics been as feeble as they are now. In other words, the critical situation is just as schizoid as much of the rest of the theatre: the good parts are getting better, the bad parts rapidly worse, and caught in the middle is the public, looking for a voice.

Who is this public anyway? How many of them are there? What do they want? Are they receiving it from Broadway? Estimates as to audience size vary enormously, and no one really knows. In a recent season, the low estimate was 7,000,000 people, the high estimate almost 11 million. But the high estimate came from Playbill magazine, which circulates in the theatres and owes its advertising rates to the size of its market. And I think its figures are high. My own guess is that probably a total of 8,000,000 people go to Broadway during a season. That means that 8,000,000 seats are sold, 8,000,000 chairs filled. Nowhere near that many different people attend. I think about 1,500,000 people attend the Broadway theatre annually, less than 1% of our total population.

Of that 1,500,000 people, approximately a third, or 500,000, come from out of town. According to the New York Convention and Visitors Bureau's 1967 report, there were more than 16 million people who came to New York as tourists. That means a lot of people aren't going to an industry that's operating on a less than 50% annual capacity. But in that respect they're just like New Yorkers, who don't go to the theatre either. About 1,000,000 people from the New York area attend Broadway. But the New York and Newark metropolitan areas have a population of over 13 million. If you want to figure out how many adults are actually working in New York City every day (and therefore within reasonable distance of the theatre), God knows how many millions more you could come up with. It would only reinforce what is already known, namely, that Broadway is a minority pleasure.

In their Theatregoers Study, the Center for Research in Marketing, Inc., actually questioned three main groups of people: New York area theatregoers, out-of-town theatregoers (from Chicago, Los Angeles, etc.) and New York area non-theatregoers (being defined as New Yorkers who have stopped attending, who haven't been to Broadway in at least a year). As an indication of how these groups differ, here is the movie preference ratings, part of which was given before, but not with the preference of the New York *non*-theatregoers listed. The five favorites of the three groups are:

New York Non-theatregoer	New York Theatregoer	Out-of-Town Theatregoer
1. "Guess Who's Coming to Dinner"	1. "Bonnie and Clyde"	1. "To Sir, with Love"
2. "The Graduate"	2. "The Graduate"	2. "The Graduate"
3. "Bonnie and Clyde"	3. "Guess Who's Coming to Dinner"	3. "Thoroughly Modern Millie"
4. "A Man and a Woman"	4. "A Man and a Woman"	4. "Camelot"
5. "In the Heat of the Night"	5. "In the Heat of the Night"	5. "Bonnie and Clyde"

From the above (and this pattern is repeated throughout the survey) it is clear that the New York non-theatregoer is much closer to the New York theatregoer than to the out-of-town theatregoer. As long as the subject of movies is with us, it's interesting to note that over *one half* (55%) of the New York non-theatregoers went to at least one movie a month. That means that New York non-theatregoers—over half of them—had seen twelve movies in the time they had seen no plays.

Why don't more people go to Broadway? My own guess, before the Theatregoers Study was made, was that people don't go because the cost of the whole evening—getting there, getting back, food and drink and baby-sitter, all in addition to whatever the theatre itself cost—was the chief barrier to Broadway.

I was wrong.

The cost of the entire evening is *a* barrier, but not more statistically important than the reviews a play received or the general over-all quality of the theatre. There are three other reasons, all of which are at least twice as important as barriers to increased (or, in the case of the non-theatregoer, to any) Broadway attendance. Following are the reasons and the percentage for each of the three groups:

New York Non-theatregoers   1. The cost of tickets   58%
                              2. The need to plan in advance 55%
                              3. Difficulty in getting tickets 45%

New York Theatregoers	1.	The cost of tickets	61%
	2.	Difficulty in getting tickets	53%
	3.	The need to plan in advance	44%
Out-of-Town Theatregoers	1.	The need to plan in advance	66%
	2.	Difficulty in getting tickets	45%
	3.	The cost of tickets	42%

These figures indicate that the cost of the entire evening isn't particularly a barrier: it's the *theatre* cost that's the barrier. People are going to be satisfied with their dinner, and they're going to be satisfied with their drinks after. The dissatisfactions come with the theatre itself: the theatre part of the evening—the center of the evening—is the weakness. One other point to be made about these figures: *of the three reasons that are listed as by far the most important barriers to increased theatregoing, two can be immediately eased, if not entirely alleviated.* There isn't much anybody can do about the cost of tickets. Everything else is costing more these days; I can't imagine why theatre tickets should or ought to be able to reverse the trend.

But it isn't hard to get tickets, not really.

And you don't have to plan in advance.

Now the above statements are not completely true; they're only true ninety-some per cent of the time. Because only two of the shows that opened this season were really ever sellouts—*Plaza Suite* and *Hair*. (The Dietrich show's grosses were switching around and subject to question.) *Joe Egg* may have sold out for as many as two weeks, and *George M!* the same. And maybe *Rosencrantz* and *More Stately Mansions* had a few weeks also when they really went clean. But for the rest, for the *Price*s and the *Brodie*s, etc., there were always tickets at the window.

If you go on the right days.

Basically, and this is crucial to the understanding of Broadway financing, the eight-performance week is really two different and distinct weeks, one of them marvelous, one terrible. The marvelous one contains the three weekend performances plus the Wednesday matinee. The terrible one—Monday through Thursday nights—is death. Several honorable producers gave me their nightly statistics over a period of a week, on the condition that I would not name the shows. Fine. These facts concern three shows—two musicals and a play—all of them enormous successes, all of them shows that have paid off at least double their investment. In other words, these are internationally famous productions. And they were all having immensely profitable weeks.

One of them, the straight play, sold 81% of its seats for the week. It sold over 97% on the four good shows and 67% on the weak shows.

The second, a musical, did slightly less well for the week, selling only 77% of its total seats. But it sold almost 99% of its seats for the four good performances, less than 63% for the Monday-Thursday night stand.

The third show, also a musical, did 82% of capacity business for the week. It managed to sell barely two thirds of its seats for the four bad shows. But the four good shows sold out completely. On a good, solid, profitable week, this show, one of the most famous and successful of all time, had over 2,000 empty seats in the Monday-through-Thursday-evening sequence, while there was standing room only on the four strong performances—the two matinees, plus Friday and Saturday nights.

These figures are simply too consistent to reflect this one seven-day period only. Theatre people all admit it's true: they die during the week. Except for *Hair* and *Plaza Suite,* this is true of every one of the 58 shows that opened this season. There's simply no one there. All the theatre people know it. They brood about it. They talk about it amongst themselves. They put forth theories.

They do everything except the one thing that could do any good —*tell the public.*

Now there's a reason for this. Here it is: theatre people are convinced that if you let the people know they can see *Mame,* they will avoid *Mame* like the plague. Bruit the news that *Fiddler* is available, and it's bye-bye *Fiddler.* Theatre people don't just think this; they know it. They know it just as surely as they know that there's such a thing as last-minute walk-in business, and so you've got to be on Forty-fifth Street or you're dead.

There is, in other words, a crippling standing-room-only notion that pervades the street, based—if it is based on anything—on the days during World War II when there weren't enough hotel rooms and gas was rationed and *Oklahoma!* changed the pattern of the Broadway run. Now, assuming that there is the least moron shred of truth in their belief, you'd think that eventually theatre people would realize they could say to the public: "Listen, folks, we're sorry we're such a smash that you can't get near us on the weekends or Wednesday mats, but it just so happens that there are a few possible pairs left at the box office for some of the other performances. Such as Monday, Tuesday, Wednesday, Thursday nights." I mean, if they think it's important that people not be able to get seats, tell them the truth: the weekends and the mats are tough. But why they die the other nights is beyond my comprehension. It seems to me that if the theatre told the public that there were seats available for nearly everything they wanted to see about half of the time and just come on down, folks, then you might actually have a thing such as walk-in business again.

You don't have to plan ahead. It isn't hard to get tickets. Go. Pick what you want to see and where you want to sit, and if anybody gives you trouble, move on to the next show that you want to see. It doesn't *have* to be an insulting experience to attend the Broadway theatre; there's no law. This holds true, by the way, for the holdover blockbusters too. Sure, some of them sell out some weeks. But if you want to see *Dolly!* or *Fiddler* or *Mame* or *La Mancha* or *Cabaret* and you go down on the spur of the moment any week-night, you'll be able to see something. *Fiddler* was the top-grossing show of the year, and it sold about 94% of its seats over the season. But that means that it's only selling maybe 88% of its seats on the bad nights. There are 1,655 seats in *Fiddler*'s theatre; that means, averaged out over the season, at least 165 seats are available to the public any week-night. You could give a spur-of-the-moment party any week-night for your 150 best friends, and you'd all be taken care of. Some of your friends could even bring friends. The point to all this is simply to emphasize and emphasize again that as far as Broadway is concerned, as far as its actual availabilities to them, the public is uninformed.

They are also disappointed.

The Theatregoers Study asked the various groups of goers and non-goers what they wanted Broadway to be and listed over 20 possible choices: funny, cynical, provocative, about ordinary people, etc. (The following pertains only to those words that were selected by approximately half of those sampled.) The New York theatregoer listed the following attributes in order: (1) entertaining; (2) good theatre; (3) funny and witty (tied). Immediately following these, separated by only a few percentage points, were the following: (4) socially aware; (5) enlightening; (6) provocative. Below this, ten percentage points below "socially aware," came "smart/sophisticated."

The out-of-town theatregoers *want* the theatre to be "smart/sophisticated." It is their third choice, after (1) entertaining, and (2) funny. They are much less interested in the theatre being, for example, socially aware. Fewer than half of the out-of-town theatre-

goers would like theatre to be socially aware, compared with the
New York theatregoers. (One sidelight on the non-goers: the single
most striking adjective that differentiates them from the goers is that
they want the theatre to be "about ordinary people" to a considerably greater extent.)

But the point that this discussion is trying to emphasize is this: in
addition to being asked what they *wanted* Broadway to be, the
people questioned were also asked what they thought Broadway was
actually like, and the only word that came close to satisfying them
was "light." They felt that Broadway was, if anything, even more
light than they wanted it to be. *In every other case, Broadway fell
short.*

Example: almost half of the New York goers wanted the theatre to
be important, while barely 10% thought it was.

Example: almost half of the out-of-towners wanted Broadway to
be provocative, but less than one fifth thought it was.

Example: over 80% of the New Yorkers wanted Broadway to be
"good theatre" but less than 40% thought it was presenting good
theatre.

On and on down the line, with the single exception of being
"light," Broadway disappoints the people. They have certain wants,
and these are simply not being satisfied.

Why?

Why does anything disappoint? Because you *expect* something of
it. And it is precisely here, in the area of expectation, that Broadway
is tremendously guilty. Over the years Broadway has set about being
something special, something better, in the way it has thought of
itself and handled itself. The plain fact is that approximately 60%
of the people who go to Broadway now go "just to go to the
theatre." For the hell of it, for the fun of it.

But looking at it from the other side, 40% are going for an
"event," a birthday, anniversary, business entertaining, theatre
party, etc., etc. Whatever the reason, four out of ten people go to
Broadway for an event. And it is this "eventness" that is damaging.
The entire mystique about opening nights is, I think, enormously
damaging. It sets up the expectation of magic and Judy Garland desperately getting the set painted in time. Movies are enjoying as lush
a period right now as any in their history, and what would you guess
to be the percentage of people who go to the movies just for fun, for
the hell of it, for something to do? I'd guess (and I don't know) *at
least* 95%, and I'd bet I'm low.

So if a movie stinks up the joint, so what? Nobody's angry. And movies are expensive too, proportionately, perhaps much more expensive than Broadway over a comparable period. It costs $3.00 to see "The Graduate" in Manhattan. If you want "Doctor Dolittle," it's $4.50. (My God, it's $2.50 to see smut like "$100 a Night" at the Globe, and it's breaking all records.) *Plaza Suite* has seats for $3.00, just as "The Graduate" does. Now obviously the *best* seat for *Plaza Suite* isn't $3.00, and no one's pretending that it is. The point here is that people will go to the movies for the hell of it and have fun or not—it doesn't matter. The main thing is that they're not angry if they don't; they just tried something and it isn't anything to get all hot and bothered about.

The "eventness" of Broadway is murderous to it. People have simply got out of the habit of "just going to the theatre." They think there aren't any seats, that they have to plan, and since they have to plan and go to bother, they might as well tie it to something special—an event.

Broadway is, in a sense, like the New York Yankees. For years the Yankees ignored the general public while pandering to big business. They sold their season tickets to companies that bought them primarily because, come October, they would have seats for the World Series, and that was sound business practice and tax deductible besides. *But they weren't fans.* And the Yankees went their profitable way, alienating the fans and making pots of money and then, when the farm system stopped producing, the Yankees found themselves in the terrible position of being without fans.

The Mets were where the aficionados were. The Mets, with their rotten teams and heartburn-producing plays, were filling up Shea Stadium, while the Yankees were in trouble. Right now the Yankees are doing their best to change their image in order to try and indicate to the fans that they do in fact care, and conceivably they will be successful. Broadway has not yet begun its wooing of the audience. There are always those comforting record-breaking money figures each year, and there is so much money in a smash and in corruption, and enough people still coming that all seems well.

But this season, for the first time, some of the pros began to sweat a little. The musicals began to dry up, and Broadway needs its musicals, because they're all that people have been really going to lately.

"But that's because the plays were bad," the pros decided. "Give 'em decent plays; they'll come." Well, they got decent plays this

year, and they didn't come. The only new drama that can be said to
have had considerable audience appeal was Miller's *The Price,* and
I think that can be accounted for by the fact that the people in the
play are like the people who see it—middle-class, middle-aged Jews.
(This is clearly a generalization, but it does, in fact, have some rele-
vance. The audiences for different kinds of shows are tremendously
varied. The typical drama goer might be said to be over fifty, is
college educated, has a very low *or* very high income, and is from
New York. The musical goer is between thirty and fifty, has less than
a college education, is in the middle-income bracket—between
$8,000 and $15,000 a year—and is from out of town. The comedy
goer tends to be the youngest: proportionately, more people under
thirty go to comedy than to the other kinds of Broadway offerings.
Education is not a factor; they are middle and lower income, and
they are from New York.)

It's an overstatement to say the people didn't come. They went to
Plaza Suite and for a while to *Rosencrantz,* but they always like Neil
Simon and they'll always suffer the Snob Hit. They went to look at
movie stars, Bergman and Finney, but that's got nothing to do with
Broadway. Going back to the Yankee parallel: they weren't the fans;
they were the World Series goers. But the "good" plays, the ones
that might make a ten-best list: most of those lost money, enough for
the business people along the street to start showing concern.

The business people—the theatre owners, the ticket brokers, the
box-office personnel, the ad men, the publicists, etc.—make up a
group that is hard to compliment. Theatre owners have been mentioned enough; they're rich and generally thieves. The dishonesty
carries over into the ticket-agency field and permeates the whole
business. As a matter of fact, this is one of the biggest problems
facing Broadway: there is a slight but discernible scummy taint over
the whole operation. It starts with the uncomfortable theatres and
includes the ticket practices, the deceptions, everything else in the
industry.

Only it isn't an industry.

Theatre people themselves recognize this as a terrible problem:
there is no feeling of industry anywhere on Broadway, no sense that
what is good for someone else might actually be good (or, as is more
usually the case, bad) for me.

Example: Ingram Ash, one of the heads of Blaine Thompson, the
biggest Broadway ad agency, had the notion years ago of taking a
small ad in the *Times* for the month preceding December 25, and

this small ad would contain the five words: GIVE THEATRE TICKETS FOR CHRISTMAS. That's all. Just a reminder. It would cost next to nothing to run the ad. And Ash's notion was based on the fact that theatre tickets cover an almost infinite price range: you can give a single seat in the balcony or a whole row on the main floor. But the main thing was, GIVE THEATRE TICKETS FOR CHRISTMAS. No special play in mind. No special interests. Nothing. Just the reminder, GIVE THEATRE TICKETS FOR CHRISTMAS.

Well, you probably haven't seen that ad much over the last decade or so in which Ash has been pushing the idea. There are various theatre groups that have more than enough money to pay the piddling amounts required. But no one will do it. There simply is not enough feeling of industry to realize that it's a good idea, even if it doesn't affect all shows equally, or any show specifically. Institutional advertising is an accepted way of life in all the business world.

Not on Broadway.

I asked a leading investment analyst to discuss a thriving industry, any industry, and explain just what some of the elements were that made the industry solid. "Right now," he said after some silence. "Right now . . . what . . . well, office equipment's very sound now. IBM, Sperry Rand. Now that's considerably larger than the theatre, but it still is an industry and that's what you asked for. What makes it sound? Well, there's an expanding demand for the market. [There isn't on Broadway.] And it's not an easy-entrance business: anyone can't suddenly decide to go into it, which keeps the caliber fairly high. [Broadway is an easy-entrance business.] Labor costs aren't the most important thing to a sound industry. [Not true on Broadway.] And they have the ability to pass on their price increases. In other words, if I'm selling nails, and I raise my price, you just might go to another store to buy. But people are willing to pay for their office equipment; it satisfies its market. [Not true on Broadway.] And there is really a tremendous amount spent on market research: What are the customer's problems? What do they want?"

This last point needs a bit of pausing over. The Theatregoers Study, initiated privately for this book, is the *first* market-research survey, the first that deals with motivational research. And clearly, any survey privately initiated cannot begin to be as complete as one that a large business or industry can undertake. But they haven't undertaken it, and it's unlikely that you can ever get enough of them to see where it might benefit them to spend some money to have something done. But I think it could make them or save them fortunes. Two examples:

1. The fact that the out-of-town audience affects musical comedy so tremendously could totally revolutionize booking patterns on Broadway. The way it works now is that there is a wild scramble in the fall and then a second wave in the spring for musical houses that have previously held failures or, in some instances, long-running musicals that eventually slowed down. But whatever the case, there is *always* a vicious booking struggle for musical houses.

And there needn't be. Because the summer is when the out-of-towners are in New York. And over the last half-dozen years, Broadway people have noted how well musicals have done in the summer. The Theatregoers Study shows why: it's the out-of-towners who go to musicals. And that means that you could open a musical in June or July or August if you wanted and not damage your chances for success.

There are always houses available in the summertime. This season, in early June, there are five empty musical houses, and they're going to stay empty until at least October. Half the year waiting for the fall flood, and by that time, the fate of the mythical summer-opening musical is set. If it's a smash and it has to move, believe me, there would be a place for it to move to. Rule: never, as long as Broadway exists, will a smash ever close because there isn't a house to play in. And if it isn't a smash, a six-month run is more than it's likely to get anyway.

Theatres are air-conditioned now. Movies have discovered that the summertime, which used to be deadly, is now their prime money-making season. There is no earthly reason why the same thing can't be done for musicals. Not only could opening musicals in summer alleviate the booking problem, but it could help lighten costs as well. Everybody else in the Broadway theatre works seasonally; they have slack times. Any theatre owner would be delighted to have a musical in his house for the summer instead of nothing, and there is no doubt that he would give the producer better terms. And the set constructer would do his work for less money. As far as the musical theatre is concerned, a twelve-month season could be set in operation immediately instead of the eight-month season—October through May—that now exists.

And of course the proof of all this has been around for years. *Wish You Were Here* opened June 25, 1952, and ran a year and a half. And *Mame* opened late in May, with a reputed advance of $750,000, mostly in parties. If *Mame* had had solid parties the first month, they could have opened late in June with a $500,000 advance sale. So the final argument against opening a musical late—no advance and no possibility of getting one—doesn't hold water either.

2. This one is really a stunner: The Theatregoers Study asked people when they most wanted to go to the theatre. Not which of the eight performances presently scheduled did they prefer but—forgetting when plays are actually done—when would they most want to go. And the survey indicated—taking both New Yorkers and out-of-towners together—that the time they would most prefer to go to theatre would be the Saturday matinee. Fine. You know when the second most popular time was?

The second most popular time was the Friday matinee!

Now obviously there is no Friday matinee, but there sure as hell ought to be. Broadway, in addition to building up its product so that it inevitably disappoints its audience, as well as making it impossibly difficult for its audience to purchase the product, has also never taken the time to find out when the market wanted the product. Can you picture Xerox making a machine that would do a terrific job of copying typed tissue paper? They wouldn't, because they'd investigate first and discover that secretaries don't like typing on tissue paper because it cuts too easily, and so they would be selling a product for which there was no market.

Broadway is selling its product without first finding out that tissue paper shreds. Now they know a little of this: they know they're dying Monday through Thursday nights, and they know that if they substitute a Sunday matinee for the Monday-night performance, they will come out ahead. But they never make the switch until the show is dying. And they also know that their matinees are enormously strong. (New Yorkers taken alone, for example, would prefer a Sunday matinee *over* a Saturday night.) The point is that, for whatever reasons, people want matinee performances now, and a Friday matinee is the total second choice of all theatregoers. The five most-requested times in order are these:

1. Saturday matinee
2. Friday matinee
3. Sunday matinee
4. Wednesday matinee
5. Saturday night

In other words, the whole weekly theatre setup is archaic and wrong. They are simply not selling their product in a way or at a time that is satisfactory to the public.

My own suggestion is that the theatre week should be changed radically—into four matinee and four evening performances. The matinees would be on Wednesday, Friday, Saturday and Sunday; the evenings, Wednesday, Thursday, Friday and Saturday. And I would drastically lower the prices for Wednesday and Thursday nights. I would raise them for Friday and Saturday nights. *And I would raise them for the matinees.*

There is no logical reason for a matinee to be so much cheaper than an evening show, as it is now. *Cabaret* costs $12.00 for an orchestra seat on Wednesday night and $6.90 for an orchestra seat on a Wednesday matinee. *And it's the same show.* If they cut a couple of numbers for the matinee, fine; charge less. But Broadway is really being silly to charge as little as it does for the same product in the afternoon compared with the evening. And the Theatregoers Study indicates—this is by no means absolutely certain, but it is indicated—that people go to matinees not so much for the bargain as the convenience. They would probably resist if you charged the identical price for the evening performance. But I can't imagine why *Cabaret* couldn't charge $9.90 instead of $6.90 if their evening price held at $12.00.

The performance week I am suggesting is difficult for actors in enormous starring vehicles—five performances between Friday afternoon and Sunday afternoon. But in the first place, there are not that many starring vehicles per season, and in the second place, the actor would have from the end of the Sunday matinee, say 4:30, until the start of the Wednesday matinee to recuperate or do anything else he wanted, and that's a three-day weekend every week for the actor.

And it's more money for the business people. By raising the matinee and weekend prices—even dropping the two more poorly attended week-night evening performance prices—they would have a higher gross total, and they would benefit with a higher percentage of attendance throughout the entire week.

Now this kind of information is just the beginning. The Theatregoers Study that I initiated, while statistically valid, was only a beginning step; we didn't really know what questions to ask. Now the questions are out in the open. And if Broadway wanted to initiate a substantial survey, it could find out an incredible amount about why things work the way they do. It was indicated earlier that *Brodie* failed to excite because the out-of-towner didn't come. Well, *why* didn't he? There was word of *Brodie:* Vanessa Redgrave's triumph in London was written up in the papers over here, and there was news throughout the year across the country, in the movie columns, etc., about the movie version being made. But people didn't pay attention. *Why?* Why, out of the many facts that we are bombarded with each day, do we retain what we retain? This is the kind of thing a major theatre study could begin to answer. It's all possible, and the theatre has the money, but I doubt that anything will come of it, because David Merrick won't see what's in it for him, Feuer and Martin will be off in some proxy fight, Hal Prince will be starting a movie, and Alex Cohen will be in London negotiating to bring over some other small revue, and *no one's watching the store.* No one who gives a damn, anyway.

Why do people retain what they retain? What causes their urges? Why does "The Dirty Dozen" go through the roof when an almost identical picture starring Mickey Rooney a few years earlier didn't? (And there's more to it than the difference between Mickey Rooney and Lee Marvin; I mean, who the hell ever heard of Dustin Hoffman?) One of the strange things the Theatregoers Study discovered is that people who want to see certain shows do so for reasons that pass understanding. Word of mouth is clearly the most important single factor, particularly for out-of-town goers. It least affects New York drama goers, who are, in turn, affected most by notices.)

But one of the questions asked the theatregoers, both local and out of town, was to name the one show on Broadway they most wanted to see. Now after they'd been asked that and had answered, they were asked, "I wonder if you recall the name of the leading man?" (And after that came female star, author, director, producer.) O.K. Not even half of any category knew any single answer.

Example: nine out of ten out-of-towners and over eight out of ten New Yorkers did not know the name of the director of the one show they most wanted to see. Nothing surprising here.

Example: over nine out of ten of the out-of-towners and over eight out of ten New Yorkers didn't know the producer. To be expected.

But 76% of the out-of-towners could not name the male star of the one show they most wanted to see. And neither could almost six out of ten New Yorkers. Statistics for female stars are not startlingly different.

I don't want to drive anybody crazy with percentages, but why the hell did these people want to see the one show they most wanted to see? (It wasn't the author, by the way; three quarters of them didn't know who he was either.) Well, what is it? I don't know. But it's got to be something, and whatever that "something" is, Broadway had better find out fast and figure some way to advertise that will appeal to that something, instead of somberly placing some ugly ad that the *Times* takes $9,000 for and which doesn't pull beans. Theatre advertising is terrible; it is probably as bad as book advertising. They both work on very small budgets, so their lack of size is excusable. What is less easy to forgive is their lack of invention. Theatre publicity is pretty standard too: the same phony interviews, the same grinny-sweet, TV talk show appearances that mean the show's in trouble. Joel Grey· wouldn't have done those *George M!* numbers on "Ed Sullivan" if the lines had been down the block at the box office. And I think the TV audience knows it now. We know that when Carol Lawrence says she's having "such fun" doing *I Do! I Do!,* what she's really saying is, "If you don't come, we'll close."

One other nutty thing about audiences: they don't remember all that much about the last show they've seen. Take New Yorkers: fewer than four out of five knew who the stars were of the last show they'd seen; less than two thirds knew the name of the author; and over three quarters could not name either the director or producer. All of this would tend to suggest that the theatre is self-deluding: you *must* get Gene Saks to direct your show or you're nowhere, only nobody knows who Gene Saks is.

That's only partially true. The party ladies and the charity chairwomen do know; that's how they sell. But as we have already said, they are not as much help to the theatre as they might be, because even though they sell seats, they have no qualms about quality. In the long run, this is going to be damaging.

Illegal ticket practices are, I think, part of the beast. John Wharton resigned this year from one of the committees or commissions he was heading, and although I don't know why, I bet despair had something to do with it. He is a fine man and has been suggesting ways to improve ticket distribution for decades now. And Broadway always nods, says "brilliant" and goes on stealing.

But even the thieves were a little worried this year. At last, I think (hope), a feeling is creeping along the street that things aren't as rosy as they might be. My God, the reasons they come up with for people not going to theatre. This year alone they blamed it on the weather, the riots, the parking strike, the fact that so many New Yorkers were taking midwinter vacations. (Listen, if you think that's reaching, there was once a time, long ago now, when the claim was made that the reason no one was going to the theatre was because too many people were riding bicycles in the evenings.) This season poor attendance was also blamed on Robert Kennedy's death, Memorial Day, daylight saving time, the post-Easter lull, Passover, Dr. King's funeral, the general business situation, the absence of a musical smash and on and on. Press agent David Rothenberg was listening to a listing of such reasons one day, nodding in pseudosympathy as one possible reason after another was ticked off. At the end of the recital, Rothenberg said, "You're absolutely right. And not only that, but over in Jersey there's a big dance tonight in Hohokus."

Finally, the creative people. Starting with the producers, because in a very real way they are responsible for what gets done. It was reported earlier, with some shock, that the best producer of straight plays doesn't exist. That's still true, but there's another little something about producers that bears on Broadway's future. But in order to get to it, I have to name who I think the leading producers are: certainly Harold Prince and David Merrick, and Robert Whitehead; probably Saint-Subber and Richard Barr; Feuer and Martin; maybe Leland Hayward; maybe Alex Cohen; maybe Kermit Bloomgarden. After that, there is a certain shortage, as I have already gone into. Let me list them and put a number after their names, and you guess what the numbers mean:

Prince	54
Merrick	54
Whitehead	47
Saint-Subber	48
Barr	53
Feuer and Martin	48
Hayward	44
Cohen	41
Bloomgarden	40

Those cynics who guessed that the numbers are their respective IQs are probably playwrights and certainly wrong. The numbers also do not pertain to the number of productions that the men have brought in. Rather, they represent, more or less accurately, the year in which the first production they were in charge of got to Broadway, and if you study the list carefully, you will detect a certain paucity of numbers beginning with "6." That means just this: not only does the best producer of American plays not exist, but neither does the best new producer of the sixties.

There's no new talent.

Among the creative personnel involved in the Broadway scene, this same theme recurs: no new talent. The talent's all old, but it's all we've got. Look at those men up there. The newest one started 14 years ago. By this time in the fifties, Hal Prince had brought in *Pajama Game* and *Damn Yankees, New Girl in Town* and *West Side Story*. By this time in the forties, Leland Hayward had done *A Bell for Adano, State of the Union, Mr. Roberts,* and *South Pacific* was on the horizon.

But the producers who started in the sixties are not to be named; there's not an agent in the business who would willingly take a client's play to a sixties producer *first*. You do it, you eventually end up there, but not by choice. And one of the damages that the lack of good new producers brings is that you end up with bad new producers.

The situation among the directors is better: there are four new ones. Mike Nichols is the most successful new figure of the sixties, and as long as he stays with trivia, he's terrific. But *The Little Foxes* showed an inability to deal with much beyond that, and besides, Nichols is becoming more of a movie man anyway.

Gene Saks is sort of a poor man's Mike Nichols, although *Mame* is a much greater success than anything that Nichols has attempted in the musical field. Saks showed genuine skill with *Nobody Loves an Albatross,* but his work since then has been disappointing. *Half a Sixpence, Generation* and *Mame* are not stretching his talents all that much, and his movie work thus far—"Barefoot in the Park" and "The Odd Couple"—has only reinforced his poor-man's-Nichols reputation.

Besides, once creative people start in movies, you just can't count on them. Especially directors. Maybe the reason for that is this: on the stage, no matter how rich or sought after he is, no matter how brilliant, the director is doomed to be primarily a traffic manager. But a director really makes a movie after all the shooting is done, when he's alone in the cutting room. The film is a much happier medium for a director than the stage, not only because he can actually be creative, but because he can look back on it later. On stage, if he gets what he wants right once, it's going to be altered during the next rehearsal or performance. On film it's his, permanently.

Gower Champion, who was choreographing on Broadway as early as the forties, only became a directing power this decade. He is, like Nichols, very gifted. And, like Nichols, superficial. Champion, with his stunning visual sense, is really the greatest window dresser of them all: his work looks gorgeous in the shop window, but take it home, and the seams start showing.

Ulu Grosbard, who directed *The Subject Was Roses,* is serious and talented but his output is still too small to talk about much. And Grosbard has just done his first film; there are rumors that he is about to do a second, and, to repeat, once a director senses the power of the camera, he is not to be counted on for the theatre.

Those are the four names that theatre people would generally agree on. But there were 44 plays that needed directors this year, and eleven book musicals, and the director shortage along the street has rarely been so acute. Example: the Neil Simon musical, *Promises, Promises* hired as its director Robert Moore, who six months before was directing his first New York piece off-off-Broadway. It was *The Boys in the Band,* and he did it beautifully. But it's still a jump from directing for free in a workshop to trying to handle the elements of a Broadway musical—all within six months. The reason that he was offered the chance to make the jump is only secondarily because he might be talented: the main reason is that *there's no one else*. Robbins isn't working much and Fosse's doing a picture and Champion's tired, and after them, the deluge. You can try some of the old hacks and *know* you'll get well-crafted mediocrity, or you can try someone new and pray. A stage manager was initially announced as director for *Dear World,* the Jerry Herman musical starring Angela Lansbury. That's like Bennett Cerf hiring the office manager of Random House to edit the new Capote.

There may have been some new faces this season: Tom O'Horgan got a lot of publicity for camping up *Hair,* and so did Donald Driver for his splendidly slick work on *Your Own Thing* off-Broadway, but then he came uptown with *Mike Downstairs.* Driver will get more work, no question about that, but the bloom is off.

Actors you can forget about. All the talent of the forties and fifties: Scott and Robards and Preston and Stapleton and Julie Harris and Page and Kim Stanley—they have not been followed. And Streisand will return to Broadway when Hollywood comes to Dunsinane. Robert Redford and Alan Alda are terrific talents, but first of all, they hit Broadway in the fifties, and secondly, naturally they're in movies now.

The musical-comedy writers, or lack of them, has already been talked about. And as for playwrights, well, there's Edward Albee. And assuming he is the most important playwright to surface in the sixties, what better example could you ask to show there's no new talent? Consider Albee's Broadway work and what have you got? Some dreadful adaptations, some soporific originals, and two good acts of *Virginia Woolf*. Yes, those first acts of *Virginia Woolf* are marvelous bitch dialogue—not as good as Mart Crowley's bitch dialogue in *The Boys in the Band*—but still marvelous. That is really the extent of Albee's skill: he writes good bitch dialogue.

It is to weep.

So Broadway's dead, right?

Don't hold your breath. Michael Smith, the drama critic for the *Village Voice,* edited a book on off-off-Broadway in which he noted that off-off-Broadway was becoming more and more an alternative to Broadway rather than a way into it. When asked about that, he said, "I don't think it's true any more. I think it was probably always wishful thinking on my part. I don't want to live by passing the hat. There's just not enough money off-off-Broadway." And there you have the secret ingredient that insures Broadway's durability: money. Just as money is at the root of many of Broadway's and the nation's problems, so is it responsible for much of both their strengths. There is more money to be made now on Broadway—from a smash—than ever before. With *Dolly!* and *Fiddler* running forever, and Neil Simon making millions for three short plays, it is simply not an industry that can vanish. It's a high-risk enterprise—it always has been—but when you hit, you are almost set for life. Any business that can hold out that promise is going to be around awhile.

And there are hopeful signs. Rumor has it that Robbins is planning a musical, and if it pans out, and if he does half a dozen more, that will help. And the batch of writers who appeared off-Broadway this season are legitimate cause for rejoicing.

And there are, at last, to be some new theatres.

That could be of incredible help. The putting up of all those new Cinema I- and Cinema II-type movie houses on the East Side has been an enormous boost to the film business in New York. The new legitimate theatres, besides being new, will have an even greater potential advantage: they will be housed in skyscrapers. That means, God willing, that for the first time a theatre will not have to produce the paralyzing income it needs annually as a real-estate venture. Rounding off the figures, Broadway grossed approximately $60 million this year. Well, $15 million to $20 million of that went to the theatre owners, because theatres take up land in an incredibly valuable part of the city, and the taxes are vicious. But with theatres in skyscrapers, the theatres' percentage wouldn't have to be such an enormous one to be profitable, and the cost spiral could conceivably be stopped, which couldn't hurt.

Also, Harold Prince is heading a theatrical advisory board for Mayor Lindsay, and maybe, as so many theatrical assemblages do, it will end up in sound and fury. But Prince is probably the producer with the broadest view of the problems of the theatre as a whole, and maybe—probably not, but maybe—he can make things happen.

So Broadway, that fabulous invalid (and no phrase on earth makes me want to upchuck faster), is going to survive.

And it's also going to change.

The standard prediction, based on the fact that Circle in the Square is soon going to take over Henry Miller's Theatre and Albee and Barr are bringing their string of successful off-Broadway plays to the Billy Rose Theatre, is to say that off-Broadway is coming up-town. I think the reverse is more likely to be true.

If I had to guess, I would say that in the next few years more and more Broadway producers will take straight plays and put them on in off-Broadway houses. The reason, of course, is that the costs of producing make doing anything but mass-appeal plays a lunatic Broadway venture. *Spofford* ran over six months and lost its entire investment. *I Never Sang for My Father,* with a great preponderance of good notices, lost $180,000 during a four months' run.

And off-Broadway is money now. Big money. Perhaps the most important cultural advancement of the season came about when Hollywood discovered off-Broadway, as it did this season to a much greater extent than ever before. (This is titanically logical on Hollywood's part: the paying of great fortunes for Broadway successes on the basis of a presold audience isn't necessarily smart. *Mary, Mary,* the longest-running Broadway play of the decade, was a disastrous financial failure as a film. *How to Succeed in Business,* the long-running musical, was a similar cinematic box-office bomb. Hollywood is discovering more and more that what pays off is the film, not the original property, as in the case of "The Graduate" and "Bonnie and Clyde.") It is entirely possible that of the five most financially successful productions of the 1967–68 year, three will have come from off-Broadway: *Your Own Thing, Scuba Duba* and *The Boys in the Band.*

A Broadway producer was explaining his options on a play that he was doing next season. "There's a strong possibility right now of a movie sale: $100,000 is the figure they're throwing. If they mean it, and I do the play off-Broadway, it's a guaranteed money-maker right off the bat. The production gets 40% of a movie sale, and that's $40,000, and it will cost me $20,000 to do the play. To do it on Broadway and take it on the road, it's got to cost me close to $150,-000. Got to. So what happens to the $40,000 share of the movie money then? It's nothing. My only trouble is—goddammit, I like off-Broadway, I go all the time to off-Broadway—I just don't want to work there, that's all. Will I? Ask my analyst."

I hope he does. I hope a lot of people do, because right now is a terrible time for original American drama. Briefly, artistic talent tends to cluster; that's why we have the so-called golden ages. We have had two talent clusters in American theatre in the last half century. The first was around the time of O'Neill, and the twenties and thirties produced, in no order whatsoever: Philip Barry, S. N. Behrman, Marc Connelly, Kaufman and Hart, Maxwell Anderson, Sidney Howard, Edwin Justus Mayer, Robert Sherwood, Paul Green, George Kelly, Elmer Rice, Sidney Kingsley, Lillian Hellman, Clifford Odets, John Steinbeck, William Saroyan, Thornton Wilder. That's an impressive list of talent even now. And when Miller and Williams happened along, they seemed simply to further the line of talent that began with O'Neill. Sadly, they were the end.

But no one minded terribly, because by the time of their arrival, the second burst had begun, this one the musical explosion that *Oklahoma!* initiated. And along with Rodgers and Hammerstein came Lerner and Loewe, Bernstein, Loesser and the rest, and Broadway became essentially a musical-comedy theatre. Now that the musical-comedy talent has thinned, the lack of playwrights becomes increasingly evident. The plain fact is that we have not had a first-rate playwright debut in almost a quarter of a century, and the wait is getting painful.

There was no Pulitzer prize awarded in drama this season, the fourth time in the past six years that such a decision was reached by the Pulitzer committee. This is by far the most arid stretch in the history of that award. Just to compare a bit, ten years ago, the award went to O'Neill's *Long Day's Journey into Night*. Twenty years ago, the winner was *A Streetcar Named Desire*. Thirty years before, *Our Town* won the Pulitzer, and ten years before that, it went to *Strange Interlude*. Broadway is desperately awaiting that third cluster, and of course there is no reason to assume it is going to come in our lifetime. Right now drama is deep in the trough of the wave.

One of the problems Broadway drama faces is that it does not attract the best talents, and when it does get a good one working for it, the talent often contents itself with second-rate work, as Gore

Vidal did this season with *Weekend*. I doubt that he would have published as trivial a novel under his own name. Worse, though, is the kind of talent that can succeed on Broadway. The following quotations are taken from the book of a playwright who had just written an enormously successful retirement-making play.

The producers constantly referred to the "well-made play" as typified by Ibsen. I had no rebuttal, never having seen or read an Ibsen play.

[When told of a good English director] How good can he be if I never heard of him? Besides, all good English directors are named Peter.

This last remark probably makes little sense to anyone outside Broadway, but three hot English directors of a few years ago were Peter Brook, Peter Hall and Peter Glenville. The upsetting thing about these quotations is that someone could be enormously successful on Broadway, know that all good British directors were named Peter, and at the same time be so completely (and unashamedly) ignorant that he had never seen or read an Ibsen play.

This is the kind of talent Broadway often has to get by with. In a sense, it's the problem Balanchine faces. A D'Amboise or Villella is luck: most of the boys with elevation play basketball. And most of the writers with talent write poems. Or novels. Or advertising copy, or God knows what, but they don't write for the theatre.

And why should they? For every $1.00 that was spent last season for theatre tickets, less than 3¢ was spent to see serious original American drama. I do not include O'Neill: *More Stately Mansions* was no more a contribution to original American drama than the APA's revival of *The Show-off*. And I don't count *Plaza Suite* either, because for all his enormous skill, Simon is still too concerned with the easy laugh, the entertainment piece.

Look, when Sander Vanocur came on NBC and gave his report of the trip back on the plane with the Kennedy people after Bobby was murdered, he said that they all felt somehow as if they were in an O'Neill play. He didn't say they felt as if they were in a Norman Krasna play or an F. Hugh Herbert play or even a Neil Simon play. O'Neill was the man. O'Neill is what Broadway is all about, not because he wrote "serious" plays, plays you didn't laugh at, but because he wanted to mean something. I personally prefer comic writing *when it means something,* but America doesn't generally produce comic writers that fit that category. So if I say "serious" drama, I don't mean it's good because you don't laugh at it; I mean it's good because the intention of the artist is greater than simply to delight.

The original American drama received two terrible shocks about ten years ago, and the repercussions are still crippling: a young girl walked, and an old man sat down. The old man was Brooks Atkinson, and when he retired as critic of the *Times,* he took some of his 35 years of influence with him. And the *Times,* through magnificent handling, has got rid of the rest. The audience for serious plays has no one to listen to any more.

The young girl was Brigitte, and it is my feeling that Miss Bardot's bottom is going to prove one of the significant cultural events of this half century. Because what it did—and the grosses that "And God Created Woman" pulled in proved this—was to show the movie people that they could make a fortune with a fragmented audience. Before that, the general theory was that *all* people had to like *all* pictures.

The following is a short list—not counting hit-play adaptations—of some of the films that have opened in New York during the sixties. These films are not necessarily artistic triumphs, but they are, incontestably, experiences.

"Psycho"
"Hiroshima, Mon Amour"
"Big Deal on Madonna Street"
"The Hustler"
"The Mark"
"L'Avventura"
"Breathless"
"Ride the High Country"
"David and Lisa"
"Jules and Jim"
"Last Year at Marienbad"
"Divorce, Italian Style"
"Tom Jones"
"Dr. No"
"Dr. Strangelove"
"The Americanization of Emily"
"The Servant"
"The Organizer"
"The Easy Life"
"A Hard Day's Night"
"The Pawnbroker"
"Blow-up"
"The Shop on Main Street"
"Virgin Spring"
"Through a Glass Darkly"
"Winter Light"
"The Silence"

"La Dolce Vita"
"8½"

Broadway just isn't in the same league. And I don't think it's going to be again until it can somehow figure out a way to do what movies did: fragment its audience.

I was talking with a young man, a Duke senior on vacation in New York. He was going to movies and not to theatre, and when asked why, he said it was because of the cost. He gave in on that when it was pointed out that the cost of two movies equaled for practical purposes one play, and wasn't there at least one play he wanted to see? The Pinter, he said after some thought. Then why not go see it? Again there was thought. Serious and considerable. Then he said this: "Frankly, I just don't want to be associated with that kind of audience."

The remark may be unkind, but I don't think it's uncommon. The kids—probably the brightest group in America, the group that playwrights would most like to reach—are away from Broadway. And let's hope they'll come back, but don't bet on it. The talent's in films now, the "new" is in films, the prestige is in films, and Broadway is stumbling along, hoping somehow it's all going to have a happy ending.

I hope so too. I started going to the theatre when I was eight and began subscribing to *Variety* before I was ten. I care for Broadway, and it's frightening. A year or so ago I was addressing a group of writers at a men's college within easy distance of New York. We started off by talking about movie writing, and how the scene construction differs from a scene in fiction. And then something led to something else, and suddenly everyone was talking away at once— going on about Bergman and Fellini, and what was this science-fiction thing that Kubrick was up to. Any time you see a dozen bright kids really excited it's a good feeling. But halfway through I cut them off and said it was time to talk a little about Broadway now. And I asked what their memorable Broadway experiences were, what moved them, what made them laugh or think or question, or anything else. These were young writers, remember, and well off financially, and within easy distance of New York.

And no one raised a hand.

April 1967–September 1968

                                                       New York City

Appendix: Oddments

1. There is no known way to get a taxi before theatre time. It is possible, however, to get one after, especially if you don't mind a little walk. Simply head west to Eighth Avenue and then go downtown until an empty one comes along.

2. *The Drama Book Shop* is at 150 West Fifty-second Street. You have to take a very slow elevator to reach it (on the fifth floor), but once there, you may never want to leave.

3. *Broadway Joe* serves as good a sirloin as any in Manhattan. It is small and very crowded. 315 West Forty-sixth Street.

4. *Pearl's* is the best Chinese. 149 West Forty-eighth Street.

5. The best hamburger is available from *McGinnis'*, Broadway and Forty-eighth Street. At the stand-up bar.

6. *The Alamo Chile House* serves cold beer and hot chili, and you can get happily stuffed for under $2.00. 142 West Forty-fourth Street.

7. *Dinty Moore's* charges you for bread and butter, which is irritating. Otherwise, there is little to fault with the place. Both the calf's liver and the beef stew are exceptional. 216 West Forty-sixth Street.

8. *Sardi's* is the most famous restaurant in the area, and it shouldn't be any good. But it's terrific, and not only that, it isn't even terribly expensive. They are famous for their cannelloni, and they should be. If they have deviled beef bones on the menu, grab it. 234 West Forty-fourth Street.

9. *The Gaiety Delicatessen,* which still serves the best two-pieces-of-bread sandwich on the isle, has reopened at 224 West Forty-seventh Street. It isn't as uncomfortable as it used to be, but otherwise they haven't hurt it.